SAFETY, NUTRITION, AND HEALTH IN EARLY EDUCATION

Cathie **Robertson**

Delmar Publishers

an International Thomson Publishing company I(T)P®

Albany • Bonn • Boston • Cincinnati • Detroit • London • Madrid
Melbourne • Mexico City • New York • Pacific Grove • Paris • San Francisco
Singapore • Tokyo • Toronto • Washington

NOTICE TO THE READER

Cover and book photos by Fred Greaves
Cover Design: Brucie Rosch

Delmar Staff:

Publisher: William Brottmiller
Senior Editor: Jay Whitney
Associate Editor: Erin O'Connor Traylor
Project Editor: Patricia Gillivan

Production Coordinator: James Zayicek
Art and Design Coordinator: Carol D. Keohane
Editorial Assistant: Mara Berman

COPYRIGHT © 1998
Delmar is a division of Thomson Learning. The Thomson Learning logo is a registered trademark used herein under license.

Printed in the United States of America
3 4 5 6 7 8 9 10 XXX 03 02 01 00

For more information, contact Delmar, 3 Columbia Circle, PO Box 15015, Albany, NY 12212-0515; or find us on the World Wide Web at http://www.delmar.com

International Division List

Japan:
Thomson Learning
Palaceside Building 5F
1-1-1 Hitotsubashi, Chiyoda-ku
Tokyo 100 0003 Japan
Tel: 813 5218 6544
Fax: 813 5218 6551

Australia/New Zealand
Nelson/Thomson Learning
102 Dodds Street
South Melbourne, Victoria 3205
Australia
Tel: 61 39 685 4111
Fax: 61 39 685 4199

UK/Europe/Middle East:
Thomson Learning
Berkshire House
168-173 High Holborn
London
WC1V 7AA United Kingdom
Tel: 44 171 497 1422
Fax: 44 171 497 1426

Latin America:
Thomson Learning
Seneca, 53
Colonia Polanco
11560 Mexico D.F. Mexico
Tel: 525-281-2906
Fax: 525-281-2656

Canada:
Nelson/Thomson Learning
1120 Birchmount Road
Scarborough, Ontario
Canada M1K 5G4
Tel: 416-752-9100
Fax: 416-752-8102

Asia:
Thomson Learning
60 Albert Street, #15-01
Albert Complex
Singapore 189969
Tel: 65 336 6411
Fax: 65 336 7411

Library of Congress Cataloging-in-Publication Data

Robertson, Catherine, 1946-
    Safety, nutrition, and health in early education / Cathie
Robertson.
        p.   cm.
    Includes bibliographical references and index.
    ISBN 0-8273-7329-5
    1. School children—Health and hygiene—United States. 2. Early childhood education—United States. 3. School health services—United States. 4. School—United States—Safety measures. 5. Day care centers—Health aspects—United States. 6. Day care centers—United States—Safety measures. I. Title.
LB3409.U5R63   1998   97-41064
372.17'1—dc21   CIP

CONTENTS

Chapter **SEVEN**
Outdoor Safety

212

Chapter **EIGHT**
Emergency Response Procedures for Child Care

239

SECTION 3   NUTRITION IN CHILD CARE

271

Chapter **NINE**
Promoting Good Nutrition in Child Care

272

Chapter **THIRTEEN**
Special Topics in Safety, Health, and Nutrition

Chapter **FOURTEEN**
Creating Linkages

Chapter **FIFTEEN**
Building Curriculum for Safety, Health, and Nutrition

Online Services

Delmar Online
To access a wide variety of Delmar products and services on the World Wide Web, point your browser to:
> **http://www.delmar.com/delmar**
> or email: info@delmar.com

thomson.com
To access International Thomson Publishing's home site for information on more than 34 publishers and 20,000 products, point your browser to:
> **http://www.thomson.com**
> or email: findit@kiosk.thomson.com

A service of

PREFACE

Cathie
Robertson

Working with children today is different than it was ten years ago. There has been a societal shift and the daily lives of children are not the cultural images of childhood popularized in the media and on children's Web sites. *Safety, Nutrition, and Health in Early Education* includes vital information for those who work with children and addresses the challenges they will encounter in today's diverse world. Although adequate preparation in the areas of safety, nutrition, and health is imperative, even the best child development knowledge for learning and teaching will not be useful if the children are unhealthy, in unsafe environments, or malnourished.

This text focuses on the safety, nutrition, and health of children in child care. The audience for this text are child development students who are or are preparing to be teachers, paraprofessionals, caregivers, family home child care owners, or who will be working in other jobs that directly relate to young children. My experience teaching a variety of students who became nannies, preschool teachers, and family home care providers has helped me understand that although each type of caregiver will have many similar experiences, there will also be differences. This text is organized so that both the similarities and differences are recognized and discussed.

ORGANIZATION

The whole child is addressed with respect to safety, nutrition, health, and special topics. All areas of the environment are examined to create policies that emphasize children's status and minimize any risk to children's well-being. *Safety, Nutrition, and Health in Early Education* combines basic information and theory, as well as practical applications, resources, and caregiving skills needed today for working with children, families, and staff.

HEALTH

Strategies for maintaining a healthy child care environment are covered in this section of the text. Tools are provided for observation, assessment, and screening of physical and mental health. Information on staff health, infection control, and health care in child care will help caregivers manage good child care with minimum health risks. Methods and strategies for using education, cultural sensitivity, role modeling, and supervision are highlighted for the student to reinforce understanding of the health needs of children in care.

SAFETY

Creating safe child care environments is the major goal of this section of the text. The type of care and the developmental ages of the children in care are carefully examined in order to produce an appropriate safety plan. Accessories, behaviors, and conditions for safety risk are carefully explained in order for the caregiver to anticipate, monitor, and modify any risks to safety in the child care environment. Both indoor and outdoor environments are examined for common risks such as toys, equipment, traffic, fires, and burns. In addition, interpersonal safety and environmental factors are considered in relation to child care.

NUTRITION

Providing nutritional balance in child care is covered in this section of the text. Using the Food Guide Pyramid, child caregivers can create nutritionally balanced menus. Infants, toddlers, preschoolers, school-age children, and special needs children are examined to help the caregiver meet the needs of children in each group. Exercise is addressed as a vital part of providing proper nutrition. Food safety and supplemental food programs are covered so that the caregiver can minimize health risks in the child care environment. Reinforcement of the information is provided through strategies and methods.

SPECIAL TOPICS

This section covers topics of special interest to caregivers, such as child abuse, inclusion of children with special needs, care of children with chronic illnesses, the impact of stress on children, and how to meet the needs of children from families where drugs are abused. Communication skills, managing diversity, accessing resources, using advocacy for improved child care, and creating teams for child care are discussed. Curriculum for children, including a large reference section, is also offered in this section. As in previous sections, reinforcement is provided through discussion of methods and strategies in education, cultural sensitivity, and supervision.

SPECIAL FEATURES

Reality Checks address current issues that have an impact on the well-being of children. They bring an in-depth approach to some of the more critical areas that are affecting child care and children today. Reality Checks include information that is often absent in the popular cultural images of children found in many textbooks and the media regarding children's development. The following issues are discussed in Reality Checks:

■ Popular cultural images
■ The resilient child
■ Second-hand smoke

- The effects of lead poisoning
- The effects of poverty on children
- Children at-risk for preventable diseases
- Otitis media in child care
- Special care for mildly ill children
- Sudden infant death syndrome
- A safety checklist for parents
- Kids and guns
- Neighborhood violence
- Hunger in America
- Effects of advertising on children's food choices
- Children of the fast-food generation
- Domestic violence and its effect on children's lives
- Children with HIV/AIDS in child care

PEDAGOGY

The chapters are organized for ease of use beginning with an outline that includes expected outcomes. The outline format is used so the student can easily assimilate the information. Each chapter section ends with **Key Concepts,** which summarize the important points of that portion of the chapter. Vignettes, or stories based on real-life observations or events, are placed throughout each chapter. Vignettes reflect practical application and can help the child caregiver improve the health, safety, and well-being of children. For example:

> Tamara, an autistic child, was acquiring some sign language capabilities. She spent part of her morning in a special school and then went to Kate's family day care before lunch. Her favorite food was watermelon, and whenever Kate served Tamara watermelon she could sign the word *more.*
>
> Kate felt that there was an opportunity for learning here, so she went to the special education teacher at Tamara's school and learned how to sign the word *watermelon.* She used it every opportunity she could when she gave Tamara watermelon for lunch or snack. Eventually, Tamara learned how to sign the word. Her mother was so excited when she informed Kate several days later that Tamara had asked through signing for watermelon for dinner. It was a real milestone in Tamara's limited language.

Generalizable skills
common skills that can be practiced and used in different settings

Important terms are highlighted in color in the text and defined on the page where they first appear. This allows students to understand the term when they come to it and be familiar with it before they continue. There is also a complete glossary at the end of the text for reference.

Chapters Two through Thirteen include **Implications for Caregivers.** This section of these chapters helps to reinforce the information given and reflects the responsibilities of the caregiver to perform the practices, strategies, and methods discussed in that chapter.

Chapter Fourteen is devoted to issues that directly relate to the caregiver's ability to provide the best environment possible for all children in care. Entitled "Creating Linkages," this chapter deals with communication, managing diversity, accessing resources, acting as an advocate, and creating teams.

The final chapter, Chapter Fifteen, addresses curriculum for caregivers to use with children. It includes the basics of curriculum planning and provides fourteen lesson plans for caregivers to use with children. There are suggestions for many more ideas for lessons. This chapter also includes an extensive list of children's books to use as resources for working with children.

The end of every chapter is entitled **To Go Beyond.** This section gives the instructor ideas for classroom discussion, individual and group projects, and assignments. It also includes extensive references and suggestions for further reading.

Tables, graphs, checklists, figures, and photos are placed throughout each chapter to help present information in an organized manner. These features reinforce important concepts. For example:

TABLE 13.2

Stressors in a Child's Life

■ Divorce/single parent family/stepfamily adjustments

■ Birth of a sibling

■ Separation anxiety

■ Loss (death) of a loved one or pet

■ Too many scheduled activities

■ A new care situation or being placed in care for the first time

■ A friend leaves child care

■ Lack of bonding or attachment

■ Financial problems at home

■ Fears, real or imagined

■ Special needs or chronic illness

■ Victim of child abuse

■ Drug abuse in the home

■ Frequent relocation

■ Cultural considerations, including language and immigration

■ Observing violence in the home, neighborhood, or other real situation

■ Poverty

■ Homelessness

SUPPLEMENTAL MATERIALS

An extensive Instructor's Manual is available for this text. It includes an outline guide, a test bank, enhancement activities, case studies, a video and film list, and other resources for each chapter. The enhancement activities offer ideas for meaningful projects that include many community linkages. The **Case Studies** provide opportunities for critical thinking and practical application of the information provided in the text. These can also be used as essay test questions. The **Video/Film List** and **Other Resources** offer up-to-date resources for the instructor that are helpful supplements to the text.

ACKNOWLEDGMENTS

The author wishes to extend her gratitude to a number of people who helped this text progress from an idea to reality. First and foremost, Jay Whitney, whose title of Acquisitions Editor is not as extensive as the job he performs. Jay pursued the idea of this text for years until I agreed to write it. From that point on, he was very involved and supportive at every turn. I would also like to thank Erin O'Connor Traylor who helped shape the text. In addition, I appreciate the work of Carol Keohane who orchestrated the photos and art and Pat Gillivan and Jim Zayicek who worked on the production of this text. My experience with Delmar Publishers has been positive and supportive and I appreciate the expertise that they were so willing to share.

I want to extend my heartfelt thanks to the following reviewers for sharing their expertise with me. Their constructive suggestions and recommendations were helpful in shaping the final product.

Josephine M. Alexander
Mohawk Valley Community College
Utica, NY

Katherine Y. Collins
Pitt Community College
Greenville, NC

Jeannie Edwards
St. Louis Community College
St. Louis, MO

Lou Ann Farrell
University of New Mexico-Los Alamos
Los Alamos, NM

Teresa Frazier
Thomas Nelson Community Center
Hampton, VA

Jeanne Goodwin
Brainerd Community College
Brainerd, MN

Charlotte M. Hendricks
JCCEO-Head Start Program
Birmingham, AL

Rosanne Pirtle, PhD
Marian College
Indianapolis, IN

Arleen Prairie
Harold Washington College
Chicago, IL

Marilyn Thomas
Petit Jean Technical College
Morrilton, AR

Cheryl Woolsey
Blackfeet Community College
Browning, MT

I have been fortunate to have two colleagues, Lorraine Martin and Barbara Chernofsky of Grossmont College, to turn to for feedback, information, and further expertise. I am grateful to them for their help to me throughout the process of writing the text and the Instructor's Manual. I must also acknowledge the support of Grossmont Community College, where I teach. The administration, management, and faculty have been very helpful in this effort, including awarding me a sabbatical to pursue the writing of this text.

THE AUTHOR

Cathie Robertson received her BS and MS degrees from San Diego State University. She teaches courses in Family and Consumer Studies and Child Development at Grossmont College. She has taught food and nutrition courses, specializing in childhood nutrition, for a number of years. She is the former president of the International Nanny Association and presently serves on several local and state committees for issues that involve child care. She has made numerous state, local, and national professional presentations. Ms. Robertson has been the recipient of a number of grants, including one that funded the writing of a curriculum and resource guide for working with prenatally substance exposed children and their families. Ms. Robertson is married, the mother of three adult children, and a grandmother.

DEDICATION

I would like to dedicate this text to my family, including my mother, Helen; my children, Annie, Matt, and Tara; my son-in-law, Eric; and in memory of my father Glen, who passed away as this was being written. Special thanks to my husband, Dan, and my granddaughter, Zarli. Dan's loving support has allowed me the time and energy needed to complete this project. Zarli is a work in progress, who has helped me rediscover the joys of childhood. Having a grandchild in my life was a major influence on my decision to take on this task, because it reinforced for me the importance of good child care and inspired me to renew my efforts to make sure all children could have what I expected for the children in my life.

Safety, Nutrition, and Health in Child Care: A Holistic Environmental Approach

Upon completion of this chapter, including a review of the summary, you should be able to:

Holistic Approach

Define a holistic approach to the health, safety, and nutrition of children.

The Environment

Describe an ecological perspective and explain how the environment may affect the health, safety, and nutrition of a young child.

Health Promotion, Protection, and Prevention

Describe and discuss the differences between health promotion, protection, and prevention as they apply to child care.

Risk and Risk Management of Children's Well-being

Define risk and discuss how risk management is crucial to the health, safety, and nutrition of children in child care.

Providing High-Quality Child Care in Health, Safety, and Nutrition

Discuss how a child caregiver would provide high-quality child care for safety, nutrition, and health.

Caregivers
persons who provide care
for children: teachers, family
child care providers,
nannies

At risk
exposure to chance of
injury, damage, or hazard

Holistic
consideration of the whole
being

Environment
all the conditions,
circumstances, and
influences surrounding
and affecting the
development of an
individual

HOLISTIC APPROACH

It can no longer be assumed that all of the health, safety, and nutritional needs of children are met at home by parents. The United States Department of Labor estimates that more than 11 million children under the age of six have mothers in the workforce and it is expected that these numbers will continue to increase. It is estimated that more than 53 percent of mothers return to work within a year of a child's birth (Young, 1994). Seventy-five percent of children whose mothers work part-time and 88 percent of children whose mothers work full-time receive nonparental supplemental care (National Health Education Consortium, 1992). Public and private center-based child care programs, family child care, and nanny in-home care are providing nonparental care for the majority of children while their mothers are working. These nonparental **caregivers** need to help the parents meet the health, safety, and nutritional needs of the children in their care.

Teachers, family child caregivers, nannies, and other nonparental caregivers spend their days working with children to provide intellectual stimulation, social and emotional support, and physical care. Good physical care is of primary importance to support the health, safety, and nutritional well-being of children. Children who are unhealthy or whose physical well-being is **at risk** may have difficulty performing cognitive tasks and relating to others in terms of social and emotional development. Cognitive, social, and emotional deficits as well as physical difficulties may result in poor health. Health should be defined in terms of a person's physical, mental, social, and emotional well-being. These areas are interrelated and a **holistic** approach will allow the effects of all areas of development to be observed for health and well-being.

Good health is the result of reducing unnecessary risk, preventing illness, and promoting the well-being of an individual. Child caregivers need to create an atmosphere for children that provides this protective type of environment. In order to accomplish this task, the child caregiver needs to focus on three basic areas: health, safety, and nutrition. Lack of good health practices, an unsafe environment, or providing poor nutrition may all contribute to failure in protecting children. The interrelationship of the areas of health, safety, and nutrition will be easier to understand if a holistic approach is used.

The **environment** of children's health, safety, and nutrition is the focus of this text. Each chapter begins with a lead-in paragraph and then points out current research findings that reinforce the need for concern for that issue. The issues presented indicate how children may be put at risk in center-based child care as well as family child care and nonparental care given to a child in the home. The body of each chapter provides the child caregiver with the information and strategies to deal with these issues.

As an example, the following research findings indicate and support the need for dealing with health, safety, and nutrition in a holistic manner:

■ Good quality child care can help reduce the magnitude of the effects of problems children may encounter such as poverty, drug abuse, and violence (Schweinhart, 1994).

Research findings support the need for dealing with safety, nutrition, and health in a holistic manner.

■ Good quality child care should meet standards that protect the basic health and safety of children and should also consider developmental needs. Most child care centers in the United States do not meet the children's needs for safety, health, or caring relationships (University of Colorado at Denver et al., 1995).

■ Children in this country are experiencing a greater number of at-risk difficulties than previously reported. These include psychological problems, emotional disorders, and chronic physical conditions (U.S. Department of Health and Human Services, 1990).

■ A holistic approach is needed to address the needs of children at risk for severe health problems and school failure (National Health Education Consortium, 1992).

■ Feeding practices related to growth can help predict the outcome of children's health, cognitive development, and social adjustment (Zeitlin, 1991).

■ Excellence of child care is directly related to compliance with a high standard of care (Grubb, 1993).

KEY HOLISTIC APPROACH

CONCEPT

A holistic approach is the sensible way to deal with the interrelationship of health, safety, and nutrition on the well-being of young children (National Health Education Consortium, 1992). Those who provide nonparental child care should consider the environment of every child in care. Growth, health, development, and safety are a result of each child's environment.

Ecological
pertaining to the relationship of the individual to the environment

THE ENVIRONMENT

Environment includes all the conditions, circumstances, and influences that surround a person. All of the complex factors in the environment can be simplified by using an **ecological** point of view (see Figure I.1). The ecological perspective examines the physical, social and emotional, economic, and cultural environments that affect a child. It relates all of the factors that might influence children's lives in terms of growth, health, safety, development, and well-being. Child care is an essential part of environment for those children who receive nonparental care. Those who are caregivers need to be aware of all the environmental factors.

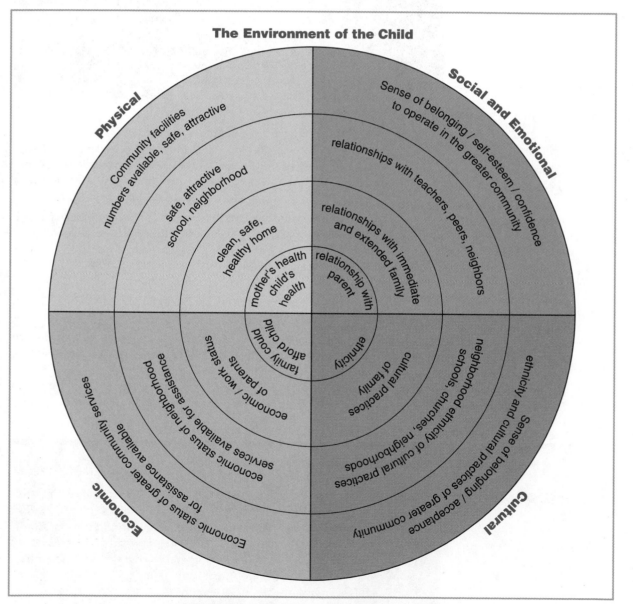

FIGURE **I.1** Holistic View Ecological Approach

The Physical Environment

The physical environment of a child begins in the mother's womb. A child born to a mother who had regular prenatal checkups and proper nutrition during pregnancy is less likely to have physical complications at birth and more likely to experience good health later in life than a child born to a mother who had no prenatal care (U.S. Department of Health and Human Services, 1990). A child whose mother had no prenatal care is more likely to be born at a low birthweight and is far more likely to have physical problems at birth and health difficulties later in life.

After birth, the physical environment includes the family, home, school, neighborhood, and greater community. Children who are raised in a safe, secure, stable environment are less at risk for poor health, injury, or accidents than children who do not have that type of environment (Wright, 1990). Children who live in neighborhoods where they are protected from harm and are carefully watched are less likely to become injured or victims of violence than children who live in unsafe neighborhoods (Cicchetti & Lynch, 1993). This is significant because in the past 15 years, violence, poverty, physical illness, and family stress have increased in the United States (Bowman, 1995).

Another factor in the physical environment is **heredity**. Heredity plays a key role in the health and nutrition of children. A child's **genetic** background can influence a number of environmental risk factors (Plomin, Reiss, Hetherington, & Howe, 1994). Body type, temperament, and inherited diseases are just some of the characteristics that are expressed through genetic contributions from both parents in the reproduction process. There can also be inherited traits that may not be present at birth but may show up later.

An example of a disease that shows up at birth is phenylketonuria (PKU). It causes an inability in the child to **metabolize** one type of protein in the normal manner. Left untreated, this condition can cause brain damage and mental retardation. These harmful effects can be prevented if PKU is diagnosed in early infancy and if the proper diet is followed. Hospitals in many states routinely test for PKU at birth. The proper environment through proper diet can eliminate the risk factor.

Diabetes, cancer, obesity, and heart disease are inherited family factors that may appear later in life. These conditions may be prevented or their effects may be reduced through proper diet and exercise throughout life. By managing the environmental factors, those risks can be diminished and possibly eliminated.

Heredity
the transmission from parent to child of certain characteristics

Genetic
the origin of features of an individual

Metabolize
change occurring by chemical and physical processes in living cells

Andrea was ten months old when she was diagnosed with diabetes. Her family struggled to control the disease through diet and insulin. Even though several members of the extended family had the disease, none had been as young as Andrea at its onset. At age two and a half, her disease was finally managed with insulin in the morning and through careful diet control. When Andrea was three, her mother went back to work part-time, and she put Andrea in a family child care home. Andrea's child caregiver worked closely with her mother to make sure Andrea's diet was closely monitored. Today, Andrea is a healthy seventeen-year-old high school senior. The cooperation of her family child caregiver contributed to maintaining a positive environment for Andrea so she could be healthy and grow. ■

Children enter child care from many different physical home environments. Some children have had good physical environments and are healthy and protected from harm. Other children may come from at-risk physical environments. Families may not provide good health practices, or children may have an inherited condition or disease. Some children may be at risk for safety due to abuse or neighborhood violence. Children who attend a good child care environment are more likely to develop properly even if they are considered at risk in their own home environments (Cesarone, 1993).

A good child care environment using the holistic approach screens for health difficulties, provides good health and safety practices, and promotes proper nutrition. Caregivers integrate health, safety, and nutrition into the curriculum and value them as highly as social skills, language, or any other aspects of curriculum. This means that caregivers include all of these areas in the program every day. By providing this instruction to children in care, a good quality child care environment can provide the foundation for good health and well-being in adulthood. Child care may offer many children a better chance for an improved physical environment for at least part of the day.

The Social and Emotional Environment

The social and emotional environment of a child begins with the parent-child relationship. As the child grows, this environment expands to include the family, neighbors, teachers, peers, and other members of the community. Children's mental health and sense of well-being are very important factors in overall health. A family that provides a stable environment and creates the opportunity for a secure **attachment** for a child is more likely to raise a happy, cheerful child. A family that exposes a child to a high-risk situation and fails to form a secure attachment is more likely to produce a child who is at risk for many social and emotional problems (Bowlby, 1988; Luster, Boger, & Hannan, 1993). Children raised in healthy, functional families are more likely to retain good mental health and be well adjusted than those raised in dysfunctional, violent households (Spaccarelli, Sandler, & Rooss, 1994).

The consistency of caregiving and emotional investment on the part of a child caregiver has a direct relationship to the healthy development of children (Brazelton, 1992). Quality care contributes to children's sense of well-being. A good child care environment is one in which there are good one-on-one relationships between caregivers and children in care. Larger child care situations may have to provide a **primary caregiver** for each child to accomplish this optimal type of relationship. The caregiver who relates to the children in care is more likely to be alert and observant. A care-

Attachment
the bond that develops between a child and another person as a result of a long-term relationship

Primary caregiver
the person assigned to be a child's main caregiver throughout the day in order to form a positive attachment bond

giver who has noticed any social or emotional effects of nonparental care can help the child adjust (Honig, 1993). The caregiver can also work with families to offer them strategies for providing a home environment that makes a child feel more secure and mentally healthy.

The quality of peer relationships may be a good indicator of a child's mental and emotional health status. A child's ability to cope with new situations, her sense of self-esteem, and her level of confidence affects how the child deals with her peers. The observant caregiver will notice these things. A child's sense of self will affect how he grows and develops into a member of the greater community as an adult. It is widely recognized that early intervention by a caregiver provides a more secure environment for children who are at risk for adjustment difficulties (Zero to Three, 1992; American Public Health Association & American Academy of Pediatrics, 1992).

Mary Elizabeth is a four-year-old with a healthy appetite, a hearty laugh, and the ability to move from activity to activity with little need for transition. When she was born to a cocaine-addicted mother, the doctors were not sure of her prognosis for growth or behavior. She was briefly removed from her mother's custody and returned when her mother went into a parent supportive recovery program. Her mother, Ellen, received help for her addiction as well as help in learning how to parent, including the importance of early bonding in the mother-child relationship. Ellen studied to be a computer operator at a local community college and has been working for the past two years. Mary Elizabeth has been in the same child care center since she was 11 months old.

The staff at the child care center have been supportive of Ellen and understood that Mary Elizabeth might need some special help as a result of prenatal substance exposure. When Mary Elizabeth exhibited a high degree of frustration in certain types of play, the staff were able to provide emotional assurance and reduce the stimulation around her while redirecting her behavior. Mary Elizabeth is a good example of what early intervention and a good environment can do for the healthy development of a child at risk. Studies that have followed substance-exposed children from birth have concluded that, in many cases, a secure and supportive environment may overcome most of any possible side effects of prenatal exposure to drugs (Robertson, 1993).

The Economic Environment

Economic
the satisfaction of the
material needs of people

The **economic** environment of the child is established in the home and is influenced by the parents' work history, the economic health of the neighborhood, the community, and the nation. Low income is the primary factor for the majority of childhood health and nutritional risks in this country (Children's Defense Fund, 1996). Many children who are economically at risk are in child care situations.

One in every four young children in the United States lives below the poverty level. There is a 59 percent poverty rate for children under the age of six living with a single parent. Forty percent of the parents of children in poverty are unemployed. The impact of financial stress on the home environment can affect children's emotions and behavior (Takeuchi, Williams, & Adair, 1991). Financial limitations can also affect children's health. Lack of good medical care, poor nutrition, and an environment where parental attention is limited can affect children's well-being. Another effect of low income may be the inability to afford quality child care. Poor children are more at risk for serious illness and death. Some childhood health problems related to poverty are:

- Low birthweight
- Accidental deaths
- Lead poisoning
- Asthma
- Lack of immunizations; deaths due to childhood diseases
- Iron deficiency anemia

Economic factors that include the lack of preventive care and access to care can seriously impair the potential of many children in this country for maximum growth, healthy development, and protection from harm.

The person who provides child care will need to be aware of the impact that the economic environment of families has on the health, safety, and well-being of children. Child caregivers may be able to improve the impact of the economic environment on children by providing good nutrition and preventive health and safety measures. Caregivers can also help families to access resources, create community linkages, and advocate for children. These efforts and collaborations may provide families with critical

How can an at-risk environment where parental attention is limited negatively affect a child's well-being?

information on health, safety, and nutritional issues. Child caregivers who collaborate with the greater community on these issues can improve their community environments.

The Cultural Environment

Cultural
relationship to traits and ascribed membership of a given group

The **cultural** environment includes the beliefs and practices of the family, the neighborhood, and the greater community. The United States has become a multiethnic society. With so many cultural traditions, practices, and values present, there may be value conflicts among different cultures. There may be bicultural conflict within families that represent several generations of values. One outcome of these conflicts may be the reinforcement of cultural values within families.

Practices for maintaining traditional cultural values in daily life, such as food choices and child care, are seen as meaningful declarations of family heritage. For example, whether or not the mother accesses prenatal care may depend upon the social practices of her cultural background (Kahler, O'Shea, Duffy, & Buck, 1993). It is important that the professional child caregiver support the family cultural values of the children in care. In instances where these cultural values put children at risk, cultural differences and legal practices will need to be addressed.

Characteristics of family health attitudes may relate directly to culture. For example, Latin-American families appear to have lower expectations for children's health and therefore may be less likely to use preventive services (Vilchez & Tinsley, 1993). The combined impact of social problems due to culture and economic hardship may cause harm to children. Children from these environments are more likely to experience social, emotional, and behavioral problems and suffer from poor mental health (Barbarin, 1993).

It is important for the child caregiver to be aware of the diversity of the children and families in care. Cultural awareness will help the caregiver better understand ways to communicate and provide information on issues concerning health, safety, and nutrition.

KEY ENVIRONMENT

Concept

An ecological perspective allows one to view the environment of a child. A risk factor in the health and well-being of children can come from any area of the environment. The physical, social and emotional, economic, and cultural environments all influence children's growth and development. Negative conditions from any part of a child's environment may place that child at risk. Poor physical and mental health, injury, or an impaired sense of well-being and self-esteem may prevent the maximum growth potential and development of a child. Using an ecological perspective, the child caregiver can approach the health, safety, and nutrition of children considering their total environment.

Health promotion
the improvement of health conditions by encouraging healthful characteristics and customs

HEALTH PROMOTION, PROTECTION, AND PREVENTION

This text deals with the developmental aspects and issues that can help promote and protect children's well-being. The text also illustrates ways to prevent childhood illness, disease, or accidents. Caregivers should establish and maintain a healthy environment using **health promotion**. Caregivers promote health by checking for immunization and encouraging the use of proper hand washing and diapering techniques. They provide adequate nutrition and arrange for hearing, vision, and dental screening tests. Caregivers protect children in care by promoting safety practices such as using childhood safety seats in travel, checking toys and other equipment for hazards, and providing a low-risk environment.

The holistic approach to child care includes other measures to promote and protect children. Many organizations and efforts concerned with the health, safety, and nutrition of children contribute to a holistic approach. Some contributions will be examined in order to understand how issues concerning children's health, safety, nutrition, and well-being impact child care. Awareness of these outside efforts may help clarify the role of a caregiver in terms of the importance of providing good health, safety, and nutrition practices in child care. This knowledge may also help the caregiver understand the necessity of community linkages and of advocacy for children.

Healthy People 2000

Healthy People 2000: National Health Promotion and Disease Prevention Objectives is a report that is a product of a national process that has set health objectives for the year 2000. The major purpose of the program is to improve the health and well-being of Americans. Many of the major targets for improvement are issues involving children. Some of the objectives that affect children are:

- Consider the environmental risks that cause emotional, physical, psychological, and learning problems.
- Provide educational and support programs for parents in high-risk environments to help reduce child abuse and other health problems.
- Increase to at least 75 percent the proportion of the nation's schools that provide nutrition education from preschool to the twelfth grade.

A caregiver can help improve the health and well-being of children in care by addressing these issues. Topics in this text provide the caregiver with a base of knowledge to effectively consider the issues.

National Health and Safety Performance Standards for Child Care

The American Public Health Association (APHA) and the American Academy of Pediatrics (AAP) collaborated and produced *National Health and Safety Performance Standards: Guidelines for Out-of-Home Child Care Programs.* Funding for this project was provided by the Maternal and Child

Health Bureau of the Department of Health and Human Services. These guidelines recognize the need for some consistency and guidance to help child caregivers provide the optimal environment for health, safety, and nutrition. The Pennsylvania Chapter of the American Academy of Pediatrics (1993) published *Model Child Care Health Policies*, which may provide caregivers with some specific tools to create the optimal environment for child care.

The National Association for the Education of Young Children is another organization concerned with the well-being of children. Although in agreement with many of the standards set by the APHA and AAP, they encourage caregivers to make decisions based on information from several points of view. Caregivers must first have the information and an understanding of specific procedures before making any decision regarding the health, safety, and nutritional needs of children in care. Caregivers need training to do this. This text was written to help caregivers acquire training in the areas of health, safety, and nutrition.

Other Efforts

Many federal and state programs such as Project Head Start, WIC (USDA's Supplemental Food Program for Women, Infants, and Children) and Project Healthy Start in Hawaii (Stein, 1995) are promoting good health and nutrition habits. Groups such as the Consumer Product Safety Commission promote safety measures that will improve the well-being of children.

Many of the initiatives that fund health promotion, protection, and prevention operate at all levels of government. There is a clear indication of the need for all entities involved with caring for young children to work together. Some collaborative efforts to promote health, safety, and nutrition for young children include:

■ Improving the health and nutrition of the developing child

■ Providing health and nutrition instruction for preschoolers

■ Providing parent education in health and nutrition

■ Preparing preschool teachers to educate children and parents to use the skills themselves for health, safety, and nutrition issues

There are implications for caregivers from these governmental efforts. Child caregivers need to be prepared to perform the preceeding tasks. They also need to understand how to communicate with families and collaborate with others in the community.

KEY HEALTH PROMOTION, PROTECTION, AND PREVENTION

CONCEPT

Health promotion, protection, and prevention are ineffective if caregivers fail to understand the effects of the environment. Clearly, some programs and initiatives are trying to help parents and caregivers promote and protect the health and well-being of children. Caregivers play an essential role in the holistic approach to child care. They should be able to provide good nutrition and healthy environments that are safe from harm for the children in care. By modeling this environment, the caregivers can help children feel secure and help parents recognize the value of quality care.

RISK AND RISK MANAGEMENT OF CHILDREN'S WELL-BEING

Risk is defined as a chance or gamble that is often accompanied by danger. Risk management is a way to minimize the chance that danger may occur. Risk management takes on specific meaning when it is applied to taking care of children. Results of health risks include illness, infection, disease, mental illness, developmental difficulty, disability, and death. Results of safety risks include accidents, disability, and death. Nutritional risk results include developmental delay, growth retardation, poor health, and lack of resistance to infection or disease.

The opposite of risk in relation to health is well-being. Well-being is measured by wellness, degree of activity, resiliency, proper growth, at-level development, and general vitality. Children who are healthy, safe, and well nourished will exhibit those characteristics. Children who are at risk for problems will display one or more of the risk factors previously discussed.

Joey, a bright, happy two-year-old boy, was small for his age and seemed not to have grown in the six months that he had been at the child care center. Occasionally, he was listless. His teacher was concerned and spoke to Joey's mother, who had noticed the same thing. Joey's mother took him to the doctor for a checkup. The doctor inquired about Joey's diet and discovered that the mother was giving Joey large amounts of fruit juice and not enough milk and other foods. The doctor put Joey on a balanced diet. The mother explained that she had had a problem of being overweight when she was a child and did not want to feed him foods that had too much fat in them. The doctor explained that too much fruit juice may hinder growth and that Joey needed some fat and more milk in his diet. To stay healthy and grow properly, children need a variety of food sources (Bittman, 1994).

Proper risk management strategies remove risk factors from children's health, safety, and nutrition. For the child caregiver, the strategies of health promotion, safety protection, and nutritional education are necessary risk management tools. Modeling good health, safety, and nutrition practices is a positive risk management strategy. The guidelines to managing risk in relation to the well-being of children are to set thorough standards and guidelines for child care facilities, training, and staffing.

KEY RISK AND RISK MANAGEMENT

CONCEPT

Risk management is an effective way to protect, promote, and prevent difficulties regarding children's health, safety, and nutrition. A number of strategies such as modeling good practices and complying with standards and guidelines are good risk management tools for child caregivers.

PROVIDING HIGH QUALITY CHILD CARE IN HEALTH, SAFETY, AND NUTRITION

According to Bredekamp (1987), high quality child care programs should provide "a safe and nurturing environment that promotes the physical, social, emotional, and cognitive development of young children while responding to the needs of families" (p.1). In terms of the health, safety, and well-being of children, the child caregiver needs to have four basic goals in mind to ensure a high quality child care program:

1. Maximize the health status of the children.
2. Minimize risks to the health, safety, and well-being of the children.
3. Utilize education as a tool for health promotion and risk reduction for both children and adults.
4. Recognize the importance of guidelines, standards, and laws as they apply to the health, safety, and well-being of children.

Goal One: Maximizing Children's Health Status

Health status
the condition of health of an individual

A person's **health status** reflects the condition of health of that person. Child caregivers have the opportunity to provide optimal conditions to maximize the health and sense of well-being of the children in their care. In order to accomplish that goal, a set of objectives for health promotion and the prevention of illness and disease should be planned, carried out, and monitored. Regardless of whether care is in a child care center, a family child care home, or in the child's own home, many of the objectives will be the same. In some instances, the objectives may apply more specifically to the type of setting in which the care is performed (see Table I.1).

TABLE I.1

Objectives for the Optimal Health and Well-Being of Children

For care of children, all caregivers should:

- Respect the developmental needs, characteristics, and diversity of each child.
- Support a child's development based on knowledge of the general health and unique characteristics of the individual child. This includes emotional support as well as attention to physical needs.
- Reduce and prevent the transmission of infectious and communicable diseases.
- Understand the management of ill children, including exclusion policies.
- Use universal health procedures for toileting, diapering, maintaining toys, and handling and storing food.
- Utilize the health status of the staff as an important component of job performance.
- Ensure good nutrition and food safety by following the requirements of the USDA child care component, the Child Care Food Program, and the Code of Federal Regulations.

For parent education, all caregivers should:

- Help parents understand the importance of developing child care routines that contribute to children's sense of well-being.
- Utilize community health and nutrition professionals to create helpful linkages for children, families, and staff.
- Promote good health and nutrition through education for children, parents, and staff.
- Provide education and support to parents for the management of infectious illness and disease.

A child care center staff should:

- Provide a **primary caregiver** for each child.
- Provide someone to communicate in the children's and parents' first language.

Family and in-home child caregivers should:

- Work closely with the parents to provide nutritional information, healthy food choices, and good food for children.
- Act as a resource and role model for the parents by providing a healthy home environment for children in care.

Primary caregiver
the person assigned to be a child's main caregiver throughout the day to form a positive attachment bond

Goal Two: Minimizing Risks for Childhood Health, Safety, and Nutrition

Proactive planning to reduce risk for children is an essential element in providing quality child care. The vulnerability of children places them at risk for many problems that can be prevented. Historically, infectious diseases have been perceived as the major risk associated with childhood. The threat of many childhood diseases has been lessened or eliminated with the availability of widespread immunizations to eliminate those diseases. However, these immunizations are only effective if they are administered to children. Other risks for spread of disease could decrease through proper sanitation practices.

Today, in reality, the major risks to children are unintentional injury, child abuse and neglect, homicide, lead poisoning, and developmental difficulties. The vulnerability of children at risk for unintentional injuries is influenced by age, cognitive development, motor skills, and the home environment (Glotzer & Weitsman, 1991). The danger of child abuse and neglect and homicide have become major issues in the health and well-being of children in America. Children are more at risk for violence when drug and alcohol abuse, poverty, and family violence are present in the environment.

Lead poisoning is another problem that poses risk to many children through environmental exposure. Developmental difficulties can cause permanent harm if they are not detected early. Intervention can reduce many problems associated with the difficulties.

This text includes a number of Reality Checks to help the reader understand the significance of current issues that affect the health, safety, or nutrition of children. The first Reality Check indicates an overview of issues that often go unnoticed due to lack of awareness.

REALITY CHECK

Popular Cultural Images

American culture is closely tied with the images that are projected to the population through mass media such as newspapers, television, movies, books, magazines, and billboards. We see and hear much about what Madison Avenue and the entertainment industry want us to see and hear. The cereal aisle of a grocery store reflects this. Ask any child what a particular cereal will do for him and one may get a good, although inaccurate, answer. Certain cereals will offer acceptance, others will make one strong, and some will allow one to be just like a hero. Adults understand that these claims should be discounted, but we often buy the cereal anyway. The selection of cereal is not often based upon nutritional content but upon children's wishes.

The majority of children's television shows would have viewers believe that all children are happy, healthy, and belong to families that care for and about them. Adult viewing can paint other more realistic pictures, but often the popular television shows and movies leave the public with the impression that everything is well. When we view the news, read news magazines, or look in the newspaper, we realize that everything is not how it seems on television or in the majority of movies.

A very popular cultural image for children today is the Camel cigarette camel. Shown as sophisticated, cute, and talented, this camel may lead children to believe that smoking is not only acceptable behavior but preferable. A reality check

continued

occurs when the public is made aware that smoking and secondhand smoke are not healthy. The Surgeon General has warned citizens against smoking and the danger of cigarettes. Are we listening? An increasing number of young women are smoking at an early age. Secondhand smoke is becoming a major health issue (American Academy of Pediatrics, 1994).

Many popular magazines present beautiful houses and show how to decorate them. This should please the public, give a sense of place, and provide our children with a healthy environment. A reality check reveals that an increasing number of homes are unhealthy and even hazardous for children due to biological pollutants and lead poisoning (Rosenblum, 1993).

The majority of popular cultural images dealing with the family portray most families as intact. If the families are headed by a single parent, they are doing well. A reality check tells us many things about this image. One out of four children is living in a single parent family. One out of two children is expected to reside in a single parent family at one point in his life. Single parent families are more likely to live in poverty than any other family group. Poverty places children at risk for problems related to safety, nutrition, and health.

In most instances, the popular image of children in our culture shows us happy, vital, and healthy children. These children may have an occasional cold or temper tantrum but nothing more. The reality check displays a very different picture. Only 56 percent of children under two are properly vaccinated for childhood diseases (Graham, 1994). In the five year span between 1984 and 1989, 30,000 cases of pertussis, also known as whooping cough, requiring hospitalization occurred. Twenty-three other nations have a lower infant mortality rate than the United States. This may reflect the fact that many women are not receiving prenatal care and good nutrition. Two and one-half million American children were

abused or neglected in 1993 (Children's Defense Fund, 1996). Increasing rates of neighborhood and family violence are threatening the lives, health, and well-being of too many of our children. Acts of violence cause the death of at least 2,000 children per year (Cicchetti & Lynch, 1993). Malnourishment and undernourishment of children in this country are not uncommon. They may be too poor to eat properly or they may have busy parents who either do not understand a balanced diet or do not take the time to plan a balanced diet.

Although popular cultural images are showing more minorities, the reality of our multiethnic society is not reflected in these images. African American, Hispanic, and Asian peoples play an important role in our society and their numbers are increasing. The number of new immigrants and refugees entering this country is growing rapidly. There are 20 million foreign-born people living in the United States and almost half of them arrived in the last decade (Loeb, Friedman, Lord, Guttman, & Kukula, 1993). Many of these people have given birth to children since arriving in this country. Conflicting cultures and cultural values may take their toll on these children (Sam, 1992).

One social analyst concluded that Americans are not doing enough to ensure the health and well-being of our children (Fuchs, 1991). A survey of data on the decline of the American family reported that children are the most affected by the decline (Popenoe, 1993). Both social observers suggest that the popular cultural image needs a reality check. However, the outlook for the health, safety, and well-being of the children in this country is good because of medical research, health promotion, and safety precautions. Lack of access to health care and proper nutrition is often the topic of today's news. Child caregivers have the opportunity to contribute to the improvement of the well-being of children in care by providing the optimum environment for health, safety, and nutrition.

Prevention, recognition, protection, and early intervention are the major tools child caregivers can use to reduce risks to children in their care. Table I.2 lists some risk management objectives for child care health, safety, and nutrition.

TABLE **I.2**

Risk Management for Child Care

All child caregivers should:

- Require proof of immunizations before admitting children to care.
- Meet immunization requirements personally.
- Follow health and safety licensing guidelines.
- Provide a safe staff-to-child ratio.
- Develop good observational skills.
- Use health appraisals and assessment as risk management tools.
- Follow sanitary guidelines for hygiene and food handling.
- Protect the facility from neighborhood violence.
- Recognize and manage mild childhood illnesses.
- Provide backup or substitute caregivers to replace ill caregivers.
- Develop an inclusion/exclusion policy for ill children.
- Communicate by written notice about exposure to communicable disease.
- Provide a hazard-free environment.
- Prevent accidents in the indoor environment by following safety guidelines and practices.
- Prevent accidents in the outdoor environment by selection and placement of equipment and by following safety guidelines and practices.
- Create a safety plan for the facility.
- Create a disaster preparedness plan for fire and other dangers.
- Prevent fire by following local fire code standards and practices.
- Post and be ready to follow emergency procedures.
- Have knowledge of pediatric first aid and be able to practice it in case of an emergency.
- Be able to perform cardiopulmonary resuscitation (CPR).
- Detect, prevent, and report child abuse.
- Understand and utilize acceptable methods of discipline.
- Arrange the facility so there is no opportunity for isolation or privacy of individual caregivers with children.
- Develop a written plan for nutritious meals and snacks.
- Provide nutritious foods.
- Provide relief time for all staff.

Family child and in-home caregivers should:

- Organize the home for child care.
- Organize for mixed age child care.

Goal Three: Education as a Tool for Children's Health Promotion and Risk Reduction

A holistic approach to health promotion and illness and disease prevention is needed because health and well-being cannot be achieved without awareness. An educational component must be present in order to create a safe and nurturing environment for children. The educational component must impact the staff, the children, and the parents involved in the child care program or relationship.

Education and training for quality child care are essential (American Public Health Association & American Academy of Pediatrics, 1992; Herr, 1991). The caregiver should be educated in promotional, preventive, and protective practices in order to provide the maximum environment and minimum risk for the child (Table I.3). A fundamental role of the child caregiver is to pass along knowledge. Modeling good health and safety measures and good food choices teaches children by example. Role modeling also allows children and their parents to see the caregiver put this knowledge to practice.

Teaching children about good health and proper nutrition helps them contribute to their own health. Instructing children in preventive and protective measures permits them to participate in their own well-being. The children can pass that information on to others by modeling and through discussion. This may motivate parents to be more receptive to the caregiver's modeling and information.

Caregivers educate parents by sending handouts, holding miniworkshops, and discussing health, safety, and nutrition directly with them. If necessary, the caregiver can access community groups help to aid with this task. Parents who are supported through continual contacts with caregivers and educational assistance are better at providing holistic health for their children (Johnson, 1993).

Knowledgeable child caregivers who work with children, parents, and the community contribute to a team effort to promote good health, safety, prevention, and nutrition. Creating these linkages allows the child caregiver to effect a holistic approach to ensure a quality environment for the children.

Goal Four: Recognizing the Importance of Guidelines, Standards, and Laws for the Health, Safety, and Well-Being of Children

Guidelines
statements of advice or instruction pertaining to practice

Standards
statements that define a goal of practice

Laws
rules of conduct established and enforced by authority

Guidelines, standards, and **laws** affecting child care have been created for the purpose of protecting children and promoting quality environments for them. Child care centers in states where there are stringent regulations tend to provide higher quality care than those in states that have less stringent regulations (Phillips, Howes, & Whitebook, 1992). When nonparental child caregivers in all settings comply with standards, there is a lower turnover rate, more sensitive care, and staff with better training, resulting in better quality child care. Compliance with minimum standards can affect environmental practices, relationships with parents, and the general attitude of caregivers (Grubb, 1993).

TABLE I.3

Educational Tools for Caregivers

A caregiver should have knowledge of:

- Health promotion and the importance of modeling health promotion behavior
- Observational skills
- Immunizations and when they are to be given
- Health appraisals and use of assessment tools
- Mechanisms of communicable diseases and how they are spread
- Universal sanitary practices
- Common childhood illnesses, including management and exclusion policies
- Environmental health and safety hazards
- Safety standards and practices for both indoor and outdoor equipment
- Disaster preparedness
- Emergency response procedures
- Cardiopulmonary resuscitation (CPR) and first aid
- Child abuse detection and reporting
- Child abuse prevention
- Nutritional needs of children
- Good feeding practices for children
- Any special health or nutritional needs of children in care
- Communication skills
- Diversity and how it can affect health, safety, and nutrition
- Advocacy for children
- How to access community resources
- How to develop family and community coalitions for improved health, safety, and nutrition

Whenever a child is injured or dies in the care of a professional caregiver, the media is quick to report it. Although the sensationalism may hurt the profession at the time, good may come from these unfortunate accidents or poor care. Parents have been calling for tougher regulations for safe child care (Chisolm, 1992). Some legislators in this country are more receptive to recommendations from organizations such as the National Association for the Education of Young Children, Children's Defense Fund, The American Academy of Pediatrics, The National Center for Clinical Infant Programs, The American Dietetic Association, and The American Public Health Association. Those organizations have developed standards and recommended guidelines for child caregivers to follow concerning the health, safety, and nutrition of young children. These and other groups are helping

Regulations
recommendations that are made a requirement by law

Staff-to-child ratio
the number of staff required to provide proper care for the number of children of a certain age group

to effect legislation that originates **regulations** or enacts laws that protect children's well-being. For example, the **staff-to-child ratio** is an issue covered by regulations.

The American Academy of Pediatrics and the American Public Health Association believe that standards and guidelines should be established for all nonparental child care. The United States Department of Health and Human Services oversees federal regulations that have been enacted to help children. Individual states can enact legislation that creates regulations for child care. Many states have strict licensing regulations for child care settings, although some states have few, if any, licensing requirements. These licensing requirements basically relate to center-based care and family child care. There are virtually no regulations for in-home child caregivers.

Guidelines, standards, and regulations affect the child caregiver. They exist to support and promote the health and well-being of children. If guidelines, standards, and regulations exist, they should be followed. In a center-based facility, it is up to the director to ensure that the staff complies with and understands the guidelines, standards, and regulations. In a family child care home, it is the caregiver who monitors guidelines, standards, and regulations to ensure compliance. A caregiver who cares for a child in the child's own home must use common sense and form guidelines based on information from classes and available support such as this text or a network of community resources.

If the state in which the child care is performed has no regulations, it is imperative that the caregiver follow guidelines and standards suggested by the organizations previously discussed in this introduction. Many of the guidelines and standards are reflected in this text. It is basic good child care practice to follow them. The caregiver who uses them will be able to provide a healthy, protective environment for the children in care.

KEY CONCEPT PROVIDING HIGH QUALITY CHILD CARE

High quality care should be the objective of every child caregiver. For good health, safety, and nutrition in child care, the caregiver should have four basic goals: to maximize the health status of children; to minimize risks to children; to utilize education as a tool for health promotion and risk reduction; and to recognize the importance of guidelines, standards, and laws as they apply to child care.

CHAPTER **SUMMARY**

A holistic approach allows the caregiver to look at the interrelationships of health, safety, and nutrition for the care of young children. An ecological perspective views the total environment of the child. The physical, social and emotional, economic, and cultural environments all have an effect on the growth and development of children. Health, safety, and nutritional risk factors may come from any of these environments.

Awareness of efforts on national, state, and local levels may help clarify the role of the child caregiver concerning health, safety, and nutrition and nutritional practices, and recognizing signs and symptoms of health problems for early intervention.

Quality child care involves maximizing the health status of children and minimizing risk. Health promotion and risk management will enable the caregiver to ensure this. A caregiver who recognizes the importance of guidelines, standards, and laws has the tools for maximizing the child's environment. These tools help the caregiver set up healthy and safe practices, risk management strategies, and other tools needed to create a quality environment for the children in care.

TO GO **BEYOND**

Questions for Review

1. Discuss the holistic approach to children's health, safety, and nutrition. How does the interrelationship affect those issues when applied to child care?
2. Describe the ecological perspective of the total environment. Consider a child that you know. How does each of these areas affect this child's health? How does it affect this child's safety? How does it affect this child's nutrition?

AS AN **INDIVIDUAL**

1. Look at your own environment. What are the risks you see in it? What could you do to minimize the risks and maximize the health and safety of your own environment? How could you improve your nutritional status?
2. Observe a child care situation. Look at it with a holistic approach. What is the caregiver or facility doing to contribute to the children's health, safety, and nutrition? How would you improve the child care using the holistic approach?
3. What are the health and safety standards or regulations for child care in your community? In your state? If possible, obtain a copy.

AS A **GROUP**

1. Discuss health promotion activities on your own campus. Are you aware of them? Are they adequate? What suggestions for improvement do you have?

2. Obtain and examine the local licensing requirements for health and safety measures in child care. Are they adequate? How would you change them? Are those changes practical?

3. Watch the video *Whatever Happened to Childhood?* List the health, safety, and nutritional practices that are causing risks to children.

4. Discuss the environment of your own community. Be sure you consider all elements: physical, social and emotional, economic, and cultural. How would you rate your community? What could be done to improve it?

CHAPTER **REFERENCES**

American Academy of Pediatrics. (1994, June/July). Warning to parents who smoke. *Healthy Kids*, 52.

American Public Health Association & American Academy of Pediatrics. (1992). *Caring for our children: National health and safety performance standards: Guidelines for out-of-home care*. Washington, DC: American Public Health Association.

Barbarin, O. (1993). Emotional and social development of African American children. *Journal of Black Pathology, 19*(4), 381–390.

Bittman, M. (1994, March 18). Eating well: Why would a child exasperate his parents by refusing to eat? Maybe he isn't hungry. *New York Times*, B7, C4.

Bowlby, J. (1988). *A secure base*. New York: Basic Books.

Bowman, B. (1995). The professional development challenge: Supporting young children and families. *Young Children, 51*(1), 30–34.

Brazelton, T. (1992). *Touchpoints*. New York: Addison-Wesley.

Bredekamp, S. (Ed.) (1987). *Developmentally appropriate practice*. Washington, DC: National Association for the Education of Young Children.

Cesarone, B. (1993). *Health care, nutrition and goal one*. Eric Digest. Champaign, IL: Eric Clearinghouse on Elementary and Childhood Education.

Children's Defense Fund. (1996). *The state of America's children: Yearbook 1996*. Washington, DC: Author.

Chisolm, P. (1992). The search for safe day care. *Maclean's, 105*(25), 30.

Cicchetti, D., & Lynch, M. (1993). Toward an ecological/transactional model of community violence and child maltreatment. *Psychiatry, 56*(1), 96–118.

Fuchs, V. (1991). Are Americans underinvesting in their children? *Society, 28*(6), 14–22.

Glotzer, D., & Weitsman, M. (1991). Childhood injuries: Issues for the physician. *American Family Physician, 44*(5), 1705–1716.

Graham, J. (1994, April/May). Immunization update. *Healthy Kids,* 58–61.

Grubb, P. (1993). The quality of regenerated family day care homes and compliance with minimum standards. *Child Welfare, 72*(5), 461–472.

Herr, J. (1991). Child care providers and parents: Let's work together for America's young children. *Personnel, 68*(9), 15.

Honig, A. (1993). Mental health for babies: What do theory research teach us? *Young Children, 48*(3), 69–75.

Johnson, D. (1993, March). *Teaching low-income mothers to teach their children*. Paper presented at the meeting of the Society for Research in Child Development. New Orleans, LA.

Kahler, L., O'Shea, R., Duffy, L., & Buck, G. (1993). Factors associated with rates of participation in WIC by eligible women. *Public Health Reports, 107*(1), 60–65.

Loeb, P., Friedman, D. Lord, M., Guttman, M., & Kukula, G. (1993). To make a nation: How immigrants are changing America for better and worse. *U.S. News and World Report, 115*(13), 47–52.

Luster, T., Boger, R., & Hannan, K. (1993). Infant affect and home environment. *Journal of Marriage and the Family, 55*(3), 651–661.

National Health Education Consortium. (1992). *Creating sound minds and bodies: Health and education working together.* Washington, DC: Author.

Phillips, D., Howes, C., & Whitebook, M. (1992). The social policy context of child care: Effects on quality. *American Journal of Community Psychology, 20*(1), 25–51.

Plomin, R., Reiss, D., Hetherington, M., & Howe, G. (1994). Nature and nurture: Genetic contributions to measures of the family environment. *Developmental Psychology, 30*(1), 32–33.

Popenoe, D. (1993). American family decline, 1960–1990: A review and appraisal. *Journal of Marriage and the Family, 55*(3), 527–542.

Robertson, C. (1993). *California community college curriculum and resource guide for working with prenatally substance exposed children and their families.* Sacramento, CA: Chancellor's Office California Community Colleges.

Rosenblum, G. (1993, November). Is your house making your family sick? *Sesame Street Parents Magazine,* 68–72.

Sam, D. (1992). Psychological acculturation of young visible immigrants. *Migration World Magazine, 20*(3), 21–24.

Schweinhart, L. (1994). *Lasting benefits of preschool programs* (ERIC Digest). Champaign, IL: Eric Clearinghouse on Elementary and Early Childhood Education.

Spaccarelli, S., Sandler, I., & Rooss, M. (1994). History of spouse violence against mother: Correlated risks and unique effects of child mental health. *Journal of Family Violence, 8*(1), 79–98.

Stein, M. (1995, July 23). We're breaking the cycle of abuse. *Parade Magazine,* 8.

Takeuchi, D., Williams, D., & Adair, R. (1991). Economic stress in the family. *Journal of Marriage and the Family, 53(4),* 1031–1041.

Too much of a good thing. (1994, July). *Tufts University Diet and Nutrition Letter, 12*(5), 1.

University of Colorado at Denver, University of California at Los Angeles, University of North Carolina and Yale University. (1995, January). *Cost, quality and child outcomes in child care centers.* [Executive Summary].

U.S. Department of Health and Human Services. (1990). *Healthy people year 2000: National health promotion and disease prevention objectives* (DHHS Publication No. 91-50213). Washington, DC: U.S. Government Printing Office.

Vilchez, K., & Tinsley, B. (1993, March). *Latino families' childhood health socialization: Theoretical and applied issues.* Paper presented at the meeting of the Society for Research in Child Development, New Orleans, LA.

Wright, J. (1990). Homelessness is not healthy for children and other living things. *Child and Youth Services, 14*(1), 65–88.

Young, K. (1994, May 1). From zero to three. *San Diego Union-Tribune,* p. G-4.

Zeitlin, M. (1991). Nutritional resilience in a hostile environment: Positive deviance in child nutrition. *Nutrition Reviews, 49*(9), 259–268.

Zero to Three/National Center for Clinical Infant Programs. (1992). *Heart start: The emotional foundation of school readiness.* Arlington, VA: Author.

SUGGESTIONS FOR **READING**

Aronson, S., Smith, H., & Martin, J. (1993). *Model health care policies.* Bryn Mawr, PA: Pennsylvania Chapter American Academy of Pediatrics.

Belsky, J. (1988). The effects of infant day care reconsidered. *Early Childhood Research Quarterly, 3*(3).

Child care and early education program participation of infants, toddlers, and preschoolers. The National Data Resource Center. NCES 95-213. Path: http://www.ed.gov:80/NCES/Sbriefs/sbielec2.html.

Children's Defense Fund. *Maybe America really is going to hell in a handbasket.* [Brochure]. Washington, DC: Author.

Griffin, A. (1993). *Preventing preventable harm to babies: Promoting health and safety in child care.* Arlington, VA: Zero to Three.

LEAD! No. 1 environmental pediatric health problem. (1994). *Young Children, 49*(4), 9.

National household education survey—Child care and early education program participation of infants, toddlers, and preschoolers. (1995). U.S. Department of Education National Center for Education Statistics [Internet].

Schweinhart, L. (1993). Observing young children in action: The key to early childhood assessment. *Young Children, 48*(7), 29–33.

HEALTH IN CHILD CARE

In this section we will discuss four areas that deal with health:

1. Promoting Good Health for Children
2. Tools for Promoting Good Health in Children
3. Infection Control in Child Care
4. Health Care in Child Care

In order to properly cover these expansive topics we will relate them to basic health policies that work well in child care settings. These policies will connect health promotion and risk management tools to each chapter's focus.

25

CHAPTER ONE

Promoting Good Health for Children

Upon completion of this chapter, including a review of the summary, you should be able to:

Health Policies

Define and discuss health policies and their use as a tool for health prevention, protection, and promotion.

Children's Health Records

Discuss the contents and importance of health records, including up-to-date immunizations.

Staff Health

Discuss the importance of health policies for staff, including staff health records and promoting staff health.

Providing a Mentally Healthy Environment

Indicate the importance that stable, responsive, and consistent caregiving has on providing a child with an optimum environment for good mental health.

Implications for Caregivers

Discuss the importance of parent and child education, role modeling positive health actions, and supervision for providing optimum health.

Health policies
framework for ensuring
health and well-being in
child care settings

HEALTH POLICIES

Health policies help the caregiver manage risks to good physical and mental health that might be found in child care. These policies provide the framework for providing protection and prevention. A child caregiver who has health policies can improve the care of children. The following information indicates the need for improving the care of children:

■ The overall quality of infant and toddler care is not good (Chiara, 1995; Willer et al., 1992).

■ Children of poor or low income families are more likely to experience substandard care (Children's Defense Fund, 1996).

■ At least one of every four children has not received one or more of the vaccinations needed to prevent childhood diseases and this can lead to epidemic levels of these diseases (Children's Defense Fund, 1996.)

■ Children in the care of others have three to four times the amount of diarrhea and a higher incidence of colds than children in their parents' care (Centers for Disease Control, 1990).

■ Negative mental health effects of children exposed to violence can be offset by child care professionals (Wallach, 1993).

Designing a Health Policy

Health policies should be developed and directed toward the children and staff. They should promote healthy practices for the child, the caregiver, and the family. Basic health policies lay the foundation for the child care atmosphere.

Health policies establish a process, assign responsibility, and offer guidance for action. Health policies may take the form of checklists, records, guidelines, practices, and strategies. When policies are being developed, the following questions should be asked (Kendrick, Kaufmann, & Messenger, 1995):

■ What needs to be done?

■ What process will be followed?

■ Who is responsible for making sure the process is followed?

■ Are there any time parameters or limitations?

The question "What needs to be done?" provides the child caregiver with information needed to create a specific health policy for a particular issue. An example of this is a state mandate that child caregivers must report any suspected abuse. The caregiver creates a policy for dealing with how, when, and where to make a report of suspected abuse.

Addressing the process involved in a health policy will help the caregiver understand how the policy should be carried out. The process explains when, and perhaps where, an action should be performed. An example of this is proper hand washing techniques for good sanitation practices. This policy should show that hand washing should be done in a certain manner, that it should be done before or after certain events, and that it should be done in a particular area under certain conditions.

Children are extremely active. In both private homes and public child care centers, it is the responsibility of the child caregiver to ensure their safety.

The child care setting will determine who is responsible for carrying out the policy. In a child care center, responsibility may fall to the director, the primary caregiver, an assigned health advocate, or a health consultant from the community. In family child care, the responsibility will usually fall to the child caregiver or the assistant. In in-home care, the nanny will probably have the responsibility. It is important to define the responsible party so that the policy does not go unenforced. A good health policy will have checks and balances for responsibility built into the policy.

Time limitations or parameters may be a critical factor in some areas of health in child care. Where applicable, time constraints should be included in the health policy. This is especially true for emergency situations. A child who has fallen and is unconscious for more than a few seconds should have immediate emergency medical care. Another example is the health record. A child's immunization record should be checked quarterly to make sure the child's immunizations are up to date. If they are not, the parent is given a date by which the child's immunizations must be updated.

Health policies should be clearly written and include guidelines, limitations, and suggested methods of communication to be used for each topic. Health policies help the caregiver develop proper practices based on knowledge of health prevention, protection, and promotion. Basic policies should also be created to cover the areas of safety, nutrition, and special topics.

Health, safety, and nutrition policies should incorporate the four major goals of high-quality child care (see Figure 1.1):

■ Maximizing health status

■ Minimizing risk

■ Using education as a tool

■ Recognizing the importance of guidelines

FIGURE **1.1**
Four Major Goals of High
Quality Child Care

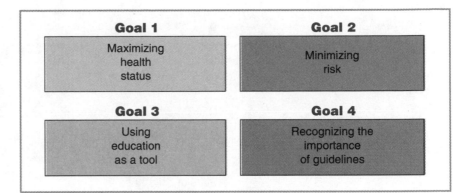

Goal 1
Maximizing health status

Goal 2
Minimizing risk

Goal 3
Using education as a tool

Goal 4
Recognizing the importance of guidelines

Basic health policies for promoting good health should cover:

1. *Health Records:* specific records for the child to be accepted and stay in care
2. *Staff Health:* using staff health and health records to promote health and protect the environment
3. *Protective and Preventive Practices for a Mentally Healthy Environment:* specific practices for creating a proactive and interventive environment for good mental health
4. *Implications for Caregivers:* strategies and practices for health education, cultural sensitivity, role modeling, and supervision in child care

KEY HEALTH POLICIES

CONCEPT

Basic health policies should be designed to provide protection, prevention, and promotion of good health in child care. These policies should include guidelines, records, and checklists. The health policy should define what is to be done and then outline the process for doing it. It should also define who is responsible and provide for follow-through. When time parameters are critical, the health policy should address them. Good health policies should address the basics of children's health records, staff health, providing a mentally healthy environment, and implications for caregivers that provide for education, role modeling, cultural sensitivity, and supervision.

CHILDREN'S HEALTH RECORDS

Increased risk for poor health and mental health is often associated with group care (Belsky, 1988). To help reduce this risk, caregivers should create a health policy for children's health records that covers certain basic information regarding each child's health and should include guidelines for all children. The contents of each child's preadmission health history form are listed in Table 1.1. Table 1.2 lists the records that are kept for all children.

TABLE **1.1**

Checklist for Child's Health History

Check for:

- [ ] Name, address, and phone number
- [ ] Physician's name, address, and phone number
- [ ] Emergency numbers (two minimum)
- [ ] State of child's health
- [ ] Record of immunizations
- [ ] Dietary restrictions
- [ ] Allergies and other conditions that may require medication
- [ ] Any condition that requires special consideration for care
- [ ] Any special problems or fears
- [ ] TB test for children over one year
- [ ] Any previous major illness or injury
- [ ] An emergency release form signed by the parent

TABLE **1.2**

Records to Keep for Each Child

Check for:

- [ ] Health history and preadmission exam form
- [ ] Immunization records
- [ ] Injury reports
- [ ] Assessment and screening results
- [ ] Medication log and permission slips, where applicable. Some states do not allow caregivers to administer medication.
- [ ] Health communication history between parents, staff, and health provider
- [ ] Reports of all illnesses that have occurred while in child care
- [ ] Growth chart
- [ ] Any update to the health history as it occurs

Parents should provide the caregiver with a release to discuss medical information with the child's doctor. What information should be included on these forms?

Orientation
meeting or discussion of a child new to care regarding health, special needs, and developmental history

Guidelines for this health policy should include an **orientation** for the caregiver for each child. This orientation would cover the special developmental needs of the child, dietary restrictions, and any special health or nutritional needs. Caregivers should have a developmental health history in order to know the child and provide for a holistic approach to care. A checklist to review with parents is found in Appendix A.

 Jon, a two-year-old boy, was new to the child care facility. The facility director read Jon's history, but Amanda, his primary child caregiver, never saw it. In his second week at school, Amanda gave Jon sliced bananas and a cup of raspberry yogurt for morning snack. In a short time, Jon broke out in hives and then went into anaphylactic shock. The child care center called an ambulance immediately. His records were provided to the emergency care technician, who noticed that Jon was allergic to bananas. The director had failed to pass on the information to Amanda. Jon recovered, but the incident frightened everyone involved with the child care facility, including all the children who witnessed it and the parents who heard about it. The center immediately changed its policy to require that all possible caregivers for each child must review the child's health history and any specific dietary information must be posted on the refrigerator, in the kitchen, and by each food serving station as a reminder. Information on other allergies was also posted in the corner of the room as a reminder to the caregivers.

Confidential
keeping information private

Although the information found in health records is very important to the caregiver, it must be a policy that this information remain **confidential** and not be discussed with anyone but the parents of the child, members

As parents drop off children, informal quick health assessments may be made by the child caregiver. Is the child lethargic and listless? Does the child look flush or pale?

of the staff, or the child's health care professional. The parents should provide the caregiver with a release to discuss medical information with the child's doctor. Discussion among staff should remain at a professional level. Certain information in the developmental history could lead to labeling a child; the professionally competent child caregiver understands the need for discretion and confidentiality.

It is important to have a review procedure included in the health policy. Keeping records current allows for periodic review to look for specific warning signs, normal development rates, and immunization.

KEY CHILDREN'S HEALTH RECORDS

CONCEPT

Health policies created for the health records of children are vitally important for the prevention of diseases and the protection of everyone involved in child care. Health histories that include currency in immunizations, special considerations, and special needs of children can prevent the spread of infectious disease as well as alert staff to possible health-related problems that may occur in the child care setting. Procedures for orientation of new children in care, as well as the management of communications and confidentiality, give the caregiver guidelines for conduct.

How can preventive and protective measures by the child caregiver help ensure a healthy environment?

Infectious diseases
diseases capable of invading the body and causing an infection to occur; may or may not be contagious

STAFF HEALTH

The health policy that covers staff health records and health care is of primary importance. The child caregiver usually cares for a number of young children and the potential for spreading **infectious diseases** to other children, other employees, and her own family is great. Other occupational health hazards will be discussed later. Every child caregiver should be able to comfortably perform the duties of the job. The policy for health records and health care for staff should reflect preventive and protective measures. The health policy should apply to all staff members, including volunteers.

Staff Records

Before any caregiver is hired or considers beginning a career working with children, he should have information available to complete a staff health record. The caregiver health history should include the information listed in Table 1.3 (see also Appendix A).

Other items that might be included in an adult health history are limitations in common situations, such as allergies to art materials, medications, and the general health status of family members residing in the household. Some states have mandated forms that will be provided.

Before a potential caregiver cares for children, a complete physical should be given. This pre-employment health examination will evaluate general health and physical condition. It will also provide the opportunity to complete the schedule of immunizations if any of the required immunizations are missing. After employment, regular health checkups will evaluate maintenance of good health.

Potential caregivers should have a complete physical, including a general health evaluation and a review of immunizations before working with children.

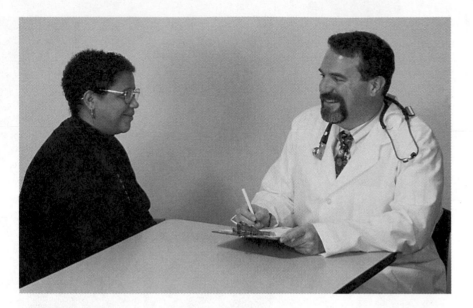

TABLE **1.3**

Checklist for Caregiver Health History

Check for:

☐ Name, address, and phone number

☐ Physician's, name, address, and phone number

☐ Pre-employment examination that includes an evaluation of general health, the physical ability to perform job duties as outlined, and any condition that would create a hazard to children or other staff

☐ Immunization records including currency in all necessary immunizations and history of childhood diseases

☐ TB test results

☐ Hearing and vision screening

Maintaining Staff Health

A child caregiver should protect the health of children and should also be a role model for good health. Maintaining the health of a child caregiver can be challenging because of the following occupational hazards:

■ Exposure to infectious diseases

■ Stress

■ Risk for back injury

■ Potential exposure to environmental hazards

Exposure to Infectious Diseases. All caregivers should be immunized against or have a natural immunity to the following infectious diseases: diphtheria, tetanus, mumps, measles, rubella, Hepatitis B, and polio. If the caregiver has had the disease, a natural immunity will have developed. Immunizations and occurrence of infectious disease should be thoroughly checked before employment. If the measles vaccine was given before the age of fifteen months, a booster should be given to an adult, especially if the adult is a female of childbearing age. Tuberculosis should also be checked before employment through a skin test. This test should be repeated approximately every two years.

Special safeguards should be in place for pregnant caregivers or women with childbearing potential. Unborn children may acquire certain infectious diseases in the child care setting that can cause birth defects and in some cases, miscarriage. Five of these infectious diseases that can be prevented by proper pre-pregnancy immunization are measles, mumps, rubella, chicken pox (varicella), and Hepatitis B. Other occupational health hazards include herpes, cytomegalovirus (CMV), parvovirus, and AIDS.

Hand washing is the number one defense a caregiver uses to avoid the spread of infectious disease. Wearing rubber gloves helps support the check of disease. Special care should be made to follow all sanitary procedures, especially those that deal with children's mucous secretions, blood, and urine and bowel movements. Caregivers should wear gloves each time a child's nose is wiped, after dealing with a cut or injury, for assisting in toileting or diaper changing, and before food is handled. Use of latex gloves is not suggested because of possible allergic reactions to the caregivers or children. Hands should be washed immediately after removing gloves.

If a caregiver becomes ill, a sick day should be taken. A staff health policy should include a substitute list of caregivers for the protection of the

Staff meetings are an excellent forum for discussing the occupational health hazards that can affect caregivers.

Child care can be highly stressful and often results in job burnout. What measures can caregivers take to cope with stress and avoid burnout?

children and the rest of the staff. There should also be substitutes or backup caregivers if a family child caregiver or nanny becomes ill. A family child caregiver may have to send the children to another family child caregivers' home. This backup care must be arranged in advance so that parents will not have to arrange for another form of care for a day or two.

Stress
nonspecific response of the body to any demand put on it

Stress.   Caring for children is a rewarding profession, but it has the potential for **stress**. There are a number of reasons why the potential for stress is present in caregiving. These reasons include:

- ■ Isolation from other adults. This is more likely to occur in family child care and nanny care.

- ■ Long hours and hard work. Working with children and needing to be constantly aware can be stressful. Breaks may be rare.

- ■ Trying to do too much in too little time. Packing the day with too many activities or expectations of yourself or the children in care.

- ■ Balancing work and the rest of life. This may include family, roommates, or school.

- ■ Low wages and lack of recognition. Children and those who care for them are not adequately valued in our society.

- ■ Lack of training. Caregivers with more training have coping skills, organizational skills, and increased knowledge of appropriate activities for children that help them get through the day with less stress.

- ■ Dealing with parents and respecting their needs.

- ■ Dealing with individual children with a variety of needs.

Job burnout
inability to perform job due
to excessive stress

Job burnout is one reaction to too much stress in life. Burnout is the combination of emotional and physical feelings of not being able to function. It is a result of the accumulation of stress, and is a hazard for caregivers. Studies show the job burnout rate for child caregivers in center-based care is 43 percent per year (University of Colorado at Denver et al., 1995). That means for every 100 people who begin the year as a child caregiver, only 57 are still on the job a year later. A major contributing factor to the significant turnover rate is too much stress.

It is important for the caregiver to learn the warning signals and signs of stress. Awareness of stress is the first step in preventing it and protecting the caregiver. Stress is the body's response to a threat. A biochemical reaction occurs within the body whether the threat is real or imagined. Stressors are people, places, or events that an individual perceives as a threat. What may be a stressor to one person may not be a stressor to another person. Causes of stress and reactions to it are unique to the individual (see Table 1.4).

A person can learn how to cope with stress and may be able to reduce or eliminate it. Changing one's perception and reaction to the stressor is one way to deal with stress. Another way is to eliminate or reduce the cause or source of stress. Time management is also a helpful tool to eliminate stress.

TABLE **1.4**

Stress Warning Signal Checklist

Check for:

- ☐ Persistent feelings of anxiety, nervousness, or depression
- ☐ Fatigue
- ☐ Frustration, moodiness, or irritability
- ☐ Difficulty in concentrating or forgetfulness
- ☐ Loneliness
- ☐ Perfectionism
- ☐ Restlessness
- ☐ Eating too much or too little
- ☐ Sleeping too much or not being able to sleep
- ☐ Job dissatisfaction
- ☐ Absenteeism

- ☐ Procrastination
- ☐ Interpersonal conflicts with adults or children
- ☐ Frequent headaches
- ☐ Neck and backaches
- ☐ Asthma
- ☐ Muscle tension and/or spasms
- ☐ Indigestion, diarrhea, or constipation
- ☐ Infections or skin rashes
- ☐ Lowered immunity to illness
- ☐ Sexual problems
- ☐ Increased smoking, use of alcohol or drugs

A child's schedule may not always agree with the caregiver's schedule, causing daily stress for both.

There are several techniques for changing perception and reaction to stressors. Sharing stress with others helps one see the problem from another person's point of view. Just talking about it with a friend or family member may reduce the level of stress or even the perception that stress exists. A person who learns to recognize limitations can help reduce stress and possibly understand why stress exists in certain situations. A person who realizes certain situations are not within her control should accept the fact that the situation cannot be changed. Instead, the person should take time to recognize what situations can be changed. At this time it is within the power of the individual to change the circumstance in order to reduce or eliminate stress.

Marcus had a difficult time with transitions, especially at lunch and snack time. First Marcus had to settle down and then he ate very slowly. His teacher, Lavonne, worked hard to follow a scheduled routine each day. She tried to get Marcus to eat faster, but he still dawdled at each meal. Lavonne's feelings of resentment toward Marcus and frustration that she was not meeting her own expectations were causing her stress. She went to Anita, her director, to discuss her feelings. They came to several conclusions. Marcus' behavior of transitioning might always be difficult at mealtimes. Lavonne would continue to try different strategies, but they agreed that in the meantime, she would try not to react to that behavior. In addition, Anita would try to give Lavonne some relief during this stressful time.

Lavonne realized that she could not fix everything, and that gave her the sense of freedom to accept the way Marcus acted at mealtime. Anita tried to provide someone to help Lavonne with the end of lunchtime as often as possible. This left the other caregiver with Marcus while Lavonne was free to continue with her plan of activities. Anita and Lavonne discussed what would happen if no one was available to help relieve Lavonne at lunchtime. They agreed that Lavonne's expectation that a schedule should be or could be followed rigidly was unrealistic. Lavonne learned to be more flexible and to not feel bad if everything did not go according to her plan. Lavonne was much happier in her work and the child care atmosphere was less stressful for everyone concerned.

Learning to manage time can also help reduce stress. Many people try to do too much. The pressure of having expectations of what can be accomplished in a certain time frame can lead to stress. To change perception about time, there are several positive techniques found in Table 1.5.

TABLE **1.5**

Time Management Checklist

Check for:

☐ Do only one thing at a time. Some people try to manage three or four activities at a time. Child caregiving is an activity that almost demands that, but one can learn to try not to do too many things at one time.

☐ Slow down.

☐ When several children ask for help at the same time, find ways for them to help each other or explain your need to finish with another task first.

☐ Learn to say no to activities or events that are not productive or enjoyable.

☐ Make a "to do" list every morning or afternoon for the following day. Allow time for this activity. Prioritize the items that must be done, and eliminate those that can be done later.

☐ Try not to be a perfectionist. Use the worst case scenario for trying to reduce perfectionism. Ask "what's the worst that can happen" if something is not done up to the self-enforced standard.

☐ If you are stuck in a line or traffic, realize it is out of your control. Try relaxing or do deep breathing exercises.

☐ Do not try to do everything yourself. If someone offers to help, let them. If help is needed, ask for it.

A number of other strategies are available to help reduce or eliminate stress as it occurs. These methods include both physical and mental coping skills. Some of the things one can do physically are to increase physical activity, eat a balanced diet, and get enough sleep. Exercise is particularly important. Exercising vigorously for 20 minutes, three times a week can be a major reducer of stress. Hormones are released during excercise that help the body cope with stress. Eliminating sugar and caffeine in the diet can also help to relieve stress because both have physical side effects that may allow stress to occur more easily. Eating healthy foods, including lots of fresh fruits and vegetables, can help the body be more resilient to stress.

People who care for others often find it difficult to care for themselves. Making more time for leisure, daydreaming, crying when it is needed, and learning to relax are ways that help a person's mind adjust to stress. Some people find it difficult to relax. Learn to schedule a quiet time each day to relax and reflect. Reading, taking a bubble bath, or watching television may be relaxing. Other leisure activities such as hobbies may be more physically active, but they can be equally relaxing. Do not try the activity at a fast pace nor focus on its competitive nature. This may eliminate the stress reduction quality of the leisure activity. Instead, focus on the enjoyment and relaxation benefits of the activity.

When stress is present, try deep breathing exercises. Breathe in slowly, hold the breath for 1 or 2 seconds, and then let it out slowly. This helps the body to come to a more neutral point. Relaxation response techniques such as holding a group of muscles taut, then allowing them to relax may also help. This process usually involves the entire body, starting with the head and moving down to end with the feet.

Caregivers should bend at the knees, not the waist, when working with children to ensure proper caregiver-child interaction and reduce the risk of back strain.

Back Injury. Back problems are very common. Most people experience back pain at one time or another. Child caregivers may be called upon to lift and carry children many times in a day. They also bend over to play, change diapers, and feed children. Lifting, bending, twisting and sitting are frequent normal daily activities for the child caregiver. If these tasks are done correctly, problems with the back can be minimized. However, if they are done incorrectly, serious back problems can result. Many child caregivers are not as careful as they need to be; therefore, back injury is considered an occupational hazard.

It is important for the caregiver to learn how to correctly bend, lift, and sit. Lifting should be done by bending at the knees, not the waist. Bending at the knees can help relieve some stress from the back; bending at the waist adds stress to the back. When the knees are bent, the legs carry most of the load. If the waist is bent, the back carries the load. Whatever is being lifted should be kept close to the body, not held away from it. During lifting, move the feet as needed but do not twist the body (see Figure 1.2). If possible, do not lift or pull heavy objects that need to be moved. Instead, push the object so that the stress on the back is lessened.

Bending over to talk to a child or to perform other common activities should also be done from the knees, not the waist. Getting at the child's level is important, but it can be done in less physically stressful ways. Position can be shifted from bending at the knees to kneeling, sitting in a chair, squatting, or even sitting cross-legged on the floor (see Figure 1.3).

Surprisingly, sitting down is more stressful on the back than standing or walking. If sitting is necessary, be sure to maintain good posture and try to sit in a way that supports the curve of the back (see Figure 1.4). When bending to sit or to stand from a sitting position, it is better to hang on to something stationary to help remove stress from the back. Child caregivers

FIGURE **1.2**
How to Lift

FIGURE **1.3**
Sitting on a chair or on the floor at a child's level is crucial for effective caregiver-child interactions, but can result in daily back strain. To relieve pressure on the back, bend from the knees when sitting or standing and hold onto something stationary.

FIGURE **1.4**
Correct Body Alignment When Sitting

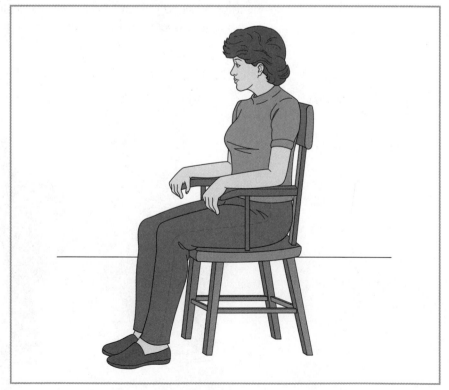

FIGURE **1.5**
Exercises for the Back

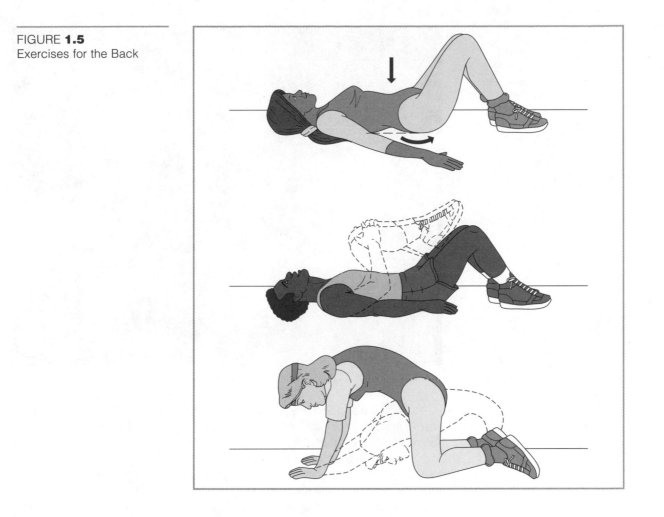

often sit in child-sized chairs. This is acceptable as long as it is comfortable, but it should be avoided if it causes back pain or discomfort.

Just as exercise can relieve stress, it can also build protection for the back. Regular exercise can strengthen the back muscles to support the spine (see Figure 1.5). This will help the back withstand the daily routine of the child caregiver.

Exposure to Environmental Hazards. There are numerous environmental hazards in child care. The most common hazards are arts and crafts materials, cleaning supplies, and pesticides. All arts and crafts materials should be examined and labels should indicate that they are nontoxic. Throw away any materials that are not labeled nontoxic. If there are any questions, call the local Poison Control office. Some paints or other craft items may cause a harmful reaction. For example, several years ago, some child care centers stopped using shaving cream as an art supply because of the rashes it caused. Others continued using it, because it did not cause rashes. If any materials are found to be harmful to the children or caregiver, their use should be discontinued. It is also important to always maintain good ventilation when working with arts and crafts materials.

Arts and crafts materials are some of the most common environmental hazards in child care. Good ventilation is essential when working with these materials.

Cleaning supplies should also be nontoxic. Cleaning supplies may be strong enough to cause skin irritation so gloves should be worn when using them. The room should be ventilated and air kept circulating during cleaning. This will help lessen any irritation to the nose, lungs, and eyes. If there should be lingering odor, continue with ventilation and air circulation until the odor lessens.

When pesticides are necessary, they should be applied by a professional exterminator when children are not present. The area that the pesticide is applied to should be well ventilated after the application. A child caregiver should be present and watch the application to make sure that the pesticide does not get on food, food preparation areas, or play areas. If minor use of pesticides, such as spraying for ants, is done by the caregiver, the same rules should apply. Gloves should be used and discarded. These cautions will help prevent skin, nose, or lung irritations.

CONCEPT

KEY STAFF HEALTH REQUIREMENTS

Staff health is an important factor in the prevention and protection of health in the child care environment. All personnel should have a pre-employment physical examination and should meet health record requirements. Staff health should be maintained by keeping up immunizations and by washing hands frequently. The caregiver should employ practices that help avoid stress, back pain, and exposure to hazardous environmental materials.

PROVIDING A MENTALLY HEALTHY ENVIRONMENT

Mental health is an area of health promotion that may be overlooked. The importance of providing a consistent, loving, and protective environment cannot be stressed enough. Warm, responsive, one-on-one care is essential to providing a good mentally healthy environment (Honig, 1993; MacDonald, 1992). Children need an atmosphere where they feel that they belong. Each child needs to feel unique and have a sense of power. The child also needs to feel the freedom to express himself through play, talk, and action.

When a health policy is being developed for mental health, several considerations need to be included. Attention to a child's family situation and cultural background is essential for developing a rapport with the child. Some stressful environmental factors that a child may have and that may negatively affect health are found in Table 1.6.

TABLE **1.6**

Caution Signs for Environmental Factors Affecting Mental Health

Warnings
☐ Poverty
☐ Divorce/single parent family/stepfamily
☐ Drug abuse in the home
☐ Child abuse
☐ Other at-risk home environments
☐ Frequent relocation
☐ Immigration
☐ Cultural considerations, including English as a second language
☐ Lack of bonding or attachment
☐ Special needs
☐ Lack of resiliency
☐ Poor health or nutrition

Self-esteem
positive sense of self

Self-esteem in a child is the general product of a mentally healthy environment. When a child has a sense of self-esteem, that child feels both lovable and capable. A child's self-esteem evolves primarily through the quality of relationships with people in her life. Responsiveness in caregiving enables the child to feel good about herself. A caregiver offering emotional security and encouragement can provide the foundation for success in later life (Zero to Three, 1992).

A primary caregiver for an infant provides emotional security through an atmosphere of caring and trust. This security is an important foundation of self-esteem.

Caregiver behaviors that promote a mentally healthy environment can not only provide this in the moment, but they can alleviate past problems and may help the child in the future. Table 1.7 outlines caregiver behaviors that are useful in providing a mentally healthy environment.

TABLE **1.7**

Providing a Mentally Healthy Environment

Check for:

- ☐ Establish a good relationship with parents, including respect and mutual communication.
- ☐ Respond with consistency, predictability, and regularity.
- ☐ Establish daily routines for a sense of security.
- ☐ Provide support and emotional assurance for the child, including attention, affection, respect, and mutual communication.
- ☐ Allow children to safely explore and master the environment.
- ☐ Help children to express and identify emotions.
- ☐ Redirect anger and aggression through play and discussion.
- ☐ Provide a quiet area so the child can remove himself from stimulation when needed.
- ☐ Value each child's uniqueness, including cultural considerations.
- ☐ Promote responsive caregiving for staff and parents.
- ☐ Be flexible and reasonable in expectations.

The health policy for mental health should include a provision for a primary caregiver for each child. Each child should have one special person to bond with and form a healthy attachment. The primary caregiver can create an atmosphere of caring and trust for the child. This offers the child a sense of stability and consistency. A child who is at risk for mental health difficulties may recognize positive qualities in the caregiver and may be able to seek those same qualities in other adults in the future (Howe, Rodning, Galluzzo, & Meyer, 1987). Stability, understanding, and consistency in the caregiving situation may help the child to become more **resilient** in the home environment (Wallach, 1993).

Resilient
the ability to recover after being exposed to risk

Lauren, a withdrawn three-year-old child whose parents had recently divorced, lived with her father, Jim. Jim hired Julie, a live-in nanny, to help care for Lauren. Jim often traveled, sometimes with little notice. Lauren was not allowed to visit her alcoholic mother due to a court order. Julie was there for Lauren whenever a change or an unexpected event happened. Although Lauren's world seemed to have turned upside down, Julie offered comfort and security. Whenever Jim traveled, Julie stayed with Lauren, and she took Lauren home with her on her days off. Julie understood Lauren's need for stability and she was willing to make sacrifices to ensure that Lauren knew she could depend on Julie. Julie was Lauren's nanny for almost two years. Jim remarried when Lauren was ready to attend kindergarten. Today, Lauren is a happy, outgoing seven-year-old who still occasionally talks to Julie on the phone.

Vulnerability
inability to protect from risk

REALITY CHECK

The Resilient Child

Some children manage to thrive despite much stress and turmoil in their lives. Other children who have very little stress and turmoil in their lives may not manage as well. According to researchers, the terminology for these two circumstances is referred to as a child's resiliency or **vulnerability** (Werner, 1986).

A child who is vulnerable may be so due to a variety of factors. These factors may be inborn and include genetic abnormalities, malnutrition, preterm birth, prenatal stress, or drug exposure. Temperament may also be a factor. Difficult children have a harder time adapting and getting into a rhythm in life. Parents may have a more difficult time coping with and attaching to a difficult child.

Outside circumstances that may make a child more vulnerable are usually related to significant relationships. The bonding process is extremely

continued

important. Children who are insecurely attached may be more vulnerable to outside environmental stresses such as poverty, abandonment, or chaotic living. A child whose physical circumstances may make him vulnerable can have that vulnerability lessened by having a secure attachment to a significant person in his life (Gelman, 1991). First-born children who begin life with no physical difficulties and who are easy in temperament are thought to be most resilient (Werner, 1986).

Another protective factor found in resilient children is high intelligence. Children who possess these qualities are more likely to form close relationships and have a greater ability to solve problems as they grow older. Children who are resilient have been found to have positive qualities from both sexes. They are outgoing and autonomous, and nurturing and emotionally sensitive (Werner, 1986). These qualities allow resilient children to adapt to many situations and circumstances.

Resilient children find it much easier to develop key trusting relationships with an adult. This adult can be a parent, grandparent, other relative, or a teacher. This relationship allows the resilient child the freedom to know that she is significant. As long as the resilient child has someone who cares for her, she can handle almost any situation that comes along.

Both vulnerability and resiliency are significant to the child caregiver. The caregiver may watch a vulnerable child who is insecurely attached have great difficulty coping with life. She may observe a resilient child cope with problems that seem insurmountable. The more supportive the environment is for either of these children, the less the stress and the risk for poor mental health.

The vulnerable child may need extra support from the caregiver through responsive and stimulating care (Bee, 1992). He may need the caregiver to adapt to his needs. The vulnerable child will definitely benefit from a secure attachment with the caregiver. This factor can help the child deal with other factors in his life.

The resilient child will need the care and support of the caregiver, much as a cheerleader helps a team play a game. Although this child is already equipped for success, he will need the secure attachment of an adult to remain successful. If a secure attachment with an adult is unavailable elsewhere but is found during child care, the child may retain his resiliency to the problems and stresses that life may bring.

KEY MENTAL HEALTH ENVIRONMENT

CONCEPT

Many children are at risk for poor mental health. Providing a stable, responsive, and consistent environment can help children acquire protective tools that will help them become more resilient to environmental factors that negatively affect mental health. Providing a primary caregiver for each child in care will help to ensure that the child can form a relationship that will provide those protective tools. A caregiver who regards a child as unique, understands the child's temperament, and is aware of the family helps to individualize the caregiving and provide the optimum environment for good mental health for each child.

role modeling
setting a behavioral example

cultural sensitivity
perceptive, responsive
behavior to cultural
differences

IMPLICATIONS FOR **CAREGIVERS**

Children's attitudes and behavior in relation to health are affected by the adults they observe. The well-being of children is influenced by caregiver training and good practices (Aronson & Aiken, 1980). Caregivers can use **role modeling**, **cultural sensitivity**, education, and supervision to influence health.

Role Modeling

A health policy for role modeling should reflect practices that will affect the actions of children through their observation of their caregivers. Good role modeling includes exhibiting the knowledge and practice of healthy behaviors. Caregivers should display good personal grooming and hygiene and face each day with a positive mental attitude.

Good modeling uses reinforcement through observation and discussion with children. A caregiver who teaches children to use healthy practices and models those behaviors can also help the parent learn. Seeing the child and caregiver modeling healthy behavior may encourage the parent to adapt a healthy practice.

A caregiver's actions set the stage for children to learn from those actions (Bredekamp, 1989). If a caregiver encourages children to wash their hands a certain way but does not do it in the same manner, the children will not readily adopt those hand washing techniques. If the caregiver comes to work ill, the children will wonder why they should stay home when not feeling well. Children often act as a video camera by repeating what they see and hear.

Haim Ginott described the effect that a teacher's actions can have on a child:

> **"** I have come to a frightening conclusion. It is my personal approach that creates the climate. It is my daily mood that makes the weather. As a teacher, I possess tremendous power to make a child's life miserable or joyous. I can be a tool of torture or an instrument of inspiration. I can humiliate or humor, hurt or heal. In all situations it is my response that decides whether a crisis will be escalated or de-escalated, a child humanized or de-humanized. **"** (p. 15)

Because children view the caregiver as a role model, under no circumstances should smoking be permitted at anytime during child care. Smoking is a definite health hazard and caregivers should be good role models for health. Many states do not allow smoking on the premises of child care centers. Secondhand smoke has a detrimental effect on children, so they should be isolated from it as much as possible (see ✓ Reality Check: Secondhand Smoke). A family child caregiver might consider not smoking or giving up the profession to prevent these effects from harming the children in care (Figure 1.6).

Caregivers should practice healthy behaviors.

Philip Morris Can't Be Trusted With America's Children

When Philip Morris looks at its future, it sees our children. Only kids can replace the 3,000 adult smokers who quit or die every day.

Now Philip Morris executives have launched a slick ad campaign claiming they don't want kids to smoke. Yet they also claim tobacco doesn't cause disease, advertising doesn't influence children and nicotine isn't addictive.

If tobacco companies **really** didn't want kids as customers, they would:

- Tell children that tobacco causes addiction and death.
- Stop fighting effective laws to protect children from tobacco.
- Stop spending billions on youth-oriented advertising, event sponsorship and merchandise that kids love.

Don't trust tobacco companies with our children. Tell your elected officials and candidates we need action to protect kids from tobacco marketing.

To contact your Members of Congress or to learn more, call **1-800-284-KIDS**.

FIGURE **1.6**

REALITY CHECK

Secondhand Smoke

Smoking has long been an acceptable behavior in our culture. For the last thirty or so years, medical research on the effects of smoking has found that smoking can lead to certain cancers, lung diseases, and heart disease. In the United States, 350,000 deaths occur every year because of tobacco use. Cigarettes, cigars, and tobacco carry warning labels about these facts. It has only recently been concluded that secondhand smoke may cause health problems for those exposed to a smoker's environment.

Children of smokers have a greater risk for health problems. Low birthweight in newborns may be caused because the mother smoked during pregnancy. If smoking were eliminated, it is estimated that there would be 25 percent fewer low birthweights. The U.S. Surgeon General also estimates that there would be a 10 percent reduction in infant deaths if smoking ceased. Recent studies have shown that the secondhand smoke of the pregnant mother's coworkers or families may pass bloodborne chemicals to her unborn child. These chemicals have been found to prelude childhood leukemia and other cancers (Husted, 1996).

Children under five whose mothers smoke at least ten cigarettes a day were found to have elevated levels of nicotine and other cancer-causing chemicals in their bloodstreams (Buhle, 1994). Secondhand smoke in the home poses great hazards for the children present. More than 350,000 respiratory diseases are found in children each year that are directly related to secondhand smoke (Males, 1995).

Other common childhood health issues of secondhand smoke are:

■ Pneumonia
■ Bronchitis
■ Asthma
■ Middle-ear effusion (hearing loss)
■ More difficulty getting over colds
■ Reduced lung function

■ Sudden infant death syndrome (SIDS)
■ Allergic complications
■ Behavioral problems

The American Academy of Pediatrics Committee on Substance Abuse has called for a tobacco-free environment for all children. The policy statement concludes that tobacco smoke has harmful effects to the health and psychosocial well-being of children and adolescents. The policy also calls for a ban on all advertising for tobacco products. It calls on parents and health professionals to be good role models who do not use tobacco products. Since a major health function of a child caregiver is role modeling, smoking is a behavior that should be avoided.

A recent study also links the deficiency of vitamin C with those who inhale secondhand smoke. Even though the vitamin content of the diets was similar, 12 percent of those exposed to secondhand smoke had alarmingly low levels of vitamin C ("Second Hand Smoke," 1994). The lower level of vitamin C raises the risk for cancer, respiratory illness, and heart disease. Another study examined the effects of tobacco smoke in the home on a child's intelligence. The study concluded that inhaling tobacco smoke in the environment has harmful effects on the cognitive development of children (Johnson, 1993). Providing smoke-free child care is an important task of the caregiver (Massachusetts Department of Public Health, 1992).

Secondhand smoke may be considered an environmental issue that goes beyond the home. Elevated levels of cotinine, a biomarker for nicotine, were found in 80 percent of inner city children in a recent study in Baltimore (PRNewswire, 1996). Many of these children were from nonsmoking homes.

Secondhand smoke has another link to health and safety. Every year, more than 10,000 children under the age of six eat cigarettes or cigarette butts. This can cause low blood pressure and seizure disorders ("Another Cigarette Danger," 1996).

Culturally diverse early childhood classrooms provide additional challenges for caregivers. It is crucial to understand cultural values and traditional background to develop a bias sensitive curriculum and effectively communicate with the children and their families.

Cultural Sensitivity

In today's world, a child caregiver is likely to provide care for children from several cultures. It is important that the child caregiver be sensitive to the needs of the children and families concerning health, safety, and nutrition. Any notes sent home to the parents should be clearly and simply written. Wherever possible, the child's native language should be used. The caregiver should make sure the parent understands what was written and why the note was sent home. The caregiver may have to have to ask a neighbor or relative of the child to help communicate with the parent so there is no misunderstanding.

Health, safety, and nutrition issues may be critical, and there should always be a clear path for communication. Conflicting cultures can make immigrant and refugee children prone to psychological problems and they may have difficulty forming a self-identity or feeling a sense of self-esteem (Sam, 1992). By utilizing a bias-sensitive curriculum and understanding cultural values and traditional background, the caregiver can help provide children with the tools needed to feel good about themselves.

Education

Education is a tool that can be used to promote health. Education for current needs and new developments in health and child care will help caregivers maintain a healthy environment. Caregivers should have the ability to understand the importance of health records for children and staff. Sound training will offer preventive measures to avoid risk to staff health. Caregivers who understand the importance of a mentally healthy environment can develop policies that provide it.

Teaching children how to recognize their own feelings can help them to be better able to cope when problems occur. Offering information to parents about creating good, mentally healthy environments may help them provide this at home.

Supervision

Supervision is an important tool for caregivers to maintain healthy environments. Supervision includes the maintenance of health records for both children and staff. In situations where the caregiver is in charge of staff, supervision should be used to prevent stress, eliminate environmental hazards, and prevent backaches. Gentle reminders may help the staff to alter behaviors.

Supervision is also necessary to ensure the maintenance of a mentally healthy environment. Behaviors of children and caregivers should be monitored. Children may be at risk due to certain environmental factors and a caregiver who notices this early can help provide intervention. The caregiver should be providing consistent, responsive care.

CHAPTER **SUMMARY**

Health policies help the caregiver manage the environment for good physical and mental health. These policies should reflect high-quality child care. Accurate child and staff health histories should be maintained, including immunization records. Staff should model and maintain good health by avoiding exposure to infectious diseases, stress, back injury, and environmental hazards. Caregivers need to be warm and responsive and give consistent care in order to provide a mentally healthy environment for children. Caregivers can affect the health environment of child care by role modeling, using cultural sensitivity, and providing education and supervision.

TO GO **BEYOND**

Questions for Review

1. Discuss how health policies impact child care. Are there more general health policies that should be considered? List and discuss them.

2. Request health policies from specific child care programs and family child care sites. Examine and discuss the elements found in these policies. Interview caregivers from these programs to determine the impact of these policies on child care.

3. What is the interrelationship between the caregivers' actions and a mentally healthy child care environment?

AS AN **INDIVIDUAL**

1. How do you respond to stress? Identify your responses. What coping mechanisms do you use? List them.

2. Compare your family of origin practices at mealtime to the rules in child care. How do they differ? Record your response.

3. How would you deal with a distressed child? What practices would you use to help the child while in the child care environment?

AS A **GROUP**

1. Observe multicultural approaches in a preschool setting that support bias sensitive curriculum. Discuss how it differs from other curriculums.

2. Compare cultural health practices that may be present in your community. List these practices and cultural origins.

3. How could stress be reduced in the child care environment? Discuss coping skills that have been used or could be used to reduce stress.

4. Watch *Standards and You,* an AAP film about child care. Discuss how the film deals with stress, illness, and injury.

CHAPTER **REFERENCES**

Another cigarette danger for children. (1996, February). *Child,* 70.

Aronson, S., & Aiken, L. (1980). Compliance of child care programs with health and safety standards: impact of program evaluation and advocate training. *Pediatrics, 65.*

Bee, H. (1992). *The developing child.* New York: HarperCollins.

Belsky, J. (1988). The effects of infant day care reconsidered. *Early Childhood Research Quarterly, 3*(3).

Bredekamp, S. (Ed.). (1987). *Developmentally appropriate practice in early childhood programs serving children from birth through age eight.* Washington, DC: NAEYC.

Buhle, E.L. (1994, September 21). Second hand smoke: Mothers and their children. *Oncolink Home Page.* http://cancer.med.upenn.edu:80/cancer_new/smoke_child.html

Centers for Disease Control. (1990). *Plan of action: Infant immunization initiative.* Unpublished paper of the Division of Immunization Services. Atlanta, GA: Center for Preventive Services.

Chiara, S. (1995, February 2). American child care called unfit. *San Diego Union-Tribune,* pp. A10, A11.

Children's Defense Fund. (1996). *The state of America's children 1996.* Washington, DC: Author.

Gelman, D. (1991, July). The miracle of resiliency. *Newsweek, Special Issue on Children,* 44–47.

Ginott, H. (1972). *Teacher and child.* New York: Macmillan.

Honig, A. (1993). Mental health for babies: What do theory and research teach us? *Young Children, 48*(3), 69–75.

Howe, Rodning, Galluzo, & Meyer. (1987). Attachment and child care: Relationship with mother and caregiver. *Early Childhood Research Quarterly, 3*(4).

Husted, A. (1996, April 23). Second hand smoke can hurt unborn babies. Internet: AJC Health Watch.

Johnson, D. (1993, March). *Tobacco smoke in the home and child intelligence.* Paper presented at the meeting of the Society for Research in Child Development, New Orleans, LA.

Kendrick, A., Kaufmann, R., & Messenger, K. (1995). *Healthy young children: A manual for programs.* Washington, DC: NAEYC.

MacDonald, K. (1992). Warmth as a developmental construct. *Child Development, 63*(4), 753–773.

Males, M. (1995, September, 9). It's the adults, stupid: A flawed war on drugs and smoking. *New York Times,* p. 50179.

Massachusetts Department of Public Health. (1992). *Smoke free child care.* A joint project of the Massachusetts Department of Health and the Massachusetts Health Research Institute.

PRNewswire. (1996, February 6). Second hand smoke news release on the Internet.

Sam, D. (1992). Psychological acculturation of young visible immigrants. *Migration World Magazine, 20*(3), 21–24.

Second hand smoke, firsthand vitamin loss. (1994, June). *Tufts University Diet and Nutrition Newsletter, 12*(4), 1.

University of Colorado at Denver, University of California at Los Angeles, University of North Carolina, & Yale University. (1995, January). *Cost, quality, and child outcomes in child care centers* [Executive Summary].

Wallach, L. (1993). 4 ways to help children cope with violence. *Education Digest, 59*(2), 29–32.

Werner, E. (1986). A longitudinal study of perinatal risk. In D. C. Ferran & J. D. McKinney (Eds.), *Risk in intellectual and psychosocial development* (pp. 3–28). Orlando, FL: Academic Press.

Willer, B., Hofferth, S., Kisker, E., Divine-Hawkins, P., Farquar, E., & Glanz, F. (1992). *The demand and supply of child care.* Washington, DC: NAEYC.

Zero to Three/National Center for Clinical Infant Programs (1992). *Heart start: The emotional foundation of school readiness.* Arlington, VA: Author.

SUGGESTIONS **FOR READING**

Cadiz, S. (1994). Striving for mental health in the early childhood center setting. *Young Children, 49*(2), 84–87.

Miller, L., Ford, D., & Liberante, D. (1990). *Providing a healthy environment for children in early childhood program.* Coolidge, AZ: Central Arizona College.

Public sector vaccination efforts in response to the resurgence of measles among school aged children. (1992). *Morbidity and Mortality Weekly Report* (29), 522–525.

Raikes, H. (1996). A secure base for babies: Applying attachment concepts to the infant care setting. *Young Children, 51*(4), 59–67.

Readdick, C., & Walters-Chapman, C. (1994, Fall). *Texas Child Care,* 3–6.

U.S. Department of Health and Human Services. (1990). *Healthy people year 2000.* Washington, DC: U.S. Government Printing Office.

When parents puff. (1996, April 22). *U.S. News and World Report,* 22.

Ziegler, T. (1996, July). Children at risk: The director's role in identification and early intervention. *Child Care Information Exchange,* 32–34.

CHAPTER TWO

Tools for Promoting Good Health in Children

Upon completion of this chapter, including a review of the summary, you should be able to:

Health Policies

Define and discuss health policies for appraising, screening, and assessment.

Recording Health Status of Children

Describe and detail the process of recording appraisals, screening, and assessment.

Assessing a Child's Health Status

Summarize the different components of a child's health and how they are assessed.

Implications for Caregivers

Relate the importance of education, observation, and the use of appraisals, screening, and assessment.

HEALTH POLICIES

Children grow and develop at different rates. They also have different levels of health and well-being. Each child must be looked at individually for accurate health assessment. Forming a health policy for appraising, screening, and assessing a child's health is a major task of the child caregiver. A child's health is a very significant factor in her overall well-being. The following indicators show the need for creating and implementing policies for observation, record keeping, and assessment:

- All child caregivers should have good tools to assess a child's development (Schweinhart, 1993).

- One of the most useful tools for good observation of health is a basic knowledge of growth and development (Miller, Ford, & Liberante, 1990).

- Child caregivers should be trained to recognize developmental delay, signs of abuse, disabilities, and other possible health problems (Zero to Three, 1992).

- Observation helps meet the needs of children from all types of backgrounds (Lakin, 1994).

- Recorded observations about the child's health, habits, and behaviors help in the early identification of possible problems (Bassett, 1995).

Using health policies for observing, recording, and evaluating a child's health will allow for uniformity in how **appraisals** and **screenings** are carried out. These policies will provide information for **early intervention**, if necessary, and will help protect other children from contagious situations. **Assessment** provides a multitude of tools and procedures that are used to support the child's healthy development and to signify difficulties as they occur.

The caregiver is the **primary health assessor**. In a child care center, the director and aides may also contribute to the assessment of the child's health. Creating open lines of communication with the parent is essential to the evaluation of a child's health status. If there is observation or other information that indicates a child needs screening and **referral**, a discussion with the parent can clarify information and a decision about the next step can be made. If the decision is for referral, then other professionals such as a speech therapist or audiologist will contribute to the overall assessment and any resulting intervention.

Appraisals
regular process of evaluation of a child's health or developmental norms

Screenings
to select or evaluate through a process

Early intervention
decision to modify a child's at-risk behavior or condition in its early stage(s) in order to lessen the impact of the behavior or condition on the life of the child

Assessment
in-depth appraisal to determine if a particular health or developmental condition is occurring

Primary health assessor
caregiver who knows the children very well and can observe for health and well-being

Referral
sending a child for further testing or screening and making available resources that will intervene and aid risk that is posed to the child

Eric, an active four-year-old, seemed to have difficulty following directions and appeared not to pay attention during group time at the child care center. Carol, his teacher, noticed this and asked the aide, Miriam, to observe Eric during those times to see if Carol was correct in her observation. Miriam observed Eric for several weeks and documented what she observed. She agreed with Carol that Eric had attention problems. Carol discussed the situation with Eric's father, Joe, and asked Joe to watch Eric at home. Joe agreed to do this, but he seemed to think that Eric's problem might be related to a recent divorce and living in a single parent family situation. Joe reported to Carol after a weekend of observation that Eric did seem to have attention problems in certain circumstances. Carol, Joe, and Raoul, the director, met to discuss the situation.

Raoul suggested that they begin with a hearing assessment. Eric went to his physician, who felt further tests were needed and sent Eric to a hearing specialist. The specialist concluded that Eric had a hearing deficit that went unnoticed during language development, but was serious enough to cause problems at his present age.

Eric was fitted for a hearing aid and the difference in his attention was remarkable. No one had realized how much Eric had done to compensate for his problem. Now that he could hear, he was like a sponge, trying to soak up information. He asked many questions and was involved in the learning process. Eric's father was grateful that Carol had noticed Eric's problem and had pursued it. ■

It is important to understand that as primary health assessor, the caregiver is a participant observer (Cartwright, 1994). Rarely in child care does a caregiver have the opportunity to stand back for long periods of time and either casually or formally observe children without interruption. In addition, the caregiver brings her own perspective as an assessor. The caregiver's temperament, ethnicity, culture, gender, and experience will affect how she assesses a child's health and development (Lakin, 1994).

All of the preceding factors contribute to the need for definite policies to evaluate a child's health status. These health policies include:

■ *Record Keeping:* specific objectives and methods of recording health information

The caregiver, as the primary health assessor, is responsible for ongoing observations of the health status of each child in his care. Recorded observations are an additional benefit of presenting a complete picture of a child's health status to parents and can aid doctors in diagnosing health problems.

■ *Assessing a Child's Health Status:* procedures for translating and evaluating information to form assessment; includes using indicators of health difficulties

■ *Implications for Caregivers:* specific practices for observation, education, cultural sensitivity, and supervision

KEY HEALTH POLICIES

CONCEPT

Specific health policies for appraising, screening, and assessment are necessary to enable the caregiver, as the primary assessor, to accurately evaluate the health status of children. These policies include record keeping and assessing health status. Implications for caregivers include practices for observation, education, cultural sensitivity, and supervision.

Observation
primary means of data gathering in order to understand children's development and behavior

RECORDING HEALTH STATUS OF CHILDREN

Observation helps present a specific picture of an individual child's health status as well as his temperament, personality, behavioral characteristics, and abilities. What a caregiver considers significant and what needs further deliberation depends on the individual's insight and intuition. These insights from observation are included in the child's permanent health record.

Record Keeping Management Tools

Health policies for record keeping should consider what may be implied as a result of what has been observed. Care should be taken to be as accurate as possible when taking notes and recording information. Caregivers should remember that they are making observations, not diagnoses. A number of different types of record keeping management tools can be used to decrease bias and to present a more accurate picture of the health status of the child.

Precise Words. The first of these tools is the use of precise words to describe the condition or event that is observed. For example, "Joey has a snotty nose" might be better recorded as "Joey's nose is constantly oozing yellow-green mucus." Children can get runny noses from colds, allergies, changes in temperature, communicable diseases, and so forth. The fact that the mucus is yellow-green and constantly oozing might infer something more serious than sniffles. If Joey's nose runs often, a comparison between more precise descriptions might show a pattern for an allergy or a more serious problem. Using adjectives that clearly describe what was observed can be a way to increase perceptions about the children in care (Cartwright, 1994).

Time sampling
occurs when an observer records a particular behavior over a specific period of time

Event sampling
when an observer records a specific preselected behavior as it occurs, everytime it occurs

Anecdotal
a brief narrative account that describes a child's behavior that is significant to the observer

Running records
a detailed narrative account that describes a child's behavior in sequence, as it occurs

Type of Record. The next health management tool for record keeping is the type of record that will be kept. There are a number of different types of records that are helpful and there are advantages and disadvantages for each type. Table 2.1 indicates the major types of records for observing health status and the conditions where each type would be most accurate.

Child Care Situation. Another matter affecting the type of record keeping used is the child care situation. A child care center might use checklists as a major source of record keeping due to the number of children assigned to each caregiver. There also may be more need for **time sampling** and **event sampling** due to the number of children involved. **Anecdotal** and **running records** would be used occasionally as time permits or as a situation demands. A caregiver in a child care center might use a tape recorder for anecdotal and running records (Benjamin, 1994). A child care center caregiver would be the most likely to use all types of record keeping.

A family child caregiver would more likely use a combination of anecdotal records and checklists as the major source of record keeping.

TABLE **2.1**

Types of Health Assessment Records

Type of Record	Definition	Best Used For	Limitations
Anecdotal	Brief narrative accounts that describe health conditions and behavior	Daily open-ended observation	Relies on memory of observer, can be out of context
Running Record	Detailed narrative account in sequence of health status conditions and behaviors	More comprehensive and keeps better track over time	Time consuming; caregiver must have time apart from children to record
Checklist	Lists of specific health status, communicable diseases, absence of sign, symptom; monthly, quarterly, and yearly growth and development observations	Daily scan	Specific traits and behaviors; does not describe
Time Sampling	Records frequency of health status condition or behavior occurrences	Good for over time, takes less time; objective and controlled	Does not describe condition or behavior
Event Sampling	Waits for health condition or behavior to occur, then records specific behaviors	Reoccurring problem; objective and defined ahead of time	Misses details of condition or behavior

Adapted from: Observing the Development of Young Children, *by Janice J. Beaty, 1994, New York: Macmillan.*

The type of record keeping tool used for health observation differs depending on the type of care. For example, a family child caregiver would be likely to use a combination of anecdotal notes and checklists, whereas a nanny might keep a daily log.

Recorded health observations should be accurate and informative. It is important that caregivers realize they are presenting observed behaviors, not diagnosing a problem.

A family child care home usually has children of mixed ages; thus, the provider has a wider age range to observe. A running record would be used only as necessary and there probably would be little need for time sampling or event sampling unless a condition or behavior were serious enough to merit their use.

A nanny or in-home caregiver would rely mostly on anecdotal records. A nanny should keep a daily log that records the child's health and developmental milestones or difficulties. A running record may be used if the nanny or parents have a specific concern about the child. Since the nanny usually has fewer children to care for and generally spends more time with each child than other types of caregivers, there would be little need for time sampling or event sampling because the behavior recurrence or conditions leading to behavior would probably already have been noted. A nanny might use a checklist for the daily quick health check, but she would be more likely to do it mentally than to record any significant factors in the daily log.

How to Keep Records. The type of record keeping used usually determines how the record will be kept. Anecdotal notes can be kept in the child's health record, on file cards, or in a notebook and later placed in the child's health file. Running records are usually recorded on separate sheets of paper and then filed. Checklists and time and event samples are usually printed forms that can be added to the child's file.

The child's health record file should include all observations made. The file will give a view of the child's health status, conditions, and development over time and may be invaluable to a health professional if a child has warning signals for specific problems. The health file is also a tool for creating good two-way communication with the parent about the child and his development. The health file can be used as part of the regular parent/caregiver conferences to discuss the child's overall development.

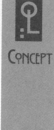

KEY HEALTH RECORDS

CONCEPT

Record keeping is a good tool for health management. The wording used to record what is observed should be accurate and descriptive. The type of record that is kept will depend on the care situation as well as the conditions or behaviors that are being recorded. The records that are kept are a valuable tool for communicating with parents and for providing information to health professionals.

ASSESSING A CHILD'S HEALTH STATUS

Appraising a child's health and well-being, screening for **developmental norms**, and evaluating the information allow the caregiver to assess a child's health status. This is done at several levels that include:

- A daily quick health check
- A general health appraisal
- Screening for growth and developmental norms
- A mental health appraisal
- A nutritional assessment

Developmental norms
statistically average age that children will demonstrate certain developmental abilities and behaviors

Daily Quick Health Check

The caregiver needs to determine on a daily basis if a child who is ill or has a health condition that may put other children at risk should be excluded from care. The health policy for daily appraisal will be an important tool for preventing the spread of illness and disease.

It is done rapidly and is often referred to as a quick health check. The child's health condition is appraised daily when the child enters care. Table 2.2 shows the signs to watch for while performing the daily quick health check observation.

If a child exhibits any of the signs listed in Table 2.2, the caregiver should inform the parents and discuss the observations with them immediately. However, if the symptoms are included in the child care exclusion policy, the parent should take the child home. If the observation is of something vague, the caregiver and parent will need to discuss how the child should be managed that day and at what point the caregiver will contact the parent. The discussion could reveal a simple explanation of the problem and may alleviate the caregiver's concerns.

TABLE **2.2**

Daily Health Checklist

Check for:

- [ ] Activity level
- [ ] Severe sneezing or coughing
- [ ] Discharge from nose, eyes, or ears
- [ ] Breathing difficulties
- [ ] Sores
- [ ] Swelling or bruises
- [ ] Rashes or unusual spots
- [ ] General mood and behavior
- [ ] Skin color (pale or flushed)

Raphael, a fifteen-month-old active toddler, was being dropped off at the family child care home by his mother, Anna. Frances, the caregiver, noticed that Raphael was not his normally happy self and that he appeared to be feverish. Anna explained that she had taken Raphael to the doctor for a checkup the day before and he had received his current series of immunizations. Anna told Frances that the doctor had said that Raphael might be cranky and have a slight fever for 24 hours. Armed with that information, Frances said good-bye to Anna and kept a close watch on Raphael. He played quietly and did not eat as much as normal, but he did not have any other symptoms.

Frances was glad to have the information because when she had first started her child care business, a mother had dropped off a child whose fever had become elevated later in the day. Frances had not been able to reach the mother and had been worried for several hours until the child's doctor returned her call. The doctor told Frances that the girl had had an immunization the day before and that the girl's reaction was normal.

Figure 2.1 shows the signs that the caregiver should be on alert for throughout the day as well as over time if there is a more serious problem.

General Health Appraisal

A general health appraisal is used when warning signs of questionable health or illness are observed. It can also be used to track the recurrence of illness or health conditions. This appraisal goes into more depth as to the signs of health and illness the caregiver might observe in the children in care.

If the caregiver notices frequent recurring conditions or that a child is not acting normally, the caregiver may want to take a closer look at the child's health. Recurring physical problems such as frequent colds or ear infections may indicate a child has an allergy or other health problem that needs to be evaluated by a physician. The frequency of a condition will be noted in the child's health record. The parent should be consulted about the frequency before gathering further information.

If the caregiver feels more information is needed, she should seek the help of a health consultant with the parent's permission. That person can help the caregiver decide if the child needs to be seen by a physician or community health clinic. Discussions with the health consultant can assist the caregiver in being better prepared to seek further cooperation with the parent about the child's specific health concern.

Screening for Growth and Developmental Norms

Screening for growth and development is an essential component of the health status assessment process. Screening identifies whether growth and development fall into the normal pattern and can indicate a potential problem or impairment. An observer should have some knowledge of the normal range of age expectations for developmental milestones. Summaries of milestones for development are listed in this section as are assessment tools, where applicable.

An alert caregiver can help detect whether a child falls within the normal range for growth and development. This could be vital in the child's future health status. A child who is small and light for her age may have a growth abnormality and should see a physician, and perhaps a dietician. A child whose speech is garbled at two-and-a-half may need a therapist or audiologist. Many different conditions that can be corrected can be uncovered through careful observation and recording. A policy of quarterly screening for developmental norms can aid in this process.

A change in a child's behavior or a child with behavioral difficulties may indicate mental health risk, a nutritional deficiency, child abuse, or a physical health impairment. Appraising a child's physical and mental health and nutritional intake will enable discussions with parents to help determine whether a referral should be made. If child abuse is suspected, reporting the observation and showing the records that have been kept to proper authorities will be necessary. A health policy for appraisals and consequent discussion or referral is necessary to allow the process to run smoothly.

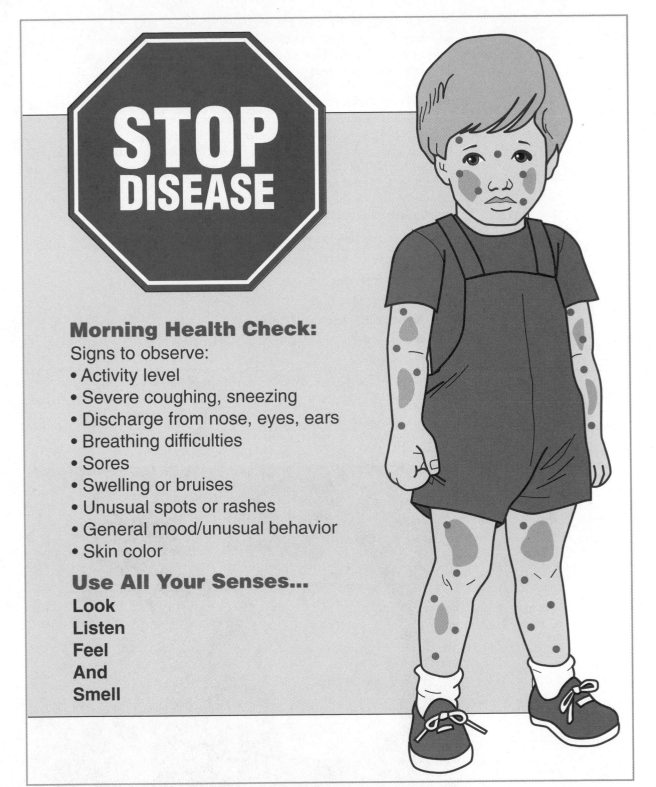

STOP DISEASE

Morning Health Check:

Signs to observe:
- Activity level
- Severe coughing, sneezing
- Discharge from nose, eyes, ears
- Breathing difficulties
- Sores
- Swelling or bruises
- Unusual spots or rashes
- General mood/unusual behavior
- Skin color

Use All Your Senses...

Look
Listen
Feel
And
Smell

FIGURE **2.1** Daily Health Check

The American Public Health Association (APHA) and the American Academy of Pediatrics (AAP) suggest that child caregivers have some form of a health consultant on whom to call when they need a resource for assessing health and well-being. The consultant can be a physician, a pediatric or family nurse practitioner, or a registered nurse (APHA and AAP, 1992). The consultant should have some knowledge about nonparental child care, the community, and available resources.

Screening is routinely done in child care centers and can easily be done in family child care homes or in the child's own home. It is neither expensive nor sophisticated. Screening takes a closer look at specific areas and can add important information to the overall assessment process. The health consultant can assist with any questions the caregiver may have about specific screening methods. Screening is used to:

- Measure height and weight
- Appraise motor development
- Check vision
- Appraise hearing
- Evaluate speech and language
- Assess nutritional intake and deficiencies

Measuring Height and Weight.   Children of all ages fall into a range of normal heights and weights that are calculated on a growth chart (see

Periodic height and weight checks are exciting for the children and foster a knowledge of and pride in their own bodies.
The height and weight assessment can be incorporated into the classroom curriculum by visually representing each child's height and weight (on a wall or piece of posterboard) at regular intervals.

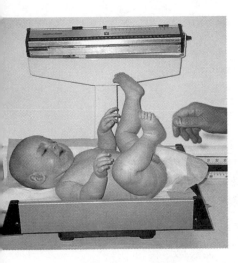

Infancy is a period of dramatic weight and height gains. Infants should be weighed regularly to ensure that they are growing at a normal rate. A weight and height that is below the normal range for their age could indicate a condition called *failure to thrive*.

Failure to thrive
failure of a child to grow physically and develop mentally according to the norms. This condition may occur because of organic defects, or may be due to lack of emotional bonding

Appendix A). Growth charts are easy to follow and are used to direct attention to body size for age that is not the norm. Physicians routinely use these charts to detect problems or abnormalities in a child's growth.

Recording a child's height and weight is part of the normal screening process that a caregiver performs on a quarterly basis. It helps familiarize children with their bodies and helps them to better understand the screening process in the doctor's office. Children enjoy knowing how tall they are and how much they weigh. Even though they do not understand what the numbers mean, children seem to gain a sense of self-identification from them.

Karla, a healthy three-and-a-half year old, was very self-confident. She enjoyed having her family child caregiver measure her and liked to get on the scale and see how much she weighed. Martine, the caregiver, had a special place on her family room wall that was used to measure the height of children in her care. Every two months Martine would bring out the scale and let the children stand against their spot on the wall to measure them so they could see how they were growing. One day when the children went through this process, Karla could not wait to tell her mother, "I'm three and a half, and three (feet tall), and I weigh 34." She looked forward to these screening opportunities and it helped her be more comfortable when she had to go to the doctor.

If a child seems unusually small, thin, obese, or tall for his age, there may be a good reason to compare his height and weight to the growth chart. These conditions may indicate poor nutrition, a hormonal imbalance, or a disease that causes retarded or accelerated growth. Sometimes children exhibit a condition called **failure to thrive** that indicates they are below the normal height and/or weight range for their age. Other children may be overweight for their height. Screening and early intervention may help prevent obesity. The results of the chart comparison should be discussed with a parent. If there is an indicator for further examination, a referral course should be planned. A discussion with the health consultant would be helpful at this point. The most common starting point for a referral of this sort would be the child's own physician. If the child does not have a primary physician, a community health clinic would be the next most likely source that the caregiver could recommend to the family.

If changes in diet are indicated, the caregiver can support those changes. The caregiver will need to be informed by the parent or health professional what should be done to help the child. The caregiver could turn to the health consultant for further assistance.

Appraising Motor Development.   As a child develops, her ability to perform physical activities and use acquired motor skills is one of the most evident areas in growth and development. It is easily observable and is

Gross motor skills
physical skills related to large body movements such as running, jumping, and climbing

Fine motor skills
physical skills related to small body movements, particularly of the hands and fingers. These skills include using scissors, holding a crayon, or working a puzzle

fairly easy to screen. A child should be able to perform the **gross motor skills** and **fine motor skills** that are normal for her age range. A certain degree of coordination should also be present. Table 2.3 indicates the developmental motor skill norms for the first two years of life.

TABLE **2.3**

Developmental Norms for Gross Motor Skills in Infants	
Motor Skill	Month at which 90% of infants master skill
Lifts head up while lying on stomach	3.2
Sits with head steady	4.2
Rolls over	4.7
Sits alone	7.8
Stands holding on	10
Walks holding on	12.7
Stands alone steadily	13.9
Walks well	14.3
Walks up stairs with help	22.0
Kicks ball forward	24.0

Reprinted with permission of DDM. © 1969, 1989, 1990 W. K. Frankenburg and J. B. Dodds © 1978 W. K. Frankenburg.

For children over age two, there are other motor skills and degrees of coordination that should be present. Between ages 2.5 and 3.5 years, a child should be able to perform the gross motor and fine motor skills listed in Table 2.4.

TABLE **2.4**

Developmental Norms for Motor Skills of Children 2.5 Years to 3.5 Years	
Gross Motor Skills	Fine Motor Skills
■ Walk well with a normal gait	■ Use eating utensils well
■ Run in a straight line	■ Copy a circle
■ Jump in the air with both feet	■ Scribble
■ Throw a ball	■ Stack blocks
■ Reach for objects with one hand	■ Manipulate large puzzle pieces
■ Climb	■ Smear paint
■ Hang by both hands	

Throwing a ball in the air is an example of a gross motor skill that children normally master between 2.5 and 3.5 years of age.

When a child does not appear to be following the development norms for his age, there are usually caution signs present. The warning signals for motor development difficulties are included in Table 2.5.

TABLE **2.5**

Caution Signs for Motor Development

Warnings

☐ Has difficulty judging distances in relation to himself

☐ Lacks large muscle control and appears clumsy and uncoordinated

☐ Has difficulty pointing out or locating parts of the body

☐ Lacks small muscle control in things like cutting and coloring

☐ Lacks steady hand or arm when reaching or stacking; arm or hand appears to tremble

Some assessment tools that can be used to further evaluate a child's motor skills are The Denver Developmental Screening Tool, The Mullin Scale, The Hawaii Early Learning Profile, the Bayley Assessment Tool, and the Gessell Assessment Tool. A health consultant could help the caregiver decide which developmental tool would be most appropriate and might also assist in the administration of the assessment tool or refer the caregiver to a source for help. These tools are not commonly administered by the caregiver because they require specialized training.

If it is determined that a child appears to have a motor skill problem, the caregiver and a parent should discuss the referral procedure. The child's physician, a community health agency, or a local **regional center** are good starting points. Physical activities may be prescribed to help the child learn to cope with the motor skill difficulties. The caregiver will be a source of support for both the child and parent during this period.

Regional center
a center in a particular geographic area dedicated to helping families that have children with special needs. The center acts as a resource, a referral agency, and a source of support for families

Checking Vision. Children use vision to take in the information about the world around them, sort it, and then make sense out of it. Visual difficulties should be caught as early as possible for correction and treatment. Children are normally screened for vision during their regular checkups with a physician. If there appears to be a problem, the physician will refer the child to an eye specialist to determine if there is a visual deficiency. Some children may not have regular physical checkups, so vision problems may not be caught. Vision difficulties can appear over time or rapidly. The signs that indicate a child may have hidden eye problems or that may be indicators of visual perception difficulties are listed in Table 2.6.

REALITY CHECK

Effects of Lead Poisoning on Children

It is estimated that at least 15 percent of all children have levels of lead in their systems that can cause cognitive deficiency. Lead poisoning may be endangering as many as 14 million children of all ages (U.S. Department of Health and Human Services, 1993). The extent of lead poisoning in the inner city may be affecting one out of two children. Lead poisoning has been called the number one environmental threat to children (Waldman, 1991).

Lead poisoning can cause mild to severe lasting effects on children. Among the effects are damage to the nervous system, the brain, and growth. The effects of damage to the nervous system and brain may manifest themselves as cognitive deficits, lack of ability to concentrate, and even to learn. Reading, writing, math, and visual and motor skills can be affected. Signs that children may have elevated levels of lead include irritability, insomnia, colic, and anemia.

Children with high levels of lead have been found to be six times more likely to have reading disabilities. They also are seven times more likely to drop out of high school (Waldman, 1991). Some experts believe that lead poisoning contributes to delinquency.

Lead poisoning knows no boundaries. Children under seven years of age live in almost four million homes that have peeling lead paint or lead dust in the environment. Families from these houses are almost equally divided between lower and middle/upper incomes. Renters and homeowners are equally likely to have this problem (Waldman, 1991). Children affected by lead poisoning come from all cultural and racial groups (AAP, 1994).

Seventy-four percent of houses built before 1980 have lead-based paint (Binder & Matte, 1993).

Lead-based paint was banned in 1978. Lead was removed from gasoline during the 1980s.

Lead poisoning is most likely to occur if leaded dust or lead paint chips are swallowed. Children are especially susceptible to lead poisoning because they put many objects in their mouths. They may play in dirt that contains toxic levels of lead, then put contaminated fingers and toys in their mouths. Children encounter lead chips or dust on window sills and railings and near baseboards, door jams, and radiators. Lead is also found in paint on old toys and furniture and in some jewelry.

Lead is absorbed into the bloodstream, then like calcium is absorbed by the bone. Lead can continue to accumulate through life (Health ResponseAbility Systems, 1995). Children's bodies are inclined to absorb more lead, especially if there is an iron deficiency.

The National Association for the Education of Young Children recommends a number of protective practices to keep children safe from lead poisoning (Kendrick, Kaufmann, & Messenger, 1995), including screening children, paint, water, and soil for lead levels. If lead is found, deleading should be done very carefully, and professional assistance may be required. The Department of Health will provide the caregiver with this information.

The NAEYC also suggests that providing an iron and calcium-rich diet and washing fruits and vegetables may be preventive measures. Frequent washing of hands, toys, and floors can cut down on lead levels if it is present. For further information, the caregiver can call the National Lead Information Center Hotline (1-800-LEAD-FYI) and the National Lead Information Clearinghouse (1-800-424-LEAD).

TABLE **2.6**

Caution Signs for Vision Problems

Warnings

Eye Problems:

☐ Persistent redness, swelling, crusting, or discharge in eyes or eyelids

☐ Excessive tearing

☐ Frequent squinting

☐ Eyes that look crooked or crossed or that do not move together

☐ Head held in a tilted position

☐ Drooping eyelids

☐ Continuous rubbing

☐ Eyes that wander

☐ Inability to see objects unless holding them close

Visual Perception Difficulties:

☐ Short attention span

☐ Visually distractible

☐ Unable to visually sequence

☐ Difficulty with color vision

Nearsightedness
lack of ability to see well, other than close up

Strabismus
a condition that occurs in children that causes one or both eyes appear to cross

Amblyopia
an unequal balance of a child's eye muscles often referred to as "lazy eye." Condition is improved through the use of eye patches to enable the weaker eye to strengthen with greater use

If the caregiver observes any of the conditions listed in Table 2.6, the concerns should be discussed with a parent. The parents may have noticed the same conditions or may already have the child in care for that condition. If that is the case, it is important for the parent to share the information. If the child is not under care, it is important for the parent to understand the potential seriousness of an eye condition and refer the child to her physician or local health clinic.

There are three common eye conditions found in children: nearsightedness, strabismus, and amblyopia. **Nearsightedness**, the inability to see distant objects clearly, is the most common visual problem in young children. It may not be readily detected before the age of two, but corrective lenses will enable the child to see normally. **Strabismus** is the misalignment of the eyes, which occurs because of an imbalance in the eye muscles. It becomes difficult for the eyes to focus on the same point at the same time. Corrective lenses, eye exercises, eyedrops, and sometimes eye surgeries help to correct this problem. **Amblyopia**, also called "lazy eye," occurs when one eye does not see well or is injured, and the other eye takes over almost exclusively. Treatment of this condition is most successful when it is caught before age three years. The child wears a patch to prevent vision in the good eye, thereby forcing him to use the inactive eye.

Vision screening is normally done during a child's regularly scheduled physician visit. However, centers and schools that have a nurse on staff may conduct this screening on site.

Caring for a child with any of these eye conditions will take patience and assistance on the part of the caregiver. A child may become easily frustrated or embarrassed over the visual difficulties he is having. It is important that other children understand and not make fun of the child.

Aaron, two-and-a-half years old, was found to have amblyopia in his right eye. The doctor prescribed glasses with a patch on the right lens. The first day at the day care center Aaron felt awkward and embarrassed. The other children were curious; some appeared to be fearful and did not understand why Aaron had the patch. At circle time, Regina, the teacher, talked about it with the children. They talked about eyes and how it felt to see things with two eyes and how different it would be to have to use just one eye to help make the other eye see better.

After hearing the comments and questions of the children and sensing Aaron's discomfort, Regina had the children make their own patches and decorate them. Regina, and the children who wanted to, wore the patches tied with yarn during afternoon snack. They were all excited and felt rather glamorous, like a group of pirates. By the end of snack the children with patches could grasp that it was not as easy to see and coordinate with one eye. They all talked about this and asked Aaron questions. These children became helpers to Aaron and their concern restored Aaron's confidence. Regina helped diffuse a difficult situation for Aaron.

Appraising Hearing.   Hearing loss is caused by a number of factors. For example, a mother may have had an illness while pregnant or there may have been a genetic factor that caused an abnormal development. Or a child may have been born prematurely or may suffer from recurrent ear infections, allergies, or colds. It is not always easy to detect a hearing loss, but the caregiver may notice some caution signals. Table 2.7 contains the ages and questions recommended by the National Association for Speech and Hearing to help the caregiver detect whether the child may have a hearing problem.

TABLE **2.7**

Developmental Hearing Norms

Check for:

Birth to 3 months	☐ Does the child listen to speech?
	☐ Does the child cry or startle at noises?
3 to 6 months	☐ Does the child smile when spoken to?
	☐ Does the child try to turn toward speaker?
	☐ Does the child seem to recognize mother's voice?
6 to 9 months	☐ Does the child respond to his name?
	☐ Does the child turn head toward where the sound is coming from?
	☐ Does the child notice and look around for source of new sounds?
9 months to 1 year	☐ Does the child listen to people talking?
	☐ Does the child look up when you call?
	☐ Does the child look around when hearing new sounds?
1 to 2 years	☐ Can the child follow two requests such as "go to the kitchen and get your cup?"
2 to 4 years	☐ Can the child point to pictures in a book upon hearing the object named?
	☐ Does the child understand conversation easily?
	☐ Does the child hear the television or music at the same loudness level as everyone else in the room?
	☐ Does the child notice normal sounds like the phone, the doorbell, or a dog's bark?
	☐ Does the child hear you when you call from another room?

Adapted from How Does Your Child Hear and Talk?, *by Psi Iota Xi Sorority and American Speech-Language-Hearing Foundation, 1986. Copyright 1986 by The National Association for Hearing and Speech Action.*

Caregivers are a good source for observations regarding a child's hearing. It is essential that the caregiver be aware of the developmental norms for speech development, which can be an identifier of hearing problems. Caregivers may also have access to resources to help parents identify the proper type of specialist to test the child's hearing.

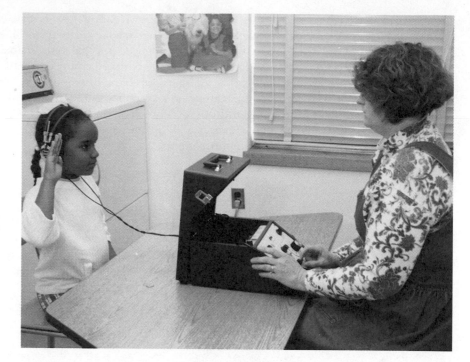

If a child's responses are not developmentally appropriate, the caregiver should discuss with a parent what has been noticed and decide with the parent what action to take for a referral. A conference with the health consultant would help the caregiver and the family know how to proceed. Early detection of a hearing problem can help a child learn to cope and adapt to hearing loss or possibly have the hearing repaired.

If a hearing referral is necessary, there are several places to send the child. A visit to the family physician is a good start. Other sources would include an **audiologist**, a speech language hearing clinic, or a community health agency. Often, school districts have a speech-language and hearing program that will help children in that district before they enter school.

If a hearing loss is detected, the caregiver can help the child adapt by speaking slowly and directly at the child, using hand gestures when applicable, and demonstrating more complex instructions where appropriate. Other children in care should be taught these same methods of communicating with the child who has a hearing loss. The child caregiver can also help to educate and support the parent in the use of these communication methods.

Audiologist
person trained to identify types of hearing losses, to interpret audiometric tests, and to recommend equipment and procedures to assist the hearing impaired

Evaluating Speech and Language. Speech and language acquisition come at varying ages in children. Girls tend to verbalize earlier than boys. Children in bilingual households may acquire speech more slowly (Brazelton, 1992). Some children do not acquire speech and language as rapidly as might be expected. These are normal speech and language patterns for children. Table 2.8 can help the caregiver notice how children use expressive language and if they have the ability to understand at the developmental level given. If a child does not follow this pattern, then the caregiver should check the list of warning signals found in Table 2.9.

TABLE **2.8**

Normal Speech and Language Developmental Patterns

Age	Expressive Language	Ability to Understand
3 to 6 months	Babbling, vocalizing pleasure	Smiles in response to speech; seeks sound source; recognizes familiar people and objects
7 to 9 months	Consonants—b,d,m,t,p,z; babbling; imitates speech sounds	Responds to gestures and "no"; can play peek-a-boo, pat-a-cake, and bye-bye
10 to 12 months	First true word may appear; intonations begin; uses all sounds in vocal play	Relates object and name; can follow simple body action commands; always responds to own name
1 to 1 1/2 years	Uses 3 to 20 single words; uses gestures	Follows simple commands; recognizes some body parts and names for objects
1 1/2 to 2 years	Uses 20 to 60 words; combines two words in sentences; 65% speech intelligible	Understands 200 to 300 words; can answer simple yes or no questions
2 to 3 years	Uses 200 to 500 words; three- and four-word sentences; grammar emerges; 70 to 80% speech intelligible	Understands 800 to 900 words; what, why, where questions; can listen to short stories
3 to 4 years	Uses 800 to 1,500 words; four- and five-word sentences; asks questions	Understands 1,200 to 1,500 words; can compare (up and down); responds to two-part commands
4 to 5 years	Uses 1,500 to 2,000 words; very intelligible speech; eight-word sentences; can tell long stories	Understands 2,500 words; answers complex questions; has some color and number concepts

Peer interaction during playtime is an ideal time to observe children's speech patterns.

TABLE **2.9**

Caution Signs for Screening and Referral

Warnings

☐ No intelligible speech by two years of age

☐ Voice is monotone, too loud or soft, or of poor quality

☐ Difficult to understand after age three

☐ Nasal quality to voice

☐ Speech too fast or too slow

☐ Difficulty in expressing self, organizing thoughts

☐ Makes very few or no attempts to speak

☐ Inability to produce all speech sounds, thus interferes with communication

☐ Difficulty following directions at appropriate developmental language level

☐ Difficulty in engaging in verbal activities with other children

☐ Stuttering

If a child exhibits any of the caution signs listed in Table 2.9 or is not at the appropriate developmental level, the child caregiver should discuss this with the parent to determine if the parent agrees that a problem may exist. A discussion with the health consultant may help the caregiver and the parent determine the best course of action. The child may have to be referred to a physician or other specialist such as a speech therapist.

A child who has a speech or language problem will need much patience and understanding. The caregiver can help the child by allowing him time to speak clearly. The caregiver can offer encouragement and reward the child's effort. The child needs caring and warmth. By modeling these supportive actions, other children will begin to imitate these actions. This support will make it easier for the child with the problem to practice for success. A child with a good sense of self will be less hesitant or self-conscious, enabling the child to attempt to use speech and language at every opportunity.

Richard, a bright, cheerful three-year-old, attended a campus child care center three mornings a week. Two full days a week he attended a special school for children with developmental difficulties. Richard was born with a problem with his tongue that was not detected until he was almost two years old. Surgery and the school helped Richard begin to learn how to verbalize. He attended the campus child care center to help him acquire language from his interaction with other children who had good language skills. In the beginning, Richard was hesitant to speak and was somewhat withdrawn. Cathy, his teacher, read several books to the children that dealt with characters who were different. These books helped bring about a dialogue that concluded, that there were more similarities than differences among these characters. After this, Richard seemed less hesitant to speak and began to relate to the other children. The children observed how Cathy listened to and spoke with Richard. They began to follow her lead. The inclusion was a success for both Richard and the other children. Richard's language was becoming more intelligible and the other children learned that differences were not threatening.

Mental Health Appraisal.   During observation, the caregiver should be aware of at-risk indicators and other behavioral characteristics that may indicate poor social, emotional, or mental health. Table 2.11 shows a number of characteristics that may indicate the child is at risk.

There are many behaviors that may be annoying to adults but are perfectly normal and a part of a child's development between the ages of one-and-one-half years and four years of age. Children often do not pay attention and do not do what they are asked. They can be hard to reason with sometimes and may sulk or cry easily. They may not be able to sit still. Some may boss other children around and try to show off.

Younger children may not want to share and will say "no" often when requested to cooperate. They may grab toys, hit, shove, or attack others who have what they want.

It is not uncommon for some children to whine and complain. Other children may have a special blanket or suck their thumbs. Some children are

shy and afraid of unfamiliar people and situations. It is not unusual for children to make up stories and tell them as truths.

These typical behaviors are not necessarily indicators of risk for mental difficulties. Behaviors that may indicate children are at risk for problems in mental health are found in Table 2.10.

When a child shows a number of disturbing behaviors, especially with increasing frequency, it is a good idea to discuss the child's behavior with a parent. If there is no explanation or if the parent expresses concern, the caregiver, with the parent's permission, may want to contact the health consultant. Many conditions that cause a great deal of stress for a child may be at the root of the problem. Collaboration on the part of the caregiver, the family, and a health professional may detect the problem and enable early intervention to alleviate the difficulty. A referral to a physician or mental health counselor or psychologist may be necessary if the difficulties are not easily solved.

Identifying at-risk indicators and behavioral characteristics that may indicate a child's poor mental health is an important part of early intervention. It is important for caregivers to recognize that normal behaviors, such as crying or shyness, do not necessarily indicate a problem and may instead be just a normal aspect of the child's personality.

TABLE **2.10**

At-Risk Indicators for Children's Vulnerability to Poor Mental Health
Warnings
☐ Aggression or acting out behaviors, without provocation
☐ Passivity, lack of response, or totally withdrawn
☐ Disorganized behavior socially or in play
☐ Poor or inappropriate attachment patterns
☐ Low self-esteem
☐ Easily over-stimulated
☐ Unresponsive to verbal cues or affectionate overtures
☐ Clingy, dependent
☐ Hypersensitive
☐ Unable to make decisions or solve problems
☐ Temper tantrums or very irritable
☐ Mood swings with no explanation
☐ Lack of attention or ability to focus
☐ Easily frustrated
☐ Overreaction or inappropriate response to everyday events
☐ Inability to transition easily
☐ Indifference to parent
☐ Avoids eye contact
☐ Anxiously follows caregiver everywhere
☐ Little or no interest in others

REALITY CHECK

Poverty and Childhood

Twenty-four percent of children under six years of age live at the poverty level (National Center for Children in Poverty, 1993). This represents a significant rise from the early 1970s (U.S. News and World Report, 1994). A correlation with this is the significant rise in single parent families, which doubled during that period of time. In total, 27 percent of the children in this country live in a single parent home. Fifty-nine percent of children under six from single parent families live in poverty, compared with only 13 percent of children from families with two parents.

There are many contributing factors to poverty, including family composition, parent education, and family income (Jones, 1994). Although there is a higher total number of Caucasian children living in poverty, the total percentage of African American and Hispanic and other children living in poverty is at a higher level. Fifty-eight percent of minority children live at the poverty rate, compared to 42 percent of Caucasian children (Atkins, 1993). Children living in urban areas represent one-third of the children living in poverty. Children who live in rural areas represent 26 percent of children living in poverty. Children living in suburban areas represent 16 percent of children living in poverty (Atkins, 1993).

Children from families in poverty make up the largest growing segment of the homeless. More than one-third of the homeless are families with children and 75 percent of those are single parent families (Eddowes, 1994). The risk to children due to poverty is even greater for homeless children because of their lack of housing.

Impoverished living conditions can result in poor health, lack of safety, and poor nutrition. Poor families are six times more likely to report that their children are in poor or fair health than families that have adequate income (Newacheck, Jameson, & Halfon, 1994). Health problems are reflected in lower blood iron levels and higher levels of vision, hearing, and dental problems. Blood levels of lead are also higher for children living in poverty. Children in poverty have more frequent, more severe, and longer lasting infectious diseases (Kotch & Shackelford, 1989). Families in poverty may seek primary medical attention in the emergency room. Homeless children are at an even higher risk. Because of living conditions, these children are more likely to have higher levels of respiratory infections and food-borne infections.

Children in poverty are also more likely to have developmental difficulties, which may be related to poor or nonexistent prenatal care for the mother. The difficulties may also relate to being born to teenage mothers. Health conditions are more likely to go untreated for these children.

Poverty appears to contribute to emotional and behavioral problems for children (Takeuchi, Williams, & Adair, 1991). Children living in poverty are more likely to be affected by drug and alcohol abuse and child abuse, which lead to increased risk for mental health problems that result in emotional and behavioral problems. Homeless children are even more likely to suffer from emotional and behavioral problems. These children are more likely to have frequent changes of residence, be at risk for safety, and suffer from domestic conflict (Burg, 1994).

Children living in poverty are more likely to be at risk for safety in their living conditions. Poor housing conditions can lead to higher levels of lead and unsafe neighborhoods. The economic stress of living at the poverty level causes higher levels of domestic abuse, including neglect and physical, sexual, and emotional abuse.

Income level affects food consumption practices. Financial resources help families meet basic food needs. The less income, the less likely the basic needs for nutrition will be met (Reicks, Randall, & Haynes, 1994). Children living in poverty are far less likely to have their needs for fruits and vegetables met. Inadequate nutrition can affect cognitive development and behavior (Kotch & Shackelford, 1989).

continued

Pollitt (1994) reported that worldwide research shows three conditions correlated with poverty and poor nutrition:

1. Effects of poor nutrition and illness on school performance
2. Relationship between poor motor and mental development and anemia
3. Positive effects of supplemental food programs

Recent evidence has shown that children need enough protein, calories, vitamins, and minerals to prevent malnutrition. Homeless children may be at greater risk for nutritional deficits because their basic food needs may depend on food programs that are not geared to children.

Caregivers can have a profound effect on the lives of poor children. They are in the position to provide an environment for a significant portion of the day that will offer children greater physical safety and good nutrition. Child caregivers can help improve the health of children through good screening and sanitation practices. They can also help families access health care and nutritional supplement programs. Caregivers can offer children emotional stability that may help to counteract the problems that poverty brings to their lives.

Nutritional Assessment. Assessment of a child's nutritional status may be warranted for a child whose growth is different from the norm, such as children who appear obese, who may have a food intolerance, or who may show an increased susceptibility to infections or illness. Assessing a child's food intake pattern may be very helpful in determining if there is a physical or organic difficulty that is affecting a child's growth, health, or well-being. The types of foods a child eats, how much food is eaten, and when and where the child eats may be pertinent information. If necessary, the caregiver and the parent can work together to provide this information for a health professional who may further assess the child's condition.

The nutritional assessment will help reveal:

■ What types of foods the child eats

■ How much food the child eats

■ When the child eats

■ Under what circumstances the child eats

■ Adequacy of nutrition provided to the child

■ Parental knowledge of nutrients offered to child

■ Adequacy of the child's diet

■ Why the child eats what she eats

■ Why the child refuses to eat certain foods

Nutritional screening is usually accomplished in several ways. The first is the 24-hour dietary recall method. This information is relatively easy to obtain and can be done in several ways. With this method, the parent and caregiver create a list of foods eaten, including an estimate of how much food is eaten. This can be done for either a one-day or three-day period. Since any one day may not reflect the child's normal diet, a three-day record may be more beneficial. Some difficulties with this method are that the estimates may not be accurate and gaining the cooperation of the parent to record more than one day may be difficult. The recall method may reveal

TABLE **2.11**

24-Hour Dietary Recall

Name: Dane Leonard   **Age:** 3 years, 2 months

G = Grains, bread, and cereals   MM = Milk and milk products
V = Vegetables   M = Meat   F = Fruits

Breakfast
½ cup sugared cereal (1 G)
1 cup milk (1 MM)
1 banana (1 F)

Lunch
1 corn dog (1 M)
chips
punch
½ cup pudding (1 MM)

Dinner
1 chicken leg (1 M)
peas (1 V)
mashed potatoes (1 V)
1 cup milk (1 MM)

Snacks
1 apple (1 F)
2 chocolate chip cookies
1 cup grape juice (1 F)
1 cup milk (1 MM)

How many servings of each in one day?
Grains, Breads, and Cereals (G)—1
Fruits (F)—3
Vegetables (V)—2
Milk and Milk Products (MM)—4
Meats (M)—2

Assessment: Low on grains, breads, and cereals; high on milk and milk products

potential patterns of consumption that put the child at risk for nutritional deficiency. See the sample in Table 2.11.

As far as diets for children are concerned, the sample given in Table 2.11 might be a typical diet for a three year old. If one were to compare this sample to the food pyramid and the recommended daily allowances, there are definite indicators that the diet is lacking in grains, vegetables, and fruits and that there is overconsumption in the milk and milk product category.

Another method of nutritional assessment is the food frequency questionnaire. This tool will show how often foods are consumed in the four food groups plus the "other" group in the period of one week. This questionnaire relies on the parent for recall, but it might be an easier tool to use to find out if the child is lacking in or excessively consuming certain food groups. This tool may also establish a cultural or ethnic eating pattern that may put the child at risk for nutritional problems.

Both of the nutritional assessment tools require understanding and cooperation between the parent and the caregiver. Working together to establish what the child's eating patterns are and making changes to help the child follow the recommended diet pattern can be an effective method for establishing respect and forming an alliance between the caregiver and the parent. Discussing the dietary pattern with the health consultant or a dietician might be helpful, if a problem is indicated. A referral to the child's physician or local health clinic may be recommended.

KEY HEALTH STATUS ASSESSMENT

CONCEPT

Assessing a child's health status is a major task for the child caregiver. Using daily health checks, general health appraisal, screening for developmental norms, screening for good mental health, and assessing nutrition are the tools that the caregiver would use to detect any problems or deficits that a child may have. Early detection may lead to early intervention to correct the problem.

TABLE **2.12**

Food Frequency Questionnaire for Children

Name _____ Age _____

Indicate how many times on average your child eats the following foods in a week by marking down the number of times in the category that most describes your child's eating pattern.
D = Daily   O = Often   S = Sometimes   R = Rarely

Food	Frequency			
	D	O	S	R
Milk and milk products: cheese, milk, yogurt, ice cream, and pudding	☐	☐	☐	☐
Meat, meat products, and meat substitutes: beef, chicken, pork, lamb, fish, egg, lunch meat, bacon, dried beans, peas, and peanut butter	☐	☐	☐	☐
Grains, breads, and cereals: rice, pasta, tortillas, grits, breads, cereals	☐	☐	☐	☐
Fruits and vegetables	☐	☐	☐	☐
Other: fats, oils, sweet bakery goods, fast foods, and candy	☐	☐	☐	☐

What type of milk does your child drink?

skim	1% lowfat	2% lowfat	whole	formula	breast
☐	☐	☐	☐	☐	☐

How many meals, including snacks, does the child eat in one day?_____
Also, explain the child's eating habits: _____
_____
_____

Are there any dietary restrictions or limitations practiced by your family? If yes, please explain.   Yes ☐   No ☐

_____

IMPLICATIONS FOR **CAREGIVERS**

Child caregivers are a key link in establishing the promotion of good health for children. Caregivers have the opportunity to contribute to the health and well-being of children in care. These areas include observation, education, cultural sensitivity, and supervision.

Observation

Observation of children is a significant portion of a caregiver's job because it allows a caregiver to get to know and understand a child's temperament, personality, abilities, and limitations. When the caregiver is specifically observing a child's health and well-being, there are several goals to keep in mind.

What Is Going to Be Observed? The first goal is to decide what is going to be observed. Is the child being observed for physical well-being, how she performs physically, or acts emotionally? Is the caregiver specifically looking for a particular health condition or communicable disease? Has the parent indicated a problem he may have observed? What is the age of the child being observed? A three-year-old has different physical and emotional capacities than a two-year-old. Some other considerations that may affect the observations follow:

- Are there cultural differences?
- Is the child at risk?
- Does the child have special needs?
- Has there been a recent event in the child's life that may affect her well-being or behavior (e.g., birth of a baby, loss of a pet, a move)?

These factors will influence what is observed.

How Will the Observation Take Place? A second goal is to understand how the observation will take place. The caregiver needs to be aware that his own childhood, feelings, and experiences will affect the interpretation of what is observed and how it is translated. Lakin (1994) suggests that the observer go through stages of observation.

- To act like a scientist and observe physical data
- To be the garbage collector and sort out feelings from the physical data
- To behave as an advocate and look at the situation from the child's point of view and consider why the child acted in a certain manner.
- To act as an artist and use what is observed to take action to support the development and interests of the child. (This method enforces a holistic approach to observation.)

The "how" of observation also includes what was physically done to carry out the observation. In order to be accurate in the first stage of observation of a child's health and well-being one needs to use all of the physical senses. The child caregiver will need to:

- Look
- Listen
- Feel
- Smell

Looking at the child includes all physical aspects of the child as well as how the child is acting. Listening to the child involves hearing what the child sounds like, as well as what the child says and how it is said. Feeling the child involves touching the child to see if she is feverish, clammy, or has swollen glands or other physical symptoms that a touch could help determine if a problem exists. Smelling a child would make the caregiver aware concerning personal hygiene as well as toileting accidents.

When to Observe?   The caregiver should also know when the appropriate time to observe is. It is very important that a health check be made daily when the child first enters child care. This quick check should be done before the parent leaves the child. If the child is ill and must be excluded from care, it should be done before other children are exposed.

It is at the drop-off time that the parent may share any particular concerns he may have about the child's health or well-being. This helps the caregiver to be on the alert for observation of that concern.

In addition to the daily quick check, a child should be observed for physical and mental health on an ongoing basis. If there has been an outbreak of an infectious disease, special care should be taken to observe for that particular disease.

A plan and health policy for monthly, quarterly, and yearly observations for health in regard to assessment and screening for growth and developmental norms should be created and carried out.

Education

Assessment is a helpful communication device between the caregiver and the parent and can lead to collaborative practices that involve all factors of the child's environment: the child, the caregiver, the parents, the school, and the community. Information about the child's growth and development is collected and recorded at certain intervals. It is important that the caregiver be trained and have a base of knowledge to perform basic assessments. Another good practice is to discuss concerns with a health consultant before talking to the parent so that you are better informed as to the implications of those concerns. The health consultant can also be a source for referrals for the child if there is a difficulty.

The daily appraisal need not be discussed unless there is a problem or concern. All other forms of assessment should be discussed thoroughly with the parent. The parent may need to be educated as to the importance of any assessment. Any difficulty with the child's health and well-being should be addressed early in the process.

When a referral is made, the caregiver should follow up. If there is a problem, the caregiver should be aware of it and should be given instructions on how best to help the child cope with any difficulty. A discussion with the parent and the person to whom the child was referred would be most helpful to give the child the continuity of care that she might need.

Cultural Sensitivity

A child whose first language is not English may appear not to follow developmental norms. A child who is exposed to two languages may have difficulty switching from the home language to the language while in child care. Patience and understanding are important. It is helpful to have a caregiver or someone that a caregiver can call upon who speaks the same language as the child to make the shift between the two languages easier.

If the caregiver notices real difficulties in hearing, speech, or language, she might want to discuss it with the parent to see if the child seems to have these same difficulties in the native language. If the child seems to have a problem, discussions with the parent and then referral should be approached with cultural sensitivity. Many cultures view any problem with a child as an imperfection that is a source of guilt and shame for the parent. An understanding of the child's native culture helps the caregiver relate better with the parent.

Dietary patterns are greatly influenced by cultural and ethnic considerations. Certain cultures such as southeast Asians and Indochinese rarely consume milk products. Other cultures may not have a varying menu that allows for the meats or fresh fruits and vegetables that a child needs in his diet. When assessing the child's diet, it is extremely important to have some knowledge of the family's customs. This will allow the caregiver to be culturally sensitive when talking to the parent. A health consultant, dietician, or family member who speaks both the child's and the caregiver's languages can help alleviate any problems that a language barrier might cause. It may be a challenge to help a family from a different cultural background adjust to dietary allowances recommended for the child. A health professional could prove to be an invaluable source of support to the caregiver.

Supervision

The caregiver needs to supervise child care to make sure that record keeping and assessments are carried out on a regular basis. A director in a child care center usually supervises the assessments and makes sure that the records are kept up to date. In family child care or in-home care, there may only be one caregiver present. It is up to this caregiver to make sure that children's health is supported through regular use of record keeping and assessment.

A communication system also needs to be established within the child care environment. Child caregivers need to work together and collaborate on promoting the good health of the child. A family child caregiver may have an aide or a substitute who could assist in appraisals and assessment. In a child care center, the child may see several caregivers and aides in one day, as well as the director and perhaps a kitchen helper. All of the staff should be trained to cooperate and help in appraising and assessing a child's health status.

KEY IMPLICATIONS FOR CAREGIVERS

CONCEPT

The child caregiver needs to promote the good health and well-being of a child. The caregiver does this by using observation, education, cultural sensitivity, and supervision as tools to promote health and prevent risk.

CHAPTER **SUMMARY**

Children must be observed as individuals to assess their health and well-being. Caregivers can appraise and assess children for physical health, mental health, and nutrition. They can screen children for growth and developmental norms. Caregivers can document their observations through several forms of records. If there appears to be a difficulty in any area, they can discuss it with the parents and offer a referral, if necessary. Caregivers need to employ observation, education, cultural sensitivity, and supervision to provide adequate assessment measures for children in care.

TO GO **BEYOND**

Questions for Review

1. Discuss the interrelationship of assessment and early intervention.
2. Describe the difference between observing children and diagnosing them.

AS AN **INDIVIDUAL**

1. Assess your physical health by self-observation. Weigh yourself and write down how the weight affects your health. Record how you feel physically for a period of three days. Be sure to use precise words. Have you been observing or diagnosing your health?
2. Observe two children in a child care situation. Use the anecdotal type of record to document your observation. Discuss how it feels to observe children with documentation in mind.

AS A **GROUP**

1. Bring several two-year-olds to class. Watch them and observe their interactions. Compare these observations for developmental norms for speech and language and gross motor skills.

2. Discuss mental health indicators that put children at risk. List the indicators that are most likely to prelude mental health risk.

 CHAPTER **REFERENCES**

American Academy of Pediatrics (AAP). (1994). *Pediatrics, 93*(2).

American Public Health Association (APHA), & American Academy of Pediatrics (AAP). (1992). *Caring for our children: National health and safety performance standards: Guidelines for out-of-home care.* Washington, DC: Authors.

American Academy of Pediatrics advices lead screening for children (1993). *FDA Consumer, 27*(6), 4–5.

Atkins, B. (Ed.). (1993). *Dilemma of the working poor. 1992 update.* New York: National Center for Children in Poverty.

Bassett, M. (1995). *Infant and child care skills.* Albany, NY: Delmar Publishers.

Beaty, J. (1994). *Observing the development of young children.* New York: Macmillan.

Benjamin, A. (1994). Observations in early childhood classrooms: Advice from the field. *Young Children, 49*(9), 14–20.

Binder, S., & Matte, T. (1993). Childhood lead poisoning: The impact of prevention. *The Journal of the American Medical Association, 269*(13), 1679–1681.

Brazelton, T. B. (1992). *Touchpoints: Your child's emotional and behavioral development.* Reading, MA: Addison-Wesley.

Burg, M. (1994, May). Health problems of sheltered homeless women and their dependent children. *Health and Social Work, 19*(2), 125–131.

Cartwright, S., (1994). When we really see the child. *Child Care Information Exchange, 49*(6), 5–9.

Eddowes, E. A. (1994). School providing safer environments for homeless children. *Childhood Education, 70*(5) 271–273.

Frankenburg, W. K., Frandel, A., Sciarillo, W., & Burgess, D. (1981). The newly abbreviated and revised Denver Developmental Screening Test. *Journal of Pediatrics, 99,* 995–999.

Health ResponseAbility Systems. (1995). Lead poisoning. Document ID: lhf00101. http://gii-awards.com.:80/nicampgn/2ffe.htm.

Jones, J. (1994). *Child poverty: A deficit that goes beyond dollars.* New York: Columbia University National Center for Children in Poverty.

Kendrick, A., Kaufmann, R., & Messenger, K. (1995). *Healthy young children: A manual for programs.* Washington, DC: NAEYC.

Kotch, J., & Shackelford, J. (1989). *The nutritional status of low-income preschool children in the United States: A review of the literature.* Washington, DC: Food Research and Action Center.

Lakin, M. (1994). Observing from a different point of view. *Child Care Information Exchange, 94*(1), 65–69.

LEAD!—No. 1 Environmental Pediatric Health Problem. (1995). *Young Children, 49*(5) 9: Author.

Miller, L., Ford, K., & Liberante, K. (1990). *Providing a healthy environment for children in early childhood programs.* Coolidge, AZ: Central Arizona College.

National Center for Children in Poverty. (1993). Study shows effect of 1990–1991 recession on children under six living in poverty. *News and Issues, 3*(3), 1.

Newacheck, P., Jameson, W., & Halfon, N. (1994). Health status and income: The impact of poverty on child health. *Journal of School Health, 64*(6) 229–234.

Pollitt, E. (1994). Poverty and child development: Relevance of research in developing countries to the United States. *Child Development, 65*(2), 283–295.

Reicks, M., Randall, J., & Haynes, B. (1994). Factors affecting consumption of fruits and vegetables by low-income families. *Journal of the American Dietetic Association, 94* (11), 1309–1311.

Schweinhart, L. (1993). Observing young children in action: The key to early childhood assessment. *Young Children 48*(7), 29–33.

Takeuchi, D., Williams, D., & Adair, R. (1991). Economic stress in the family and children's emotional and behavioral problems. *Journal of Marriage and the Family 53*(4), 1031–1041.

U.S. Department of Health and Human Services (1993). *Learning readiness: Promising strategies.* Washington, DC: Author.

U.S. News and World Report. (1994, August 1). 1 child in 4 in a single parent home. *U.S. News and World Report,* 6.

Waldman, S. (1991, July 15). Lead and your kids. *Newsweek Magazine,* 42–48.

Zero to Three/National Center for Clinical Infant Programs. (1992). *Heart start: The emotional foundations of school readiness.* Arlington, VA: Author.

SUGGESTION **FOR READING**

Barness, L. E. (Ed.) (1993). *Pediatric nutrition handbook.* Elk Grove Village, IL: American Academy of Pediatrics.

CHAPTER THREE

INFECTION CONTROL IN CHILD CARE

Upon completion of this chapter, including a review of the summary, you should be able to:

HEALTH POLICIES FOR INFECTION CONTROL

Define and discuss health for the prevention of childhood infectious diseases.

MECHANISMS OF INFECTIOUS DISEASE SPREAD

Explain the mechanisms of communicable disease spread.

IMMUNIZATIONS FOR DISEASE PREVENTION

Relate the importance of immunizations in the prevention and reduction of communicable diseases.

UNIVERSAL SANITARY PRACTICES FOR THE CHILD CARE ENVIRONMENT

Summarize sanitation methods used in the prevention of spread of disease in child care.

ENVIRONMENTAL QUALITY CONTROL FOR DISEASE PREVENTION

Discuss factors in the environment that quality control can help to curb the spread of disease.

IMPLICATIONS FOR CAREGIVERS

Describe the importance of education, supervision, and role modeling in the prevention of communicable diseases.

Infection control
control of infectious agents
by sanitary practices

Immunization
vaccines given in order
to protect individuals
through the development
of antibodies against
specific infectious diseases

Hygiene
protective measures and
sanitary practices to limit
the spread of infection and
help to promote health

HEALTH POLICIES FOR INFECTION CONTROL

Policies for **infection control** are essential to maintain the health and to prevent serious illness of children. Children in child care are more likely to become ill than children who stay at home. **Immunization** and **hygiene** can provide barriers to the spread of infectious diseases and illness of children who are in child care. The need for these policies is reinforced by the following:

■ The United States ranks behind sixty-nine other countries in its immunization rate. Forty-four percent of two year olds are not properly immunized (Graham, 1994). In urban areas this figure is even higher (U.S. Department of Health and Human Services, 1993).

■ Good practices in sanitation and hygiene can greatly reduce disease in child care (Griffen, 1993).

■ Children under three years of age are more vulnerable to disease than are older children (Kendall & Moukadden, 1992).

■ The risk of meningitis is more than twelve times greater in child care centers than in home-based child care for children under the age of one year (Klein, 1986).

■ Children are contagious three to five days before they develop any symptoms, so in addition to exclusion, preventive measures should be taken (Child Care Action Campaign).

The key tools of risk management for health are prevention, protection, and promotion. In order to utilize these tools properly, there must be an understanding of how disease is spread and how it is controlled. It is also important to know that educating caregivers, parents, and children can help prevent the spread of disease.

Developing health
policies is essential for the
control of infection and
the spread of disease.
Even more important is
communicating these
policies to caregivers and
parents. The distribution
of written policies, meetings
to articulate and reinforce
the written policies, and
new staff and parent
training sessions are ways
to communicate health
policies.

There are many people involved in the child care setting, both directly and indirectly. The potential for the spread of infectious diseases is increased as these numbers increase. There are the caregivers, the children, and the families whose interactions with each other make them more vulnerable than the general population. An added risk is present for a caregiver who is pregnant. A fetus is particularly vulnerable to certain infectious diseases. Health policies for the control of infectious diseases are critical for all people involved in the child care environment. These health policies should include:

1. *Mechanisms of Communicable Disease Spread:* understanding the mechanisms that spread disease and practices that will prevent it.

2. *Immunizations for Disease Prevention:* understanding the importance of immunizations for protection and prevention and implementing strategies to be sure that children and adults are properly immunized.

3. *Sanitation for Disease Prevention:* practices for sanitation, hygiene, and cleanliness that offer protective and preventive measures.

4. *Environmental Quality Control for Disease Prevention:* strategies that help prevent the spread of disease in the rest of the child care environment.

5. *Implications for Caregivers:* methods and practices that provide minimum risk and maximum health protection for child care.

KEY HEALTH POLICIES FOR INFECTION CONTROL

CONCEPT

Health policies for the control of infection and the spread of disease are essential in child care. These policies should cover the mechanisms of disease control, the immunizations, and sanitation needed for disease prevention. Health policies should also address environmental quality control and education for disease prevention. The caregiver needs to understand the methods and practices that provide protection and prevention.

MECHANISMS OF INFECTIOUS DISEASE SPREAD

To many people, child care is thought of as a barrier to health. Infectious diseases are common in child care. Some child caregivers often complain about frequent illnesses. What most people do not understand is that the frequency of infectious diseases and the potential for disease spread can be greatly reduced through use of sanitary practices.

In order to place barriers against infectious diseases and to try to control them in child care, one must fully understand how disease is spread. It does not matter whether in child care, in an office, or in a home, **germs** are always present. The fact that they cannot be seen does not mean they are not there.

Germs
microscopic organism that can cause disease

Child care centers present a challenge for germ control. The frequent exchange of toys among children who have not yet mastered personal hygiene is one example. Important prevention measures are regularly disinfecting mouthed toys and frequent hand washing.

There are several major reasons why the spread of infectious diseases is more likely in child care. The young children present have not yet learned good hygiene practices and germs multiply in warm, moist places. Child care and the children present offer germs many warm, moist places in which to grow. Diseases are spread through the air and person-to-person contact.

Certain practices or lack of practices in child care greatly contribute to the spread of infectious diseases. Table 3.1 lists those practices.

TABLE **3.1**

Child Care Practices that Contribute to the Spread of Infectious Disease CAUTION
Warnings
☐ Failure to wash hands as needed
☐ Presence of children in diapers who put toys in the mouth
☐ Mixed ages where older children play with children in diapers
☐ Large numbers of children present, especially if within a contained area
☐ Improper diaper changing procedures, including disposal and cleanup
☐ Staff who have dual duties, such as preparing food and working with children
☐ Lack of facilities, such as not enough bathrooms, small rooms, or diaper area not separated from rest of care
☐ Water tables or wading pools that are not sanitized or do not have the water changed frequently
☐ Pets in the environment that are handled by children or caregivers
☐ Not requiring or checking immunization records for completion or update for all children in child care
☐ Not requiring or checking immunization records for all staff
☐ Failure to perform daily health check
☐ Not excluding ill staff
☐ Not having a good backup substitute list for replacing ill caregivers
☐ Not having a policy for exclusion of ill children
☐ Not properly informing families when the children are exposed to a communicable disease
☐ Lack of proper sanitation and cleaning, especially of toys and food preparation, bathroom, and sleeping areas
☐ Improper storage of food
☐ Lack of hygiene in food handling
☐ Inadequate circulation of air
☐ Children sharing sleeping space or equipment

For greater understanding of why the practices in Table 3.1 are so careless, it is helpful to know exactly how germs are spread to cause infectious diseases. There are four basic ways diseases are spread:

1. Respiratory tract transmission
2. Fecal-oral transmission
3. Direct contact transmission
4. Blood contact transmission

Respiratory Tract Transmission

Respiratory tract transmission is perhaps the most common method of disease spread in child care. Tiny droplets from the eyes, mouth, or nose get into the air when a child sneezes, coughs, drools, or even talks, and these droplets are transmitted to another person through the air they breathe. These droplets can also land on toys, food, and other things in the environment. Germs can live for many hours and activate once they come into contact with the mouth, nose, throat, lungs, or eyes of an uninfected person. When germs come into contact with an uninfected person, they can multiply and cause illness. Colds occur more often in the winter when children spend more time in a confined environment, and are spread by sharing tissues, food, and cups. They can also be spread when coughing or sneezing without covering the mouth.

The best ways to prevent germs from spreading are to disinfect toys that are put in the mouth often, wash hands at appropriate times (see Table 3.4), and teach children to protect others when they cough, sneeze, or blow their noses.

Fecal-Oral Transmission

Fecal-oral transmission occurs when the germs from one person's feces get into another person's mouth and then are swallowed and introduced into the digestive tract of that person. The most common way for germs to spread is when hands are not washed after toileting, before eating, or before preparing food. Fecal-oral transmitted diseases can affect a number of children. Approximately 11 percent of children under five years of age are hospitalized for diarrhea diseases (Griffen, 1993).

In child care another common way that germs are spread is in the water. Water tables that are not **sanitized** and do not have the water changed frequently are hosts to germs that are transmitted from unwashed hands. The APA and AAHA do not recommend water tables in the child care environment for this reason. However, many child caregivers feel the benefits of having a water table outweigh the risks. Therefore, special care must be taken to maintain these water tables so they are not good hosts to germs and do not encourage the spread of disease.

Hand washing at proper times, proper care of a water table, and proper food safety can help obstruct the spread of disease through the fecal-oral route.

Respiratory tract transmission
germs that are passed through the air from the respiratory tract of one person to another person

Fecal-oral transmission
passing of germs from an infected person's bowel movement through the hand into another person's system through the mouth

Sanitized
removal of bacteria, filth, and dirt that makes transmission of disease unlikely

TABLE **3.2**

Infectious Disease Spread in Child Care

Method	How Spread	Diseases
Respiratory tract	Infectious droplets from the mouth, nose, and eyes get in air via talking, sneezing, coughing, and blowing nose.	Colds Strep throat Meningitis Chicken pox Measles Flu, Hib flu Tuberculosis Whooping cough Ear infections Fifth disease Sixth disease
Fecal-Oral	Germs from stool of one person get in mouth of another person and are swallowed. Not washing hands after toileting, before preparing food, before eating, and not disinfecting toys that have been put in the mouth. Also handling pets such as birds, snakes, and lizards can spread bacteria from salmonella.	Hepatitis A Giardia Shigella Salmonella Diarrhea
Direct Contact	Infected articles or secretions from infected area. Spread through touching toys, faucets, food, tables touched by infected person. By parasites through bedding, clothing, shared hats, combs, brushes, or dress-up clothing.	Impetigo Lice Scabies Cold sores Pink eye CMV
Blood	Infected blood from one person entering bloodstream of another person. Infected blood can come in contact through cuts, chapped hands, a hangnail, and other broken skin, or lining of mouth eyes, nose, and rectum. In child care common transmitters are child biting, bloody noses, and skinned knees.	Hepatitis B HIV-AIDS

Direct contact transmission
passing of germs from one person's body or clothing to another person through direct contact

Secretions
saliva, mucus, urine, and blood produced by the body for specific purposes

Direct Contact Transmission

Direct contact transmission occurs when one person has direct contact with **secretions** from an infected person. Secretions can be left on toys, doorknobs, or other objects that come in direct contact with the uninfected person. Direct contact transmission also occurs when a person picks up parasites from infested objects such as bedding, toys, clothing, or combs. Diseases can spread easily through direct contact among children and caregivers in a child care environment if precautions are not taken to curb it. Good hygiene, including hand washing, sanitizing, and proper food handling, can help block the spread of disease through direct contact.

Blood Contact Transmission

Blood contact
passing of germs through the blood from one person's circulatory system to another person's circulatory system

Transmitting disease through **blood contact** occurs when the infected blood of one person enters the bloodstream of another person. The infected blood can be transmitted and absorbed easily. For example, spread can occur when an infected person has a cut, scraped skin (such as from a skinned knee), or a bloody nose and is treated by a person with a hangnail, chapped hands, or a small cut. Spread also can occur when mucous membranes such as the inside lining of the mouth, eyes, and nose come in contact with another person's blood through a broken surface. The major risk for this would be child-biting. Caregivers should wear disposable gloves when caring for a child with an open wound and any secretions. Any child-biting should be handled immediately.

Following guidelines set up in the remainder of this chapter, the caregiver should be able to forestall or deter the spread of disease in the child care environment as shown in Table 3.2. Figure 3.1 shows the five most effective ways to prevent the spread of disease in child care.

FIGURE **3.1**
Five Fabulous Forestallers of Disease Spread in Child Care

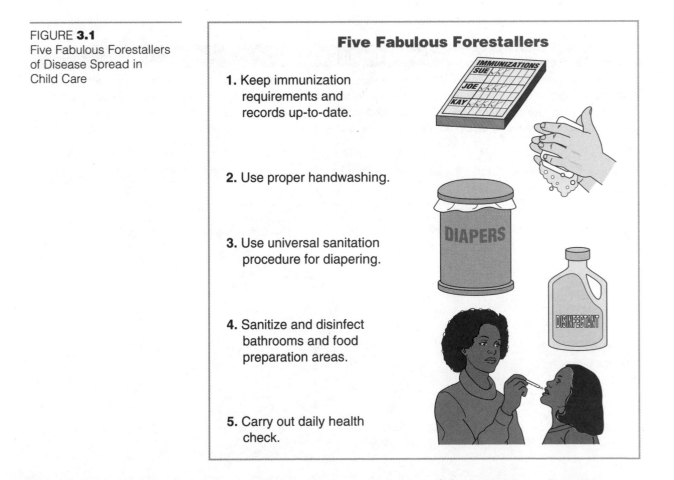

Five Fabulous Forestallers

1. Keep immunization requirements and records up-to-date.

2. Use proper handwashing.

3. Use universal sanitation procedure for diapering.

4. Sanitize and disinfect bathrooms and food preparation areas.

5. Carry out daily health check.

KEY MECHANISMS OF DISEASE SPREAD

CONCEPT

Infectious diseases are common in child care. In order to protect children's health, barriers must be in place. The caregiver must understand how diseases spread. The four methods of transmission are respiratory tract, fecal-oral, direct contact, and blood. This knowledge will provide a foundation for the caregiver to construct barriers to disease spread.

IMMUNIZATIONS FOR DISEASE PREVENTION

Communicable diseases
a disease spread from one person to another through means of respiratory spray or infected body fluids

One of the major deterrents of **communicable disease** spread is immunization against those diseases. Immunizations can protect children from diseases that caused epidemics. These outbreaks could make children violently ill, disable them, and even kill them. Through medical science, a number of these diseases have been controlled by a regular schedule of immunizations for children at particular ages (see Table 3.3 for an immunization schedule).

TABLE **3.3**

Recommended Immunization Schedule for All Children

Vaccines are listed under the routinely recommended ages. Bars indicate range of acceptable ages for vaccination. Shaded bars indicate *catch-up vaccination:* at 11–12 years of age, Hepatitis B vaccine should be administered to children not previously vaccinated, and Varicella Virus vaccine should be administered to unvaccinated children who lack a reliable history of chickenpox.

Age ▶ / Vaccine ▼	Birth	1 mo	2 mos	4 mos	6 mos	12 mos	15 mos	18 mos	4–6 yrs	11–12 yrs	14–16 yrs
Hepatitis B	Hep B-1		Hep B-2		Hep B-3					Hep B	
Diphtheria, Tetanus, Pertussis			DTaP or DTP	DTaP or DTP	DTaP or DTP			DTaP or DTP	DTaP or DTP	Td	
H. influenzae type b			Hib	Hib	Hib[5]	Hib					
Polio			Polio	Polio		Polio			Polio		
Measles, Mumps, Rubella						MMR			MMR or	MMR	
Varicella						Var				Var	

Approved by the Advisory Committee on Immunization Practices (ACIP), the American Academy of Pediatrics (AAP), and the American Academy of Family Physicians (AAFP). From The Centers for Disease Control and Prevention.

Vaccinations
inactivated, dead, or
weakened live organism of
infectious diseases to which
the body builds resistance

There are immunizations or **vaccinations** available for a number of diseases that are associated with children and child care. Diseases that can be prevented include measles, mumps, rubella, whooping cough (pertussis), diphtheria, Hib (Haemophilus Influenza Type B—Meningitis), chickenpox, and Hepatitis B. Immunizations for these diseases are recommended by the American Academy of Pediatrics and are required for entrance into elementary schools. There is also a vaccination available for Hepatitis A, and although no recommendations have been made, it is expected that this will be included in a child's immunization schedule (Graham, 1994).

Immunizations against disease are effective as a preventive measure only if they are administered according to schedule. Parents do not always realize that many serious childhood diseases can still pose threats and they need to prevent those threats through immunization. In recent years, whooping cough and measles have greatly increased because enough children have failed to be vaccinated against them. Adult caregivers need to make sure that boosters are administered as scheduled.

Children in child care not only need protection from the classic childhood diseases, but also from those diseases that seem to flourish in child care environments if proper precautions are not practiced. Recent outbreaks of childhood diseases seem to be traced to child care situations. These outbreaks include Hepatitis B, Hepatitis A, and Hib, which is a flulike form of meningitis. There are now vaccines available for each of these diseases that help protect children.

Completion of the
immunization schedule
for both children and child
care providers is essential.
Children who come to the
center after receiving their
immunization shots may
exhibit a low-grade fever
or sleepiness.

REALITY CHECK

At Risk for Preventable Diseases

Although immunizations are available for many childhood diseases, recent studies show that large numbers of children are at risk for these preventable diseases because they have not been immunized. There has been an increase in reported cases of measles and mumps (Cesarone, 1993). In fact, a sharp increase has been seen in cases of measles ("Public Sector Vaccination Efforts," 1992). Whooping cough or pertussis was thought to have been eradicated, but there have been a number of reported cases recently that required hospitalization. In 1993, there were over 6,500 cases of pertussis reported—the largest number in more than twenty-five years (Graham, 1994).

The Carnegie Institute's Task Force on Meeting the Needs of Young Children reported that 60 percent of two year olds in this country are not immunized for childhood diseases. A report by Mustin, Holt, and Connell (1994) indicated that poverty, lower levels of maternal education, and lack of access to health care are associated with the large number of children who lack proper immunizations.

Following the recommended series of childhood immunizations can prevent children from becoming ill and even dying. Every disease that a child has not received an immunization for becomes an issue for child care and the caregiver. Until the diseases are eliminated, children will spread the disease and nonimmunized children will become ill. Caregivers can help eliminate these childhood diseases by requiring immunizations before children enter care. They should also update their records and report any childhood diseases to the public health authority in their area.

As a child caregiver, it is imperative to protect the children and the caregivers in the child care environment by requiring the completion of the immunization schedule. Parents of children in care must provide an immunization record filled out by a physician or local health clinic on the form provided by the state in which the child resides. A copy of this record should be on file with each child's health record and should be periodically updated if the child is in the process of receiving a series of vaccinations.

Children who have not followed the immunization schedule, and have missed a particular vaccination will not be protected from that particular disease. If a child has not met all of the requirements of an immunization schedule he must do so immediately. A quarterly check of children's records can help keep them up to date. To simplify record keeping, the caregiver can place a "red flag" or special sticker on each child's file who must still complete the immunization schedule.

If a child in child care has not completed the schedule and the parents do not have any plans to complete this schedule, the child should be excluded from care until the process of immunization is resumed. An exception to this would be a child who, for medical or religious reasons, is exempt from the immunizations. An exemption or release form must be signed by the parent before the child is admitted or readmitted into care.

The more children in child care who are properly immunized, the less the risk for the spread of those childhood diseases. Caregivers also need to verify their own immunity to childhood diseases and should follow the vaccination schedule for Hib, Hepatitis A, and Hepatitis B.

KEY IMMUNIZATIONS FOR DISEASE PREVENTION

CONCEPT

Immunizations are a major deterrent to disease. In order to be effective, they must be administered according to schedule. Both the children and caregivers in the child care environment should meet the immunization requirements.

Sanitary practices
practices that remove bacteria, filth, and dirt that cut down on disease transmission

Virus
a small microorganism that is produced in living cells and that can cause disease

Otitis media
infection of the middle ear

Disinfecting
procedures to eliminate all germs through use of chemicals or heat

UNIVERSAL SANITARY PRACTICES FOR THE CHILD CARE ENVIRONMENT

One of the most effective tools you have to create a healthy environment for the child is to incorporate universal **sanitary practices** to keep the environment as clean and germ-free as possible. These protective and preventive actions can greatly reduce risk for infection or disease. Proper sanitary practices can help in the prevention of the spread of **virus**, bacteria, parasites, respiratory diseases, and **otitis media**.

Cleaning, sanitation, and disinfection procedures should be the main points of a health policy for a sanitary environment. These procedures should include:

■ Hand washing
■ Diapering
■ Toileting
■ Cleaning and **disinfecting**

It is very important that a written explanation of the sanitary practice policy be sent home with children so that parents understand that an effort is being made to keep the environment healthy and germ-free. Cooperation may also be elicited to encourage children to use these sanitary practices in the home by providing parents with a flyer on correct hand washing procedures.

Hand Washing

Washing the hands is perhaps the single most important thing the caregiver can do to prevent illness personally and to keep it from spreading to the children in care (see Table 3.4). It is essential that the caregiver develop the habit of frequent hand washing. Often when the pace of life is hectic, it is easy to forget that hand washing should be done. If it is developed into a routine and becomes a habit, hand washing will be second nature and will be done regardless of the pace.

The times for routine hand washing shown in Table 3.4 reflect when the caregiver should wash hands and help the children wash their hands. By modeling hand washing behavior, the children can easily follow the caregiver's direction. Caregiver hand washing should be part of training, as well as monitoring the environment. The combination of training and monitoring

Friction
rubbing together

TABLE **3.4**

Universal Sanitary Hand Washing Practices

When:

Both the Child and the Caregiver

■ Upon arrival at child care

■ Before eating or drinking

■ After touching a child who may be sick

■ After using the toilet or changing diapers

Caregiver

■ After handling body secretions (vomit, mucus, and so forth)

■ Before and after handling or preparing food

■ After cleaning

■ Before and after giving medication, if applicable

How:

■ Use running water that drains. Do not use a stoppered sink or container.

■ You must use soap. Liquid soap is preferable, because germs can grow on soap bars.

■ Use **friction.** Rub hands together for germ removal. Rub between fingers and around nails.

■ Rinse thoroughly in running water.

■ Turn off faucet with paper towel. Touching the faucet can recontaminate your hands.

Adapted from Control of Communicable and Infectious Diseases: A Manual for Child Care Providers, *California Child Care Health Project.*

Fecal contamination
contamination occurring
through exposure to feces

leads to a very significant decrease in diarrhea in children in child care (Griffen, 1993).

Diapering

Fecal contamination in the child care environment leads to the spread of infection from the carrier to others. Containment of fecal matter, use of disposable changing table pads, proper hand washing, and use of disposable gloves are protective measures that control this spread. These measures manage the risk of contamination and spread of disease. Bacteria can also be spread through urine and the same protective measures help to manage this risk.

The area where diapering occurs should be isolated and equipped for cleanliness and safety (see Table 3.5). A correct procedure for changing diapers should be developed and placed above the diaper changing area.

Routine hand washing should be a part of training in the day for any child. It is important to have sinks at a child's level, or safe footstools, so the child can comfortably wash.

Maintaining the procedure as well as a clean and sanitary area to change diapers greatly reduces risk (see Table 3.6).

If a child uses cloth diapers, the diapers should be placed in a second plastic bag and sent home with the child. There is too much risk of spreading disease by rinsing or laundering diapers at a child care facility.

Proper diapering procedures should be followed to avoid the spread of infection. A sanitary diapering area as well as using disposable rubber gloves are examples of proper diapering procedures.

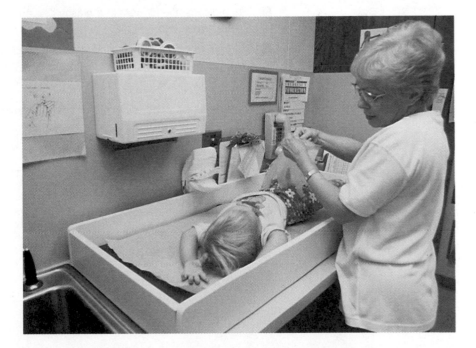

TABLE **3.5**

Creating a Sanitary Diapering Environment

■ Use area for diapering only.

■ Provide running water to wash hands before and after.

■ Put it as far away from food preparation area as possible.

■ Surface should be flat, safe, and preferably three feet off the floor.

■ Make sure surface is clean, waterproof, and free of cracks. Use disposable covers such as squares, rolls of paper, paper bags, or used computer paper. Throw away immediately after use.

■ For safety, keep all lotions out of the reach of children. Restrain child. Never leave child unattended.

Adapted from Control of Communicable and Infectious Diseases: A Manual for Child Care Providers, *California Child Care Health Project.*

TABLE **3.6**

Universal Sanitary Diapering Procedures

■ Have area and supplies ready.

■ Put on disposable gloves.

■ Pick up child. If diaper is soiled, hold child away from you.

■ Lay child down on diapering surface.

■ Remove soiled or wet diaper. If clothes are contaminated, remove them.

■ Place disposable diapers in a plastic bag and then throw away in a lined, covered trash can.

■ Clean child's bottom with moist disposable wipes. Wipe from front to back, using towelette. Use another towelette if needed.

■ Pat dry with paper towel.

■ Dispose of towelette and towel in lined, covered trash can with lid.

■ Wipe your hands with moist towelette and dispose of in lined, covered trash can with lid.

■ Diaper child and dress.

■ Wash the child's hands.

■ Remove disposable covering from diaper surface.

■ Wash area and disinfect with bleach solution.

■ Remove disposable gloves.

■ Wash your own hands thoroughly.

Adapted from Control of Communicable and Infectious Diseases: A Manual for Child Care Providers, *California Child Care Health Project.*

Toileting is a good opportunity to teach children about the importance of hand washing. Some states require that caregivers use disposable gloves when helping children with toileting.

Toileting

Toileting in a center is easier to control than toileting in a family child care or the child's own home. In most cases, centers have child-sized toilets that need to be cleaned and sanitized daily. If the toilet is contaminated with

Recording information about a child's progress during toileting can be useful for the parents who must further the progress at home.

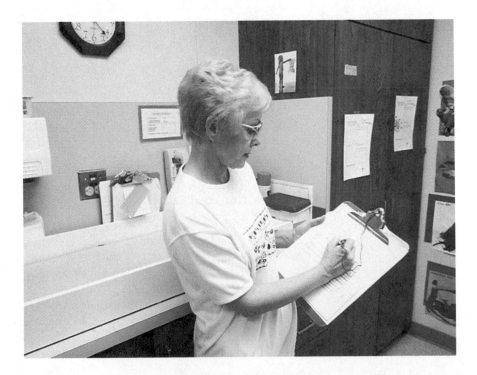

diarrhea, it should be cleaned and sanitized immediately. When training children to use the toilet they should be taught about the importance of washing hands. Instruction in hand washing should be given before and after toileting. Observing the children when they wash their hands will help to know which children need assistance in thorough hand washing.

Toileting in a home environment often involves a potty chair. Ideally, each child learning to toilet should bring his own potty chair to the caregiver, because it decreases the risk of spreading germs. The potty chairs should be kept out of the reach of children and away from other surfaces that may have germs. Table 3.7 reviews sanitary procedures for potty chair use.

TABLE **3.7**

Sanitary Procedures for Potty Chairs

- ■ Wash child's hands.
- ■ Empty into toilet.
- ■ Rinse with water. This should be in a sink used for no other purpose. If it is used for hand washing of the child, clean and sanitize sink after toileting.
- ■ Wash chair with soap and water. Empty into toilet.
- ■ Rinse again and place contents in toilet.
- ■ Spray with bleach solution.
- ■ Air dry.
- ■ Wash hands.

Adapted from Control of Communicable and Infectious Diseases: A Manual for Child Care Providers, *California Child Care Health Project.*

The use of disposable gloves is also helpful in reducing the risk of spreading disease. Caregivers should check the requirements of their state licensing agencies, as some require the use of disposable gloves for helping with toileting.

Cleaning and Disinfecting

The best way to stop the spread of germs is to both clean and disinfect. Neither is adequate alone. Cleaning gets rid of dirt and some surface germs while disinfecting rids the surface of the remaining germs by using a sanitizing solution. In child care, the most common effective and least expensive sanitizing solution is bleach.

Several strengths of the solution are necessary for disinfecting different surfaces or contaminants. Figure 3.2 shows a general purpose sanitation mix.

The solution is placed in spray bottles and used in the bathroom, kitchen, diapering area, and on other surfaces and toys. This mix is also used

A standard solution of bleach to water should be used to clean and sanitize the classroom, toy surfaces, and floors. What other surfaces should be sanitized?

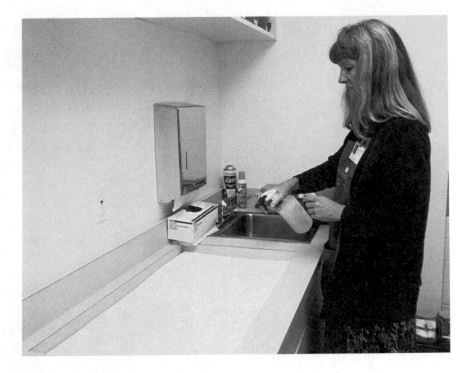

on floors and to clean sleeping mats. See Table 3.8 for frequency of cleaning and disinfecting needed in the child care environment.

For cleaning more infectious items such as blood, blood spills, and body fluids, including vomit, a stronger solution is needed. This stronger mix is found in Figure 3.3. The contamination cleaning solution is also used for regular cleaning when outbreaks of infectious disease occur.

FIGURE **3.2**
General Purpose Cleaning Solution. Use in the bathroom, kitchen, diapering area, and on toys.

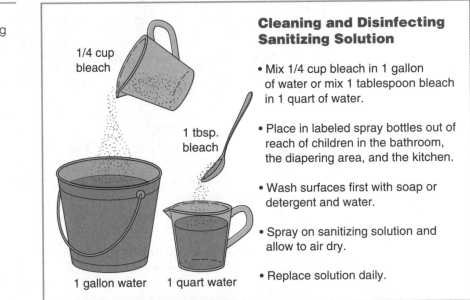

Cleaning and Disinfecting Sanitizing Solution

1/4 cup bleach

1 tbsp. bleach

1 gallon water   1 quart water

- Mix 1/4 cup bleach in 1 gallon of water or mix 1 tablespoon bleach in 1 quart of water.

- Place in labeled spray bottles out of reach of children in the bathroom, the diapering area, and the kitchen.

- Wash surfaces first with soap or detergent and water.

- Spray on sanitizing solution and allow to air dry.

- Replace solution daily.

TABLE **3.8**

Cleaning and Disinfecting Guidelines

- Clean objects and surfaces with detergent and water first.
- Next apply bleach solution by spraying from bottle or dipping object in bleach solution and allow to air dry.

Cleaning and Disinfecting Schedule:

Object or area	Frequency
Diaper changing area, toilets, and potty chairs	Clean after every use. Spray with sanitizing solution after cleaning.
Bathroom	Clean thoroughly one or more times daily.
Kitchen	Clean thoroughly one or more times daily.
Play Areas	Mop or vacuum daily. Remove litter or food immediately.
Cribs and Cots	Change linen when wet or soiled; otherwise, weekly. Disinfect weekly.
Toys	Clean and sanitize all mouthed toys daily. Machine wash stuffed toys frequently. Sanitize water tables and wading pools after each use. Throw away mouthed play dough or clay immediately. Change frequently.

Cleaning: All-purpose liquid detergents and water are used to remove dirt, urine, or vomit by washing and scrubbing.

Sanitizing: Soap, detergents, and abrasive cleaners are used to remove filth, soil, and a small amount of bacteria. To be considered sanitary, surfaces must be clean and germs must be reduced to a level at which disease transmission is unlikely.

Disinfecting: A solution of bleach and water is used to eliminate practically all germs from surfaces. For normal disinfecting, a general-purpose solution is used. When working with blood or stools from bowel movement, a contamination solution is used.

When a child has soiled her clothing with fecal or bodily fluid, the item should be removed immediately and placed in a plastic bag for the parent to take home and launder. Parents should be informed of this policy when the child enters care. A reminder note should be attached to the soiled clothing bag.

FIGURE **3.3**
Contamination Cleaning
Mix. Use to clean blood,
body fluids, and vomit.

Contamination Cleaning Mix

1 tablespoon of bleach in
3/4 cup of water

Clothing and hats used for dress-up in play areas should be laundered frequently with bleach. Hats should be sprayed frequently with a disinfectant such as Lysol. If an outbreak of lice or skin infections such as scabies occurs, these clothes should be temporarily removed, laundered, and placed in airtight plastic bags for at least two weeks.

Each child should use his own bedding only. These items should be stored separately in bins or boxes labeled with the child's name. Regular weekly laundering can keep them fresh and clean. If they become contaminated with mucus, feces, urine, vomit, or blood, send them home with the parents to wash.

When soiled or contaminated items are sent home with the child, a reminder note accompanying the items is an effective communication tool. It will explain to the parents why the item was not rinsed and alert them that they should closely observe their child for illness. The prevention, protection, and control of infectious disease are not always easily understood, but are very necessary in maintaining a sanitary environment.

KEY UNIVERSAL SANITARY PRACTICES

CONCEPT

Universal sanitary practices are some of the most effective risk management tools a child caregiver can employ to create a healthy environment. A clean, sanitary environment will help curb the spread of germs and infectious diseases. Proper techniques for hand washing, diapering, toileting, cleaning, and disinfecting are the main tools the caregiver uses to provide a healthy environment.

Water play is an engrossing and enjoyable activity for young children, but opens up the playing field for germs when the table or container is not properly cleaned.

ENVIRONMENTAL QUALITY CONTROL FOR DISEASE PREVENTION

There are certain other areas of the child care environment that may contribute to the spread of disease. These special areas of consideration include water play, play dough, air quality, and contamination.

Water Play

Water play occurs in a container which, if not properly cleaned, can be an environment where germs multiply. If the water becomes warm, it offers the warm, moist place where germs thrive and rapidly multiply. For optimal use of a water table in the child care environment, follow the water table health tips found in Table 3.9.

TABLE **3.9**

Water Table Health Guidelines

■ Clean and sanitize the water table with the general-purpose sanitation mix daily.

■ Change water at least daily; more frequently, if it gets warm (over 72°F). Use fresh, cool water.

■ Children should wash hands before playing in water table.

■ Wash water play toys daily either with general-purpose solution or in the dishwasher.

■ Use plastic throw away items when possible.

Play dough is a classroom staple, but health precautions should be taken to make this fun manipulative germ-free and safe for children.

Play Dough and Clay

Play dough and clay are also good hosts for germs because they are moist and get warm through frequent contact with children's hands. Safety tips for having play dough and clay in the child care environment are included in Table 3.10.

TABLE **3.10**

Play Dough and Clay Health Guidelines

- ■ Children must wash hands before and after playing with the play dough.
- ■ Do not use scents in play dough because it encourages mouthing.
- ■ Replace play dough frequently and always after being mouthed or when dirty.
- ■ Store play dough in the refrigerator.
- ■ Keep clay in a cool, dry place and make sure it is well covered.
- ■ Clean and sanitize tables before and after play dough or clay is used.
- ■ Allow only a small amount of clay at a time so it can be replaced more often and the expense will not be as great.
- ■ Do not use play dough or clay for a day or two if a fecal-oral disease has been identified in the environment.

During naptime at least 3 feet of space should be maintained between cribs and cots.

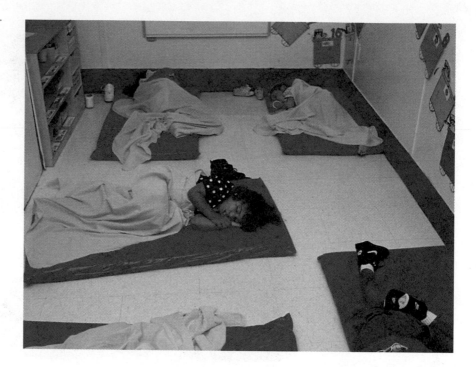

Air Quality

Air flow in the child care environment is especially important to help control the spread of germs. If the air is not moving or if there are too many children in one area, the air will not flow as well as it should, resulting in a better environment for germs. To avoid poor air quality, follow the air quality health guidelines in Table 3.11.

TABLE **3.11**

Air Quality Health Guidelines

- Keep air temperature cool; under 72°F helps prevent disease spread.
- Circulate fresh air as much as possible—open windows as daily weather permits.
- Make sure children get outside to breathe fresh air daily, weather permitting.
- Heating and cooling equipment should be checked several times a year and should be cleaned every three months. Any filters should be replaced when serviced to prevent buildup of molds and dust.
- Arrange your environment so that there is plenty of open space. This discourages the spread of germs.
- Keep at least 3 feet of space between cribs and cots in the sleeping area.
- Follow guidelines of indoor space per child so that there is no crowding.

Contamination in Child Care

Special precautions should be taken to minimize the effects of contaminants such as blood, vomit, urine, and loose stools or diarrhea in the child environment. For proper health precautions see Table 3.12.

TABLE **3.12**

Health Guidelines for Disease Prevention

- Minimize the number of people who handle contaminated materials.
- Use disposable gloves and paper towels to clean up spills from diarrhea, blood, urine, or vomit.
- Clean and disinfect surfaces involved with contamination sanitation mix.
- Dispose of cleanup materials, disposable gloves, and so forth in a plastic bag, covered and tied, and placed in an outside trash can immediately.
- If any contaminated materials soil the child's or caregiver's clothes, they should be changed immediately.
- Wash hands immediately.
- Place contaminated clothing in a plastic bag with tie. Double bag it in another plastic bag and send home with child or caregiver to launder the clothing at home.

KEY ENVIRONMENTAL QUALITY CONTROL FOR DISEASE PREVENTION

CONCEPT

There are special areas of need for environmental quality control for infectious disease spread found in the child care environment. These areas include water tables, play dough and clay, air quality, and contamination. Using preventive strategies and techniques for these items can help the child caregiver control the spread of infectious disease.

IMPLICATIONS FOR **CAREGIVERS**

Child caregivers must use a number of tools to prevent the risk of infectious disease spread. These tools include education and role modeling, cultural sensitivity, and supervision to make sure protective measures are carried out.

Education and Role Modeling

Education is one of the best preventive tools a caregiver has to help control the spread of infectious disease in child care. The effort to prevent the spread of germs and disease needs to be a cooperative venture. Caregivers need to model proper health behaviors. Children need to be taught to perform proper health practices. Parents need to understand the need for these practices and help children remember to carry these out at home so they get into the habit of good hygiene.

Children need to focus on several things to play their role in prevention. Good hand washing techniques at the right times is the most important tool for children to prevent the spread of disease. This can be done in a number of ways. Modeling the hand washing techniques is important.

Modeling hand washing should include:

- Showing
- Helping
- Telling
- Feedback

When the caregiver is washing her hands or helping a child to wash his, the caregiver should talk about what is happening and why. Reinforcing the conversation and hand washing method with feedback is important for the caregiver to see that the child is grasping: (1) why hands are being washed; (2) when hands should be washed; and (3) how hands should be washed.

Reminders should be given throughout the day at times when hand washing is a must. A poster or line drawing showing proper hand washing procedures placed by the hand washing sink offers a visual reminder when the caregiver is not present.

To ensure a healthy environment, one of the caregiver's most important tasks is to help children form the good hygiene habit of hand washing. If hand washing is made a fun task, the children will more likely participate and remember when and how to use the hand washing techniques. Caregivers who develop or use songs that focus on hands while in circle groups or at the sink at hand washing times may make it easier for some children to

Hand washing at scheduled intervals throughout the day can be a fun activity and teaches the children good hygiene.

grasp good hand washing behaviors. Using books that focus on hands or good hygiene will also help.

Cultural Sensitivity

Cultural sensitivity may be needed, especially when dealing with the issue of immunization. A parent may be unaware of the need for immunizations or may lack access to immunizations. Recent immigrant families may not be aware of the need for immunization or may even feel it is unnecessary. It is important for the caregiver to help the parents understand how vital it is to follow the immunization schedule. Following this schedule is vital to the child's own health as well as the child care environment.

Supervision

Parents have a significant degree of responsibility in preventing the spread of disease in the child care environment where their children attend. Parent education is critical in the prevention of outbreaks of whooping cough and rubella (U.S. Department of Health and Human Services, 1993). Parents can make sure their children are immunized according to schedule. They can reinforce the hygiene practices that children learn at school and they can make sure not to send their children to school when they are ill. Some of the supportive behaviors that are essential on the part of the parents may need some special effort on the part of the caregiver. It is up to the caregiver to supervise the environment so that the children come into care as risk-free as possible.

There are five basic commandments for infectious disease control that must be monitored by the child caregiver. These include:

- ■ Prevent the spread of disease.
- ■ Require and monitor immunizations.
- ■ Report some illnesses.
- ■ Exclude some children.
- ■ Be prepared.

KEY IMPLICATIONS FOR CAREGIVERS

CONCEPT

The effort to prevent the spread of infectious disease is a cooperative venture. The child caregiver can educate and model behaviors to the children. Modeling will also help the parent reinforce these behaviors at home. The caregiver must be especially culturally sensitive about the need for immunizations and help the parents understand the necessity of a current immunization schedule for children. The caregiver must supervise the child care environment to make sure sanitary practices are carried out.

CHAPTER **SUMMARY**

Health policies for infection control maintain health and prevent some illnesses in children and adults present in child care. Two practices that contribute to this are good hygiene and sanitary practices. Checking the immunization schedule is another preventive practice. Food safety and storage are other practices that help manage the spread of disease. The four methods of infectious disease spread should be understood and proactive measures taken to reduce the spread.

TO GO **BEYOND**

Questions for Review

1. Discuss the methods of transmission of infectious diseases. Relate them to sanitary practices that can be performed.
2. Discuss the importance of immunization schedules. How much have these schedules changed in recent years, compared to when the students were young children?

AS AN **INDIVIDUAL**

1. Observe hand washing practices in a child care environment. Were universal hand washing procedures used at appropriate times? Record your observations.

AS A **GROUP**

1. Discuss environmental quality control. What further measures can be taken to improve the health of the environment?
2. Watch *Basic Caregiving,* an AAP video. How do they handle diapering and hand washing? Discuss what was observed.

CHAPTER **REFERENCES**

California Child Health Project. (1990). *Control of communicable and infectious disease: A manual for child care providers.* San Diego, CA: Author.

Cesarone, B. (1993). *Health care, nutrition and goal one.* Eric Digest, Champaign, IL: Eric Clearinghouse on Elementary and Early Childhood Education.

Child Care Action Campaign (CCAC). *Finding good child care: The essential questions to ask when seeking quality care for your child.* [CCAC Information Guide 19]. Author.

Graham, J. (1994, April/May). Immunizations update. *Healthy Kids,* 58–61.

Griffen, A. (1993). *Preventing preventable harm to babies: Promoting health and safety in child care.* Arlington, VA: Zero to Three/National Center for Clinical Infant Programs.

Kendall, E., & Moukadden, V. (1992). Who's vulnerable in infant child centers? *Young Children, 47*(7), 72–78.

Klein, J. (1986). Infectious disease and day care. In M. Osterholm, J. Klein, S. Aronson, & L. Pickering (Eds.), *Infectious diseases in child day care: Management and prevention.* Chicago: University of Chicago Press.

Mustin, H., Holt, V., & Connell, F. (1994). Adequacy of well-care and immunizations in U.S. infants born in 1988. *Journal of the American Medical Association, 272*(14), 1111–1115.

Public-sector vaccination efforts in response to the resurgence of measles among school aged children. (1992). *Morbidity and Mortality Weekly Report, 41*(29), 522–525.

U.S. Department of Health and Human Services. (1993). *Learning readiness: Promising strategies.* Washington, DC: Author.

SUGGESTIONS FOR **READING**

Adler, S. (1989). Cytomegalovirus and child day care: Evidence for an increased infection rate among day care workers. *New England Journal of Medicine, 321*(19), 1290–1296.

Arnold, C., Makintube, S., & Istre, G. (1993). Day care attendance and other risk factors for invasive Haemophilus influenzae type b disease. *American Journal of Epidemiology, 138*(5), 333–340.

Wood, S. (1996, February). Should your child get the chicken pox vaccine? *Child Magazine,* 72–73.

Young, K. (1994, May 1). From zero to three: Millions of American children are at risk because of improper parenting, neglect. *San Diego Union-Tribune,* p. G-4.

CHAPTER FOUR

HEALTH CARE IN CHILD CARE

Upon completion of this chapter, including a review of the summary, you should be able to:

HEALTH POLICIES

Describe and discuss health policies for the identification and management of childhood communicable diseases.

IDENTIFICATION OF INFECTIOUS DISEASES

Describe the methods and means of identifying childhood infectious diseases for early interventions and prevention of disease spread.

MANAGING INFECTIOUS DISEASES IN CHILD CARE

Describe the methods and practices for managing childhood infectious diseases for early identification and disease spread.

MANAGING CARE FOR MILDLY ILL CHILDREN

Summarize and indicate the importance of policies and protocols for care of mildly ill children in child care situations.

IMPLICATIONS FOR CAREGIVERS

Indicate the need and importance of education, observation, and supervision for early intervention to manage childhood communicable diseases in the child care setting.

HEALTH POLICIES

Health policies for health care in child care are essential to keep children as healthy as possible, to prevent disease spread, and to care for mildly ill children. The following are indicators of the need for good health care policies for child care:

- Children under the age of three years are more vulnerable to infectious diseases because their immune systems are not fully developed (Kendall & Moukadden, 1992).

- The chances of diseases being transmitted depend on three things: (1) the characteristics of the children in the group; (2) the nature of the disease; and (3) the health policies and practices of the child care facility (Kendrick, Kaufmann, & Messenger, 1995).

- With most illnesses, children are contagious for at least three to five days before they develop any symptoms (Child Care Action Campaign, 1993).

- Women who work full time have children who are 50 percent less likely to stay home when they are ill (Hewison & Dowswell, 1993).

- Being clean or dirty has nothing to do with getting head lice. It is transmitted from child to child or by sharing objects, such as combs or hats with people who have lice (County of San Diego Department of Health Services, 1993).

Health care in child care is a complex issue. A child caregiver must be able to identify the signs and symptoms of illness and parasite infestations. The identification process helps put an exclusion policy into operation. The exclusion policy enables the caregiver to separate those children who are very ill or who are contagious and have to leave from those children who are not contagious or very ill and may remain in child care. If children are

A center's health policy should specify that when a child exhibits signs and symptoms of a contagious disease or infection, the parents must be notified and an authorized person contacted to come pick up the child.

not excluded from child care, the caregiver needs to manage the care for mildly ill children without putting others at risk in the child care setting.

Parents and caregivers need to work together to help identify and manage risks to the health of the children in the child care environment. Caregivers need to supervise child care to intervene and minimize risk, and to help maintain the health of all of the children in their care.

To provide the child care environment with the optimum health care there should be policies for:

■ *Identification of Childhood Infectious Diseases:* practices for recognizing signs and symptoms of infectious disease for early intervention.

■ *Management of Childhood Infectious Diseases:* practices for managing childhood infectious diseases, including exclusion.

■ *Managing Care for Mildly Ill Children:* strategies and practices for managing the care of mildly ill children.

■ *Implications for Caregivers:* methods and practices to provide minimum risk and maximum protection for health in child care through education, observation, and supervision.

KEY HEALTH POLICY

CONCEPT

Managing health care in child care may be a challenge to the caregiver, because it includes a number of aspects. The caregiver must learn how to identify infectious diseases and know when to exclude children from care. The caregiver must understand how to prevent the spread of infectious disease and protect the health of the children in care.

IDENTIFICATION OF INFECTIOUS DISEASES

The first line of defense for illnesses in child care is the control of infectious diseases through good hygiene and sanitary practices.

Identifying Infectious Diseases and Illness in Children

The second line of defense is the caregiver's ability to identify illness as quickly as possible. Many illnesses may be present several days before signs or symptoms appear. Guidelines for helping a caregiver recognize signs and symptoms provide a barrier to the spread of an infectious disease.

Signs and Symptoms of Illness. Children may show few signs of illness, then may suddenly appear to be ill. The caregiver needs to observe for certain signs and symptoms that will help identify an ill child (Figure 4.1). Observation can help determine if the illness is the type that may spread rapidly and necessitate excluding a child from care. Some signs and symptoms are serious, while others need special consideration because they may signify an oncoming illness.

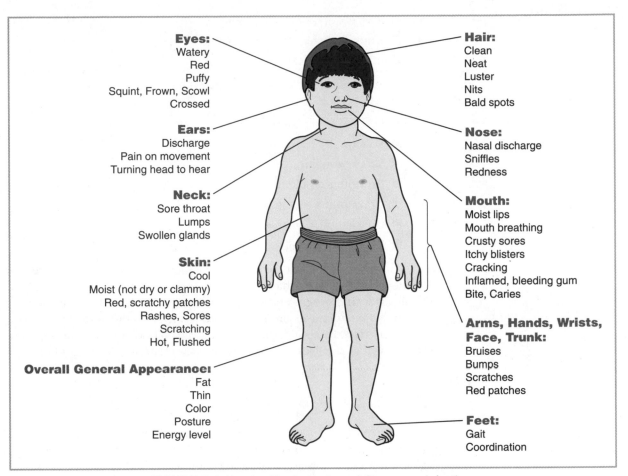

Eyes:
Watery
Red
Puffy
Squint, Frown, Scowl
Crossed

Ears:
Discharge
Pain on movement
Turning head to hear

Neck:
Sore throat
Lumps
Swollen glands

Skin:
Cool
Moist (not dry or clammy)
Red, scratchy patches
Rashes, Sores
Scratching
Hot, Flushed

Overall General Appearance:
Fat
Thin
Color
Posture
Energy level

Hair:
Clean
Neat
Luster
Nits
Bald spots

Nose:
Nasal discharge
Sniffles
Redness

Mouth:
Moist lips
Mouth breathing
Crusty sores
Itchy blisters
Cracking
Inflamed, bleeding gum
Bite, Caries

Arms, Hands, Wrists, Face, Trunk:
Bruises
Bumps
Scratches
Red patches

Feet:
Gait
Coordination

FIGURE **4.1** Head to Toe Indicators of Disease or Infection

Conducting a daily health check as the child arrives is the first point of the day to watch for caution signs for health or illness. The health policy for child care should state that any child who exhibits infectious disease signs and symptoms be excluded from child care. This should be strictly enforced. (Table 4.5 presents the conditions for exclusion.)

The child who appears to be below the normal level of mood or activity should be monitored for further symptoms. Signs or symptoms may not be exhibited in the first stages, yet the child may indeed be ill.

The following are some common primary indicators of whether a child is ill:

■ Unusual crankiness or listlessness

■ Complaint of sore throat or difficulty swallowing

■ Runny nose (clear discharge indicates allergies; green or yellow indicates infection)

■ Complaint of stomachache or cramping

■ Diarrhea

■ Complaint of headache or earache

- Red, watery, or draining eyes
- Unusual rashes or spots
- Infected skin lesions

More serious indicators of illness that need *immediate attention* include:

- Fever
- Vomiting
- Severe coughing
- Breathing problems
- Urine with a strong odor
- Unusual drowsiness
- Excessive crying

The caregiver must determine whether the child is just under the weather or is ill and may have an infectious disease. The caregiver can identify illness with the signs and symptoms listed in Tables 4.1 through 4.4.

Infectious diseases are spread through four methods of transmission: respiratory tract, fecal-oral, direct contact, and blood contact. The signs and symptoms that diseases exhibit may directly relate to the method of transmission.

Respiratory Tract Transmitted Diseases

Respiratory tract infectious diseases range from a mild cold to bacterial meningitis, which can be life threatening. Many of these diseases affect all age groups. Other diseases are more common in children like Haemophilus Influenza Type B (Hib). Table 4.1 describes the identification of and management methods for respiratory tract transmitted diseases.

TABLE **4.1**

Respiratory Tract Transmitted Diseases

Disease	Signs/Symptoms	Caregiver's Role
Colds	Sneezing, runny nose, stuffy nose, watery eyes, sore throat, fever Most contagious 2 to 3 days before and 3 to 5 days after symptoms appear	Wipe runny noses; use gloves. Wash hands often. Do not share food, drink. Disinfect mouthed toys. Teach children to cover mouth when coughing.
Influenza	Fever, chills, headache, drowsiness, muscle aches, nausea, vomiting	Wipe runny noses; use gloves. Wash hands often. Do not share food, drinks.

Respiratory Tract Transmitted Diseases *continued*

Disease	Signs/Symptoms	Caregiver's Role
Influenza *continued*		Disinfect mouthed toys. Call parent if fever or vomiting is present.
Strep Throat	Painful, scratchy throat, tender/swollen glands, fever, spots on throat	Wash hands often. Do not share food, drink. Disinfect mouthed toys. Call parent if fever is present or child is unable to swallow. Notify all parents if strep throat is present. Be alert to outbreak. Exclude child from care until antibiotic treatment has begun.
Scarlet Fever	Same as above Red, sandpapery rash on trunk, neck, groin Red tongue, flushed cheeks	Wash hands often. Do not share food, drink. Disinfect mouthed toys. Call parent, if fever is present. Be alert to outbreak. Exclude child from care. Notify all parents.
Chicken Pox	Fever, runny nose, blistery rash, cough	Exclude if chicken pox is suspected until doctor confirms. Readmit after rash is crusted and dry. Follow same procedures as listed under Colds. Children in care should be immunized.
Fifth Disease (Parvovirus)	Headache, body ache, sore throat, fever, chills, lacy rash	Follow same procedures listed under Colds. If pregnant, report to doctor.
Sixth Disease (Roseola)	High fever, lacy rash	Follow same procedure listed under Colds.
Meningitis	Fever, lethargy, poor feeding, fine red rash, stiff neck, headache, irritability	Exclude if suspected. Report to local health department. Notify all in contact with child immediately. Those in contact begin rifampin antibiotic treatment in 24 hours. See doctor immediately if symptoms appear. Same as colds.

continued

Respiratory Tract Transmitted Diseases *continued*

Disease	Signs/Symptoms	Caregiver's Role
Hib (Haemophilus Influenza type B)	Same as meningitis, earache, rapid onset of difficult breathing, red/swollen joints, red/purple area of skin	Follow procedures listed under Meningitis. All should be immunized. See doctor immediately if symptoms appear.
Measles	Brownish/red rash beginning on face, fever, white spots in mouth, runny nose, cough	Exclude if suspected. Allow to return 6 days after rash appears. Report to public health. Notify parents. Wash hands often; use gloves. Do not share food, drink. Disinfect mouthed toys. All in child care should be immunized.
Rubella (German Measles)	Joint pain, red rash, enlarged lymph glands	Follow procedures listed under Measles. If child caregiver is pregnant, notify doctor. All in child care should be immunized.
Mumps	Fever, at least one swollen salivary gland near jaw, earache, headache	Exclude if suspected. Allow to return after 9 days. All in child care should be immunized.
Whooping Cough	Coughing spells with whoop sounds, vomiting, runny nose	Exclude if suspected. Notify local health department. Notify parents. Allow to return 5 days after antibiotic regime or 3 weeks after onset of cough. Do not share food, drink. Disinfect mouthed toys. Wash hands often; use gloves. All in care should be immunized.
Otitis Media (Ear Infection)	Fever, difficulty hearing, pain, drainage from ear	Wash hands often; use gloves. Do not share food, drink. Children with frequent ear infections should be followed for speech or language difficulties.
Tuberculosis	Cough, fever, weight loss, or no symptoms present	Exclude anyone with active TB. Allow to return when no longer contagious. Notify the health department. Notify parents. All in care should be tested before entrance to care, then every two years.

REALITY CHECK

Otitis Media and Child Care

Ear infection, or otitis media, is the second most frequently diagnosed childhood disease (Teele, Klein, & Rossner, 1984). These infections are probably the most common bacterial infection found in children. It is estimated that as many as 50 percent of cases are missed because they have no symptoms (Feagans, Kipp, & Blood, 1994). Children in child care are more likely to have these ear infections than children who are cared for at home (Droom & Culpepper, 1991).

By the age of three, more than half of children have had three or more bouts of otitis media (Wessel, 1990). These children could be classified as having chronic otitis media (Feagans, Kipp, & Blood, 1994).

Otitis media is an infection in the middle ear that is directly behind the ear drum. The ear infection commonly begins as a cold. It is suspected that children in child care are more likely to get otitis media because of the number of colds found in that environment.

The bacteria and virus germs move up the Eustachian tube, which is a passageway between the throat and middle ear. If the bacteria settles in the middle ear, pus forms and pressure develops. This causes the pain that is experienced. If left unchecked, the infection can spread to the bone behind the ear and cause a condition called mastoiditis. Fluid from otitis media may remain in the ear for months after the infection is gone. This condition can cause hearing loss for the child.

Otitis media is diagnosed by a doctor and treated with antibiotics. The medication should work within several days. For children with chronic otitis media, antibiotics may not be as effective. In these cases, children may require surgery for placement of small tubes to allow the fluid to drain.

It is important for the caregiver to recognize symptoms of otitis media so that treatment is begun early. Signs of otitis media include fever, irritability, ear pain, hearing loss, loss of appetite, and ear discharge. Nonverbal children often pull their ears or cry (Watt, Roberts, & Zeisel, 1993). Lack of attention during story or group time may also be a sign that the child has an ear infection. It has been found that high-quality child care with a low teacher-child ratio may cushion the effects of these ear infections (Feagans, Kipp, & Blood, 1994). It is important for the caregiver to alert the parent to these conditions. The caregiver may need to recommend a referral for hearing or speech problems.

The caregiver can help reduce otitis media in the child care environment by washing hands, keeping toys clean, not propping bottles for babies, and not allowing children to go to sleep with a bottle (Watt, Roberts, & Zeisel, 1993). Also, the caregiver should never use cotton swabs on children's ears and should watch for any sign of hearing or speech problems (Kendrick, Kaufmann, & Messenger, 1995).

Ear infections are not contagious and children can stay in care if they are comfortable. If allowed, the caregiver may administer medication. The caregiver may try to reduce the distractions and sound level for a child with an ear infection (Watt, Roberts, & Zeisel, 1993).

Infectious Diseases Transmitted Through the Fecal-Oral Route

Diseases spread by the fecal-oral route are caused by bacteria, parasites, and viruses that grow and spread in the intestines. The stool is the main vehicle of disease spread to others. Child care environments that have infants and toddlers in diapers are especially at risk for these types of diseases. The best course for preventing the spread of disease is to always use special precautions. Table 4.2 relates how to identify and manage diseases transmitted through the fecal-oral route.

TABLE **4.2**

Diseases Transmitted Through the Fecal-Oral Route

Disease	Signs/Symptoms	Caregiver's Role
Giardia	Diarrhea, gas, poor appetite, weight loss, cramping, bloating	Frequent hand washing according to schedule. Use sanitary procedures and gloves during diapering, toileting, and before handling food. Exclude if diarrhea is uncontrolled. Allow return once diarrhea is gone.
Shigella	Diarrhea, fever, pain, mucus or blood in stool, vomiting, headache, convulsions	Wash hands following schedule. Use sanitary procedures and gloves during diapering, toileting, and before food handling. Exclude if fever is present. Call parent immediately if convulsion occurs.
Salmonella	Stomach cramps, diarrhea, fever, fatigue, poor appetite	Wash hands following schedule. Use sanitary procedures and gloves during diapering, toileting, and before food handling. Notify local health department. Notify parents. See doctor if diarrhea occurs.
Hepatitis A	Fever, jaundice, nausea, poor appetite, dark-brown urine	Wash hands following schedule. Use sanitary procedures and gloves during diapering, toileting, and before food handling. Exclude; allow to return one week after onset and when fever is gone. Notify local health department. Notify parents. All exposed should have immune globulin treatment.
Campylobacter	Fever, vomiting, stomach cramps, diarrhea or severe bloody diarrhea	Wash hands following schedule. Use sanitary procedures and gloves during diapering, toileting, and before handling food. Notify local health department. Notify all parents. See doctor if diarrhea occurs.
E. Coli	Diarrhea or blood diarrhea	Wash hands following schedule. Use sanitary procedures during diapering, toileting, and before handling food. Cook all hamburger meat to 155°F. Notify local health department. Notify parents. Exclude until diarrhea is gone and stool specimen is negative.

Diseases Transmitted Through the Fecal-Oral Route *continued*

Disease	Signs/Symptoms	Caregiver's Role
Cocksackie virus	Fever, stomach pain, sore throat, rash with tiny blisters on hands, feet, and mouth, diarrhea	Wash hands following schedule. Use sanitary procedures and gloves during diapering, toileting, and before handling food. Notify parents. Notify staff.
Pinworms	Anal itching, worms that crawl out during sleep or no symptoms present	Follow procedures in Cocksackie virus. Each child should have own crib, mat, or cot. Exclude only until treatment has begun.

A clean and sanitary diapering area, as well as the use of disposable gloves, are essential in preventing fecal-oral transmission of disease.

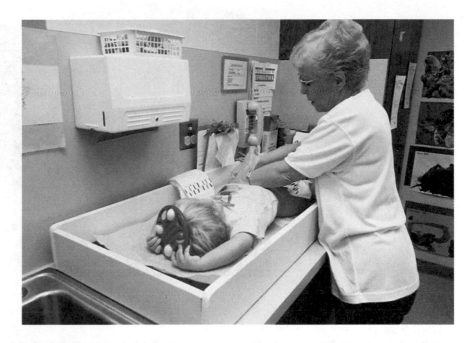

Infectious Diseases Transmitted by Direct Contact

Diseases transmitted by direct contact are spread from the secretions of one person that penetrate through the skin or mucous membranes of another person. These germs may be in the form of bacterial infections, parasites, or viral infections. Contact may be made directly through the infected or infested skin areas or by touching an infested article of clothing, a brush, or bed linens. The child caregiver should provide protective measures to prevent the spread of these diseases. Two methods of protection are offered through identification and management as shown in Table 4.3.

After diapering, both the caregiver and the child should wash their hands to prevent the spread of infectious disease. It is good to start the hand washing routine with young toddlers, who are at a higher risk for infectious disease due to mouthing and diapering/toileting activities.

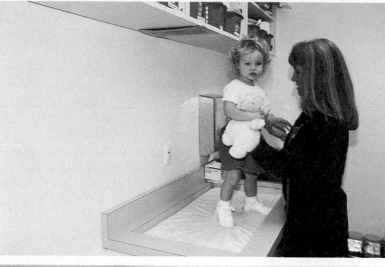

TABLE **4.3**

Infectious Diseases Transmitted by Direct Contact

Disease	Signs/Symptoms	Caregiver's Role
Conjunctivitis (Pinkeye)	Mucus in eye, watery eyes, red/pink eyes, painful eyes, red eyelids, itchy eyes	Keep eye wiped free of discharge. Always wash hands after wiping. Teach children to wipe eyes and wash hands. If child's eyes come in contact with any toys, clean them well. Have child see doctor. Exclude only if white or yellow discharge is present. Allow to return 24 hours after start of antibiotics. Notify parents and staff.

Infectious Diseases Transmitted by Direct Contact *continued*

Disease	Signs/Symptoms	Caregiver's Role
Impetigo	Red/cracking/oozing pimples, scaly rash, often on face or a sore that will not heal	If suspected, wash and cover rash with a bandage or gauze. If child scrapes or cuts another area, clean thoroughly. Follow good hand washing procedures. Have child see doctor. Follow sanitary cleaning schedule. Notify parents and staff.
Ringworm (Tinea)	Flat, growing ring-shaped rash, often scaly, may be in between toes, on scalp, or body	Keep environment clean, cool, and dry. Wash hands thoroughly. Follow sanitary cleaning schedule. Have child see doctor. If more than one case in care, notify parents and staff.
Head Lice	Lice (sesame seed sized insects) on scalp or hair, nits (eggs) behind ears or nape of neck	Learn to identify nits and regularly check near scalp, of children for them (see Figure 4.2). Notify parents with handout concerning procedures. Machine wash all possibly infested items using hot water. All nonwashable items go in dryer for 20 minutes. All other items placed in sealed plastic bags for 30 days. Soak all combs and brushes for one hour in bleach solution. Vacuum rugs, furniture, and mattresses; then throwaway vacuum bag.
Scabies	Very itchy red bumps or blisters, often between toes or fingers, head, neck, feet	Wash and dry all items contacted by the child 72 hours before outbreak. Use hot cycle wash and dry. Vacuum as for ringworm. Have child see doctor. If a serious problem exists, all children and caregivers need treatment. Notify parents.
Cytomegalo-virus (CMV)	Often no symptoms, fever, swollen glands, fatigue, jaundice	Always wash hands after contact with urine, saliva, or blood. Do not share food or drinks. Do not share utensils or glasses. Do not kiss children on mouth. Have child see doctor. Can cause problems for pregnant caregivers; notify doctor if pregnant.
Herpes Simplex (Cold Sores)	Fever, painful, small blisters on lips, mouth, or gums; may ooze	If blisters are oozing and child bites or is drooling, exclude until sores are crusted over. Do not share food, utensils, or glasses. Do not kiss children on mouth. Wash hands often. Follow sanitary cleaning schedule.

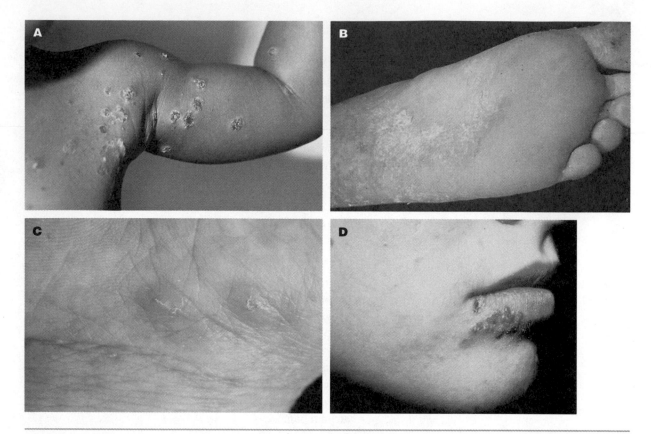

A. Impetigo. **B.** Ringworm. **C.** Scabies. **D.** Herpes Simplex I (Cold Sore).
(Courtesy of Robert A. Silverman, MD, Clinical Associate Professor, Department of Pediatrics, Georgetown University)

FIGURE **4.2**
Cycle of Head Lice
Treatment

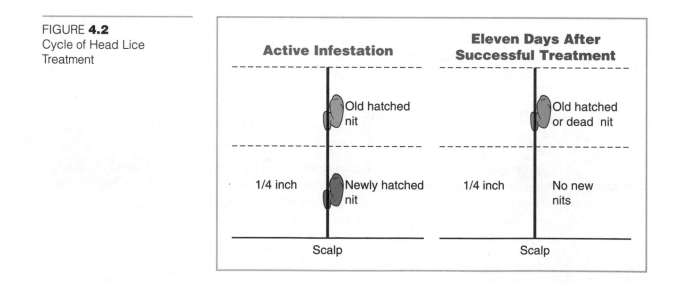

Bloodborne Infectious Diseases

Infectious diseases are spread through the blood when blood containing the virus in one person enters the bloodstream of another person. This usually occurs if the infected blood comes in contact with broken skin or mucous membranes such as the inside of the nose, mouth, eyes, anal area, or sex organs. The two diseases that are transmitted in this manner are Hepatitis B and HIV/AIDS. These viruses may be present without any symptoms. It is important that all blood and body fluids contacted in child care be treated as if they were contaminated. Prevention of these diseases is critical. All blood spills should be cleaned up immediately and the area disinfected.

All surfaces should be thoroughly disinfected with the bleach solution for contaminated items. If the caregiver is aware that another adult or child in care has Hepatitis B or HIV/AIDS, then the stronger solution should be used in all cleaning and disinfecting tasks. Table 4.4 lists bloodborne infectious diseases.

TABLE **4.4**

Bloodborne Infectious Diseases

Disease	Signs/Symptoms	Caregiver's Role
Hepatitis B	Fever, loss of appetite, nausea, jaundice, pain in joints, skin rash	All present in care should be immunized. All blood and bodily fluids should be cleaned up immediately and treated as if contaminated. All disposable items with blood should be thrown out in plastic bags, then placed in covered trash cans. Everyone washes hands often. Do not share personal items that could be contaminated. Send home contaminated personal clothing with instruction for parents to wash them with bleach and hot water. Discourage aggressive behaviors. Children infected with Hepatitis A who demonstrate behaviors such as biting, have no control over bodily secretions, and other risky behaviors will need to be supervised closely. Where this is not possible, the child may have to be excluded from child care. Consult with health department and health consultant. If someone is bitten by an infected person, contact doctor.
HIV/AIDS	Failure to grow and develop, enlarged lymph and gland, frequent infections, illness	Follow procedures as in Hepatitis B except for immunization. Protect those with HIV or AIDS from infectious disease outbreaks by exclusion. Allow to return when outbreak is over. Maintain confidentiality of child with HIV or AIDS. Provide staff with information.

Sick children who are isolated from the group need a comfortable place to rest and, if possible, the company and reassurance of a caregiver until the child's parents or emergency contacts arrive.

KEY IDENTIFICATION OF INFECTIOUS DISEASE

CONCEPT

It is an important task of the caregiver to be able to identify infectious diseases. Child caregivers must have a base of knowledge to recognize signs and symptoms of infectious diseases. They must be able to identify symptoms that are serious for the child and that indicate the presence of a contagious disease.

MANAGING INFECTIOUS DISEASES IN CHILD CARE

Caregivers who use universal sanitary practices and can recognize and identify signs and symptoms of illness protect the environment and prevent disease from spreading. An additional way to provide management of infectious diseases is to require that everyone involved in child care be immunized for those infectious diseases that have vaccines and immunization schedules. (Refer to Table 4.5 for the immunization schedule for children.) Children's records should be kept current and checked for compliance on a regular basis. The same process should be performed for staff. No one should be hired or should care for children if they do not comply with all of the required immunizations. (Refer to Tables 4.1 and 4.4 for those diseases that should be complied with for immunizations.)

Certain symptoms in children, such as fever, may not necessarily indicate an illness. A fever may be a result of too much activity, warm weather, teething, or the body overheating due to other circumstances. If the child does not appear to be ill, a fever may not be a problem. The child caregiver needs to learn how to take a temperature, how to read it, and how to evaluate whether or not it is a serious indicator of illness (see Figure 4.3).

The caregiver who recognizes serious symptoms knows when to call a parent and when to exclude the child from care. The ability to identify serious symptoms will help the child caregiver know when to notify parents that children in care have been exposed to an infectious disease. Parents can monitor children for further signs and symptoms. Children who need medical attention should go to the doctor immediately. Certain infectious diseases must be reported to the local public health department. This information is available at the local health department that has jurisdiction over the area in which the child care is performed.

When a child shows some signs of illness, the caregiver should observe the child and write down the symptoms. Do not draw conclusions. Report measurable facts, such as "Joanna has a temperature of 101°F and looks flushed." If the symptoms are mild and do not affect the child's ability to participate, continue observing the child, and go on with regular activities.

Exclusion

If a child shows symptoms that are serious or that might be highly contagious, the child should be isolated from the rest of the children in care. The child caregiver needs to have an area set aside that will allow for isolation.

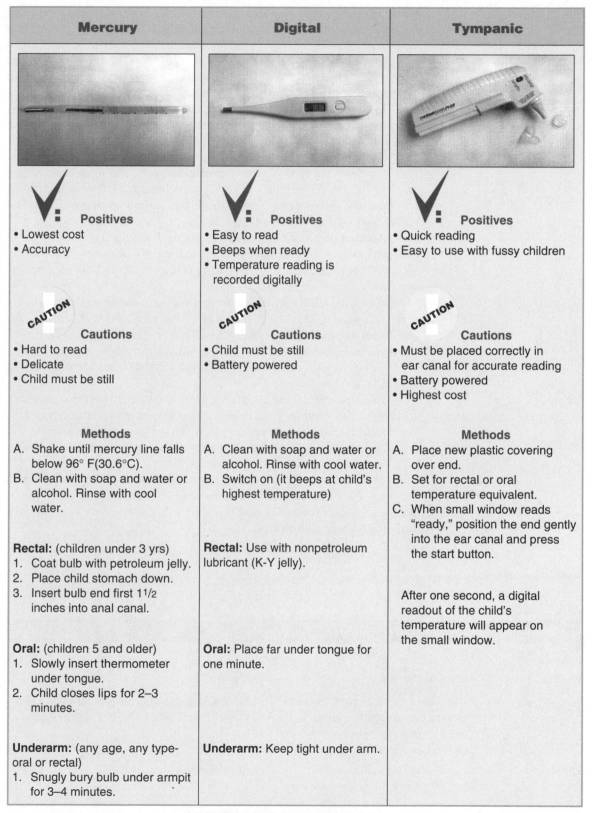

Mercury	Digital	Tympanic
Positives	**Positives**	**Positives**
• Lowest cost • Accuracy	• Easy to read • Beeps when ready • Temperature reading is recorded digitally	• Quick reading • Easy to use with fussy children
CAUTION **Cautions**	**CAUTION** **Cautions**	**CAUTION** **Cautions**
• Hard to read • Delicate • Child must be still	• Child must be still • Battery powered	• Must be placed correctly in ear canal for accurate reading • Battery powered • Highest cost
Methods A. Shake until mercury line falls below 96° F(30.6°C). B. Clean with soap and water or alcohol. Rinse with cool water.	**Methods** A. Clean with soap and water or alcohol. Rinse with cool water. B. Switch on (it beeps at child's highest temperature)	**Methods** A. Place new plastic covering over end. B. Set for rectal or oral temperature equivalent. C. When small window reads "ready," position the end gently into the ear canal and press the start button.
Rectal: (children under 3 yrs) 1. Coat bulb with petroleum jelly. 2. Place child stomach down. 3. Insert bulb end first 1 1/2 inches into anal canal.	**Rectal:** Use with nonpetroleum lubricant (K-Y jelly).	After one second, a digital readout of the child's temperature will appear on the small window.
Oral: (children 5 and older) 1. Slowly insert thermometer under tongue. 2. Child closes lips for 2–3 minutes.	**Oral:** Place far under tongue for one minute.	
Underarm: (any age, any type-oral or rectal) 1. Snugly bury bulb under armpit for 3–4 minutes.	**Underarm:** Keep tight under arm.	

FIGURE **4.3** Guide to Thermometers

Once serious symptoms are recognized, the parents should be notified immediately. If the parents cannot be reached, there should be backup or emergency contacts in the permanent health file for who to call next. The caregiver should ask the parent on a regular basis whether the emergency information is still current. While the child waits for the parent, or other emergency contact person, it is important to reassure the child.

In addition to any serious signs or symptoms of illness, conditions such as uncontrolled diarrhea, a yellowish tint to the skin, and discharge of the eyes also indicate the need to immediately isolate the child and call the parent.

Table 4.5 indicates the guidelines for exclusion of ill or infected children. It relates the type of illness or disease, gives the signs and symptoms, and the conditions for return to child care. These guidelines are a major tool for the child caregiver to help manage the spread of infectious disease in child care and are the basis for the health policy for exclusion.

Another important consideration for exclusion is the adults in the child care environment. If a caregiver has any of the signs or symptoms in Table 4.5, he should also be excluded from participating in care and not return until the conditions for return are met.

When the child is excluded from care, there are several things the caregiver will need to do. The parents should be provided with information on the infectious disease that caused the child to be excluded. This is usually in the form of a letter or handout. The information includes the exclusion policy for that disease, the period of time the disease lasts, and the conditions for return to child care.

Information on how to care for the disease or condition should also be included. For example, if the child has lice, the information given to the parent would include consulting the physician for the type of shampoo to use, how often to use it, and what else needs to be done to rid the child's home of lice so the process does not repeat itself.

The caregiver should discuss the return to care policy for that particular disease or condition at the same time. Parents like to know the time parameters of a child's illness, if possible, so that necessary work or back up care arrangements can be made.

TABLE **4.5**

Guidelines for Exclusion of Ill or Infected Children

Illness or Infection	Sign or Symptom	Return
Temperature	Oral temperature of 101°F; rectal temperature of 102°F; may be accompanied by behavior changes or other symptoms	Until doctor releases child to return to care
Symptoms of severe illness	Unusual lethargy; irritability; uncontrolled coughing; wheezing	Until doctor releases child to return to care

Guidelines for Exclusion of III or Infected Children *continued*

Illness or Infection	Sign or Symptom	Return
Uncontrolled diarrhea	Increase in number of stools, water, and/or decreased form that cannot be contained in a diaper or underwear	Until diarrhea stops
Vomiting illness	Two or more episodes in 24 hours	Until vomiting stops and child is not dehydrated or doctor determines illness not infectious
Mouth sores with drooling		Until condition is determined to be noninfectious
Rash	Rash accompanied by fever or behavior change	Doctor determines it is noninfectious
Conjunctivitis	White or yellow discharge in eye(s) accompanied by eye pain and/or redness around eyes	Until 24 hours after treatment has begun
Head lice, scabies, or other infestations	Infestation present	Until 24 hours after treatment has begun; no remaining lice on hair or scalp
Tuberculosis	Cough; fever; chest pain; coughing up blood	Until doctor or health official allows child to return to care
Impetigo	Rash-blister to honey colored crusts; lesions occur around mouth, nose, and on chin	Until 24 hours after treatment has begun
Strep throat	Fever; sore throat; throat drainage and tender nodes in lymph	After cessation of fever or 24 hours after antibiotic treatment
Chicken pox	Sudden onset of slight fever, fatigue, and loss of appetite followed by skin eruption	Until 6 days after eruption of rash or until blister eruption has dried and crusted over
Whooping cough	Severe, persistent cough	Until 5 days after antibiotic treatment to prevent infection
Mumps	Tender/swollen glands and/or fever	Until 9 days after onset of gland swelling
Hepatitis A virus	Fever, fatigue, loss of appetite, abdominal pain, nausea, vomiting, and/or jaundice	Until 1 week after onset of illness or as directed by local health department; immune serum globulin should be administered to staff and children who have been exposed
Measles	Rash, high fever, runny nose, and red/watery eyes	Until 6 days from onset of rash
Rubella	Mild fever, rash, swollen lymph nodes	Until 6 days after onset of rash
Unspecified respiratory illness	Severe illness with cold, croup, bronchitis, otitis media, pneumonia	Until child feels well enough to participate
Shingles	Lesions	Until doctor allows child to return to care or if child can wear clothing that covers lesions
Herpes simplex (1)	Clear, painful blisters	Until lesions, involving face and lips, that ooze have no secretions

Notification of Public Health

A number of infectious diseases should be reported to the local health department so that they may track the disease for patterns of outbreak. This helps to prevent the spread of infectious illnesses in the community. The types of disease typically requiring reporting are those that can spread rapidly and may cause serious illness. Table 4.6 gives a list of infectious diseases that most health departments want reported. It is also a good idea to notify the health department if a large number of cases of infectious diseases not requiring reporting should occur at the child care site.

TABLE **4.6**

Checklist of Commonly Reported Childhood Infectious Diseases

Check for:

- ☐ AIDS
- ☐ E. Coli
- ☐ Giardia
- ☐ Hepatitis
- ☐ Hib (haemophilus influenza type B)
- ☐ Measles (rubeola)
- ☐ Meningitis
- ☐ Mumps
- ☐ Polio
- ☐ Rubella (German measles)
- ☐ Salmonella
- ☐ Shigella
- ☐ Tuberculosis
- ☐ Whooping Cough (pertussis)

The child caregiver should be familiar with the reporting procedures of the local public health department. The health advocate caregiver at the child care site should be the person to contact the health department.

Notification of Parents

It is important to notify all families in care of infectious disease occurrences that will cause exclusion or will need a follow-up by the parents. This notification provides them with information such as signs, symptoms, and incubation period (Figure 4.4).

If the infectious disease is serious and is one that has preventive measures such as Hepatitis A, the caregiver should notify the parents. This will allow the parents to take the child in care to the family physician, who may administer a course of treatment. It is critically important for the parent of a child exposed to a serious infectious disease to understand the need for taking the child to a physician. The caregiver needs to make sure that parents understand the role they play in the prevention of disease and preserving the child's health.

FIGURE **4.4** Sample Notice to Parents

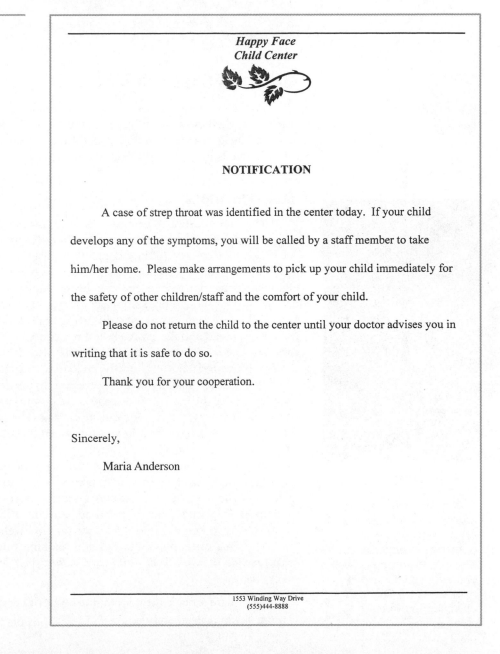

Happy Face Child Center

NOTIFICATION

A case of strep throat was identified in the center today. If your child develops any of the symptoms, you will be called by a staff member to take him/her home. Please make arrangements to pick up your child immediately for the safety of other children/staff and the comfort of your child.

Please do not return the child to the center until your doctor advises you in writing that it is safe to do so.

Thank you for your cooperation.

Sincerely,

Maria Anderson

1553 Winding Way Drive
(555)444-8888

KEY MANAGEMENT OF INFECTIOUS DISEASES

The role that the caregiver plays in managing the infectious diseases must be clearly perceived. The first line of defense is the use of sanitary procedures for hand washing and the use of gloves. The next step is to make sure immunizations are current for everyone in the child care environment. The child caregiver must understand the procedures and policies for exclusion from and return to child care. The caregiver must recognize when to notify the public health department and when to notify the parents of children in child care.

MANAGING CARE FOR MILDLY ILL CHILDREN

The child caregiver has a number of tools that will help make the decision as to whether or not to care for mildly ill children. The most effective tool for managing care for mildly ill children is a series of three questions that the caregiver should ask (see Figure 4.5).

Three Questions

The first question a caregiver should ask is: *"Is the child's infectious disease highly communicable or communicable at this time?"*

There are certain childhood infectious diseases that do not pose a health threat. Some of these infectious diseases may be viruses that are no longer contagious once the symptoms appear or the infectious disease might be one that is not highly contagious. For example, colds are very common in young children. Most children average six to ten colds in the period of a year. Ear infections are not easily spread and therefore should not cause a child to be excluded from care. The child caregiver needs to be familiar with those diseases that are not at risk for spread and that will allow the child to participate in care.

The decision-making process proceeds to the next step once it has been established that the infectious disease is not highly communicable or does not pose risk to others in care. The question *"Does the child feel well enough to participate in child care?"* addresses the issue of whether or not the child feels well enough to be in care.

Families are busy and parents may have deadlines or have difficulty missing work. It may be tempting to take a child who is ill but not contagious to school. The daily quick health check is an effective tool for the caregiver to help prevent this from happening. Parents need to understand their responsibility to keep a child who does not feel well at home.

The final question in the decision making process is *"Can the child care provide the mildly ill child adequate care?"* This question addresses several issues:

- Is there a place for the child to rest or play quietly?
- Is there a caregiver who can be responsible for caring for the mildly ill child?

FIGURE **4.5**
The three questions a caregiver should ask are: (1) Is it a highly infectious or communicable disease? (2) Does the child feel well enough to participate in child care? (3) Can the child care provide the mildly ill child adequate child care?

■ If not, are the parents willing to pay extra for care so the caregiver can hire a helper?

There may be a number of additional tasks that have to be performed and the child caregiver should only agree to provide care for the mildly ill child if the quality of care is consistent with regular child care.

If the answers to any of the three questions indicate that the caregiver would have difficulty caring for the child, the parent must take responsibility for caring for the ill child. There may be an alternative care site that specializes in caring for mildly ill children. Contact the local resource and referral agencies for information.

Special Considerations for Care of Mildly Ill Children

If the decision to care for the mildly ill child is made, the child caregiver should be prepared to provide the degree of care needed. Table 4.7 provides a checklist of strategies that will help the caregiver meet the needs of the mildly ill child.

TABLE **4.7**
Care Checklist for the Mildly Ill Child
Check for:
☐ Observe the child for signs and symptoms of the illness. Share this information with the parents at a midday phone call and when the child is picked up.
☐ Record the signs and symptoms.
☐ Frequently check with the child to provide the extra attention and care she may need while ill.
☐ Provide quiet activities that will hold the interest of the child, such as tapes, videos, books, stories, and artwork.
☐ Set aside a quiet corner or separate space for the child to be quiet, rest, or nap.
☐ Administer prescribed medication as directed, if allowed.
☐ Supply foods and beverages that provide good nutrition and follow guidelines as indicated by illness or recommended by a physician.

If the illness requires the administration of medications, there are special procedures that should be followed. In some states administering medication is prohibited. Caregivers should check with the local licensing agency. The procedures are found in Table 4.8.

TABLE **4.8**

Procedures for Administering Medication in Child Care

■ No medication will be administered without the written order of a doctor, which would be on a prescription bottle, but over-the-counter medications should have a doctor's note attached. The child's name should appear on the original container. Over-the-counter medications should have the manufacturer's label and contain clear instructions for use.

■ Parents must provide written permission authorizing the administration of medication. This should include the frequency, dose, and method of administering the medication. The note should be dated and should be done each time a child is ill, unless it is for a chronic condition such as allergies or asthma (see Sample Medication Policy in Appendix A). Monitor those medications that are kept in case of emergency and should not be used beyond the expiration date. If a child has had over-the-counter medicine prescribed, it should be administered according to the directions on the bottle.

■ Always wash hands before and after administering medication.

■ Administer medication according to method, dose, time, and frequency prescribed. Explain to the child what you are giving and why. Never refer to medicine as candy (see Figure 4.6). Always give medication away from diapering, toileting, or food handling areas.

■ Maintain a medication log. Record the administration of the medication in the log, the instructions for giving medication, and attach parents' consent form. This log will be kept in the child's permanent health history.

■ Have a list of possible side effects of medication to watch for.

■ Keep medications at proper temperature as directed. Some liquid antibiotics need to be refrigerated.

■ Store all medications out of the reach of children, preferably in a locked cabinet, on a high shelf, or in the back of the top shelf of a refrigerator.

REALITY CHECK

Special Care for Mildly Ill Children

Many companies experience high absenteeism rates from their employees because their children are ill. A child's illness causes missed deadlines, parents who feel guilty, and coworkers who must do extra work because of the absent worker (Child Care Action Campaign, 1993). This situation can cause many problems for the parents and discomfort for the child. Children are most comfortable in a familiar setting with familiar people when they are ill. This familiarity offers emotional support for the ill child. It is not always possible to provide this familiar comfort so parents may have to settle for physical care alone.

Care for mildly ill children may take place in several ways.

- Care in the child's own center, family child care, or in-home care
- Family child care homes or centers that specialize in caring for mildly ill children
- Corporate on-site care for ill children of employees
- In the child's home by specialized caregivers

Many centers and family child care homes are providing this care within their regular programs. Most states permit child care centers to offer get-well care for mildly ill children. Some centers provide a designated caregiver for these mildly ill children. Some caregivers specialize in the care of mildly ill children.

To address this situation, many corporations are cooperating by providing care for mildly ill children. New York City Emergency Child Care Services and Tucson Association for Child Care Inc. are two examples of in-home care services that have contracted with companies to provide mildly ill care (Cassidy, 1991). Johnson and Johnson provides on-site care for mildly ill children at their headquarters in New Brunswick, New Jersey. This is offered at their child care center in an infirmary.

There are centers specifically designed for the care of mildly ill children. These centers must meet licensing standards that are more stringent than the regular standards. They must also be very careful of preventing the spread of infectious diseases. The AAHP and APA suggest that these special centers have the following for each child:

- Information concerning the diagnosis and the attending physician's name
- Prognosis for illness, including activity level, diet, and so forth
- Health care plan
- Open communication line with parents

Mildly ill children can still be relatively active. Mildly ill child care should include provision of toys, games, and other activities that provide children stimulation as needed.

The licensing regulations should be determined for the local area and state where the care will take place, if the caregiver intends to provide this type of care for mildly ill children.

KEY SPECIAL CONSIDERATIONS FOR CARE OF MILDLY ILL CHILDREN

CONCEPT

Taking care of mildly ill children is not something all caregivers or child care situations are prepared to do. Determining the ability to handle this type of care will be based on three questions:

1. Is the infectious disease contagious or will it put others at risk?
2. Is the child able to participate in care?
3. Can the caregiver accommodate the needs of the mildly ill child?

When the determination is made, the caregiver will need to understand the issues of the special care he will be providing for the child. One of the special considerations is the administration of medication. The caregiver should follow exact procedure for this.

FIGURE **4.6**
Children can very easily mistake medication for candy. Medications should be stored in a locked cabinet at all times. *(Courtesy of Payless Drug Stores)*

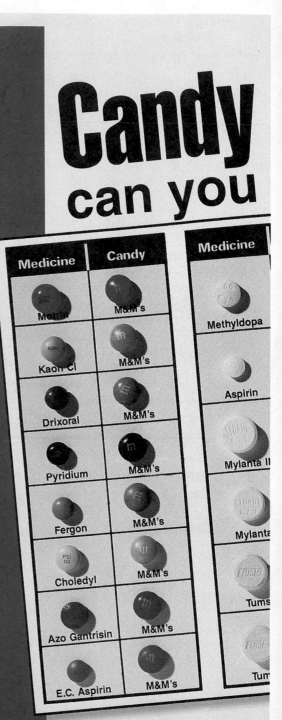

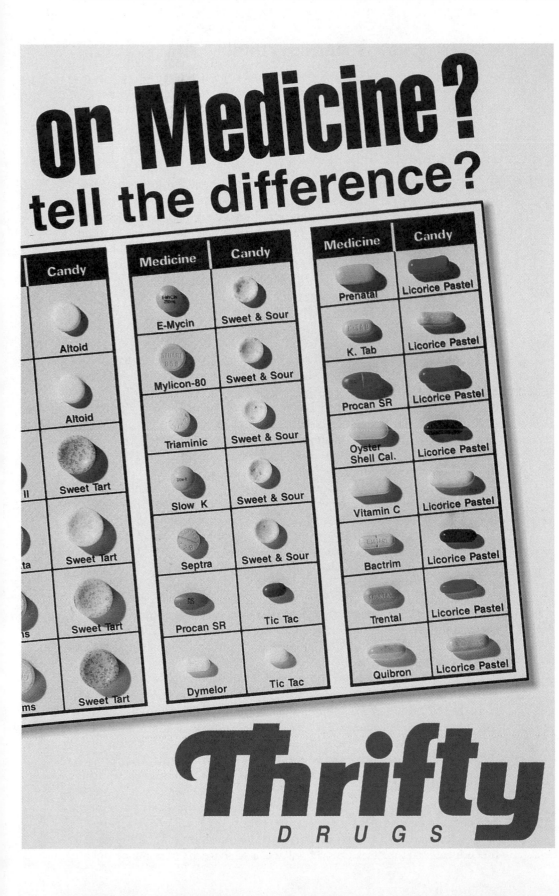

IMPLICATIONS FOR **CAREGIVERS**

Caregivers need the tools of observation and supervision in order to provide and maintain a healthy environment. Education and cultural sensitivity also help them to manage the spread of disease as well as to manage mildly ill child care.

Observation

Observation provides the caregiver the ability to recognize any symptoms of infectious disease early. The daily quick health check allows the child caregiver to monitor the health of a child on a regular basis. Recording any signs, symptoms, or irregular behaviors can give the caregivers indicators of illness. When a child is observed, the question, "Is the child able to participate?", can be answered more readily. A caregiver who knows a child well will recognize whether or not the child is acting in a normal enough manner to be in the child care setting.

Supervision

Supervision is a powerful tool that helps the caregiver to manage health care in child care. Supervising the setting for proper immunizations and sanitary hand washing and cleaning procedures can reduce the amount of infectious diseases seen in child care. Supervising for exclusion and return policies help keep contagious diseases from child care.

Notifying the public health department allows the caregiver to help manage the spread of infectious diseases both in and out of child care. When the health department tracks infectious diseases, another child care setting may benefit from the notification. This may prevent further outbreaks.

Caregivers need to notify all parents when a child in care has an infectious disease that is highly contagious and/or can cause serious diseases. The parents can observe for the signs and symptoms and can prepare for follow-up care after exposure to the infectious disease.

Education

Education provides a wonderful tool for the promotion of healthy habits and the prevention of disease. All participants in the child care environment should be educated to avoid exposure to and reduce the spread of infectious diseases.

Education offers caregivers the base of knowledge and training needed to carry out their daily task of creating a healthy environment. Caregivers who have the ability to identify the signs and symptoms of infectious diseases protect the environment against any further spread of the infectious disease.

Education helps parents work with the caregiver as a team. It also allows the family to offer a more protective environment in the home. Teaching parents about hand washing and the importance of immunizations will help them understand their own responsibility to protect their children and to prevent disease. Parents who understand proper procedures for the care of a child with an infectious disease may be able to reduce the seriousness of the disease.

Education for children in child care incorporates several things. The first educational tool the caregiver will use is to share the importance of hand

Parents may not have children immunized because of fears, cultural beliefs, or lack of understanding of the importance of immunizations. Although caregivers need to respect the beliefs of different cultures, the "no immunization, no care" rule must be enforced to protect all children in care.

washing along with the "how-tos and when to." Teaching children to recognize when they feel ill may help the caregiver identify an infectious disease before outward symptoms appear. This may provide another level of protection for all of the children in care. Teaching children at their own level about an infectious disease that is present in child care may reinforce the information sent home concerning that disease.

Cultural Sensitivity

The caregiver needs to understand that early access to health care for ill children is perhaps the major issue for cultural sensitivity. This may be especially true of recent immigrants. Certain cultures may have had little access to health care. Parents of these children may not understand the importance of early health care for children. For example, there appears to be a pattern of delayed care for Latin-American children (Zambrana, Ell, Dorrington, Wachsmur, & Hodge, 1994). Emergency medical services appear to be the primary care for many of these children.

When a child becomes ill, the caregiver may have to help the parent access health care. Many cultures use the emergency room as their first contact of care. This is dangerous for the child and it is not protective for the child care environment. It may take extra effort on the part of the child caregiver to help parents from other cultures provide the health care needed for these children.

Immunization may be another culturally sensitive issue. Many families do not understand the need for immunization. If the child is from a country where immunizations are not readily available, the thought of having a child stuck with needles may be fearful (Gonzalez-Mena, 1997). The need for immunization should be dealt with when the child enters care. The rule, "No immunization, no care," must be understood by both the caregiver and the parents. No exceptions should be made. The caregiver may need to educate potential child care parents of the need to adhere to the immunization schedule. When a child is in care, it is up to the caregiver to follow up and make sure that immunizations occur.

The child caregiver should understand the sanitary habits of the different cultures that are represented in care. The caregiver may have to provide extra education or acquire interpreters to inform parents of their responsibility in keeping their children well.

C 4.5

CONCEPT

KEY IMPLICATIONS FOR CAREGIVERS

The implications for the child caregiver are the tools of observation, supervision, education, and cultural sensitivity that help the caregiver create the holistic approach needed to deal with the many issues raised. Observation can identify infectious diseases early and thus provide some protection for others in care. Supervision will give the caregiver the tools needed for exclusion and notification. The caregiver must be educated, and must educate parents and children in methods that will forestall the spread of infectious diseases. Cultural sensitivity should be practiced to help the caregiver include all children and parents in providing the best preventive environment possible.

CHAPTER **SUMMARY**

Caregivers need to prevent disease spread and to care for mildly ill children. They need to form exclusion policies and understand reporting procedures. Caregivers need to determine if they have the ability to care for children who become ill and are not contagious. Observation and supervision will help the caregiver identify and manage infectious diseases. Education will help the caregiver teach healthy habits to children and their parents.

TO GO **BEYOND**

Questions for Review

1. Discuss the identification and management of infectious diseases. How does this compare to what has been observed in child care situations?
2. Describe the skills needed to manage infectious diseases. How do they compare to those skills that you presently possess?

AS AN **INDIVIDUAL**

1. Call the local licensing agency and obtain the guidelines for exclusion. How do they compare to those in this text?
2. Describe the type of care you intend to participate in, then ask the three questions about caring for ill children. How do they relate?

AS A **GROUP**

1. Watch *When Children are Ill,* an AAP film. How does it deal with planning for the care of an ill child? How does it handle exclusion? What other procedures does it cover? Compare these to what you have learned in this section of the text.
2. Discuss the availability of mildly ill child care in your area. Are there any special centers for this type of child care? If not, why do you think there are none? If so, describe these centers.

CHAPTER **REFERENCES**

Cassidy, A. (1991, January). When your child is ill. *Working Mother,* 74–76.

Child Care Action Campaign (1993). *Temporary care for the mildly sick child.* [CCAC Information Guide 21]. New York: Author.

County of San Diego Department of Health Services. (1993). *Head lice.* [Brochure]. San Diego, CA: Author.

Droom, J., & Culpepper, L. (1991). Otitis media in day-care children. A report from the International Primary Care Network. *Journal of Family Practice, 32*(3), 289–294.

Feagans, L., Kipp, E., & Blood, I. (1994). The effects of otitis media on the attention skills of day-care-attending toddlers. *Developmental Psychology, 30*(5), 701–708.

Gonzalez-Mena, J. (1997). *Multicultural issues in child care.* Menlo Park, CA: Mayfield.

Hewison, J., & Dowswell, T. (1993). *Child health care and the working mother: The juggling act.* London: Chapman Hall.

Kendall, E., & Moukadden, V. (1992). Who's vulnerable in infant child care centers? *Young Children, 47*(7), 72–78.

Kendrick, A., Kaufmann, R., & Messenger, K. (1995). *Healthy young children.* Washington, DC: NAEYC.

Teele, D., Klein, J., & Rossner, B. (1984). Otitis media with effusion during the first years of life and development of speech and language. *Pediatrics, 74,* 282–287.

Watt, M., Roberts, J., & Zeisel, S. (1993). Ear infections in young children: The role of the early childhood educator. *Young Children, 48*(11), 64–72.

Wessel, J. (1990, September). Not another ear infection. *Working Mother,* 76–78.

Zambrana, R., Ell, K., Dorrington, C., Wachsmur, L., & Hodge, D. (1994). The relationship between psychosocial status of immigrant Latina mothers and use of emergency pediatric services. *Health and Social Work, 19*(2), 98–102.

SUGGESTIONS FOR **READING**

American Academy of Pediatrics. *Health in day care: A manual for health professionals.* Elk Grove, IL: American Academy of Pediatrics.

Aronson, S., Smith, H., & Martin, J. (1993). *Model child care health policies.* Bryn Mawr, PA: Pennsylvania Chapter of the American Academy of Pediatrics.

California Child Health Care Project. (1990). *Control of communicable and infectious diseases: A manual for providers.* San Diego, CA: Author.

Frieman, B., & Settle, J. (1994). What the classroom teacher needs to know about children with chronic medical problems. *Childhood Education, 70*(4), 196–201.

Seattle-King County Department of Public Health. (1991). *Child care health handbook.* Seattle: Washington State Department of Social and Health Services.

2

SAFETY IN CHILD CARE

In this section, we will discuss elements of safety in child care:

5. Setting Up and Managing a Safe Environment

6. Indoor Safety

7. Outdoor Safety

8. Emergency Response Procedures for Child Care

CHAPTER FIVE

SETTING UP AND MANAGING A SAFE ENVIRONMENT

Upon completion of this chapter, including a review of the summary, you should be able to:

SAFETY POLICIES

Define and discuss safety policies and their use as tools for safety, risk prevention, protection, and promotion.

CREATING SAFE ENVIRONMENTS

Discuss the importance of safe environments and describe a safe environment for all types of child care.

INJURY PREVENTION MANAGEMENT

Discuss the factors involved in childhood injury and describe strategies for use in injury prevention.

CONSTRUCTING A SAFETY PLAN FOR CHILD CARE

Explain the development of a safety plan for a child care setting.

IMPLICATIONS FOR CAREGIVERS

Describe the importance of and strategies for education, supervision, and observation for maintaining a safe environment.

Because children may lack the capacity to judge whether or not an activity is safe, they must be provided with a secure, safe environment to ensure their well-being and protection.

SAFETY POLICIES

Developing safety policies for the caregiver to manage risk, provide protection, and promote safety in child care is important. Some factors that indicate the need for these safety policies are:

- Unintentional injury is now the leading cause of death in childhood (Mickalaide, 1994 and U.S. Department of Health and Human Services, 1990).

- Every year 7,250 children die and another 50,000 are permanently disabled from preventable injuries (National Center for Health Statistics [NCHS], 1991).

- Forty percent of parents believe that children's serious injuries are "random acts of fate or accidents" and therefore they do not think in terms of prevention (NCHS, 1991).

- We can no longer assume that children are safe in their own environments of home and school (Hatted, 1994).

- Inattention to playground design, firearms, and choking hazards were found to be the major gaps in safety regulations and standards in child care (Runyan, Gray, Kotch, & Kreuter, 1991).

- Children's sense of safety may be at risk as a result of what they observe in their world (Levin, 1994).

Caregivers should realize that most injuries to children are preventable. An accident infers a chance occurrence that is accompanied by no control or responsibility. Many injuries that children suffer can be prevented and do carry with them a degree of control for prevention and responsibility for protection. Because of developmental factors that limit children's physical, cognitive and emotional abilities, they are more vulnerable to injury. Children are natural risk takers who attempt actions for which they may lack skills. Children want to test and master their environments. Children need a sense of trust and security that their environment is friendly and safe. Depending on their developmental level, children may lack the capacity to judge the safety of their environment. See Table 5.2, page 158, for a discussion on developmental levels.

Designing a Safety Policy

Caregivers need to take responsibility for providing the safest environment possible in the child care setting. Caregivers also need to provide examples of safe practices and accident prevention strategies and model them for children and their families.

The first part of the process for designing a safety policy is to understand what safety hazards are in the child care environment. The caregiver needs to know what hazards are addressed by the local licensing regulations and fire boards. This is a good beginning point for putting together safety policies. The local licensing regulations can provide this information. These regulations should be checked carefully to make sure the child care environment is in compliance. Measures that keep the child care environment in compliance would be included in one or more safety policies. Some local areas have county or city fire regulations and zoning codes that may affect the design of safety policies. The caregiver should check with the local agencies responsible to obtain this information. In addition, caregivers receiving federal monies have to comply with federal regulations.

The NAEYC and the National Family Child Care Association have an accreditation process that supports higher than minimum standards for all areas of child care, including safety. Applying for and receiving accreditation can help the caregiver provide higher quality care standards.

Next, the caregiver should be aware of what safety hazards exist in the environment. The caregiver needs to check both the inside and outside environments for hazards while applying special safety considerations concerning small children. Viewing the environment through the eyes of a child will help the caregiver find safety hazards and create safety checklists that offer maximum protection. It is essential that the caregiver have knowledge of the developmental abilities of the children in care. These developmental level safety checklists are used to manage the environment for risk.

Knowledge of environmental hazards will help the caregiver create specific policies for the child care environment. Each type of safety hazard should have a process of actions to be followed to avoid risk. For example, if field trips will be taken, there should be a definite policy for travel with children. This would include actions to prepare for the trip as well as actions needed during the trip. A safety policy should be clearly written and should be specific to the hazard or group of hazards involved. Safety policies include guidelines, checklists, and charts that help to protect the environment from hazards.

Safety policies should name the caregiver who is responsible for carrying out the safety process that is developed. All staff should be encouraged to understand all of the safety precautions needed for the child care environment. Every caregiver should be encouraged to carry out actions that provide for the greatest degree of safety.

A responsible caregiver would help to encourage safety and safe behaviors. Educating the children and their families so that they also know how to recognize dangers in any setting will ensure further protection. There should be several policies addressing the educational aspects for safety.

General child care safety policies should cover:

- *Creating Safe Environments:* practices for creating and managing safe facility specific environments.

- *Injury Prevention Management:* understanding of injury and practices for preventing injury and protecting children.

- *Developing a Safety Plan:* strategies for developing guidelines for prevention and protection in child care.

- *Implications for Caregivers:* methods and practices for conducting education, observation, and supervision that provide maximum safety and minimum risk.

Injury prevention
forestalling or anticipating injury risk

Something as simple as making sure all footwear is properly worn and tied may prevent an accident from occurring. What are other preventive measures to avoid accidents?

CREATING SAFE ENVIRONMENTS

The caregiver will need to use all the risk management and **injury prevention** tools available in order to create the safe environment children need to grow to their greatest potential. Knowledge of the ABCs of potential for injury will help the caregiver be aware of what is needed to create the protective and secure environment (Table 5.5). Safety policies for modifying the environment, modifying behavior, monitoring children, and teaching

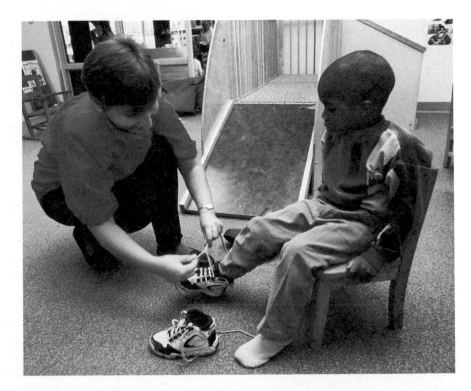

injury preventive behaviors to children will help the caregiver to provide more safety, protection, and prevention in every child care situation. Most of the practices and behaviors that create a safe environment can be applied to all child care environments. See Table 5.1 for a guide to safe practices and injury prevention. Safety policies can be created from the list.

TABLE **5.1**

A Caregiver's Guide to Safe Practices and Injury Prevention for a Safe Environment

■ Know all applicable safety practices for the child care environment.

■ Screen environment for hazards and remove, where possible.

■ Use safety devices, where applicable.

■ Monitor environment for hazards that are part of the environment.

■ Know developmental levels of children including capabilities and limitations.

■ Promote safety through action, word, and deed.

■ Role model safety practices to children and parents.

■ Be aware of conditions that contribute to injury.

■ Closely observe children, giving special consideration during at-risk conditions.

There may be some differences in child care safety policies that are dependent upon several considerations. How these policies apply to specific safety protection, prevention, and promotion practices may relate to:

■ What type of environment are you applying these safety practices?

■ What is the age of children in care?

■ What is the greater community surrounding the environment like?

■ What is the child's family environment?

The Type of Environment

The type of child care environment has a definite impact on the degree of safety the caregiver is able to provide. Protective and preventive measures may differ depending upon the type of environment. Child care centers may be able to control for safety more than a family child care home. The level of safety in an in-home care situation may vary widely.

Child Care Centers.   Child care centers are different from homes. In most states, child care centers must follow certain licensing safety codes and practices (APHA and AAP). These basic codes and practices help the caregiver lay the foundation for normal safety practices for that environment. Child care centers generally are not **multi-use facilities.** The sole purpose of the

Multi-use facilities
child care sites that are
used for other functions

Depending on the environment, different degrees of protective and preventive measures must exist.

child care center is to perform care and to provide a safe environment for the children in care.

Some child care centers are very different from single-purpose child care centers. A child care center in a church-related environment may not be subject to the same safety rules and regulations as those in the public sector. In addition, the church facility may be used by a number of different groups for a number of different activities, thus introducing a greater degree of safety risk factors.

The same hazardous situation may be true for child care center environments that are located in some public facilities. Ski resorts, fitness centers, and elementary schools may have child care centers on site. These sites may not be subject to the same licensing safety codes or regulations and may be used for other purposes at other times. Modifying the environment in these unregulated, multi-use facilities may be a challenge to the caregiver. Modification would be a constant, ongoing process. These unregulated environments may make it more imperative that the caregiver know safety practices, be a role model, and promote safety through actions, words, and deeds. Teaching the children about these safety risk factors may help the caregiver have an added level of monitoring for these environments. The responsibility for maintaining a safe environment rests with the caregivers. Some examples of shared space are:

■ A college or university preschool used in the evenings for classroom space

■ A ski lodge that uses a corner of its lounge for child care while parents ski

■ A church preschool room, used as a Sunday school and meeting room

■ A corporate child care center that is used for meetings and training classes on weekends

■ A community recreation center that has child care while parents attend classes

Family Child Care Homes.   Family child care homes are multi-purpose by definition. If the state or local area requires licensing, the home must pass certain safety requirements, such as a fire code. Some states or local jurisdictions do not require licensing for family child care homes. Other states may only license larger family child care homes with twelve or more children. This puts the responsibility of providing safety and protection directly on the caregiver in whose home the child care takes place. Self-regulation and monitoring the environment are vital for the prevention of injuries and protection of the children.

There may be local programs through the resource and referral services that help to support the family child caregiver. This support can help the family child caregiver create a safe environment using specific safety policies that are similar to licensing regulations in other areas. Another source of help for the caregiver is the National Family Child Care Association. This organization offers a program for accreditation that includes safety standards, policies, and practices.

In-Home Child Care.   An in-home situation where the caregiver comes to the child's home presents different challenges. Both the family child care home and child care center have the caregiver as the person responsible for creating and monitoring the environment for safety. An in-home child caregiver shares this responsibility with the parents. It would be easy to assume that this is a fairly straightforward task. Unfortunately, this is not always the

The caregiver at a home care center with a pool should take all appropriate safety steps to avoid the possible "accident waiting to happen."

case. Some parents do not understand the need for making the environment as safe as possible. The environment is the home they have carefully selected and decorated for comfort and style and it meets their needs.

When an infant arrives in the home, that child makes no demands on the home environment other than a place to sleep. As the child grows older and goes through the developmental stages, the need for modifying the home environment becomes important. Some parents are intent on making these modifications, while others do not see the need because "Joey is just going through a phase." It is on the shoulders of the nanny or in-home caregiver to make sure the parents participate in modifying and monitoring the home environment for safety. If the parents choose not to childproof the home environment, it is recommended that the caregiver not stay in this situation.

Damon was a quiet, curious toddler. Mary Ann, his nanny, was concerned that as he was becoming more mobile, Damon would get into unsafe situations. Mary Ann asked Damon's parents to remove the cleaning chemicals from under the sinks in the kitchen and bathroom. She asked that they install a safety gate at the stairs. Mary Ann also requested that they remove small decorative objects from his reach. Some of these objects had sharp edges; while others were small enough for him to choke on if he put them in his mouth. The parents did not see the need. They felt that Mary Ann should rely solely on monitoring the child, and not worry about the environmental hazards.

Mary Ann served her two-week notice when they refused to cooperate. The following weekend, while in the care of his aunt, Damon got under the sink and drank some cleaning solution. He was rushed to the hospital and had his stomach pumped. He was very lucky that the cleaning product he swallowed did not do permanent damage. The aunt felt terrible, the parents realized their mistake, and Damon had to go through a very scary situation. The family begged Mary Ann to stay and offered their full cooperation for childproofing their home.

Not all situations like this one turn out so well. A home environment needs to be just as safe as any child care environment.

The Age of Children in Care

Because of the developmental stages children go through (see Table 5.2, page 158), the age of children in care will affect the type of safety policies that the caregiver will need. If the environment is for a particular age group where children are all at about the same developmental level, as is true in most large child care centers, the safety modifications that the caregiver makes to the child care environment will be standardized to fit that age range.

Children who are at the same developmental level in a child care setting should be provided with a safe environment that accommodates their developmental stage.

Cephalocaudal
development from the top to the bottom of the body or from the head down toward the toes

Proximodistal
development of the body from the inside toward the outside or the torso through the arms and out to the fingers

Gross motor skills
physical skills using large body movements such as running, jumping, and climbing

Fine motor skills
physical skills using small body movements particularly of the hand and fingers

Infants.   Some child care may involve caring for infants. This may be a center where infant care is available, a family child care that specilizes in infants, or it may be a nanny caring for one or two infants. Infants are totally dependent and thus very vulnerable to injury if not carefully monitored. Infants develop their motor abilities in the **cephalocaudal** and **proximodistal** direction. Development in the cephalocaudal direction moves from the head to toe. As a child grows, development progresses down the body. For example, one of the first milestones for an infant is the ability to lift his head. One of the last infant milestones is the ability to walk. These **gross motor skills** develop earlier than **fine motor skills.** Proximodistal direction motor development works from the center of the body to the outside. An infant can roll over and use the arms long before he can reach and grasp (see Figure 5.1, page 158).

During the first few months of life infants are not mobile and do not encounter many risks. The major risk that infants of all ages encounter is Sudden Infant Death Syndrome (SIDS). The caregiver should use protective and preventive measures to reduce the possibility of a child being at risk for SIDS.

Once an infant rolls over, mobility, thus risk, increases. A child could turn over and fall from a changing table or infant seat set on a counter. As the cephalocaudal motor direction develops, skills, thus mobility, increase. Children who creep, then crawl are apt to get into more and more territory that may pose risk to them. The need for safety devices increases at this stage. This is the time for safety gates on stairs, closed doors to bathrooms, and so forth.

REALITY CHECK

Sudden Infant Death Syndrome

Sudden Infant Death Syndrome (SID) claims more lives of children per year between the ages of one month and one year than childhood deaths from cancer, child abuse, AIDS, cystic fibrosis, muscular dystrophy, pneumonia, and heart disease combined (SIDS Network, 1996a). It is estimated that as many as 7,000 babies die every year from SIDS (Gorman, 1993). SIDS strikes without warning to children of all racial, ethnic, and economic levels.

The medical community still cannot explain what causes SIDS. Speculation includes a vulnerability period, a birth defect, stress caused by infection, and/or failure to develop (SIDS Network, 1996b). Recently, they have found several risk factors that contribute to SIDS deaths. Although these risk factors are not the cause of SIDS, they can have a negative effect and make children more prone to the cause.

These risk factors include:

■ Sleeping on the stomach in the prone position

■ Pre- and postnatal exposure to cigarette smoke

■ Sleeping on materials that are too soft, such as sheepskins and foam pads

■ Overheating of the baby

A caregiver can help reduce risk by offering protective measures for each of these risks.

A major discovery has revolutionized how parents and caregivers put babies down to sleep. Studies in Europe in the late 1980s found that when babies were put to sleep on their stomachs in the prone position they were twice as likely to die from SIDS as children placed on their sides or back. In the early 1990s the American Academy of Pediatrics recommended that all babies be put down to sleep on their backs or sides and not on their stomachs, which had long been the preferable sleeping position for babies (Gorman, 1993). SIDS deaths have decreased by approximately fifty percent through risk reduction (Carroll, 1996). Sixty-five to 70 percent of this reduction has been attributed to putting children to sleep on their backs or sides. There is speculation that this factor alone could reduce SIDS deaths by 50 percent (Willinger, 1995).

Cigarette smoke is considered the second greatest risk factor for SIDS. It is believed that this risk factor may account for 20 to 40 percent of SIDS cases (DiFranza and Lew, 1995). Exposure to cigarette smoke as an infant may put babies at twice the risk for SIDS. If babies are also exposed *in utero,* they are three times more likely to be at risk for SIDS (SIDS Network, 1996b). Caregivers can provide a smoke-free environment for children in their care. They can also provide information about this risk to pregnant mothers of children in their care.

Babies should sleep on firm, flat mattresses. Parents and caregivers should avoid placing them on beanbags, sheepskins, foam sofa cushions, synthetic pillows, and foam pads, either alone or covered with a comforter (SIDS Network, 1996b).

The final contributing risk factor is overheating of a baby. Too much bedding, clothing that is too heavy, and an environment that is too warm can contribute to SIDS. Overheating may occur when babies have a cold and efforts are made to keep the child warm. Unfortunately, babies may be kept too warm. Babies who are overheated may exhibit sweating, damp hair, heat rash, rapid breathing, and fever. It is recommended that the indoor temperature be kept at 70°F or less (SIDS Network, 1996b).

The American Academy of Pediatrics recommends one further protective measure. When placing a child to sleep, using clean hands, check the mouth for food or foreign objects that the baby may have been keeping in his mouth (AAP & APHA, 1992).

These preventive measures can greatly reduce risk, but they cannot guarantee that SIDS will not strike. Realizing this will help parents and caregivers to withhold blame if SIDS were to happen to a baby in their lives.

FIGURE **5.1**
An Infant Showing
Proximodistal and
Cephalocaudal
Development

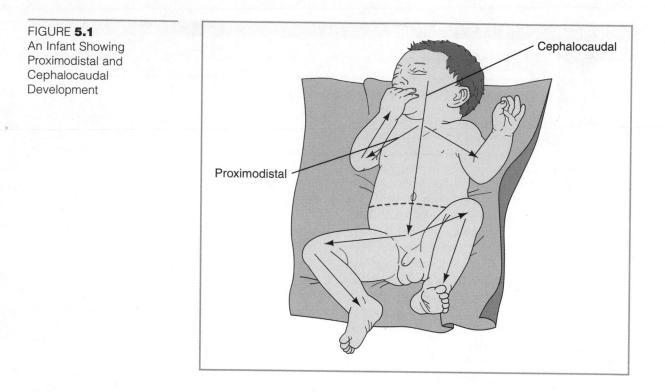

Sensorimotor cognitive development
first stage of cognitive development that utilizes motor abilities and senses

Proximodistal motor development allows children to become more agile when using their hands and arms to reach for things and pick up things. Combined with **sensorimotor cognitive development** (see Table 5.4, page 164), this can lead to danger. Children who are able to pick up objects

	TABLE **5.2**	
Piaget's Sensorimotor Developmental Stages		
Stage	**Age**	**Actions**
1	0–1 month	Mostly sucking and looking.
2	1–4 months	Make interesting things happen repeatedly with the body, like kicking legs or sucking a finger. Pleasure from repetition.
3	4–8 months	Repeated actions focusing on objects and events. Picking up rattle and shaking over and over. Pleasure from repetition.
4	8–12 months	Combine actions to reach a goal.
5	12–18 months	Experiments to find new and different ways to solve problems or reach goal. This stage often referred to as "little scientist."
6	18–24 months	Beginning of thought using symbols or language to solve problems mentally.

usually explore those objects by placing them in their mouths. The agile infant can get into practically any cabinet and may also be able to open containers in those cabinets. Safety latches should be used for cabinets, doors, and so forth. Any cleaning solutions or other chemical hazards should be removed to a high, locked cabinet. All electrical sockets should have safety plugs blocking inspection by curious infants.

Toddlers.　Once a child has begun walking, his skills as well as his abilities to access dangerous situations increase. Cephalocaudal development will progress to abilities that include running and climbing. At the beginning of this stage the balance of the toddler is somewhat unsteady. Being mobile allows the toddler different ways to look at the environment. It can also give the toddler the ability to overcome obstacles that may have previously prevented action.

Proximodistal development leads to greater manipulative abilities. Sensorimotor development presents cognitive abilities in children that will challenge any caregiver to keep one step ahead. Children at this stage are perhaps most at risk for dangerous situations. They are exploring and trying to master their environments, but they do not have the cognitive abilities to understand cause and effect. This can be a deadly combination.

Children in the toddler stage need to be supervised very closely. Their physical abilities and cognitive limitations will have them performing dangerous acts, so they must be carefully watched. All physical and environmental hazards need to be examined. Safety devices should be in place and all hazards that can be, should be removed.

Preoperational stage
second stage of cognitive development in which logic is limited

Preschoolers.　Preschool children have mastered most of their gross and fine motor skills. They are capable of most physical tasks. Cognitive abilities of children this age have also developed and they are in the **preoperational stage** that offers some limitations in their thought processes. These limitations cause preschool children to see the world from their point of view. Children of this age may not perceive risk when it is present. For example, a four year old may be certain that she can climb to the top of playground equipment, jump off it, and land on the ground without getting hurt because she saw her favorite cartoon character do this very thing.

This age group responds well to role modeling and education. Preschool children are less likely to need safety devices such as stair gates and plastic plugs in electrical sockets, because they understand the perceived risk from these items. The preschool child can be trained to understand much risk from their environment. They will need monitoring, but not at the intense level of the older infant and toddler.

Concrete operational stage
third stage of cognitive development in which logical ideas can be applied to concrete or specific situations

School Age.　School-aged children are at far less risk for safety because they have cognitive abilities that can help keep them out of danger. Children of this age are at the **concrete operational stage** of cognitive development and have the ability to understand most situations that involve safety risk or hazards. Children of this age like to test their abilities to perform. Accidents and injuries involving this age group are often from sports activities such as bicycling, skating, or organized sports such as soccer and baseball. Another area of concern for this age group is the curiosity about firearms. Guns are

TABLE **5.3**

Limitations of the Preoperational Stage

Limitation	Meaning
Egocentrism	World is centered around "me." Nothing else exists. Sharing is hard. All toys seem to be "mine."
Centration	Child focuses only on one aspect of a situation or object. Child sees a toy, heads for it, regardless of what is in the way.
Fantasy	Children love to make believe and role play.
Irreversibility	Inability to reverse a situation or an action. Difficult for child to retrace steps of thoughts or action.
Animism	Everything is "alive" and all objects are capable of human feelings or actions.
Transductive Reasoning	Child cannot relate general to specific or a part to the whole. They only relate specific to specific. For example, if Sparky, the dog is friendly, any dog that is encountered is friendly.

objects that provide great risk to children of any age, but this age group is more likely to be able to access them.

School-aged children respond well to education and role modeling. The issue of firearms and the risk they pose should be discussed with these children. School-aged children can be excellent examples when they role model safety to other children. Although school-aged children need some monitoring, they can also be their own monitors for safety if they are armed with safety knowledge.

Multi-age Groups. If the children in care are of varying ages and thus developmental levels, the caregiver will need to take a different look when planning for safety in the environment. If the environment needs to be designed for multi-age groups, then it should be modified as closely as possible to fit the youngest child's developmental abilities. This may cause some frustration for older children, but safety issues must come first. Role modeling and talking with the older children about the need for safety can help buffer their frustration and lead to greater understanding. Depending on their ages, older children may even help the caregiver monitor the potential risks in the child care environment and observe unsafe behaviors that younger children may exhibit.

The Community Surrounding Child Care

The safety of the children in care can no longer be taken for granted. It is impossible to consider the environment of child care as only the premises and the surrounding yard or outdoor play area. Child care takes place in the middle of cities, in suburbs, and in rural areas. The holistic approach for child care safety must consider the community area that sur-

In addition to violence and traffic, discarded drug paraphernalia may be a potential hazard and liability for child caregivers using inner city public playgrounds with their children.

Liabilities
safety risks or hazards

Maslow's Hierarchy of Human Needs

Self-Actualization

Self-Esteem

Social

Love, Friendship

Safety and Security

Food, Shelter, Clothing

FIGURE **5.2**
According to Maslow's Hierarchy of Human Needs, a person's needs for such basics as food, shelter, and clothing must be met before higher level needs can be addressed.

rounds the care site. No matter where the child care takes place, there are safety hazards, conditions, and behaviors that may affect the child care situation.

It is the caregiver's responsibility to be aware of the safety aspects or **liabilities** surrounding the child care premises. In some inner city areas violence may be a liability while in other areas, traffic may be the key liability. Rural and suburban areas may be isolated and distance may be a liability in case of an emergency. Rural areas may be more likely to have hazards such as animals in the environment.

It is the caregiver's responsibility to understand the risks and liabilities of the surrounding neighborhood community. The children should be taught safety and prevention strategies that apply to the community surrounding the child care. The promotion of safety should not end at the door of the child care situation.

The Child's Family Environment

A child's family environment may affect the child care environment. If the child's home environment is safe and secure, the child trusts that the caregiver's is also. A child who is free to explore and master a safe environment at home will also explore the child care environment. It is essential that the caregiver teach the child the rules and limitations for the care environment that will help to keep the child safe while in care.

A child who comes from an environment that is less safe and secure will also need consideration. Low income or poverty can affect the home environment. Maslow explained that the most important basic needs of humans are shelter, food, and clothing. Safety and security are second level needs (Maslow, 1968) (see Figure 5.2). If the family is poor, the parents may be trying to meet the basic needs and may not have the time nor energy to think about safety and security as being as important. Nine of ten Native American children, one in two African American children, one in three His-

Children living in poverty situations may be unaware of the potential safety and health risks their environment presents.

panic children, and one in five white children live in poverty. Families with children account for one-third of the homeless population (Children's Defense Fund, 1996).

Note: Before the needs of a particular level can be addressed, the needs of the previous level must be met. For example, before the needs of safety and security can be met, one must already have food, shelter, and clothing.

The number of children living in poverty is significant considering the safety risks that may be present. Children from low-income families may need help understanding the need for safety and protective measures. In this case, role modeling and safety promotion will be important tools. Some of these children may also be unfamiliar with a secure environment that allows them to explore and develop a sense of independence. These children will need a predictable, supportive environment so they can develop a sense of trust.

Violence and child abuse are also safety risks that may come from the home environment of some children.

KEY CREATING A SAFE ENVIRONMENT

CONCEPT

Creating a safe environment by using safe practices allows the caregiver to provide the sense of security and protection from harm that children need to be free to develop, learn, and grow. Developing safety policies should directly relate to the type of child care that is being provided. Understanding the developmental needs, capabilities, and limitations due to the age of children in care helps the caregiver to lay a foundation of safety and protection. Knowing about the community and the family will enable the caregiver to more adequately prepare the safest environment possible for the children in care.

INJURY PREVENTION MANAGEMENT

A safe environment for a child is one that provides freedom from harm and offers a sense of security in which to play, develop, and learn. The caregiver is responsible for providing this type of environment for the children in care. A major goal for a caregiver is to manage the child care environment for injury prevention. Injury prevention promotes safety, protects the child, and minimizes risk. Injury prevention also offers a plan to manage injuries as they occur with the least distress to everyone concerned. The child care environment should prepare for reducing risk, protecting children from harm, and planning for occurrence of injury. Injury prevention offers children the sense of safety and security needed to develop to the fullest potential.

ABCs of Childhood Injuries

Every accident has a cause and effect. Accidental injuries generally occur when a risk is taken or a hazard is present in the environment. To avoid unintentional injuries, causal factors must be understood and anticipated.

The injury triad is a valuable tool for injury prevention (see Figure 5.3). When an injury occurs, certain questions can be asked to understand the circumstances:

■ What type of injury occurred?

■ How did the injury happen?

■ Why did the injury occur?

■ Where did the injury occur?

■ When did the injury happen?

FIGURE **5.3**
The injury triad is used to understand the circumstances surrounding an injury to help prevent future injuries.

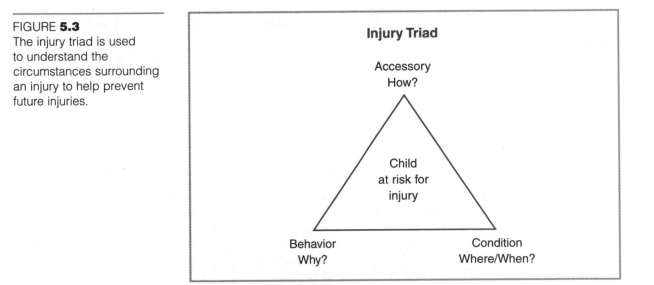

As these questions are explored, a clearer picture may form as to what could have been done to prevent the injury to a child. Table 5.4 provides common factors for childhood injury.

TABLE **5.4**			
The ABCs of Injury Risk to Children			
A =	**Accessory**	=	**How**
	Physical and environmental hazards Lack of safety devices		
B =	**Behavior**	=	**Why**
	By Child: Developmental level Mastery/Exploration Don't know/understand Lack of physical ability Don't grasp cause and effect Lack of fear Inattention Emotions Stress Imitation *By Adult:* Inattention, no supervision Lack of knowledge/understanding Lack of communication Lack of safety precautions Emotions Stress		
C =	**Conditions**	=	**Where or When**
	Where: Place Indoors/outdoors *When:* Time of day Tired, hungry, in a hurry		

Accessory. Accessories that are involved in injuries include physical and environmental hazards and lack of safety devices. Accessories help explain how the injury happened. An accessory is a known factor. A physical hazard could be an object, such as a penny on the floor, a cleaning solution stored under a sink, or a piece of equipment, such as a jungle gym. Environmental hazards might include a swimming pool or traffic around the child care center. Lack of safety devices might include an open electrical outlet without a plug cap or a car without a proper safety seat.

The most effective risk management tool to remove accessories as a risk factor in the injury triad is to use preventive and protective strategies and practice. Since accessories are known factors, the caregiver can modify the environment to remove risk due to them. Modification might include moving cleaning solutions to a high, locked cabinet or installing electrical outlet plug covers.

Behavior.   Behaviors contribute action or inaction that leads to an injury. This can help explain why an injury occurred. Behavior bears most of the responsibility for injury. Action of a child is the most common behavior to the injury triad. The majority of behaviors the child displays are related to the developmental level of the child. The common developmental tasks children perform as they go from stage to stage are the very behaviors that lead them to injury. A child explores his environment, masters his skills and abilities, and uses his cognitive processes to solve problems. These behavioral factors can lead a child into situations that can cause injury.

Knowledge of the developmental levels of children can help alleviate risky situations. Being aware of the developmental stages and situations a child is prone to encounter at a particular age can help the caregiver monitor the environment and be a keen observer of the child.

Regardless of the cause, when an injury occurs it must be taken care of properly by a child caregiver or nurse.

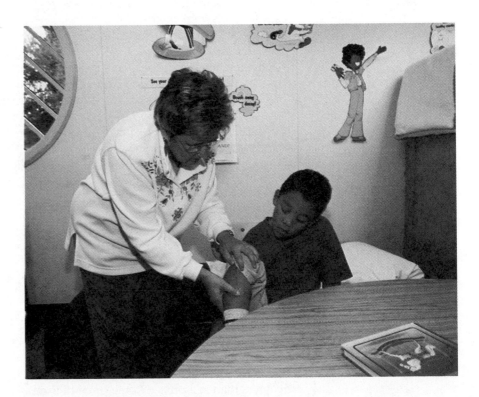

Rodney was a caregiver for two year olds at an inner city day care center. The two year olds and three year olds shared a large room and often played together during free time. Rodney was well aware of the differences of the younger twos in his group and the older three year olds in the other group. He carefully monitored the free play time. One morning he stopped Joshua from putting a small toy part in his mouth. Kelley, a three year old, had brought a small car from home. One of the wheels had fallen off and Joshua picked it up and attempted to put it in his mouth. Although Rodney had no choice about his group playing with the older children and their toys, he was very careful in what he watched for, because he knew the developmental level limitations of his two year olds.

The adult behaviors that can contribute to a child's injury can be active or inactive. In the case of child abuse, violence, or running over a child with an automobile, the adult behavior is active. In the majority of cases, however, the adult contributes inactive behavior to an injury. Lack of supervision, knowledge, communication, and understanding of a situation are causes of inaction. Inattention to what is going on around oneself can also be inaction. A caregiver who is under stress or who is experiencing emotional difficulties may not be as attentive as normal. Inaction presents itself as the absence of preventive, protective, and promotional safety measures.

The same risk management tools for safety that are used for children apply to adult behaviors. A full knowledge of safety practices through education are critical to provide the necessary supervision for a safe and secure environment for children. The caregiver also needs to be aware how his stress and emotions may affect the care given to the children. The use of education, promotion, and good role modeling by the caregiver can help children learn more safe practices. The caregiver should also be practical and use good judgment. These risk management tools may also lead children to an earlier understanding of cause and effect and provide them with preventive strategies that would protect them from harm in dangerous situations. Using education, role modeling, and communication, the caregiver can also help the parent lay the foundation for a safer, more secure environment in the home.

Condition

circumstance or situation under which safety is at risk

Condition. The **condition** factor of the injury triad indicates the circumstances surrounding an injury. The questions as to when and where the injury took place are answered as conditions are explored. The place, the time, and the situation under which an injury takes place may have contributed to the injury. Injuries take place in child care centers, in homes, on playgrounds, and many other places.

Certain types of injuries are more likely to happen in certain places (Figure 5.4). For example, falls from equipment such as climbing structures are more likely to occur on playgrounds or in child care centers than in a home because this type of equipment is more likely to be found at child care centers than in a private home. A child is more likely to have a bicycle acci-

FIGURE **5.4**
Pie Chart with Common
Conditions for Childhood
Accidents

dent in the street than on a sidewalk because streets have traffic and pedestrians, while sidewalks contain pedestrians only. Certain types of injuries are more likely to happen indoors, while other injuries commonly occur outdoors.

Time may be a critical factor that contributes to injury. Children are more likely to get injured in late morning or late afternoon when they are tired. If a child or adult is in a hurry, an injury is more likely to occur. A shift in environment or routine at child care can present distractions or conflicts that are stressful and lead to accidents. Developing an awareness that certain conditions in child care contribute to injury can help the caregiver be more alert when those conditions are present in the child care situation.

Table 5.5 applies the causal factors from the injury triad to specific situations that may be found in injuries that might occur during child care.

When Injury Does Occur

Even in the safest environments, injuries do happen. How the caregiver handles the injury can contribute to keeping the child care environment as secure as possible. Careful planning for injury prepares the caregiver

TABLE **5.5**

Causal Factors in Childhood Injuries

Who = Children of all developmental stages and ages

What	How	Why	Where	When
Motor vehicle accident	Lack of seat belt or safety seat Inattention of driver	Inattention to importance of using safety device	In automobile	Anytime
Riding bicycle near cars	Darting in front of car	Inattention Don't grasp cause/effect Lack of fear In a hurry	Near home, school neighborhood	Anytime Unsupervised
Fall	Unsafe equipment Mastery Exploration	Lack of safety knowledge Lack of ability Don't grasp cause/effect Imitation	Outdoor playgrounds Indoor climbing	Late morning Late afternoon Unsupervised Tired
Collision with objects	Mastery Exploration	Hazards in environment Lack of ability Don't grasp cause/effect In a hurry Imitation	Anywhere	Anytime Tired Unsupervised
Poisoning	Exploration Mastery	Hazards in environment Don't grasp cause/effect Imitation Inability to read	Kitchen, bathroom bedroom, garage living room, yard	Unsupervised Anytime
Choking	Exploration	Hazards in environment Don't grasp cause/effect	Anywhere	Unsupervised Anytime
Burns	Lack of safety devices Mastery Exploration	No smoke detector Water too hot Don't grasp cause/effect Imitation Access to fire device	Anywhere Bathroom Kitchen	Unsupervised Anytime
Drowning	Exploration Mastery	Lack of ability Imitation Lack of safety precautions Lack of understanding cause/effect Hazards in environment	Bathtub Pool Any body of water	Unsupervised Anytime
Child abuse	Parent Someone child knows Stranger	Repeat of cycle of abuse Poverty Dysfunction	Anywhere	Anytime Under stress
Violence	Lack of safety precautions Firearms available	Guns and other hazards Inattention to safety	Neighborhood/Home School	Anytime Unsupervised

to handle accidents and injuries as they occur with as little stress as possible. This can help reinforce the trust of the children present in child care environment. Safety policies should include injury response methods and practices to help provide good injury management.

KEY INJURY PREVENTION MANAGEMENT

Injury prevention is a major responsibility of the child caregiver. To prevent injury and protect children, the caregiver must first understand how injuries occur. A caregiver who understands how accessories, behaviors, and conditions contribute to injury will have the ability to anticipate injury. Monitoring the children and modifying the environment will allow the caregiver to prevent injury and promote safety.

CONSTRUCTING A SAFETY PLAN FOR CHILD CARE

The safety policy designed for each type of child care situation includes the construction of a safety plan. This plan prevents risk and promotes safety, and consists of the guidelines the caregiver develops to promote safety in the child care environment. The guidelines address the areas where risks are anticipated and the environment is modified and monitored for safety. These applications will lessen risk due to accessories, behaviors, and conditions.

Anticipation

The anticipation process begins with a room by room indoor inspection and overall outdoor inspection for safety with checklists that the caregiver creates for that particular child care environment. These checklists apply to the type of child care, the ages of the children in care, the surrounding community, and the family environments the children represent.

Caregivers should search for the accessories, behaviors, and conditions that affect injury prevention. The caregiver should anticipate from the developmental level of the children who are present in child care. Seeing the environment room by room from a child's eye view will help the caregiver to identify risks that an adult-only point of view may have missed.

The next step is to anticipate the behaviors that lead to injury that might occur in the caregiver's type of child care environment. In order to best meet the needs of the children in the child care environment the caregiver must consider the factors of age, community, and family. Knowledge of behaviors that contribute to injury helps the caregiver prepare to promote safety through education and good role modeling. Children who learn safe practices and preventive strategies are less at risk for behavior factors that contribute to injury.

Conditions that contribute to injury must be anticipated next. Creating a plan for safety and careful observation during times when children are more likely to be injured will help to reduce the possibility of injury. The

Teachers or caregivers can role model safe behavior in a variety of ways.

caregiver who understands the conditions and common times that injuries occur will be especially alert when faced with those circumstances.

Children who come to child care from conditions that make them more at risk for injury can especially benefit from efforts to help them understand safety and prevention. Children need a supportive and caring environment to explore in and be protected from harm. Children from at-risk environments may not feel this protection at home. Children in violence prone neighborhoods may feel especially vulnerable. For these children, child care or school may serve as a safe haven. Giving these children tools of safe practices and the sense of security in the child care environment may help them to be more resilient in their home environment (Levin, 1994). It may also help them be more alert in their community environment.

Communicating with parents about conditions, such as stress, that contribute to injury may help them avoid situations that can lead to injury. Role modeling for safety under stressful conditions delivers the message to the parent that injury can be prevented and that a safer environment can be created for children.

Modifications

Careful screening of the environment for hazards, removing the hazards, and placing safety devices where needed are simple tasks that a caregiver can perform to ensure a safe and secure physical environment for children. The use of checklists can assist the caregiver in this process.

Behaviors can be modified through teaching and exhibiting safe, protective, and preventive practices. The caregiver's safety plan would use the most applicable and suitable mode of communication for child care situations. Injury prevention can be taught at all levels, to some extent. Preschool children are more receptive and have greater capabilities than toddlers or infants. School-aged children are very receptive to safety behaviors and practices. There are several steps that the caregiver can use to help children of all ages modify their behaviors to protect themselves and prevent injury. The three most important teaching tools for promoting behavior change are:

- Feedback
- Modeling
- Role playing through practice drills

Feedback about safety can include **positive reinforcement** for good safety behavior practices, **diversion** away from unsafe situations and practices, and a two-way communication channel about both safe and unsafe practices.

Modeling can include role modeling by the caregiver, the use of safety posters and signs, and the use of videos, stories, and other modes of communicating about safety and how it is achieved.

Role playing helps prepare children to act in unsafe or dangerous situations. It is a preventative tool that allows children to be better equipped in a real emergency. Drills for fires, earthquakes, and other types of disasters are practiced on a regular basis in many child care environments. Role playing is often recommended for other types of dangerous situations such as child abuse prevention, gun safety, and neighborhood safety.

Feedback
a technique for encouraging desired behaviors in children through communication

Positive reinforcement
something pleasant that occurs after a behavior that increases the likelihood of the repetition of that behavior

Diversion
something that changes the focus of attention

Modification works well when applied to the factor of condition. The caregiver cannot change the time of day when injuries are most likely to happen. However, she can teach the children to avoid certain activities when they are tired. Caregivers can also modify activities at times that children are more prone to injuries, for example, making a climbing apparatus off limits during high injury times such as late morning. The caregiver might also make that a time when children gather together to relax over stories, instead of playing outside. Role modeling and communicating about safety conditions offer children greater protection. Older children who are able to learn safety practices and understand certain conditions that can lead to injury can have a greater sense of safety and security.

Monitoring

Monitoring the physical environment of child care for accessories is an ongoing process. Change is a constant process. A caregiver should develop an intuition for the changes, but the monitoring process should be formalized. The use of checklists allows the caregiver to evaluate changes and check for hazards.

Monitoring the child care environment for behaviors includes observing whether or not safety practices have changed. This involves keeping track of whether injuries have decreased or increased and examining the behaviors present in the environment. Regularly scheduled weekly examination of injury reports is a good idea because it helps the caregiver to recall any incidence of lack of safety precautions in the environment while they are still fresh in mind. The child care environment should be reviewed for changes on a monthly basis. Changes can occur with the arrival of new children, in the developmental levels of the children in care, in the community, or in family situations. Monitoring helps to manage change by once again anticipating and modifying the environment.

Careful observation under conditions that lead to injury is the foremost activity of monitoring. Mishaps can be prevented through observation. Ongoing evaluation for conditions that lead to injury will help to find changes. If changes in conditions occur, this type of evaluation can lead to early intervention to prevent injury and protect the child. Evaluation of conditions is accomplished through observation, active listening, and communication.

S 5.4

KEY CONCEPT CONSTRUCTING A SAFETY PLAN FOR CHILD CARE

Constructing a safety plan for child care environments is a process that involves anticipation, modification, and monitoring. The three-step process considers the accessories, the behaviors, and the conditions that lead to injury or lack of safety and protection of the children in care. Some of the tools for the process include checklists, feedback, modeling, practice drills, education, and other promotional techniques. Other effective tools include careful observation, active listening, and communication.

IMPLICATIONS FOR **CAREGIVERS**

The caregiver should use preventive and protective measures to prepare and maintain a safe child care environment. The risk management tools that will help the caregiver to provide a good measure of safety include role modeling, education, observation, and supervision.

Role Modeling

Children like to imitate the adults in their lives. Safety and protection of children from harm can be influenced by caregivers who role model good safety practices and create a safe, secure environment.

A safety policy for role modeling should reflect those behaviors the caregiver wishes to instill in the children. Some of the knowledge and practices the children should be able to observe the caregiver role model are listed in Table 5.6.

TABLE **5.6**

Role Modeling Behaviors for Safety

- ■ Verbalizing safety actions to the children
- ■ Caregiver safety actions in the child care and community environments
- ■ Presence of safety devices such as smoke alarms and electrical outlet plugs
- ■ Caregiver being attuned to unsafe conditions
- ■ Caregiver safety behaviors during practice drills and role playing
- ■ Good caregiver/parent communication level about safety measures
- ■ Daily routines for safety checklists
- ■ Removal of hazards to ensure a safe physical environment
- ■ Promotion and education on safety issues and practices
- ■ Caregiver predictability and support given the importance of safety in the child care environment

---

REALITY CHECK

A Child Care Safety Checklist for Parents

Children's safety can be increased by parents and caregivers using preventive and protective measures, but some parents think that nothing bad will happen to their children. It is imperative that a child's safety be a major consideration of parents and caregivers. The caregiver needs to provide a safe environment. Parents should protect their children by checking the child care environment for safety. The Child Care Action Campaign provides information guides for parents. Their guide, *Finding Good Child Care: The Essential Questions to Ask When Seeking Quality Care for Your Child,* provides a checklist for parents seeking child care. A number of these items refer to children's safety and protection. The following is a listing of the items that pertain to safety, printed with permission of the Child Care Action Campaign:

- The staff to child ratio is at a safe level. The safest level includes:

For family child care	1 adult per 5 children, including the caregiver's children. No more than two infants.
Child care centers:	1 adult per 4 infants and toddlers
	1 adult per 4 to 6 two year olds
	1 adult per 7 to 8 three year olds
	1 adult per 8 to 9 four year olds
	1 adult per 8 to 10 five year olds
	1 adult per 10 to 12 school-age children

- Caregivers have some training in child care. They continue to learn by reading books, taking courses, and belonging to professional organizations.

- Caregivers pay attention to children and interact with them, rather than chatting with other caregivers or attending to personal things.

- Caregivers change their style of supervision to suit the age and abilities of the child; very close supervision for infants and toddlers, more independence for three- and four year olds. Children are never left unsupervised.

- Reasonable discipline is maintained through careful supervision, age-appropriate explanations, clear limits, use of "time out." No spanking or corporal punishment is ever used, nor is harsh discipline such as shouting, shaming, or withholding food.

- Caregivers avoid conflicts between children by listening and watching carefully so that they can step in early, before the situation escalates.

- Children, including babies and toddlers, have easy access to safe toys.

- Safe and easy-to-use art materials, such as nontoxic crayons, paints, and play dough, are provided so that children can create their own work as soon as they are able.

- There is enough safe crawling space for infants and toddlers that encourage exploration of the environment.

- Challenging materials, such as scissors or toys with many pieces, are introduced, with supervision, as children are ready for them. A caregiver stays with the children as they use these materials.

- Children play outdoors in a safe area every day, except in bad weather.

- Electrical outlets and heaters are covered, and stairs have safety gates.

- Equipment is maintained to ensure safety, and there is enough space for active physical play outdoors (and to some degree, indoors) for all age groups.

- Cleaning fluids, medicines, and other harmful substances are stored in locked cabinets out of the reach of children.

- The outdoor play area is fenced and cleared of debris and poisonous plants.

- There are fire extinguishers in the building and an adequate number of working smoke detectors.

- Emergency numbers for the fire station, rescue squad, police, poison control, and so forth, are posted near the telephone.

- There is an emergency exit plan so that the caregiver can get all the children out quickly. Fire drills are held monthly, so that children and caregivers know what to do in case of an emergency.

- Safety restraints and car seats are used every time a child is in a car, bus, van, or other moving vehicle.

- There is an "open door" policy for parents: you are welcome to visit your child and the child care at any time of day.

- The facility is registered or licensed, if required.

Caregivers should provide this list to prospective families interested in their child care center or family child care home. Complying with this list will offer the parents the knowledge that their children are in safe hands while in child care.

Education

Safety education should involve the child caregiver, the children, and the parents. To provide safety in child care, the caregiver must be aware of strategies and methods to reduce risk. The caregiver must develop a keen awareness of the risks posed by the accessories, behaviors, and conditions of his particular child care environment.

Children can learn safe practices as they watch the caregiver model safe practices and behaviors. The caregiver can talk to the children about safety and share books and videos that promote safety and safe behaviors.

Educational materials provided for the parents may help them understand the importance of safe practices and behaviors for children in all environments. A parent who is aware of conditions or behaviors that may put a child at risk for safety is able to offer an extra measure of protection and prevention.

Observation

A child caregiver can use observation to protect children from risk and to prevent risk to safety. Observing for accessories, behaviors, and conditions keeps the caregiver aware of all areas of injury risk management. The caregiver should watch for safety from hazards and equipment. He should observe for the need for safety devices. Behaviors of both children and adults should be observed for safe practices and risk from injury. The caregiver should observe the conditions in the environment that are known to lead to risk of injury and reduction of safety.

Supervision

Using the ABCs of injury risk management helps the caregiver offer the greatest degree of constant supervision in order to maintain the safest child care environment possible. Supervision can also help ensure that all strategies and practices that promote safety, prevent risk, and offer protection are used.

KEY IMPLICATIONS FOR CAREGIVERS

CONCEPT

The child caregiver needs to use all tools at her disposal to help promote safety, prevent injury, and offer protection. Role modeling, education, observation, and supervision provide the practices, strategies, and methods needed to provide these for the children in care.

CHAPTER **SUMMARY**

Safety policies that manage risk and prevent injury promote and protect the safety of the child care environment. Caregivers should be aware of the environmental hazards such as accessories, behaviors, and conditions in their particular child care. Children's developmental levels should be understood and addressed when considering safety. Caregivers should learn to anticipate, modify, and monitor child care for injury prevention. Role modeling is a key to promoting safe practices. Education and supervision also help the caregiver maintain a safer child care environment.

TO GO **BEYOND**

Questions for Review

1. Discuss the interrelationship of accessories, behaviors, and conditions of child care and safety for child care.
2. Describe how the anticipation, modification, and monitoring process occurs in a typical child care center. In a family child care home. In an in-home care situation.

AS AN **INDIVIDUAL**

1. Interview a child caregiver about how he or she manages risk and tries to prevent injury in child care. After the interview assess whether or not this caregiver was considering the developmental level of the children in care. What modifications were made to the child care environment? What did you learn from this assignment?
2. Go to a local park. Observe the community around the park. Would you consider this a safe environment for children? What if a child care center or family child care home were near it? Would it put that place at risk? Record your observations and conclusions.

AS A **GROUP**

1. Watch *Setting Up for Health and Safe Care,* an AAP video. What safety measures were observed? Discuss two indoor and two outdoor measures that were promoted.
2. Working in groups of 4 to 5 people, create a safety checklist that will be used in a new child care situation. Compare the lists.

CHAPTER **REFERENCES**

American Academy of Pediatrics and American Public Health Association (1992). *Caring for our children: National health and safety performance standards: Guidelines for out-of-home care.* Washington, DC: American Public Health Association.

Carroll, J. (1996). Update on risk reduction and SIDS prevention—1996. Presentation handout, Johns Hopkins Children's Center. Path: http://SIDS-Network. ORG:80//RISK.htm.

Child Care Action Campaign. Finding good child care: Essential questions to ask when seeking quality care for your child [CCAC Information Guide 19]. New York: Author.

Children's Defense Fund. (1992). *The state of America's children 1992*. Washington, DC: Author.

DiFranza, J., & Lew, R. (1995). Effect of maternal cigarette smoking on pregnancy complications and sudden infant deaths. *Journal of Family Practice, 40*(4), 385–394.

Gorman, C. (1993, July 5). Safer sleep. *Time Magazine,* 50.

Hatted, A. (1994). Safety and children: How schools can help. *Childhood Education, 70*(5), 283–286.

Levin, D. (1994). Building a peaceable classroom: Helping young children feel safe in violent times. *Childhood Education, 70*(5), 267–270.

Maslow, A. (1968). *Toward a psychology of being*. New York: Van Nordstrom.

Mickalaide, A. (1994). Creating safer environments for children. *Childhood Education, 70*(5), 263–266.

National Center for Health Statistics. (1991). Firearms mortality among children, youth and young adults, 1–34 years of age 1979–1988 [Supplement]. Washington, DC: U.S. Department of Health and Human Services.

Runyan, C., Gray, D, Kotch, J., & Kreuter, M. (1991). Analysis of U.S. child care safety regulations. *The American Journal of Public Health, 81*(8), 981–985.

SIDS Network. (1996a). What every parent should know: Facts about sudden infant death syndrome (SIDS). Path:http://SIDS-Network.ORG: 80//RISK.htm.

SIDS Network. (1996b). Reducing the risks for SIDS: Some steps parents can take. Path: http://SIDS-Network.ORG:80//RISK.htm.

U.S. Department of Health and Human Services. (1990). Healthy people year 2000. Washington, DC: U.S. Government Printing Office.

Willinger, M. (1995). SIDS prevention. *Pediatric Annals, 24*(7), 358–364.

SUGGESTIONS FOR **READING**

Ciccheti, D., & Lynch, M. (1993). Toward an ecological/transactional model of community violence and child maltreatment. *Psychiatry: Interpersonal and Biological Processes, 56*(1), 96–118.

Elders, J. (1994). Violence as a public health issue. *Childhood Education, 70*(5), 260–262.

The quiet crisis. (1994). *Young Children, 49*(7), 60.

Sewell, K., & Gaines, S. (1994). A developmental approach to childhood safety education. *Pediatric Nursing, 19*(5), 464–466.

Smoke signals (1995, June/July). *Healthy Kids,* 8.

Wood, S. (1996, July/August). How to protect your baby from SIDS. *Child Magazine,* 26–28.

CHAPTER SIX

INDOOR SAFETY

Upon completion of this chapter, including a review of the summary, you should be able to:

INDOOR SAFETY POLICIES

Describe and discuss safety policies for indoor environments as tools for risk prevention, protection, and promotion.

INDOOR SAFETY GUIDELINES

Indicate and discuss specific guidelines for making any indoor child care environment free from risk and protected for safety.

INDOOR EQUIPMENT

Relate and discuss the safety hazards of indoor equipment as it relates to child care situations.

TOY SAFETY

Describe and discuss the importance of safe, risk-free toys for infants, toddlers, and preschoolers.

INTERPERSONAL SAFETY

Describe and discuss clear rules for consequences of behavior and appropriate methods of conflict resolution.

POISON CONTROL

Indicate the methods and means of poison control and risk prevention in child care environments.

FIRE AND BURN PREVENTION

Describe and discuss methods of fire and burn prevention in child care.

IMPLICATIONS FOR CAREGIVERS

Indicate the need for education, observation, and supervision to maintain a safe indoor environment.

INDOOR SAFETY POLICIES

The safety risks of indoor and outdoor environments vary widely. Because the variation is so widespread, we will look at these environments separately. The indoor child care environment can include many physical hazards that pose risk through choking, interpersonal violence, poisoning, burns, lead poisoning, and others. The following factors indicate the need for policies to cover indoor safety:

■ Twelve percent of child care centers were reported as unsafe in a study conducted in 400 centers throughout the United States (Chiara, 1995).

■ Over 140,000 children are injured every year in toy-related accidents. Of these, one-half of the deaths (11 of 22) were related to choking on small parts of toys (Langlois, Walker, Terrt, Bailey, Hershey, & Peeler, l991).

■ Each year, 30,000 children are treated in emergency rooms for scald burns. Foods and hot liquids prepared in the kitchen account for over 25,000 of the burns. Another 4,000 children are burned in the bathroom by hot water. Approximately one-half of these victims are under the age of five (Mickalaide, 1994).

■ One in six children under age seven has dangerous levels of lead in the blood from dust from old lead paint, window seals, water systems, and crystal or ceramics commonly found in households (Cowley, 1993).

■ Using violence to solve interpersonal problems has become common in children. Every two hours an American child loses his life to a gunshot wound ("Children's Defense Fund Reports," 1994).

To ensure the safety of the children in their care, child caregivers must make sure toys are developmentally appropriate. This child is not at risk because playing with small blocks is appropriate for his age and developmental level.

The indoor environment includes a multitude of levels that can pose risk. Hazards come from household items, toys, animals, stoves and other kitchen equipment, children's furniture, foods, firearms, fireplaces, paint, ceramics, medications, plants, electrical outlets and cords, among others. Other indoor risks include unsafe caregiver practices, unmonitored conditions, and children's behavior based on developmental levels, physical abilities, and emotional health. The child caregiver must have an awareness of all accessories, behaviors, and conditions that may lead to an accident or injury (see Figures 6.1 and 6.2, and Tables 6.6 and 6.7). The caregiver must also be in compliance with all regulations affecting the safety in care such as those from licensing and fire boards.

Indoor environment risk management process should include:

1. *Indoor Child Care Environments:* understanding indoor safety practices and applications for risk management as they apply to specific child care environments.

2. *Indoor Equipment Safety:* practices for preventing injuries and managing safety on indoor equipment.

3. *Toy Safety:* practices for preventing injuries, removing unsafe toys, and managing selection of toys for children in care.

4. *Interpersonal Safety:* strategies for developing guidelines for interpersonal safety and conflict management for the children in care.

5. *Poison Control:* strategies for developing guidelines for poison prevention and protection in child care.

6. *Fire and Burn Prevention:* educational and promotional strategies to model good fire and burn prevention behaviors and practices.

7. *Implications for Caregiver:* methods and practices of conducting education, supervision, observation, and utilizing outside resources.

KEY SAFETY POLICIES

CONCEPT

Safety policies should be planned as a tool for prevention of injuries, the protection of children, and the promotion of safe practices in the child care indoor environment. These policies should consider the specific environment and should be applicable to the accessories, behaviors, and conditions present indoors. Use of these policies minimizes risk to children and maximizes the child's care environment for safety.

EXAMINING CHILD CARE ENVIRONMENTS FOR INDOOR HAZARDS

Some hazards are common to all child care environments. The most common indoor childhood accidents are related to:

■ Falls

■ Choking

■ Burns
■ Drowning
■ Poisoning

Screening the environment for these risks to safety should be done in an organized fashion. Applying the ABCs of injury risk (see Table 5.4) allows the caregiver to anticipate, modify, and monitor the child care environment. This chapter will provide indoor safety checklists that can be used as a basis to help prepare to minimize risk.

Environmental Hazards

The indoor screening should include environmental hazards such as lead, asbestos, chemicals, and so on, that might also be found in the environment, but not necessarily at a child's reach. All environmental hazard risks should be removed or modified wherever possible.

Ventilation. Adequate ventilation is a safety risk that is considered an environmental hazard. Air needs to move sufficiently so there is no gathering of fumes, germs, or other safety risks to children. Children inhale two to three times more air than adults, so adequate ventilation is necessary (Rosenblum, 1993). APHA and AAP standards can be found in *Caring for Our Children: National Health and Safety Performance Standards: Guidelines for Out-of-Home Child Care Programs* published by the APHA.

Pets or Animals. Pets or animals in the environment can also provide safety risks through injury, infection, and allergic reactions. Any animal that

Family pets, although vaccinated and clean, may still be a conceivable safety and health risk to children in a home care center. Animals must be supervised and monitored regularly to avoid unpleasant incidents.

FIGURE **6.1**
Caregivers should teach children the meaning of the poison sign.

Safety latches and electric outlet covers are just two of the numerous safety devices available. As with any device, these must be properly installed and utilized to be truly effective.

is present should be friendly and healthy. Puppies and kittens can carry infections that cause a variety of serious diseases in children. Dogs and cats should be fully immunized and under a veterinarian's care for flea, tick, and worm control. Never allow turtles, parrots, or lizards to be handled by children because these types of pets often carry diseases that are contracted by direct contact. Do not allow other wild or aggressive animals such as ferrets to be present in a child care environment. If pets are present in child care, they should be kept in a supervised and confined area of the facility and regularly checked for disease by a veterinarian. Pet living quarters should be cleaned often and animal waste kept to a minimum. Children should always wash their hands immediately after handling pets. Follow the AAP/APHA guidelines for animals present in child care.

Another risk factor that pets may present is allergic reactions. Some children may be allergic to certain pet hair or dander. Parents may be unaware of the allergy if there are no pets in the home environment. The caregiver should observe children for any reactions to the pets in the child care environment.

Cleaning and Other Supplies. Cleaning supplies are a risk to children whether or not they are poisonous. These items can cause burns or rashes and other possible problems. All cleaning supplies or chemicals that might present danger to children should be kept at a level where children cannot reach them. Paints and some craft supplies may present a risk if a child ingests them. Anything that might be poisonous should be kept at a high level in a locked cabinet. These items should be well labeled with the poison sign. The caregiver can teach the children about the danger present when they see the sign (see Figure 6.1). This may not help the toddler or crawling infant, but it will help the older children.

Safety Devices

Safety devices should be present wherever applicable in the indoor child care environment. All wall sockets should be covered with difficult-to-remove plastic plugs. All drawers that can be pulled out and fall onto a child's head or upper body should have safety latches in them that make them child-proof. All doorways that might lead to danger should be shut and lockable. Safety gates should be installed for doorways without doors that may lead to danger or risk. All stairways where infants and toddlers are present should have safety gates to prevent the children from crawling up or falling down the stairs. The child caregiver should check local hardware stores and child care catalogs for safety devices.

Developmental Level

Prevention is the single most significant factor in risk management for safety. The caregiver begins this process by defining the boundaries for indoor safety and screening the environment for hazards with the developmental levels of the children in care in mind. Safety hazards can be broken down by developmental age and vulnerabilities associated with that particular stage as shown in Table 6.1.

Most children under the age of three are not developmentally ready to use scissors. Even children who are three and older should be regularly monitored for safety reasons.

TABLE **6.1**

Indoor Safety Hazards

Age	Hazards	Prevention Tips
0–6 months	Scalds	Set hot water temperature to 120°F or less and always test bath water before immersing baby.
	Falls	Never leave infant alone on bed or table.
	Choking/Suffocation	Buy toys larger than two inches in diameter. Keep crib free of plastics or pillows. Crib slats should be less than 2⅝″ apart and space between mattress and slats should be less than 2 fingers wide.
	Toys	Should be larger than 1½ inches in diameter and should have smooth round edges and be soft and flexible.
	Drowning	Never leave child in bath unattended.
6 months–1 year	Burns and scalds	Check water temperature (see above). Keep hot foods and liquids out of reach. Put guards around hot pipes, radiators, and fireplaces.
	Poisons	Store household products, cosmetics, and medicines in high, preferably locked cabinets. Keep syrup of ipecac on hand. Post poison control number by phone.

Indoor Safety Hazards *continued*

Age	Hazards	Prevention Tips
6 months–1 year *continued*	Choking	Check floors and reachable areas for small objects such as pins, coins, buttons. Avoid raw vegetables, nuts, hard candy, popcorn, and other foods that are difficult for child to properly chew and swallow.
	Toys	Should be large, unbreakable, and smooth.
	Drowning	Always carefully supervise when bathing.
1–2 years	Falls	Put toddler gates on stairways and keep any doors to cellars, attics, and porches locked. Remove sharp-edged furniture from child's frequently used area. Show child proper way to climb up and down stairs using handrails.
	Burns	While cooking, turn pot handles to back of stove. Keep electric cords out of reach. Use shock stops to cover used and unused outlets. Teach child the meaning of the word hot and talk about different types of hot.
	Poisons	Keep poisons locked in high cabinets. Have child tested for lead poisoning during regular check-up.
	Drowning	Always supervise child's bath.
	Choking	Remove small objects.
2–3 years	Poisons	Teach child about the difference between food and non-food and what is not good to eat. Watch child during art projects so he does not put art supplies in mouth. Keep poisons locked in high cabinets.
	Burns	Keep matches, lighter, and cigarettes out of reach and sight of children. Put screen around fireplaces and wood stoves. Reinforce the meaning of "hot."
	Toys	Check for sharp edges, hinges, and small parts that could be swallowed. Remove toy chest lids.
	Drowning	Always supervise.
	Guns	Keep any firearms unloaded and locked away out of reach.
3 years and up	Burns	Teach child drop and roll to prepare for clothing catching fire. Practice fire drills with escape route meeting place and sound of smoke alarm. Train to bring found matches to adult.
	Tools and equipment	Teach child safe use of scissors. Keep sharp knives out of reach.
	Guns	Keep firearms unloaded and locked. Teach safety precautions about guns, by telling an adult immediately when they see a gun and not to touch! Discourage use of toy guns or violent play.

Infants. Young infants are relatively helpless and must be carefully watched to protect and prevent risks. Older, more mobile infants develop new motor skills at a rapid rate that lead them into an increasing number of hazardous situations. Children at this stage are particularly at risk for choking on small objects that they can mouth. The environment should be constantly and carefully monitored for small objects if infants are present, and expanding hazards should be anticipated.

Toddlers. Toddlers probably represent the developmental group with the most potential for unsafe practices. They are at a cognitive level that allows them new ways of thinking and solving problems, but they do not understand cause and effect. Toddlers try to stretch their limits and test their environment, which they now have the physical ability to accomplish. Toddlers like to explore places that may not be in view. Poisons and chemicals that are kept in cabinets, drawers, or on shelves are a major risk for this age group. Toddlers need careful, constant monitoring and potential hazards need to be constantly anticipated. Therefore, the environment should be modified as needed (see Figure 6.2).

FIGURE **6.2**
Common Indoor Hazards

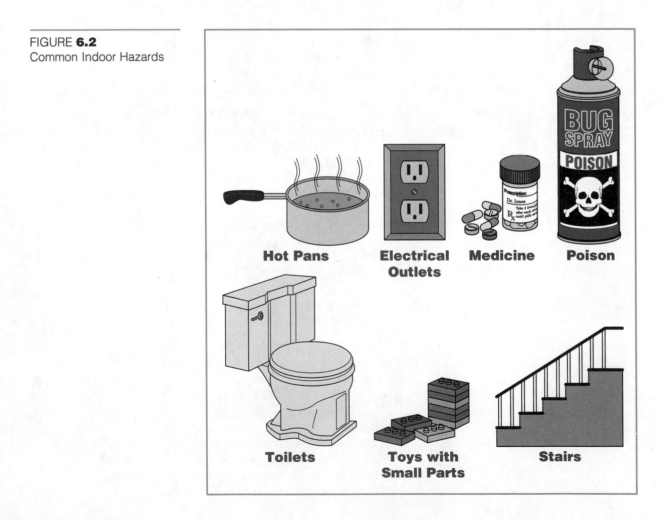

Adequate floor space in a clear and organized environment will aid in the prevention of injury.

The Preschooler. Preschool-aged children have more physical and cognitive abilities and are beginning to understand cause and effect. Indoor falls pose risk to these children. Although they know about cause and effect, physical mastery often takes precedence over thought processes. Besides monitoring the conditions and safety risks, the caregiver can teach a preschool child preventive measures and help them to anticipate hazards. Children of this age can be good helpers to monitor the indoor environment for hazards.

School Age. School-aged children are much less prone to indoor safety hazards than children who are younger. Firearms may be the greatest threat to school-aged children. This age group has intense curiosity about things they see in movies and on television. They may not understand the danger guns pose. It is important that if guns are present in a child care environment, such as a family child care home, that they be stored unloaded and locked up. Children of this age can learn preventive measures and can help the caregiver monitor the environment and younger children.

Space

Specific child care environments present unique conditions and circumstances that can lead to environmental hazards. There should be adequate space to move around the equipment and not have to compete for space with other children. Most child care centers, Head Start programs, and state preschools are licensed and do comply with spacing required by the licensing agencies.

Recommended indoor space is 35 square foot per child of play space, which does not include kitchen, bathroom, closet, laundry, or staff facilities (APHA & AAP, 1992). This space usually translates to 50 square feet per child when furnishings are included in this measurement. Family child care homes that are informed try to keep to this standard. Unlicensed or license-exempt sites also need to follow this standard for space.

Adequate floor space is essential. How the child caregiver sets up the environment in the space available is a critical factor in prevention of injury. Enough space should be provided for crawling, keeping separate play areas for infant/toddlers and older children. Caregivers should not have barriers that impair their ability to watch all the children at the same time. These considerations need to be remembered as the child care space is planned and organized. Child care space planning should include the arrangement of interest areas of the classroom with the interest of safety in mind (see Figure 6.3).

Shared Space

Another indoor environmental hazard for child care may be shared space. Some child care situations are located in areas that have multiple uses. These shared spaces may carry risks that the caregiver must anticipate, continually assess, and be prepared to eliminate (see Table 5.1).

FIGURE **6.3**
How to Set Up an
Environment—Dos and
Don'ts

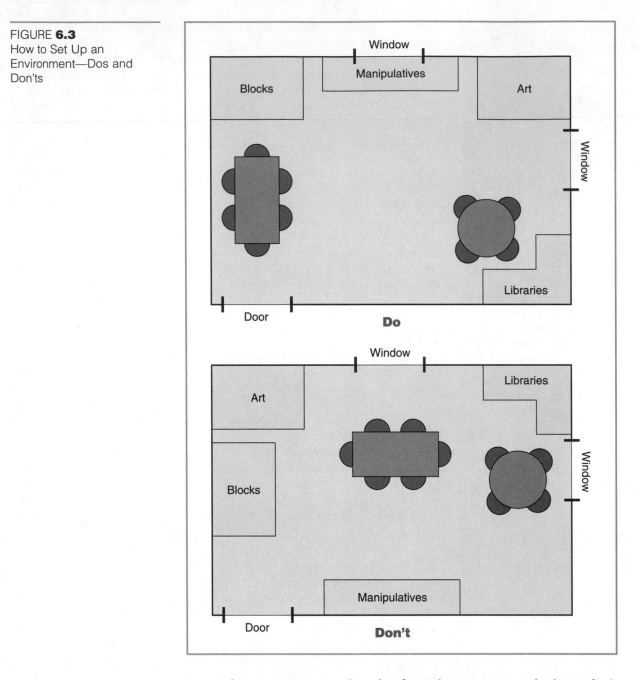

Whenever spaces are shared, safety risks can occur. Multiple use facilities need thoughtful anticipation for possible hazards, and the environment should be carefully screened before resuming child care in a shared space that was used for another purpose.

Screening a shared space may require coming to the site 15 to 30 minutes before the children arrive. Using a shared facility checklist created for the particular multiple uses helps organize and speed up this process. Table 6.2 contains a checklist for a family child care home's morning check that could also be used by a nanny upon arrival at a child's home.

It was Monday morning at the church preschool. Monica, the teacher, was pleased to see that someone had filled the juice pitchers for her and had them ready in the refrigerator. The children had come to school either tired or still excited from a busy summer weekend, so Monica really appreciated the extra help.

Sally, the director, had a habit of taking time to sit with the children at their morning snacks on Mondays to see how they were doing and to hear about their time on the weekends. She sat down after the snacks had been handed out and the juice had been poured. Sally took one sip of the juice and commented to the children, "You know this juice doesn't taste quite right, let's all throw it out and get some new juice." Sally had a very organized reaction to drinking punch with alcohol that had been left over from a wedding at the church over the weekend.

It turns out that the people cleaning up didn't want anything to go to waste, so they saved the punch in the only containers available—the preschool pitchers. Monica should have checked to see what it was first, and fortunately Sally had the presence of mind to solve the problem before anyone had a chance to take more than a sip of juice.

TABLE **6.2**

6 A.M. **Checklist**

Check for:

REMOVE:

- [ ] All food, beverages, and dirty dishes
- [ ] Scissors, knives, or other sharp items
- [ ] Pesticides, medications, or other products that might be poisonous
- [ ] Standing water left around in buckets or other containers
- [ ] All craft supplies, game pieces, and so forth
- [ ] All breakable objects
- [ ] All matches or flammable items
- [ ] Any small toys or other objects that could cause a child to choke
- [ ] Any object that attracts a child to climb, such as a stepladder or stool

REPLACE as needed:

- [ ] Safety latches
- [ ] Safety gates by stairways
- [ ] All other safety devices
- [ ] All doors, gates, and other openings that could cause safety hazards

FIGURE **6.4**
Sign for Shared Use Facility

> **Please Remember**
> **Child Care Takes Place Here!**
>
> • Pick up all small objects.
>
> • Put any dangerous objects out of reach.
>
> • Check electrical outlets for safety covers.
>
> • Lock all cabinets that contain nonchildproof objects.

It is also helpful to post signs in the shared facility about hazards so that others who use the facility are aware of safety risks to the child care environment (see Figure 6.4). Speaking with the person in charge of the other uses helps to keep the risks at a minimum. People who are responsible for the cleaning and care of the facility should be encouraged to cooperate and watch for the possible safety hazards that will keep the children from undue risks. Parents should also be trained and utilized as environmental scanners whose extra "eyes" can help check for risks when they drop off their children.

KEY EXAMINING THE ENVIRONMENT FOR INDOOR HAZARDS

CONCEPT

Examining the indoor environment for safety hazards allows the caregiver to provide protection for the children and may help prevent unnecessary accidents. Indoor environmental hazards include ventilation, cleaning and other supplies, and pets. Safety devices can be used to prevent risk. The environment should be screened to meet the risk due to the developmental levels of children. Adequate space and setup for indoor child care are factors that should be considered to prevent undue risk. Shared spaces pose many risks and need extra supervision to promote safety and prevent risk.

INDOOR EQUIPMENT SAFETY

Equipment used in child care shall be sturdy and free of sharp points or corners, splinters, protruding nails or bolts, loose rusty parts, hazardous small parts, or paint that contains lead (APHA & AAP, 1992). Furniture should be durable, easy to clean, and where appropriate, child-sized. Equipment should be placed so that children have enough freedom of movement to prevent accidents and collisions with equipment and each other. Refer to Figure 6.3 for improper equipment placement and proper placement of the same equipment.

Safety gates and latches
should be routinely used.

Some infant equipment is regularly tested and must comply with certain standards (APHA & AAP, 1992). Cribs, high chairs, strollers, and safety gates fall into this category. For information regarding the specifications of the standards, the caregiver can write to:

The American Society for Testing and Materials

1916 Race Street

Philadelphia, PA 19103

Cribs should be made of wood, metal, or plastic, and should have non-lead based paint. Cribs should also have:

■ Slats that are no more than $2\frac{3}{8}$ inches apart.

■ A mattress that is fitted so that no more than two fingers can be wedged between the mattress and the crib side.

■ A minimum height of 36 inches between the top of the mattress and the top of the crib.

■ Secure latches, which when dropping the sides shall hold the sides in the raised position. The latches should be inaccessible to the child in the crib.

Never leave a large stuffed toy in a crib. Children can use it to climb out of the crib. Never place a crib near a window because children can fall out of windows, hurt themselves on broken glass, or get caught up in cords from window shades or curtains. Bumper pads should be securely tied to the crib. There should be a minimum of six evenly placed tie strings that prevent children from crawling into an opening and suffocating. Make sure the tie strings are less than 12 inches so that children do not strangle in them.

When high chairs are used in child care, they should have a safety strap that goes between the legs and around the waist. The legs should have a wide enough base so the high chair will not tip over. If paint is used on the high chair, it should be lead-free. Strollers should clearly display the ASTM seal of compliance with the number F833. Safety gates should display the seal with the number F406 (APHA & AAP, 1992).

If the caregiver is using a changing table, it should have a lip around it that discourages a child from rolling off the changing table. The changing table should have a safety strap and the strap should always be used. The child should never be left unattended when being changed.

Preventing Falls

Falls are one of the most common injuries related to indoor equipment. A child's changing abilities to move about and manipulate the environment is a major contributor to causing safety risks with indoor equipment. A tiny baby can wiggle and move and push. An older baby can roll over, crawl, and creep. Changing tables vary greatly and can be the cause of an infant's fall if the infant is left unattended, even if the safety strap is used. Although infant walkers are tested, they are the cause of more injuries than any other infant equipment, so the American Academy of Pediatrics recommends against their use.

Toddlers can climb to get to places that were formerly inaccessible. Discouraging climbing on furniture and other equipment will help prevent risk. Using safety devices such as window guards will help prevent falls if the toddler does try to climb.

Preschoolers are coordinated enough and fast enough to do almost any physical activity. Using only safe, sturdy equipment that is in good repair also helps protect children from falls. Table 6.3 presents a list for checking indoor equipment to help prevent falls.

TABLE **6.3**

Checklist to Prevent Falls in the Indoor Environment

Check for:

- [ ] Use infant and child equipment that is in good repair and inspected for safety.
- [ ] Use durable, balanced furniture that will not tip over easily.
- [ ] Do not allow climbing on furniture, stools, or ladders.
- [ ] Place safety gates at stairways.
- [ ] Remove all objects from stairs.
- [ ] Repair or remove frayed carpeting or other flooring.
- [ ] Install window guards on upstairs windows.
- [ ] Secure all window screens.
- [ ] Clean up spills quickly.
- [ ] Avoid highly waxed floors and stairways.
- [ ] Do not use loose throw rugs.
- [ ] Keep toys picked up as often as possible.
- [ ] Never leave a baby alone in a high place.

Indoor Water Safety

Water safety is also a consideration in the use of indoor equipment. Drowning can occur in a relatively small amount of water; for example, a bucket of standing water that someone forgot to clean up and put away. A curious infant or toddler could look into the bucket, fall in, and drown. Toilets, tubs, and sinks also pose risk for drowning. Toilet lids should always be closed. Some child care environments do not have lids for toilets, in which case, the area should have a door that shuts and should be carefully monitored. Water should never be left standing in tubs or sinks.

Hot water faucets also pose risk. Hot water can cause burns by scalding. All hot water heaters should be set at 120°F (see Figure 6.5). Children

FIGURE **6.5**
Hot water heaters should be set to 120°F to prevent burns.

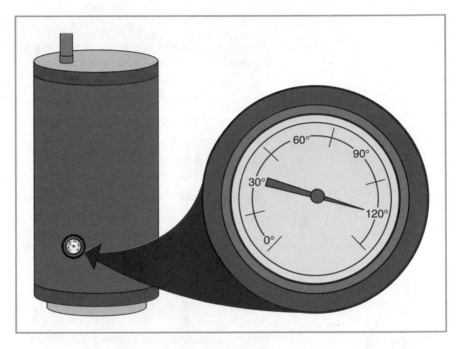

should never be left unattended near hot water faucets. When turning on water for children, always turn on the cold water first.

Toilets and water tables may also carry germs that put children at risk. To promote indoor water safety, the basic rules in Table 6.4 should be followed.

Equipment that utilizes water, such as toilets and sinks, should be carefully monitored and cleaned often, and children and staff should be encouraged to wash hands often.

TABLE **6.4**
Indoor Water Safety Guidelines
■ Any equipment that utilizes water such as toilets, sinks, tubs, and buckets should be carefully monitored and cleaned often.
■ Keep hot water temperature at 120°F.
■ Never leave standing water unattended.
■ No child should ever be left unattended in a tub or other device used to bathe a child.
■ Where toilet lids are present, when possible, keep them down.
■ In a family child care home keep the door to the bathroom closed when not in use, if very young children are present. Keep a set of jingle bells on the door to hear the door opening and closing.
■ Keep lid on diaper pail securely fastened.
■ Keep lid on water table when not in use.

KEY INDOOR EQUIPMENT SAFETY

CONCEPT

Using safe, sturdy indoor child care equipment can help eliminate some risk. Safety devices, safety practices, and good supervision will help the caregiver add a greater degree of protection for the children. Some indoor equipment that involves water poses risks. The risk of drowning and of burns from scalding water can be reduced through safe practices and supervision.

TOY SAFETY

Toy-related accidents cause more than 140,000 children to be injured each year. Over half of these accidents involve choking or inhaling of small parts (Langlois et al., 1991). Other typical toy-related accidents involve inhaling balloons, toy chest lids falling on or pinching a child, projectile toys that pierce the body, and strangulation on toys with ropes or strings that may be inappropriately used. These accidents may be avoided if the toys were examined for **age appropriateness** of the children playing with them. Art supplies may also pose risk to children and should be checked for safety and age appropriateness.

Age appropriateness
consideration of the developmental abilities of a particular age group in the selection of toys, materials, and equipment

Choking and Suffocation Hazards

Choking and suffocation are major hazards to very young children who still mouth things such as toys, foods, and small objects in their environment. The developmental level for that mouthing, along with new cognitive abilities to master the environment can lead children to risk their safety (Table 6.5).

Children in the oral stage need to be carefully watched and provided with a safe environment free of small toys and objects.

TABLE **6.5**

Choking and Suffocation Hazards for Young Children

Toys	
Marbles	Game tokens
Balloons	Game pieces
Dress-up jewelry	Jacks
Plastic bags	Toy chest with no air holes
Any toy less than 1½ inches in diameter	

Foods	
Hot dogs	Peanuts
Grapes	Popcorn
Gum	Olives
Lollipops	Hard candy and cough drops
Carrots, celery, and other raw vegetables	

Small Objects	
Pins and safety pins	Crayons
Toothpicks	Nails
Tacks	Pencils and pens
Jewelry	Staples
Coins	

FIGURE **6.6**
Device for Measuring Small Parts to Prevent Choking. Notice that the domino gets caught in the tube, but the die passes through the tube, indicating a choking hazard.

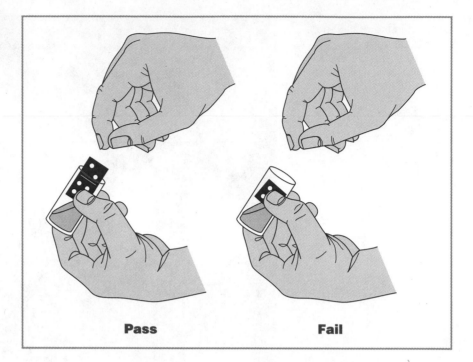

Pass   **Fail**

Ensuring that small toys and other objects are too large for mouthing is an important criteria for finding choking and suffocation hazards (see Figure 6.6). As consumers, we are probably more conscious of foods and small objects causing choking hazards than we are of toys. One purchases a toy and expects that toy to be safe. However, what is safe for a five year old may be very dangerous to a two year old. The Consumer Product Safety Commission has a small parts standard that prohibits manufacturers from marketing toys with small parts to children under the age of three years. Their toll free phone number is 1-800-638-2772.

Marty had been a family child caregiver for about six months. She had children in care from 4 months old to five years old. The older children were very active and helpful. Dana, the older four year old, and Holly, the five year old, really liked to do things that were grown-up. They especially enjoyed helping Marty. Marty appreciated their help and liked to give them little tasks to do. One of those tasks was to help her go through the child care setting looking for any safety risks. The girls often caught things that Marty might have missed because they explored the environment from a child's level.

One day Ramsey, a toddler, was chewing on something. Holly went to Marty and brought her to Ramsey right away. Even though they had all searched for hazards that morning they had missed a playing piece from a Monopoly game. The safety consciousness in this child care setting helped save Ramsey from a hazard that could have caused a real problem.

Age Appropriateness

The age group for which a toy is intended is often included on the package. However, contents of the package including small parts are not always listed, and safety precautions are often not included in the packaging or instructions. If a caregiver fails to see the package or if she does not understand other safety precautions that should be taken with a toy, she may put the children in care at risk for injury.

Consumer awareness of toy safety is imperative, especially in child care settings where there is a population of mixed age children. Age appropriateness is one of the most important tools for removing hazardous toys from the environment. Table 6.6 shows age appropriate toy suggestions.

TABLE **6.6**

Age	Toys
Up to 6 months:	squeeze toys, colorful mobiles, large pictures of faces or simple patterns, and nonbreakable mirrors
6 months to 1 year:	cradle gyms, sturdy books, drums, manipulative toys, toys that make noises and busy boards
1 year to 18 months:	stacking toys, balls, large blocks, pounding toys, push-pull toys, books, simple puzzles, and tapes with simple stories or music
18 months to 3 years:	large blocks, crayons, puzzles, trucks, dolls, dramatic play toys, musical instruments, outdoor climbing equipment, sandboxes, sand toys, and water toys
3 years to 6 years:	dramatics play toys, puppets, playhouses, art materials, chalkboards, tricycles, bicycles, balls, simple games, books, simple board games

The caregiver needs to check the environment for the age appropriateness of toys, because different developmental levels affect the way children play with toys. Table 6.7 gives the caregivers a checklist for toy safety.

Art Supplies

Art supplies present some potential hazards. The hazards may be from inhaling, lead, or other dangerous substances, and mouthing the various materials used for art. The Federal Arts Materials Labeling Act took effect in 1990. Hazard-free art products should be labeled CP or AP. Products that may be potentially toxic should carry a health label that indicates caution or warning. Table 6.8 will help the caregiver lessen risk to safety when using art supplies.

TABLE **6.7**

Toy Safety Checklist

Check for:

- ☐ Age appropriate for the children playing with toy.

- ☐ Set safety rules for mixed age groups to keep toys for older children out of younger children's reach, and secure a place in the care environment where the older children can use these toys.

- ☐ No toys or toy parts smaller than 1½ inches.

- ☐ Check for sharp parts, points, rough edges, pinch points, and loose small parts.

- ☐ Check toys for durability—if it is easily broken, it is dangerous.

- ☐ Examine toys for construction, including stuffed animals that might have seams that would open easily or eyes that could be pulled off and swallowed.

- ☐ Throw out all pieces of broken toys, crayons, and games.

- ☐ Regularly check pacifiers that children use for nipples that resist pulling and for guards that cannot fit inside a child's mouth.

- ☐ Check instructions for art and craft supplies and make sure that they are nontoxic, washable, and environmentally safe.

- ☐ Check toys that are mouthed but too large to be swallowed to make sure they are washed after use.

- ☐ Check paint on toys to make sure it is lead-free.

- ☐ Toys with projectile parts are not present.

- ☐ Toy chests with lids are not present.

- ☐ All toys are flame resistant.

- ☐ Mobiles and other hanging toys are not used when infants are able to sit up.

- ☐ Toys are cleared and put away when not in use.

- ☐ Toys with pull strings are restricted to use for when an adult is present.

- ☐ Play areas are away from electrical cords, and other cords, such as telephone wires.

Common household products are often used to make art materials. Examples of these are play dough, cornstarch clay, and goop. If these items are used in the child care environment, children should be instructed in how to use them. Children should not mouth these materials and toddlers should be well monitored when these materials are used.

TABLE **6.8**

Keeping Art Safe

■ Avoid using any art supplies like tempera paint and clay that are dry and could be easily inhaled.

■ Avoid using any materials that contain lead or other hazardous substances that can cause poisoning if ingested.

■ Use poster paints, liquid paints, and water-based paints that are nontoxic.

■ Do not use rubber cement, epoxy, or instant glue. Use glue sticks, double sided tape, paste, or school glue. These should have the AP or CP label. Use only water-based glues, glue sticks, and paste.

■ Do not use permanent markers. Use only washable markers and avoid using scented markers that tempt children to put them in their mouths.

■ Avoid using empty film canisters for art projects as lids can be mouthed and have the potential hazard for choking.

■ When using small items such as beans, rice, or small styrofoam shapes for projects, always keep special watch because children may mouth their art materials and might choke on them. It is better to use these items only with older children.

KEY TOY SAFETY

CONCEPT

The child caregiver needs to supply toys and other play materials that are safe and as risk-free as possible. Toys should be examined for hazards. By using such tools as the choking hazard checklist and the toy safety checklist, the child caregiver can eliminate those toys that may present risk. Knowledge of age appropriate toys will help the child caregiver select toys that are safe for the care environment. If the environment is mixed age, supervision and safety practices should be used to make certain younger children are not playing with toys that may present risk to them. Art materials may pose risk. The child caregiver should be aware of these risks and do whatever is necessary to minimize them.

INTERPERSONAL SAFETY

Injuries to children by other children such as biting, kicking, scratching, and fighting are common in child care settings. Caregivers need to be prepared to intervene when behaviors that threaten interpersonal safety occur. They need to understand the background for such behavior and

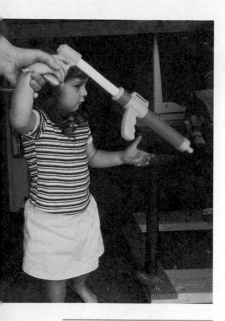

Even plastic toy guns pose a potential safety risk for children since they do not teach how dangerous guns are.

know strategies for eliminating that behavior and utilizing conflict resolution. The NAEYC's position statement on violence reflects this.

Exposure to Violence

Violence as a means of handling conflict has filtered down into early childhood. Children are seeing violent behavior modeled on television, on the streets, in their neighborhoods, and even in their homes. When children are angry, tired, or upset they may resort to behaviors that reflect their exposure to the violence in our society.

Interpersonal behaviors that threaten safety include biting, fighting, kicking, hitting, stealing, screaming, spitting, hard pushing, and threatening violence. These behaviors show aggression that may indicate a child has personal problems that may have to be addressed if the behavior continues.

Research has shown that children who have witnessed or been direct victims of violence can suffer from post-traumatic stress disorder. This disorder can be displayed by reliving the violence in play (Timnick, 1989). Children who display especially violent behavior may need special help, including psychological referrals. A conscientious caregiver can often handle violent behavior by observation, communication, and redirection.

Kevin lived in a neighborhood where he saw much violence. His child care center was in an inner city area. Jacob, Kevin's primary caregiver, noticed that Kevin seemed to become more and more aggressive in his play. One day Jacob decided to track Kevin's behavior. He counted four physical confrontations with friends, two biting incidents, and several threats. Jacob did not know what might have occurred to change Kevin's usually good behavior. Jacob spoke with Kevin's mother, Mona, and found that Kevin's older brother had been beaten up and Kevin had witnessed it. Jacob decided to try several things to help Kevin deal with his emotions.

First, Jacob talked to Kevin about his brother and what had occurred. He explained to Kevin how violence did not solve problems and that talking out feelings was better than acting on them. Jacob knew that this was not always easy. He decided to bring in a punching bag and placed it in a corner of the child care center so that using it would not put children at risk.

Jacob showed Kevin how to use the bag and he instructed Kevin to come and use it whenever angry feelings started to grow. Kevin began using it the next day. In fact, he spent a lot of time punching the bag. After a week or so, Kevin's behavior was noticeably improved, as was the interpersonal safety of the other children. Jacob noticed an interesting result in helping Kevin. Without discussing it, many of the children began using the punching bag when they were angry.

The amount of violence shown on television is increasing. It can be harmful to children and may cause children who watch it to be more aggressive with other children (ERIC Digest, 1990). The use of guns has escalated even among young children. Real firearms, not just toy guns, are a threat to many young children in their neighborhoods and their homes (Elders, 1994).

REALITY CHECK

Kids and Guns

Kids and guns cause a serious safety issue for this country. Approximately 1.2 million children over age six have access to guns in their homes. One in every four households contains a handgun ("Keep Kids Away From Guns," 1994). One in two households owns at least one gun. In the United States a child dies every 2 hours of a gunshot wound ("Children's Defense Fund Reports," 1994).

It is estimated than one in five high school students carries a gun or other weapon on a regular basis and may take it to school with them (Levin, 1994). Children are witnessing violence on the streets and in their homes. A Harvard poll revealed that 77 percent of the public believe that children's lives are at risk due to the number of guns available in this country ("Children's Defense Fund Reports," 1994). Statistics indicate that the number of juveniles who commit crimes will dramatically increase in the next decade ("Hopes and Fears," 1996). Many of those crimes will be committed with guns.

Children's development can be influenced by their exposure to violence (Levin, 1994). This exposure can be in the home or in the neighborhood. Children witness violence on television on a daily basis. Violence and the use of firearms is often treated humorously, such as on cartoons (Cohen, 1993/94).

Children need a sense of trust and safety so they can grow and develop to their potential. Children are witnessing that they may not be safe or protected in many of their life situations.

❝Children need to feel that they can direct part of their existence, but children who live with violence learn that they have little say in what happens to them. Beginning with the restrictions on autonomy when they are toddlers, this sense of helplessness continues as they reach school age.❞ (Wallach, 1994)

As they grow up, many children exposed to violence may begin to carry guns in order to feel safe and protected.

Children's curiosity about guns and how they work is encouraged by the violence they see on television. They are tempted by manufacturers of children's toys. Guns are everywhere. They are in poor neighborhoods and middle-class schools (Achenbach, 1994). All children are at risk for safety because of guns.

The child caregiver can do several things to protect children from guns. The family child caregiver can ensure that any firearm present in the home is kept out of sight, locked away, and separate from the ammunition. Caregivers can provide children with alternative forms of handling disagreements in a prosocial manner by teaching children to resolve their conflicts. Caregivers can insist that no toy guns be available for children to play with while at child care. They can forbid play with guns and use substitutes such as blocks or Legos. Caregivers can help educate parents about the dangers of guns. If television is available in the child care situation, caregivers can monitor programming and turn off violent programs or those programs that promote the use of guns to settle disagreements.

Strategies to Promote Positive Interaction

Caregiver awareness of unsafe behavior is the primary tool for safety promotion and prevention of injury in interpersonal relations among the children. Children learn best when appropriate behavior is modeled for them.

Strategies that the caregiver can use to promote positive social interaction and conflict resolution are listed in Table 6.9. The use of these strategies will be helpful to ensure a greater degree of interpersonal safety in the child care environment.

TABLE **6.9**

Strategies for Promoting Interpersonal Safety

- Help children recognize the difference between appropriate and inappropriate behaviors.

- Help children recognize that violence and antisocial behavior cause problems.

- Provide limits and consistent behavior.

- Acknowledge needs, fears, and wants of children.

- Realize negative behavior may indicate unmet needs of a child.

- Verbally redirect children's behavior.

- Model a full range of emotions in acceptable ways.

- Allow, identify, and react to a child's expression of emotion.

- Label expressions of emotions so children learn to identify those emotions.

- Use play, role playing, conversation, books, and pictures to explore and help the child express a range of feelings.

- Do not allow the use of toy guns.

- Avoid storing firearms in the child care environment, if possible. If present, the guns must be locked up and ammunition stored in a separate location.

- Support and encourage cooperation among the children during play.

- "Catch them being good" by acknowledging positive behaviors.

- Encourage those behaviors that promote conflict resolution.

KEY INTERPERSONAL SAFETY

CONCEPT

The child care environment may have situations involving behaviors that put interpersonal safety of those present at risk. Biting, kicking, and other aggressive behaviors can pose threats to other children and the caregiver. The effect that television and other media may have on how children behave in relation to violence needs to be addressed. Some types of child care environments may have guns present that would pose great risk if children were to gain access to them. It is very important that the caregiver use all the strategies for positive social interaction in order to resolve conflict and protect the interpersonal safety of those present in the child care environment.

POISON CONTROL

The most common emergency involving children is accidental poisoning. Although most poisoning occurs in the home, it also occurs in child care. Children under four years of age are the most likely to ingest poisons. Because children are so mobile, the caregiver must use prevention as the primary means of poison control.

The first order of prevention is vigilance in monitoring the children in care. This is only effective if the environment has been modified for safety. Removing all hazards and risks for exposure to poisons provides a protected environment.

Medications and poisonous substances should be either kept out of reach of small children or securely locked in cabinets with safety latches.

Examining the Environment

Poisoning occurs from many common items found in a household or child care environment. Cleaners, medicines, laundry supplies, cosmetics, plants, pesticides, garden supplies, automobile fluids, and certain foods can poison a child who ingests them. The caregiver should make a room by room inspection for poisons in the child care environment. If the child care is performed in a home, special care should be taken to inspect the entire environment. Bathrooms, bedrooms, kitchens, and garages are full of poisonous substances that may go unnoticed in daily life, if children are not

TABLE **6.10**

Common Hazardous Substances Found in the Home

Bathrooms	
■ Prescription drugs	■ Antacids
■ Over-the-counter medicines, creams, and lotions	■ Hair care products
■ Peroxide, alcohol, mercurochrome, and other medications for injuries	■ Makeup and skin care products
	■ Nail products such as polish and polish remover
■ Vitamins, iron pills, and other dietary supplements	■ Hair removal products
■ Cleaning solutions	■ Electric blow dryers, curling irons, and radios

Bedroom	
■ Birth control pills, foams, and so forth	■ Hair care products
■ Body lotions	■ Makeup and skin care products

Kitchen	
■ All-purpose cleaning products	■ Alcoholic beverages
■ Detergents	■ Bleach
■ Polishes for silver, brass, chrome, and so forth	■ Oven cleaning products
■ Baking sprays and oils	■ Waxes and other appliance care products
■ Insecticides	■ Floor care products

Garage	
■ Gasoline	■ Laundry products
■ Motor oil, lubricants, and other engine care products	■ Solvents
■ Waxes, detergents, and other car care products	■ Paint and paint removal products
■ Insecticides and pesticides	■ Glue

present. Table 6.10 gives the caregiver a list of common substances that are poisonous to children that are found in the home.

Strategies for Removal of Risk from Poison and Toxins in Child Care

The caregiver who anticipates, modifies the environment, and monitors children carefully should be able to avoid risk due to poisoning. Poisonings can occur in five ways:

1. Ingestion
2. Contact
3. Inhalation
4. Animal, insect, or reptile bites
5. Injection

Ingestion is swallowing the poison. Children are attracted to bright colorful packages, pills, and odd shapes. They often encounter containers that have been used for food or drink that now contain poisonous substances.

Contact occurs when poisonous substances or plants come in contact with the skin. This type of poisoning is indirect; the poison is absorbed through the skin into the bloodstream. *Inhalation* occurs when children breathe fumes from pesticides, certain types of art materials, or dust that may contain lead. The exchange of air in the lungs allows the poison to come in direct contact with the lungs, after which it then enters the bloodstream.

Animal and insect bites can cause allergies in children. Some allergic reactions are very toxic and can lead to death. Certain insect bites can cause health and safety risks. These include ticks, which cause Lyme disease or Rocky Mountain spotted fever. Reptiles such as rattle snakes and copperhead snakes can bite children and cause the poison to enter the bloodstream. Other safety hazards such as cat scratch fever, rabies, and salmonella can come from bites or other types of direct contact with animals.

Injection occurs when there is a puncture wound. The danger may come from the substance that was injected or remnants of tetanus on the item that caused the puncture. Today there is an extra threat of children finding needles that have been used to inject drugs. An accident like this can cause the child to be exposed to HIV.

Table 6.11 includes caregiver strategies for promoting poison control protection in the child care environment.

Plants that Pose Risk

Plants are another poisonous hazard found in the indoor environment. The caregiver should be familiar with the types of plants that may be present. All plants should be out of reach of children. Any plants that are potentially hazardous to children should be removed from the child care environment. Table 6.12 lists indoor plants that pose risk for poisoning.

Some common indoor plants such as this philodendron are poisonous. To protect the children in their care, caregivers need to know which plants are poisonous and keep them out of the children's reach. *(Courtesy of Interior Plantscape, division of ACLA)*

TABLE **6.11**

Strategies for Promoting Poison Control

■ Always supervise children in your care.

■ Keep poisons out of sight and reach of children and in a locked cabinet.

■ Keep medicines, household cleaners, and laundry products in their original containers. Never store nonfood items in food containers.

■ Use childproof safety caps.

■ Use safety latches or locks on all storage cupboards.

■ Never call medicine candy and do not take medicine in front of children—they love to imitate.

■ Inspect your child care location from a child's eye view—on your hands and knees to check the environment for poison risks.

■ Determine that all the plants in your environment are nonpoisonous (see Table 6.12).

■ Keep pets in a regulated environment.

■ Keep the environment free of insects.

■ Teach poison prevention to the children and child care providers who are in the child care facility.

■ Keep the local poison control center number on your phone.

■ Keep parents informed about poison control.

■ Keep a bottle of syrup of Ipecac at your facility.

■ When prevention fails, learn to act immediately in an educated manner.

TABLE **6.12**

Common Indoor Plants that Pose Risk for Poisoning

Plant	Reaction
Philodendra Schefflera Pothos	Burning and irritation of the lining of the mouth, tongue, and lips. Can be fatal. May also cause skin reaction.
Diffenbachia Elephant ear	Intense burning and irritation of the lining of the mouth and tongue. If tongue swells it may cause blockage to air passage and result in death.
Hyacinth Narcissus Daffodil	These bulbs are often found indoors in late winter and early spring. Nausea, diarrhea, and vomiting. Can be fatal.
Castor bean Rosary pea	Fatal. A single pea or bean is enough to kill a child.
Poinsettia	Nausea, skin reactions

KEY POISON CONTROL

CONCEPT

Poison control is an essential task of the caregiver. The environment should be examined for poisons. Safety risks from poisons in the child care environment can be reduced through removal, proper storage, supervision, and using as few poisonous products as possible. Good safety practices and supervision help prevent accidents involving poisoning. Plants in the environment should be nonpoisonous and should be kept away from children.

FIRE AND BURN PREVENTION

Children are very susceptible to fires and burns because they are so curious and do not yet recognize dangers. Injuries from these accidents are the second leading cause of death among American children. Thirty-five percent of all burn injuries happen to children; scalding is the chief cause of burns to children of preschool age. Fires caused by playing with matches and lighters are the number one cause of fire-related deaths among young children. The concept of cause and effect is not operational enough to help children protect themselves unless they are repeatedly taught fire and burn prevention and safety.

Environmental Hazards

The caregiver must be aware of all the things in the child care environment that can present hazards and present fire and burn risks. Table 6.13 gives an overview of typical environmental hazards that may be present.

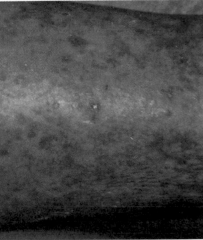

First, second, and third degree burns. In second degree burns, such as shown here, the outer and inner skin layers are burned and usually blister. If nerve endings are exposed to air or are affected by swelling, the injury may be very painful.

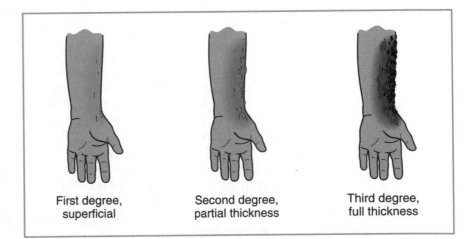

First degree, superficial

Second degree, partial thickness

Third degree, full thickness

TABLE **6.13**

Environmental Hazards for Burns

Scalding

- ■ Boiling liquids or food on or off stove
- ■ Steam
- ■ Hot coffee or cocoa
- ■ Hot bath water or water out of tap more than 120°F

Electrical

- ■ Sticking a foreign object into an electrical outlet
- ■ Touching a live wire
- ■ Water contact with an electrical appliance

Contact

- ■ Hot pan on stove
- ■ Touching fire in fireplace
- ■ Candles or candle wax
- ■ Cigarettes, cigars, or pipes
- ■ Matches, lighters
- ■ Flammable clothing or sleeping materials

Chemical

- ■ Strong household chemicals
- ■ Automobile chemicals
- ■ Lawn and garden chemicals

Strategies for Fire and Burn Prevention

It is up to the caregiver to help the children be aware of hazards that can cause fires or burns. Children should regularly be taught to avoid matches and lighters. These items should be stored out of sight and not used unless necessary. Children should also have regular practice drills for fire evacuation and should know how to "Stop, Drop, and Roll." Safety devices such as fire extinguishers and smoke alarms should be present and in working condition. As with any safety hazard, the caregiver is ultimately responsible for keeping children safe. Modeling preventive behaviors will reinforce fire and burn accident prevention. Table 6.14 gives the caregiver some strategies that will help prevent fires and burns in the child care environment.

TABLE **6.14**

Strategies for Fire and Burn Prevention

■ Use only correct size fuses in the fuse box.

■ Install and regularly check smoke detectors. Change batteries frequently.

■ Teach children to Stop, Drop, and Roll. Be sure to include keeping their faces covered with their hands during the Roll portion.

■ Keep a fire extinguisher on hand, know how to use it, and refill it immediately upon use.

■ Place and maintain barriers around fireplaces, heaters, radiators, and hot pipes.

■ Try not to use matches or lighters around children. If present, store out of sight in a locked cabinet or drawer.

■ Teach children to bring you any matches they find. If they find a lighter have them immediately tell you so that you can pick it up.

■ Use safety devices to cover electrical outlets.

■ Inspect and clean heating systems including stoves and fireplaces once a year.

■ Make sure there are sufficient outlets for all appliances to prevent overloading electrical wiring.

■ Place smoke alarms around the child care and check the batteries on a regular basis.

■ Keep extension cords exposed; do not run them under furniture or rugs.

■ Keep all flammable liquids stored in safety cans and out of reach of children.

■ Keep furnaces, heating equipment, and chimneys and flues cleaned regularly.

■ Never allow children in food preparation area without supervision.

■ Do not drink or carry anything hot when close to a child.

■ Test hot food before giving it to a child.

■ Never warm a bottle in the microwave.

■ Set water heaters to no higher than 120°F.

■ Never bathe a child in water you have not tested.

■ Never leave children unattended in the bath or near a faucet. They might turn on the hot water.

■ Turn pot handles in toward center or rear of stove and only cook on rear burners when possible.

■ Never use portable, open-flame, or space heaters.

■ Never smoke around children.

■ Never store flammable liquids such as gasoline near the child care environment.

KEY FIRE AND BURN PREVENTION

CONCEPT

The caregiver should actively practice fire and burn prevention. Burn hazards to children come from many areas. Children can be burned from scalding hazards, electrical hazards, hazards that are directly contacted with heat or fire, and by chemical hazards. The child caregiver needs to use all strategies available to protect the children in child care from any hazards that might cause fires or burns.

IMPLICATIONS FOR **CAREGIVERS**

The child caregiver should use observation, supervision, and education to provide a safe indoor environment. These risk management tools provide preventive and protective measures for the child care environment.

Table 6.15 shows is a safety policy for the child caregiver to prevent choking and suffocation. This measure uses all of the risk management tools previously mentioned.

TABLE **6.15**

Preventing Choking and Suffocation in Child Care

- ☐ Remove loose parts from toys.
- ☐ Use a choke testing device on small toys. Always do this before adding a questionable toy to the environment.
- ☐ Keep diaper and other pins, toothpicks, and nails out of your mouth.
- ☐ Do not wear dangle type jewelry like necklaces and earrings.
- ☐ Check toys, games, and art supplies for broken pieces and throw away.
- ☐ Teach children not to run with anything in their mouths.
- ☐ Teach children to chew well and not allow playing when eating.
- ☐ Never prop a baby bottle.
- ☐ Never use styrofoam cups—children like to chew them.
- ☐ Regularly hand out consumer toy alerts as you find them. Newspapers and magazines carry this information, particularly around Christmas.

Observation

Observation for accessories, behaviors, and conditions offers the caregiver the awareness needed to prevent risk in the indoor environment. Knowledge of hazards in equipment, toys and craft supplies, and poisons helps the caregiver remove these items and reduce risk. Observation adds another layer of protection. The caregiver needs to also be aware of unsafe interpersonal behavior practices. This may help the caregiver to stop or redirect action before it causes injury. The child care environment should also be inspected for fire and burn hazards. Children should be carefully observed to avoid burns or fires.

Supervision

The greatest concern for supervision is the constant monitoring of children for safety in all situations. In addition, all safe practices, methods of prevention, and means of promotion should be monitored by the caregiver. This will ensure that every measure possible is being used to provide a safe environment. Checking for compliance with licensing standards, local fire safety guidelines, and other safety related ordinances is another way to monitor the environment for safety. Communication is a tool that the caregiver can use to make sure safe practices are being used by all adults in the child care environment.

Education

Prevention of safety risks is promoted through education of child caregivers, children, and their parents. The more tools everyone has for becoming aware of hazards, developmental limitations, and the child care environment, the greater the opportunities that are available to prevent accidents and injuries.

Children can be taught many safe behaviors through a number of methods and curriculum. Visitors such as firefighters and police officers can show children how to keep safe. Caregivers can be role models of safe behaviors everyday. They can read books and provide videotapes that will help children become aware of the need for safe practices. Caregivers can conduct regular drills for fire and other safety threats. They can practice "Stop, Drop, and Roll" with children on a regular basis. Caregivers can talk with children about appropriate and inappropriate interpersonal behaviors.

Caregivers can provide parents with information about safety by handing out information sheets or handouts supplied by agencies such as fire departments, poison control, and police departments. They can request parents and children to practice fire drills at home on a regular basis.

KEY IMPLICATIONS FOR CAREGIVERS

CONCEPT

The child caregiver should use all measures possible to protect the children and prevent injury. Tools such as observation, supervision, and education can provide practices for the caregiver to ensure safety through promotion, prevention, and protection.

CHAPTER **SUMMARY**

There are a number of threats to indoor safety, including indoor equipment, toys, interpersonal behaviors, poisons, and fires and burns. Safety policies are necessary for the caregiver to monitor and protect the environment. An understanding of the developmental level of the children present is essential. The caregiver should use checklists to monitor and modify the child care environment. All items, including cleaning supplies, pets, plants, and art supplies, should be examined for safety, and should be removed if they present risk. Caregivers should promote and practice safe behaviors by using observation, supervision, and education.

TO GO **BEYOND**

Questions for Review

1. Compare the safety policies for the indoor environment found in a child care center and a family child care home. How are these policies affected by the ages of children in care?
2. Discuss the need for safe, risk-free toys. How does age appropriateness affect toy selection?
3. Discuss the importance of conflict resolution for interpersonal safety in child care.

AS AN **INDIVIDUAL**

1. Visit a child care center and survey it for indoor safety. Write down the risks observed and bring back to class to share.
2. Take the list of indoor plants found in this chapter to a local nursery or flower shop and identify poisonous indoor plants that you find there. Have you seen any of these plants in a household that has children in it?

AS A **GROUP**

1. List the developmental level risks for an 18-month-old toddler in an indoor environment at a day care center, then a family child care home.
2. Design a child care center room for two years olds that includes all the amenities, while being low risk.

CHAPTER **REFERENCES**

Achenbach, J. (1994, September/October). Guns and kids. *Family Life,* 67–72.
American Public Health Association & American Academy of Pediatrics (1992). *Caring for our children: National health and safety performance standards:*

Guidelines for out-of-home care. Washington, DC: American Public Health Association.

Children's Defense Fund Reports. (1994). Violence: Every two hours a gun kills a child. Washington, DC: Children's Defense Fund.

Chiara, S. (1995, February 2). American child care called unfit. *San Diego Union-Tribune,* A-10,11.

Cohen, S. (1993/94, Winter). Television in the lives of children and their families. *Childhood Education,* 103–104.

Cowley, G. (1993). Children in peril. *Newsweek,* Special Issue, 18–21.

Elders, J. (1994). Violence as a public health issue. *Childhood Education, 70*(5), 260–262.

ERIC Digest. (1990). *Guidelines for family television viewing.* Champaign, IL: Eric Clearinghouse on Elementary and Early Childhood Education.

Hopes and fears: Working together to find solutions to youth violence. (1996, June 16). *San Diego Union-Tribune,* Special section.

Keep kids away from guns. (1994, November). *Parent's Magazine.*

Langlois, J., Walker, B., Terrt, S., Bailey, L., Hershey, H., & Peeler, M. (1991). The impact of specific toy warning labels. *Journal of the American Medical Association, 265*(21), 2848–2850.

Levin, D. (1994). Building a peaceable classroom—Helping young children to feel safe in violent times. *Childhood Education, 70*(5), 267–270.

Mickalaide, A. (1994). Creating safer environments for children. *Childhood Education, 70*(5), 263–266.

Rosenblum, G. (1993, November). Is your house making your children sick? *Sesame Street Parents,* 68–72.

Timnick, L. (1989, September 3). Children of violence. *Los Angeles Times Magazine,* 6–15.

Wallach, L. (1994). *Violence and young children's development.* ERIC Digest. Champaign, IL: Eric Clearinghouse on Elementary and Early Childhood Education.

SUGGESTIONS **FOR READING**

Chiara, S. (1994). Television in the lives of children and their families. *Childhood Education, 70*(2), 103–104.

Latona, V. (1996, August/September). What on earth? Healthy Kids, 43-46.

Protecting your baby from environmental hazards (1994. February). Child Magazine, 75-79.

Violence threatens our youth. (1993/94, Winter). *Childhood Education,* 96-E.

Outdoor Safety

Upon completion of this chapter, including a review of the summary, you should be able to:

Safety Policies for the Outdoor Environment

Describe and discuss safety policies for outdoor environments as tools for risk prevention, protection, and promotion.

Examining Childcare Environments for Outdoor Hazards

Indicate and discuss specific guidelines for making the child care playground environment free from risk and protected for safety.

Playground Equipment Safety

Relate and discuss the safety hazards of outdoor equipment as they relate to child care situations and general safety.

Traffic and Transportation Safety

Relate the guidelines for safe transportation and traffic involved in child care situations.

Water Safety

Describe and discuss the water safety hazards in outdoor child care.

Implications for Caregivers

Indicate the need for education, observation, and supervision to maintain a safe outdoor environment.

SAFETY POLICIES FOR THE OUTDOOR ENVIRONMENT

Unintentional accidents and risks to safety are more likely to occur in the outdoor environment than indoors. Some risks may be similar, such as drowning, falling, choking, and poisons. Other hazards, such as automobiles and bicycles, are responsible for a large number of childhood injuries and deaths each year. The following factors indicate a need for outdoor safety policies:

■ More than half of the injuries in child care centers result from falls. Falls from playground equipment account for almost half of the serious injuries (Aronson, 1994).

■ Playgrounds should provide both play value and safety for health development (Frost, 1994).

■ Approximately 3 million thefts and violent crimes occur near public schools each year (Levin, 1994). Many child care centers and family child care homes are close to schools; thus, they are at risk for safety.

■ Motor vehicles cause most accidental deaths of children (Windome, 1992). The majority of these fatalities could be prevented with the use of a safety seat restraint.

■ Nearly 400,000 children each year are treated in an emergency room for bicycle related injuries (Mickalaide, 1994).

Even something as common as duct tape covering a damaged slide is a potential safety risk for the children using this piece of playground equipment.

Safety policies for the outdoor environment need to cover a wide range of areas. Not all the policies in this chapter will apply to all child care environments. Vulnerability to safety will come from a number of risks. These risks may come from playground equipment, travel, traffic, bicycles, bodies of water, and the nearby neighborhood. Some of the hazards are related to accessories such as improper equipment or lack of proper cushioning under equipment. Behaviors such as lack of attention or a child trying a physical act he is not capable of performing may present risks. Conditions such as the child being tired or the caregiver talking to another adult can cause risk.

Policies should cover monitoring accessories, conditions, and behaviors. They should comply with local licensing regulations and suggestions for accreditation, if applicable. Planning and promoting safe practices should be based on children's physical and developmental abilities as well as their emotional needs. Safety policies should include:

1. *Outdoor Child Care Environments:* understanding outdoor safety practices for the child care environment and applications for risk management as they apply to the type of outdoor environment.

2. *Playground Equipment Safety:* practices for preventing injuries and managing safety on playground equipment.

3. *Travel and Traffic Safety:* practices for preventing injury, promoting safety, and strategies for developing guidelines for travel and traffic as it applies to child care.

4. *Water Safety:* practices for removing hazards, promoting safety, and preventing injury as it applies to water in the child care environment.

5. *Implications for Caregivers:* methods and practices for conducting education, supervision, and observation and using outside resources for safety in the outdoor environment.

KEY OUTDOOR SAFETY POLICIES

CONCEPT

The outdoor environment offers a large degree of risk for child care. Outdoor safety policies should begin with examining the child care environment. Policies should be created for playground equipment, traffic and travel safety, water safety, and implications for the caregivers.

EXAMINING CHILD CARE ENVIRONMENTS FOR OUTDOOR HAZARDS

Outdoor environments may vary greatly from one child care situation to the next, but they all have common features that contribute to outdoor childhood accidents. These relate to:

■ Falls

■ Motor vehicle and other transportation accidents

■ Poisons

■ Equipment

The environmental screening for safety should address the ABCs of injury risk (refer back to Table 5.5). The caregiver must anticipate problems, modify the environment, and monitor the children in care for unsafe practices. The caregiver must also be aware of conditions and behaviors that lead to injury in the outdoor environment.

Outdoor Environmental Hazards

The child care outdoor site should be free of hazards. Protective measures and preventive practices can help reduce the risk that accessories may provide in the outdoor environment of the child care site. General environment hazards include lack of barriers, poisons, insects, and extremes of temperature. Other considerations may also present risk to the outdoor environment.

Barriers. The play area should have a fence or other barrier that surrounds it and be at least four feet high. A fence should separate the play area from all automobile traffic and any hidden corners of the outdoor area that may go unobserved if a child wanders into that corner. Fences should be constructed of safe materials and kept intact and in working order. Gates should fasten securely and should have latches high enough to be out of the reach of children or should have a safety latch that is child proof.

Poison Control. Poison control in the outdoor environment is essential. Toxic plants are the most common hazard for poison in the outdoors. Table 7.1 has a comprehensive listing of toxic outdoor plants.

Other poison hazards include pesticides, insecticides, other gardening materials, and barbecue supplies. If these are in the environment, they should be placed up high and in a locked cabinet. If a garage or workshop is present on the site where automobile repair fluids or gasoline are present, this area should be off limits and fenced off or have a locked door as a barrier to this area.

Keep the outdoor area as free from pollutants as possible. Use insect sprays sparingly and only when children are not present. If lawns are sprayed with weed killers or fertilizers, wait several days before allowing children to play on them. Also, keep the environment free of poison ivy, poison oak, and sumac, which can cause rashes that may spread on contact. Remove these plants from the environment but do not burn them as the fumes can damage the lining of a child's lung.

Insects. Insect safety is important. Although bites and stings do not usually seriously harm a child, some children may be especially sensitive. To avoid stings, do not use scented soaps or lotions and make sure children wear shoes. Children in bright colors seem to attract insects, so remind parents of this during high insect season. Do not let children in areas where insects gather or where food is left uncovered.

TABLE **7.1**

Common Outdoor Poisonous Plants

Flowers	
Azaleas	Hyacinth
Bleeding heart	Iris
Calla lily	Jonquil
Daffodil	Larkspur
Delphinium	Lily-of-the-valley
Foxglove	Lobelia
Four o'clock	Rhododendron

Shrubs and Trees	
Black locust	Oak
China berry	Oleander
Holly berries	Poison hemlock
Elderberry	Pencil tree
Jerusalem cherry	Wild cherry
Mistletoe	Wisteria
Night blooming jasmine	Yellow jasmine
Nightshade	

Vines	
Boston ivy	English ivy
Devil's ivy	Morning glory

Vegetable Plants	
Tomato vines	Potato sprouts and leaves
Rhubarb leaf	

Teach children what beehives and wasp's nests look like. The outdoor environment should be inspected and rid of insect infestation and ant hills. No standing water that allows insect breeding should be present in the child care environment.

Some areas of the country have problems with ticks that can cause Lyme disease in children. In these areas children should be dressed in high socks and their clothing should be checked for ticks before coming indoors. Remind parents to check children during bath time. If pets are in the child care environment, inspect them daily and remove any ticks that are found.

Temperature.   Extremes of temperature are potential hazards for children. Protection from heat stroke or heat exhaustion is a major consideration for outdoor play areas. Shade should be present in the outdoor area. If it is not naturally available, provide a shade structure. Children need the relief from the sun and heat to prevent overheating. All facilities should also have a safe outdoor source of drinking water to protect children from overheating or becoming dehydrated.

Freezing temperatures and snow on outdoor equipment may result in slippery surfaces that cause children to fall more easily. Before going outdoors in these conditions, check equipment surfaces to make sure they are safe and not slippery. Children should be dressed warmly when playing outdoors in the cold.

Other Considerations. Other backyard safety considerations for the outdoor area include keeping bushes and trees trimmed so children do not run into branches and injure themselves. Trimming trees will also discourage or prevent climbing. If there is dirt in the environment, make sure it is not so fine that it will cause breathing problems for some children. Always check the outdoor environment after storms, high winds, and heavy rains.

Some family child care backyards or shared facilities may have barbecues present. This implies potential for harm from lighter fluid, barbecue utensils, and the barbecue itself. Other common hazards in these two environments are gardening tools and equipment. All of these hazards should be kept in a garage, barn, or out of the reach of children.

Items such as toxic fumes, gases, and air conditioner units should not impact the outdoor environment. Child care environments should not be less than 30 feet from high-voltage power stations, railroad tracks, and electrical substations. The facility should be maintained in a safe condition by removing any sharp rocks, building supplies, or dilapidated structures. The outdoor area should be free of unprotected ditches, cesspools, wells, and utility equipment (APHA and AAP, 1992). Abandoned appliances should not be present in the child care environment.

Limit children going barefoot to areas where the surfaces are safe. Confine pets to certain areas during child care and remove animal feces often. Treat the feces as you would disposing of a diaper, following the same procedure as in Table 3.6.

Developmental Level

The impact that behavior has on risk for safety is especially crucial in an outdoor environment. The majority of accidents happen outdoors. Children's developmental behaviors such as lack of fear, curiosity, inattention, and going beyond physical capabilities can easily put them at risk for injury. Caregivers may not be paying adequate attention or may not properly communicate the risk of certain outdoor hazards.

Using developmental levels to define the boundaries of the outdoor environment will help the caregiver screen for accessories, behaviors, and conditions that lead to injuries. Prevention is the key to risk management. Planning and evaluating the environment based on the vulnerabilities of the children in care will help increase protection. Developmental levels of the children in care should be used as the starting point for screening the outdoor environment for hazards. Table 7.2 indicates the relationship of outdoor safety hazards to the developmental levels by age. This chart also indicates the greatest threats to safety at particular ages.

TABLE **7.2**

Outdoor Safety Hazards by Developmental Levels of Age

Age	Hazards	Prevention Tips
0–6 months	Motor Vehicle	Infant should always be in rear-facing infant safety seat.
6 months–1 year	Motor Vehicle	Continue using safety seat; switch to toddler seat when able to sit up by self.
	Poisons	Watch child for mouthing of objects. Check area for poisonous plants.
	Choking	Watch child for mouthing of objects.
	Drowning	Keep pool covered, fenced, and lock gate.
1–2 years	Motor Vehicle	Continue using safety seat.
	Falls	Carefully watch while climbing on outdoor equipment. Teach child safe play practices.
	Equipment	Check playground equipment for rough edges, rust, loose parts. Wood chips or soft sand are best ground coverings under play equipment.
	Poisons	Place all outdoor chemicals, and so forth, in high place, preferably locked. Check area for poisonous plants.
	Drowning	Cover, fence, and lock gate to pool. Always supervise child when playing near pool or any body of water.
2–3 years	Motor Vehicle	Keep child away from streets and driveways using supervision, fences, and firm discipline. Role model pedestrian behavior such as crossing street. Role model wearing seat belt in car and use safety seat for child.
	Falls	Carefully supervise when on equipment. Reinforce safe behavior on equipment.
	Poisons	Keep poisons up high and locked. Check for poisonous plants.
	Drowning	Always supervise when near any body of water. Begin to teach water safety, including role modeling. Cover, fence, and lock gate to pool.
	Equipment	Check equipment for hazards. Supervise and role model safety.
3 years and up	Motor Vehicle	Use safety seat or seat belt for child. Teach pedestrian and traffic safety rules. Role model this behavior.
	Equipment	Reinforce safe play habits. Supervise when using tools. Check equipment for hazards.
	Drowning	Children should have swimming lessons if they are in care near a body of water. Teach water safety.
	Violence	Teach children neighborhood safety, including safe houses and familiarity with law enforcement.

To avoid collisions, there should be a separate tricycle path on the playground and traffic on the path should be one-way only.

When the caregiver realizes the hazards that make children at risk by age level, it will be much easier to carry out safe practices, appraise risks, and avoid potential dangerous situations.

As the caregiver inspects the outdoor environment, age appropriateness should be kept in mind. If there are children of different ages and they play at the same time, the caregiver will need to provide low barriers that prevent infants and toddlers from using equipment intended for older children. These barriers provide the caregiver more time to watch the children for safety and less time for worry.

Infants and Toddlers. The outdoor play area for infants and toddlers should consist of flexible materials that offer no hazards due to the common "mouthing" of children of this age. The emphasis for this age group is sensory motor activity, so the outdoor equipment for this age group should reflect that need. These children will be exploring and mastering their environment so it is imperative that there be a safe place for them to investigate.

Preschool. As the caregiver looks at the environment with preschool children in mind, the task is to see if enough space has been provided for the children to be as active as this age group is likely to be. Are there areas for exercise play, construction play, and dramatic play, as well as solitary play? Are the climbers and swings at appropriate heights or are they too high or too low? Does this inappropriate height level provide risk? The AAP standard for children six years old and under is that no structure shall be more than 5½ feet tall. When structures are more than that, research indicates that injuries are more serious. Do the climbers, swings, and slides have appropriate cushioning materials under them? Are these structures free of loose or rusty parts? A complete checklist for these pieces of equipment is found in

Table 7.4. The caregiver should ensure that the children have been given guidelines for the use of swings, slides, and climbing equipment and should remind them on a constant basis of proper use.

School Age. Children of this age have good coordination and are physically capable of most activities. The caregiver should provide equipment that will offer children the ability to use their skills. Is there enough equipment available so that children do not become bored and find inappropriate activities to engage in that may pose risks? Does the equipment provide options for degree of difficulty for children of different ability levels? For example, does the climbing structure provide different heights, a number of exits, and areas that challenge skills yet does not threaten the safety of a child with less physical abilities? Managing risks by age appropriateness will minimize the risk and provide greater protection.

Space

Child care facilities vary greatly. Each facility's outdoor area will be unique and present conditions that may be unsafe or lead to risk. Adequate outdoor space is important to prevent crowding of children and equipment. Space must also be provided to allow safety zones around large equipment so there is no encroachment by other equipment or potential for collision with other children playing in the area. The rule of thumb is a clearance of 9 feet around stationary equipment and 15 feet around equipment with moving parts, such as swings.

The outdoor play area should provide 50 square feet of space for each child. If equipment areas are figured in, this generally translates to about 75 square feet per child (APHA & AAP, 1992). If this is not possible in the child care environment, but there is a large indoor activity area such as a gym

This playground provides children with a safe environment; children are visible to the caregiver at all times, swings are not in a walking area, and the entire playground is fenced to keep strangers out while protecting children from wandering.

available, then that area can be used for some outdoor types of activities and space is less likely to be a risk factor.

The total outdoor play area may not be utilized by all the children at once, so the total area need not reflect space for all children present. The general standard in that situation is that there be enough space for one-third of the children in care to play at any one time and that the outdoor scheduling accommodate all children over a period of time without space being an issue. If the entire play area is utilized at the same time then space becomes a more critical issue.

The outdoor space should be arranged so that all play areas are visible to the caregiver at all times. This allows for prevention of injury and abuse and gives children a more secure feeling. Bathrooms should be close enough to the outdoor play area so that the caregiver can keep an eye on the children in the outdoor area and the child who is using the toilet facilities.

Shared Space

A shared space facility can present a distinctive set of dangers that need to be managed for risk. The outdoor environment of these facilities may not meet child care safety standards. Close inspection and constant observation are vital to the children in care under these situations.

Using a list similar to Table 6.3, the outdoor environment should be inspected every morning before it is used. Remove all debris, trash, and anything else that may have been discarded in the play area. Inspect the area for animal droppings.

For public multi-use facilities in inner city areas, particular caution should be taken to inspect for sharp objects such as broken glass, razors, and needles from syringes. Also inspect the area for discarded condoms, clothing, and so on that may pose risk for infectious diseases.

Maureen and Sara were two child caregivers at an inner city child care center. One Monday morning they decided to take the children to the park next door. Several of the children were excited and really wanted to get on the slide, the swings, and the climbing structure. The children had seen their caregivers go through an inspection process before, but they rarely found any hazards. Several of the children voiced displeasure about the inspection but Maureen and Sara insisted the children wait. On this morning they were very surprised to find razor blades placed on the slide. The caregivers showed the children this hazard and explained what might have happened. The children never complained about the safety inspection again. ■

In cases where the facility includes a swimming pool or other body of water, particular care should be taken to make sure that all safety devices are in place, including shutting the gate to this area of the facility before children are allowed outside to play.

When the multi-use facility is a family home in the evenings and on the weekends, the caregiver should routinely inspect the outside for hazards he knows might remain after normal family use. For example, if there are pets, a check for animal feces should be a regular morning event, or if someone barbecued the night before, a check for matches and lighter fluid might be necessary.

Time of Day

Many outdoor accidents can occur at any time of day. Poisoning, choking, drowning, and burns occur because of the potential hazards in the environment. Many accidents and injuries occur because children cannot understand cause and effect. This may relate to developmental level.

Some accidents seem to occur at particular times of day, when children are tired or hungry and are not concentrating on what they are doing. The caregiver should be aware of the times in the child care environment that a child appears to be tired or indicates that she is hungry. Monitoring can help prevent risk. The caregiver can modify the environment by changing the schedule to avoid the outdoor environment at the times of day that seem to pose a higher risk.

The Neighborhood

The neighborhood contributes to the child care environment. It may offer conditions that support child care or it may offer risks to child care. The caregiver needs to be aware of the neighborhood and plan for safety for the child care accordingly.

A supportive environment is one that has little traffic, no noise pollution, and poses little risk for the safety of children. It may be a neighborhood where people know and support each other and the safety of the area. There may be community resources such as a park or recreation center that pose no risk for violence or injury.

Many neighborhoods do not offer an environment that supports safety. A number of risks may come from a neighborhood where the child care is situated. There may be traffic, people who do not belong coming in and out of the area, and noise pollution. There may be community resources that are not safe areas for children. It is up to the caregiver to determine what the risks are in the neighborhood. Once these risks are determined, the caregiver should do everything possible to minimize the risk to the children in care.

REALITY CHECK

Neighborhood Violence

Someone is raped, murdered, assaulted, or robbed every sixteen seconds in the United States (Moyers, 1995). Children are often victims of violence and may react by being instruments for violent behavior themselves (Clemente, 1995). Many children are finding that the world is no longer a safe place. It is dangerous and people use violence to hurt each other (Levin, 1994).

Exposure to neighborhood violence can put children at risk for safety as well as for good mental health. It can also put them at risk for performing violent crimes later in life. A Los Angeles psychiatrist, Dr. William Arroyo, has worked with a number of children affected by violence. He reports that as children become more exposed to violence, they become desensitized to it (Timnick, 1989). Children may lose their perspective of what is right and what is wrong.

Violence is becoming a standard in our society (Figure 7.1). It permeates neighborhoods in the inner cities and is reaching out to suburban and rural areas. Neighborhood violence is severely affecting the children in this country. More children are reported to have post-traumatic stress disorder (Molnar, 1992). Many of the victims and perpetrators of violence may be parents of young children (Zero to Three, 1991).

Children's ability to cope with violence and the resulting trauma may depend on several factors:

(1) age, (2) developmental stage, (3) the availability of resources to help them, and (4) the ability of the children to use those resources (Groves, 1991).

Another factor affecting children's development is that if the people who surround them are viewed as possibly dangerous, they are less likely to interact with them (Haberman, 1994).

Caregivers can offer children a safe haven from a violent world. They can monitor their neighborhood environment for safety on a constant basis. They can access resources such as police and public health to help offer children a greater degree of protection. Caregivers can encourage children to become less violent and be more gentle (Haberman, 1994). They can help children acknowledge their feelings. When children become angry, caregivers can show them appropriate ways to express their anger. Caregivers can offer children a person they can trust and relate to. For part of every day, neighborhood violence can be eliminated from children's lives.

FIGURE **7.1**

Continuum of Violence in Children's Lives *(Reprinted with permission from* Teaching Your Children in Violent Times: Building a Peaceable Classroom *by Diane E. Levin, 1994. Cambridge, MA: Educators for Social Responsibility.)*

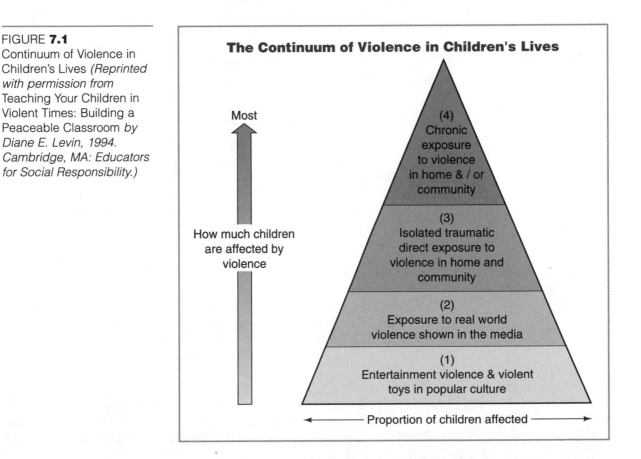

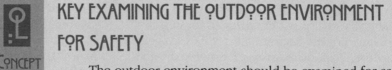

KEY EXAMINING THE OUTDOOR ENVIRONMENT FOR SAFETY

CONCEPT

The outdoor environment should be examined for safety on a regular basis. Hazards that pose risk may be items such as lack of barriers, poisons, insects, temperature, and others. Developmental behaviors and mixed age play may pose risk. Lack of space or space not properly organized can pose risk through collision and falls. Shared space allows certain conditions such as debris or trash that may cause danger to children. The neighborhood may pose risk for outdoor safety and should be carefully monitored.

PLAYGROUND EQUIPMENT SAFETY

Playground equipment is a major source of childhood injury and accident. Fifty-one percent of injuries occurring to children in child care occur on playground equipment (Aronson, 1994). The greatest number of these injuries are results of falls to the ground, onto other children, or onto other equipment. Play equipment that is properly designed, well maintained, and correctly placed can help minimize risk and provide greater protection from serious injury.

Using a general inspection list is a good idea for the caregiver to review the safety of the playground equipment. The list in Table 7.3 is suggested as a tool for regular inspection (Packer, 1993).

Climbing Equipment, Slides, and Swings

In addition to inspecting equipment for general hazards, climbing equipment, slides, and swings must meet standards set by the U.S. Consumer Product Safety Commission. Figure 7.2 shows areas to check on the playground.

In addition to these quick safety inspection checks, there are other considerations for minimizing risk in the outdoor environment. All playground equipment should have energy absorbing resilient surfaces under and around them to cushion falls and prevent serious injury. Materials such as soft, loose sand, pine or bark mulch, or pea gravel are **shock absorbers**, and should have a minimum depth of 12 inches. Asphalt, grass, and dirt are more dangerous and should not be used around play equipment. The surface material should be raked every several days to keep it from getting compacted and therefore losing some of its shock absorbency.

Shock absorbers
materials that lessen the force of a fall

Riding Toys

Toys that children ride should be sturdy, have a low center of gravity, and be well balanced. These toys should also be age-appropriate. There should be no sharp edges and pedal and hand grips should be in good con-

TABLE **7.3**

General Inspection for Outdoor Equipment

Check for the presence of the following hazards:

- ☐ Inadequate fall zone
- ☐ Protrusion and entanglement hazards
- ☐ Insufficient equipment spacing
- ☐ Age-inappropriate activities
- ☐ Platforms with no guardrails
- ☐ Equipment, such as swinging exercise rings and trapeze bars, not recommended for public playgrounds
- ☐ Broken, cracked, bent, or warped surfaces
- ☐ Sharp parts or edges
- ☐ Squeaky parts in need of lubrication
- ☐ Loose nuts and bolts
- ☐ Rotting wood, splinters
- ☐ Defects in moving parts
- ☐ Broken or missing parts
- ☐ Peeling paint, rust
- ☐ Tripping hazards
- ☐ Hard surfaces under equipment
- ☐ Worn out parts
- ☐ Open tubes or pipes that need to be capped

Adapted from "Is Your Outdoor Setting Safe?" by Barbara Packer published in SCHOLASTIC'S PRE-K TODAY, May/June 1993. Copyright © 1993 by Scholastic Inc. Reprinted by permission, and National Recreation and Park Association Safety Guidelines.

dition. The area for riding should have a flat, smooth surface and not be slippery. There should be barriers protecting this space from other play areas as well as from traffic and walkways.

Sandboxes

Sandboxes should be kept clean and raked at least once a week. If the sandbox is in a shared use facility, it should be carefully checked and raked daily for broken glass and other sharp objects. Where possible, the sandbox should have a cover in place when the sandbox is not being used. A sandbox also tends to attract cats that may use it as a litter box. Cats' feces can

FIGURE **7.2** Potentially Harmful Areas on a Playground:

A. The end of the slide is too close to the border.

B. The slide faces South and will get hot during the warm months. Locating the slide in a shaded area will minimize the risk of burns for children wearing shorts.

C. The structure is built on asphalt where rubber, sand, pea gravel, wood chips, bark, or turf cushions falls.

D. Decks above 3 feet need a safety barrier to prevent falls.

E. The climbing net and posts are too close to the main structure and maximize the risks of collisions and injury during accidental falls.

F. The border is too close to the swing area; children jumping from the swings are likely to fall against the border.

pose risk. Surfaces around the sandbox should be swept often to prevent falls. If standing water remains in sandbox after a rain, it should be removed as soon as the rain stops.

Other Equipment

Seesaws and trampolines are not recommended as regular equipment in child care. If a seesaw is present, it should be designed so children are protected from parts that can pinch. If a trampoline is present, it should have a protective surface underneath and surrounding it just like other large equipment. Only one child should use the trampoline at a time and only when there is an adult observer present who is dedicated to that one task.

All equipment, including equipment assembled or made at home, must meet the basic criteria of the standards set for manufactured equipment. Close inspection and adaptation to United States Consumer Product Safety Commission standards will lessen risk. If someone donates equipment to a child care facility, follow the same procedure. Proceed with caution because one can never assume that playground equipment is always safe.

KEY PLAYGROUND EQUIPMENT SAFETY

CONCEPT
Playground equipment safety is essential in the child care environment. Risk is posed to the environment because the equipment may not have met national safety standards. Climbing equipment, swings, and slides should be properly placed to prevent accidents. There should be shock absorbing material beneath this equipment. Riding toys should be sturdy and not tip over easily. If seesaws and trampolines are in the environment they should be closely observed and have rules for use. All equipment should be regularly inspected to keep the playground safe.

TRAFFIC AND TRANSPORTATION SAFETY

Approximately 170,000 children are injured per year in motor vehicle accidents. In the United States, motor vehicle accidents are the number one killer and crippler of children under four years of age. Motor vehicle injuries to children occur in three ways:

1. When children are pedestrians and are hit by an automobile
2. When children are riding in a car that stops suddenly or crashes
3. When children are riding bicycles and crash into or are run into by a car

To protect the children in care, safety policies should be developed for each case.

Pedestrian Safety

Children being let off at and picked up from school account for the great majority of pedestrian accidents. There should be a plan devised for safe dropping off and picking up of children. Pick up and drop off points for children should be located in an off-street area or directly at a curb near the child care facility under an adult's supervision. In the majority of cases this adult would be the parent bringing the child to school or taking him home. Parents should be reminded of the importance of close supervision of their children in a traffic situation. The outdoor play area should be as far away from traffic as possible and should be fenced.

Motor Vehicle Safety

Car travel and field trips are likely to be special events and not common occurrences in most child care situations. Planning for these events should be well organized and use accessories, behaviors, and conditions as the guidelines for safety.

The safest place for children in a motor vehicle is riding in the back seat and in an approved, secured car seat.

The Vehicle. The accessories in motor vehicle travel are the vehicle itself and the safety seats utilized. Vehicles should be in good working order, and be cleaned and inspected inside and out on a regular basis. Special care should be taken to see that brakes, lights, and other safety features of the car are working properly.

Vehicles should have heating and air conditioning features working in locations where temperatures go below 50°F and over 75°F. Children are susceptible to cold and heat and need to have the vehicle climate controlled.

Safety Seats. Safety seats are very important to the prevention of serious injury in motor vehicles. Although there are laws in every state that require a child riding in a car to be safely restrained, many drivers still do not follow the "buckle up" rule. As many as 59 percent of toddlers involved in motor vehicle accidents were not in car seats at the time of the accident ("Please Be Car Seated," 1994). As many as nine out of ten safety seats are not properly used even when the driver makes sure a child is buckled up (Mickalaide, 1994). Drivers should become familiar with the manufacturer's installation instructions for the safety seat used by the child.

Each child should be in an appropriate safety seat, harness, or seat belt that corresponds to the child's weight and age. These features shall be approved in accordance with federal safety seat standards and used in compliance with the manufacturers' directions. If a small bus or van is used, seat belts shall be provided for all children. The caregiver should always model safety by using a seat belt.

Pretravel Guidelines. Safety behaviors are necessary in the preplanning stage as well as in actual travel in the motor vehicle. Begin pretravel planning by using the guidelines in Table 7.4.

TABLE **7.4**

Pretravel Safety Guidelines

Caregiver:

■ Obtain authorization slips for all children participating in travel. Check your insurance coverage.

■ Make sure driver is licensed, is familiar with vehicle, and knows how to drive defensively.

■ Carefully plan out route, including placement of emergency care facilities along the way.

■ Explain route to children and point out highlights.

■ Prepare children for travel by explaining why buckling up and safe passenger behavior are important.

■ Arrange for backup vehicle in case of car emergency.

■ Understand safety precautions and child supervision for travel.

■ Know how to handle emergency situations, and be certified in pediatric first aid and CPR.

■ Make sure the vehicle is in good working condition. This check should include checking the gas, oil, and tires.

Children:

■ Understand the importance of travel safety, including buckling up.

■ Practice safe travel behaviors, including hands inside the car.

■ Understand rules for play in car, including no yelling or screaming.

Travel Guidelines. If the pretravel guidelines have been met, the next step is to follow the travel guidelines in Table 7.5. These guidelines are to help the caregiver be prepared for all contingencies and offer a greater degree of protection for a safe journey for the children in care.

Travel Conditions. Try to plan any travel with the children for a time when the conditions are optimal. Avoid high traffic times or times when children will be most tired or hungry and less alert. If the weather is bad, it is best to postpone the trip until it improves. Prepare a back-up activity that will excite the children to lessen the disappointment if the trip is postponed.

Make sure children are constantly under supervision during travel. At a minimum, keep to the proper adult-child ratio, but it is a good idea to ask for volunteers to accompany the caregiver. If travel is by walking and away from the neighborhood or across streets, the ideal ratio would be one adult for three to five children, depending upon age. The caregiver must prepare any volunteers with rules of supervision, by giving them handouts and talking to them several days before the trip so that they understand what is expected of them. It is also helpful to remind them of basic travel safety before leaving so it is fresh in their minds when the trip begins.

TABLE **7.5**

Child Care Travel Safety Guidelines

Caregiver:

■ Have trip authorization forms in your possession for all children present.

■ Provide the proper ratio of adult to child and assign specific children to each adult.

■ Do not allow loud music or tapes.

■ Stop and pull off road to calm children down, if they are unruly and noisy.

■ Do not be under the influence of drugs or alcohol, including prescription or over-the-counter medications that can make you drowsy.

■ Provide soft books or toys and conversation and songs for children so driver can concentrate on traffic safety.

■ Provide a first aid kit to carry in each vehicle.

■ Make sure everybody buckles up, and never allow child out of seat restraints while car is moving.

■ Pay special attention to traffic and the children when exiting and entering the vehicle.

■ If the trip is more than a few minutes, have juices and snacks for children allowing them to keep their focus on safety and not on being hungry or thirsty.

■ Do not allow children to ride up front in vehicles that have passenger airbags (1996).

Children:

■ Observe car safety rules.

■ Buckle up.

■ Ride quietly, keeping hands to yourself.

■ Be extra alert for traffic when exiting and entering vehicle.

Travel information sheet
check-off sheet that monitors all conditions for travel safety

The caregiver should always leave a **travel information sheet** with a responsible person left at the child care site. This sheet should include the following:

■ Date and time of trip, including approximate return time

■ Destination, including address, telephone number, and contact person

■ Planned route; be specific: "Main Street to Laurel Ave., left on Center Circle, right on Pine two miles to Fourth"

■ Names of children participating

■ Names of caregivers and parents providing supervision

FIGURE **7.3**
Helmets are available in
different sizes.

Bicycle Safety

School-aged children in family home child care, nanny care, or after school care should be taught about bicycle safety. Every year 300 children are killed in bicycle related crashes (National Center for Health Statistics [NCHS], 1991). Nearly one-half million other children are injured. The majority of these crashes involve head trauma. Using bike helmets can reduce the risk of injury by 85 percent (Schaaf, 1996).

Helmets.   Practicing safety by using bike helmets for children riding tricycles and small bicycles in child care can reduce risk while riding the vehicles in the outdoor environment (Figure 7.3). It can also help prepare them for a future of greater safety by being in the habit of wearing a helmet. The Consumer Product Safety Commission sets mandatory standards for helmets so the caregiver must make sure the helmets provided meet these standards.

One important and necessary element of bicycle safety is to wear a helmet properly.

Riding Safety.   Helping children learn proper tricycle behaviors can begin in the child care environment, using the same rules as for the riding toys. The skills and precautions in Table 7.6 will help the caregiver set guidelines for teaching children bicycle riding safety.

The riding safety guidelines will help the caregiver set up the child care environment to minimize risk. If children all ride in the same direction the number of crashes or collisions with other riders will be reduced. Keeping nonriders out of the area also reduces the number of collisions. A caregiver who observes the children for speed, reckless riding, and two hands on the handle bar can prevent accidents and ensure a safer experience for them. Risk will also be reduced by checking the riding toys for proper working order.

Other Riding Conditions.   Optimizing the conditions in the outdoor environment should not be too difficult. Creating a riding area in which riders have a nice, flat, nonslick surface is important. Enforcing the rule that riders only go in one direction will be a matter of changing habits and most children will readily adapt and will change direction when reminded, whereas others may need more effort.

TABLE **7.6**
Guidelines for Safe Bicycle Riding

- ■ Always ride in the same direction so all traffic goes the same way and not against each other.
- ■ Always be careful of other people and other traffic in the riding area.
- ■ Keep hands free to hold handle bars with both hands. Never carry anything with your hands.
- ■ Never show off, fool around, or ride recklessly.
- ■ Do not ride too fast, so if you do see someone or other traffic you can slow down or stop to avoid colliding with them.
- ■ The tricycle, bicycle, or other riding vehicle is appropriate for the age of the rider.
- ■ The riding vehicle is in good working order.
- ■ Stay clear of pedestrians.

Setting the time of day when children are most alert for outdoor riding activity decreases risk. Providing necessary and active supervision will also help offer greater protection to the children in the outdoor environment.

KEY TRAFFIC AND TRAVEL

CONCEPT

Traffic and travel pose risk for children in and out of care. Children should be protected and learn good travel safety practices. Pedestrian, motor vehicle, and bicycles are the three areas where there should be safety promotion and prevention from risk. Checklists, guidelines, use of safety devices, travel information sheets, and using optimum conditions will help the caregiver set up the environment for travel and traffic safety.

WATER SAFETY

Water safety presents its own set of challenges to the child care environment. Two-thirds of all drownings occur in the outdoor environment in standing bodies of water such as swimming pools, wading pools, hot tubs, ponds, and ditches. Covers for these items that are left with standing water after a rain become potential drowning hazards even though they may have originally been meant to protect. These bodies of water also have the potential for spreading disease.

Gates that enclose a pool should be self-closing and have locks that are at least 55 inches high.

Water Hazards

Safety precautions must be taken to keep the water in the child care environment as risk-free as possible. Any body of water poses a threat so screening the outdoor environment for hazards that may lead to the risk of drowning should be thorough. Young children can drown in as little as one inch of water.

Water hazards in the outdoor environment must be secured to prevent children from reaching them. Drownings occur in surprisingly short periods of time. Children have been seen playing indoors or outdoors away from a water source, and adults have been present nearby, yet these children have still drowned. Table 7.7 lists ways to child-proof the child care environment from the hazards that may lead to drowning.

Children's Behavior Around Water

Children themselves pose a threat when a body of water is present in the outdoor environment. They move fast, are curious, and do not understand cause and effect. They may lack fear or overestimate their physical abilities. Adults may underestimate children's abilities to manipulate their environment and therefore get into trouble. The majority of drownings occur within a very short period of time after a caregiver has seen a child. It is imperative that the caregiver *never* leave a child alone, even for a moment when there is a body of water in the outdoor environment.

The children should be taught safe practices for swimming and playing in the water to further protect them if they will be using the pool or wading

TABLE **7.7**

Water Safety Guidelines

■ Any hazard should be enclosed with a fence that is at least five feet tall and that is not easy to climb. A door or sliding glass door is not a safe substitute for a fence.

■ Gates should have locks that are at least 55 inches high and should be self-closing. Keep gate keys in a safe place away from children.

■ Remove chairs and objects children can use to climb over fences or gates or into spas.

■ All bodies of water that are man-made such as swimming pools, hot tubs, and cesspools should have rigid covers to protect the children from falling in, if they get past the gate.

■ If an inground pool is present in the child care environment, it should have a nonskid surface that surrounds the pool to prevent slipping and falling.

■ Always drain standing water from pool or spa covers.

■ Do not use floating spa or pool covers. Children can slip underneath and out of sight.

■ Avoid the use of floating devices that can give children a false sense of safety.

■ Remove all toys from pool after children are out of pool.

■ If a portable wading pool is used in child care, it should be filled with water, used immediately, and drained and put away as soon as children leave the pool.

■ Always carefully supervise children if there is a body of water present in the outdoor environment. *Never leave children without adult supervision, even for a few seconds.* Maintain visual contact with children.

■ Keep a rescue device, such as a long pole right next to the pool.

■ Have telephone access to pool for emergencies.

Reprinted with permission of Children's Hospital of San Diego.

pool. Table 7.8 offers guidelines for teaching safe behavior around and in the water.

When outdoors and near the water, always reinforce safety for the children. If the children are allowed to play in water, plan the time of day for this activity for when they are least tired and most alert. Always be sure there is adequate supervision and maintain sufficient ratios of adult to children. *Anyone attending children in the water should know how to swim and be competent in pediatric cardiopulmonary resuscitation.*

TABLE **7.8**

Water Safety Behaviors for Children

- Do not run, push, or play around swimming areas
- Do not swim with anything in your mouth.
- Be on the lookout for other children who may be having difficulty.
- Do not swim in very cold water. It increases risk of drowning.
- Never go near pool unless supervised.
- Never run around a pool.
- Wait at least an hour after eating before entering water.
- Do not roughhouse or fool around in water.
- Do not scream for help unless you mean it.
- Never swim alone, always have a buddy with you.

KEY WATER SAFETY

CONCEPT

    Water in many forms poses risk for children in the outdoor environment. Swimming pools, ponds, or any type of standing water may cause safety to be endangered. The caregiver needs to understand water hazards and how to eliminate them, if possible. Children's behavior poses risk and caregivers should be prepared to promote and teach children water safety behaviors.

IMPLICATIONS FOR **CAREGIVERS**

    Outdoor safety poses a number of risks to children in child care. The risks may come from different areas of hazards, such as environmental hazards, playground equipment, traffic and travel, and water. The risk may come from specific hazards, behaviors, and conditions. The caregiver should provide observation, supervision, and education that promote safe behaviors and prevent risks.

Observation

    There are many areas of outdoor safety for which observation is the best method of prevention of accident and injury. Learning to use the ABCs of safety as it applies to outdoor accessories, behaviors, and conditions can help the caregiver. A child caregiver who understands specific risks can be on guard for those risks.

Supervision

Children need to be constantly supervised in the outdoor environment. The child caregiver should supervise all aspects of the environment for risk posed by accessories, behaviors, and conditions. These are effective tools for managing outdoor risk to children.

Supervision also supplies the caregiver with methods and practices that provide a check and balance system in environments where there are more than one caregiver. Communication about outdoor safety should be a regular occurrence between the caregivers. Constant supervision can also reinforce that outdoor safety training and promotion take place on a regular basis.

Education

The caregiver, children, and parents can be educated for outdoor safety. The caregiver should access training that will provide the knowledge and awareness needed. The caregiver who has a knowledge base of outdoor safety can maximize the environment to protect the children.

Children can be taught safe behaviors and items or conditions to look for that may pose risk. The children can be encouraged to use safety devices that will protect them. Communicating with children on a regular basis and reminding them about outdoor safety can offer a greater degree of protection both in and out of child care. The caregiver can use educational methods such as reading books, showing videos, and circle time to reinforce safety measures and methods.

Parents can be educated to help promote and provide for greater protection from outdoor safety risk. Methods such as an outdoor safety awareness week with handouts, videos to borrow, and a parent group meeting can help the caregiver provide the educational support needed.

KEY IMPLICATIONS FOR CAREGIVERS

CONCEPT

The child caregiver can promote and protect for outdoor safety in a number of ways. Observation for safety risks can prevent injury. Supervision for making sure safe practices are followed can promote safety and provide protection. Education for caregivers, children, and parents can provide extra measures of protection.

CHAPTER **SUMMARY**

Risks for accidents are greater in the outdoor environment. These risks can occur on playgrounds, backyards, bicycles, streets, in water, and in automobiles. Caregivers should monitor the children and the outdoor environment and make modifications using safety checklists. Safety devices such as helmets and safety car seats should always be used. Caregivers should use observation, supervision, and education to protect their environment and to promote safe behaviors.

TO GO **BEYOND**

Questions for Review

1. Discuss the relationship between outdoor activities and risk to safety.
2. Describe some of the safety hazards that might be found in a shared risk environment. How do these differ from child care that does not share space?

AS AN **INDIVIDUAL**

1. Find a child care setting in the local area that reflects shared space. Visit the facility and observe the environment. Record your observations.
2. Find an elementary school playground. Observe the equipment and the surface under it. Do they meet the safety standards discussed in the text?

AS A **GROUP**

1. Working in groups of four to five people, make a safety checklist for a shared space environment. Use the information collected as individuals and compile a checklist.
2. Collect handouts from community resources that deal with outdoor safety. These resources might include auto clubs, poison control, or the American Red Cross.

CHAPTER **REFERENCES**

American Public Health Association and American Academy of Pediatrics (APHA and AAP). (1992). *Caring for our children: National health and safety performance standards: Guidelines for out-of-home child care programs.* Washington, DC: American Public Health Association.

Aronson, S. (1994, September/October). Early childhood checklist #5: Playgrounds. *Child Care Information Exchange,* 46–65.

Clemente, J. (1995). Therapeutic interventions for child victims of violence. *New England Journal of Medicine, 92*(2), 100–101.

Frost, J. (1994, April). Preventing playground injuries and litigation. *Parks and Recreation,* 53–60.

Groves, B. (1991). In *Can they hope to feel safe again? The impact of community violence on infants, toddlers, their parents and practitioners* (pp. 19–27). A report from the Seventh Biennial National Training Institute.

Haberman, M. (1994, Spring). Gentle teaching in a violent society. *Educational Horizons,* 131–135.

Levin, D. (1994). Building a peaceable classroom—Helping young children feel safe in violent times. *Childhood Education 70*(5), 267–270.

Mickalaide, A. (1994). Creating safer environments for children. *Childhood Education, 70*(5), 263–266.

Molnar, A. (1992, September). Too many kids are getting killed. *Educational Leadership, 50*(1), 4–5.

Moyers, B. (1995, January 8). There is so much we can do. *Parade Magazine,* 4–6.

National Center for Health Statistics (1991). *Vital statistics of the United States.* Washington, DC: Public Health Services.

Packer, B. (1993, May/June). Is your outdoor setting safe? *Scholastic Pre-K Today,* 27.

Please be car-seated. (1994, Winter). *Scholatic Parent and Child,* 6.

Schaaf, R. (1996, August). *Safe cycling.* Parent's Magazine, 35–36.

Timnick, L. (1989, September 3). Children of violence. *Los Angeles Times Magazine,* 6–15.

Windome, M. (1992) Kids and accidents. *NEA Today, 11*(5), 29.

Zero to Three. (1991). *Can they hope to feel safe again? The impact of community violence on infants, toddlers, their parents and practitioners.* A report from the Seventh Biennial National Training Institute.

SUGGESTIONS **FOR READING**

Crist, D. (1995, October/November). Car seat Q & A: Everything you need to know about car seats—but forgot to ask. *Healthy Kids,* 44–52.

Frost, J., Bowers, L., & Wortham, S. (1990). The state of American preschool playgrounds. *Journal of Physical Education and Recreation, 61*(8), 18–23.

Munson, M. (1994). Simple ways to safeguard your kids. *Prevention, 46*(10), 60–64.

CHAPTER EIGHT

Emergency Response Procedures for Child Care

Upon completion of this chapter, including a review of the summary, you should be able to:

Safety Policies for Emergency Response

Describe and discuss safety policies for response to childhood accidents and injuries.

Identifying an Emergency

Define and discuss the differences between what constitutes an emergency and what necessitates only basic first aid.

Basic Emergency Response Procedures

Indicate the steps to go through in addressing the proper responses to a real emergency and how it is to be performed.

Basic CPR

Define, discuss, and summarize the methods of basic cardiopulmonary resuscitation.

Basic First Aid

Define, discuss, and summarize the basic methods of first aid to infants and children.

Implications for Caregivers

Indicate the need for supervision, observation, and education for basic response procedures for childhood injuries and accidents.

SAFETY POLICIES FOR EMERGENCY RESPONSE

Emergencies occur in many situations. Automobiles, playground equipment, and natural disasters all pose risk for accidental injury that might be classified as an emergency. A chronic illness or a childhood disease might manifest as an emergency situation. It is important that the caregiver in any child care situation be prepared to handle emergencies. The following show the need for preparedness for emergency response in child care:

■ In a survey of over 400 child care centers, 12 percent were found to be unsafe (Chiara, 1995).

■ The most common types of childhood injury that may constitute an emergency are pedestrian injuries, motor vehicle passenger injuries, burns, firearm injuries, and drowning ("American Red Cross," 1993).

■ 140,000 children are injured by toys each year (Langlois, et al., 1991).

■ Firearms, choking hazards, and outdoor playground equipment pose great hazards to safety in child care due to lack of standards or guidelines (Runyan, Gray, Kotch, & Kreuter, 1991).

■ Child care environments should be prepared for emergencies with a code blue emergency plan (Copeland, 1996).

Child caregivers need to avoid emergencies by providing prevention and protection in the care environment. They do this with constant supervision and by anticipating, modifying, and monitoring for accessories, behaviors, and conditions that pose risk. These proactive behaviors reduce risk.

To provide the maximum protection in the child care environment, the caregiver needs to be prepared for the possibility that an emergency may occur. The caregiver needs to plan for emergencies, be prepared to handle emergencies, and be equipped with the training necessary to deal with life threatening emergencies as they occur.

In order to carry this out, the caregiver needs to plan for policies in the following areas:

1. *Defining an Emergency:* understanding what constitutes an emergency situation.

2. *Basic Emergency Response Procedures:* understanding of methods and practices for response to emergencies in child care.

3. *Basic CPR and First Aid:* Understanding when and how to use basic CPR and first aid to handle emergencies in child care.

4. *Disaster Preparedness:* methods and practices for preparing for disasters such as fire, weather, and earthquakes.

5. *Implications for Caregivers:* methods and practices for preparing the child care environment to deal with emergencies through education, observation, and supervision.

IDENTIFYING AN EMERGENCY

In order to understand how to prepare for an emergency, the caregiver must first understand what constitutes an emergency. There are common factors that indicate an emergency exists. The child caregiver needs to be able to identify these factors to help determine if an emergency is occurring. Three major factors have been used to indicate that an emergency is taking place.

Bleeding, Breathing, and Poison

The three basic factors that always indicate an emergency exists are bleeding, breathing, and poison. These emergencies are fairly easy to recognize. They are also rapidly life threatening and must be acted upon quickly. There may not even be time to call 911 right away if there is only one person present besides the victim. Any of these three factors could occur in child care and the caregiver should be prepared to recognize them and act immediately and appropriately (see Figure 8.1, page 242).

A person who is bleeding **profusely** may die if the bleeding is not stopped. Stopping the bleeding is of foremost importance, and first aid is needed immediately. If someone else is present, that person can call the emergency number (usually 911).

If a person has difficulty breathing, brain damage can occur in a matter of a few minutes and the heart may stop and death will follow. Offering **rescue breathing** may be the only alternative. Calling an emergency number is also vital, if possible.

When someone has ingested or has contacted poison directly through the skin, or has inhaled it, emergency procedures should begin immediately. Call the local poison control number to get help for the victim. In most cases, the person who answers will walk the rescuer through the exact method of treating the particular poison.

Profusely
pouring forth freely or abundantly

Rescue breathing
the process of steps to help a person who is not breathing resume normal breathing

FIGURE 8.1
In an emergency situation, there may not be time to call for help; the caregiver may have to take action.

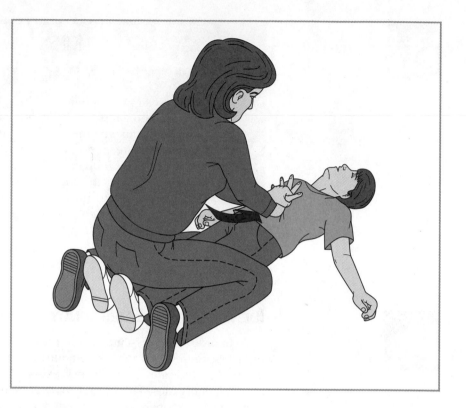

Other Emergency Indicators

There are a number of other indicators that show when an emergency may be present. The American Red Cross suggests that using one's senses is a good tool to help recognize when an emergency may exist. Hearing,

Emergency numbers such as the local poison control number should be located next to the phone for immediate use.

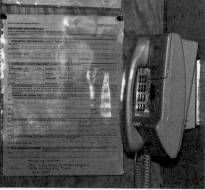

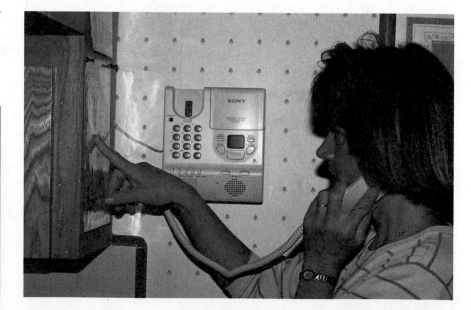

seeing, smelling, and feeling can all be tools of recognition as listed in Table 8.1.

When any of the conditions in Table 8.1 are present in child care, an emergency may exist and the child caregiver should act promptly (Figure 8.2). The caregiver should follow through with any unusual sights, sounds, smells, and sense of touch. The follow-up may prove that nothing was out of order; on the other hand, it may establish that an emergency is

TABLE **8.1**

Indicators of Emergencies

Sight

Unusual Appearances or Behaviors

- Difficulty breathing
- Unusual skin color
- Clutching the throat or chest
- Unexplained drowsiness or confusion
- Sweating for no apparent reason
- Slurred, confused, or hesitant speech

- A bone protruding from skin
- Unconsciousness
- Uneven pupils after a fall
- A rash of hives or welts that quickly appear
- A child having a seizure with no history of seizures
- Bleeding from a deep cut

Unusual Sights

- A spilled medicine container
- Broken glass
- Smoke or fire

- Downed electrical wires
- An overturned pot or pan

Hearing

Unusual Noises

- Screams, yells, moans, or calls for help
- Sudden, loud voices
- Breaking glass, crashing metal, or screeching tires
- Changes in equipment or machinery noises

- A loud crack, pop, or bang
- An explosion nearby
- A choking, gasping, or high pitched sound from inability to get breath

Smelling

Unusual Odors

- Odors that are stronger than usual
- Unrecognizable odors

- Smoke or a burning electrical odor
- Chemical odors

Feeling

Unusual Conditions

- Cold, clammy skin
- High fever

- Skin more moist than usual, possible sweating
- A bone that feels broken

Adapted from American Red Cross Community First Aid and Safety, 1993, St. Louis: Mosby Lifeline.

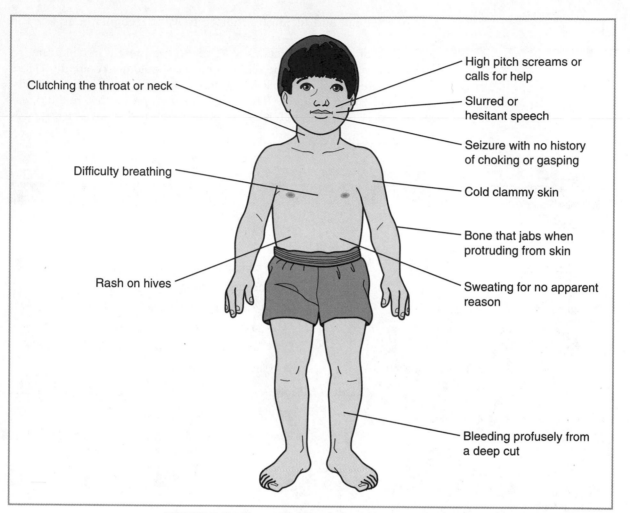

Clutching the throat or neck

Difficulty breathing

Rash on hives

High pitch screams or calls for help

Slurred or hesitant speech

Seizure with no history of choking or gasping

Cold clammy skin

Bone that jabs when protruding from skin

Sweating for no apparent reason

Bleeding profusely from a deep cut

FIGURE **8.2** Illustration of Indicators of Emergencies

taking place. The child caregiver needs to remain calm, act quickly, and follow emergency procedures.

There are a number of risks that regularly contribute to childhood injuries. These risks can be found in Table 8.2.

TABLE **8.2**

Contributors to Child Care Emergencies

- Garage door injuries (family child care)
- Choking from toys and other hazards
- Falls from playground equipment
- Firearms, poisons, and bodies of water
- Burns from fires, scalding, or electric wires
- Natural disasters such as floods, earthquakes, hurricanes, and tornadoes

Several dangerous items exist in this garage. How many can you find?

KEY IDENTIFYING AN EMERGENCY

CONCEPT

The child caregiver needs to identify what constitutes an emergency. Profuse bleeding, difficulty breathing, and ingestion or direct contact with poison always present emergency conditions that need prompt action. Other emergency indicators may be observed through the use of the senses of sight, hearing, smell, and touch. Once the caregiver has observed a questionable condition, follow-up can eliminate or determine the need for emergency response procedures.

BASIC EMERGENCY RESPONSE PROCEDURES

The child caregiver should be prepared for an emergency at all times. In order to lessen risk as an emergency occurs, the child caregiver should be prepared with proper planning, organizing, and responses based on knowledge and training. Copeland (1996) suggested the child caregiver establish an emergency plan similar to the medical plan "Code Blue."

Organization for Emergency

When an emergency occurs, the caregiver should remain calm and act immediately. This is hard enough to do under normal conditions, but is even more difficult in emergencies if one is not prepared to follow emergency procedures. There are a number of ways to prepare for the possibilities of emergencies and organize the child care environment to cope with them.

The procedures in Table 8.3 should be followed to prepare the environment for emergencies.

TABLE **8.3**

Emergency Preparedness Procedures

■ All child caregivers should have basic training and certification for first aid for children, including how to offer help to a choking victim. There should be one caregiver on site in child care who is certified in basic CPR and all other caregivers should be trained in rescue breathing.

■ All emergency information forms and health records should be readily available for each child present in child care.

■ Emergency numbers should be posted next to each phone. In addition, a list of vital information that the emergency operator will need should be posted.

■ Have a list of back-up helpers in case the caregiver must accompany a child to the hospital, away from child care.

■ In case of fire, natural disasters, or other major emergencies, an evacuation plan should be prepared.

■ Have available a first aid kit that is comprehensive enough for most emergencies.

Basic Training.   All child caregivers should have basic training for and certification in first aid for children, including how to offer help to a choking victim. This training should be updated as required by certification and the follow-up should be recorded to keep track. Any new caregivers should have this training before they start. One caregiver at the child care site at all times should be trained in basic CPR and should renew that certification yearly. All other caregivers should know how to perform basic rescue breathing.

All child caregivers should be familiar with the procedures to be followed for first aid and rescue breathing. Keep reminders of this training available in a notebook or on the wall where it is readily available. Posting pictures that depict emergency responses are helpful as reminders. These reminders can be invaluable in a real emergency. Reference books for this training should also be available for the caregiver to look at on a regular basis to help keep current.

Emergency Information.   All emergency information forms and health records should be readily available for each child present in child care. These forms include:

■ Emergency information forms filled out by parents including health information, the parents' work and home phone numbers, emergency phone numbers of other people listed by the parents in case of an emergency, the physician's phone number, the name of the hospital that has a treatment release on file, and any allergic reaction information.

■ A parental release form to treat the child in case of an emergency.

■ All "ouch" or injury reports filled out for the child.

Emergency Response Plan
Posted at a Child Care Site

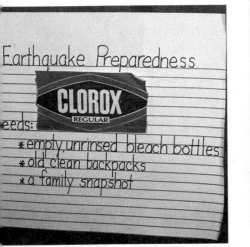

■ All health records, including immunizations.

■ A master log of injuries that occurred in the child care environment.

Emergency Numbers. Emergency numbers should be posted next to each phone. In addition, a list of vital information that the emergency operator will need should be posted as a reminder of what the caregiver needs to provide. This emergency information includes:

■ Caregiver's name and address

■ Type of emergency (e.g., burn, fall)

■ Where and how accident occurred

■ Child(ren)'s name, sex, age, and condition

■ Directions to child care site

■ Assistance already given to child

■ Always stay on the line until the emergency operator hangs up

The child caregiver should be informed about the local area emergency system. Knowing where the emergency care is coming from, how it is dispatched, and the location of the nearest hospital emergency room are helpful bits of information that may come in handy in an actual emergency.

A list of emergency contact numbers for all children in care should also be posted by each phone. These will be readily available and can be grabbed if an evacuation takes place or a field trip is planned.

Emergency Back-Up.   A list of back-up helpers should be available in case the caregiver must accompany a child to the hospital, away from child care. The back-up person could be an off-duty child caregiver, a substitute, a friend, neighbor, or volunteer to the child care environment. It is essential that these people be familiar with the child care environment and have been introduced to the children. A familiar person adds a sense of protection to the children who may already be very upset. Leaving the children with a stranger would be more upsetting. If the caregiver must leave with an injured or ill child, she should have the peace of mind that the children are in familiar good hands.

Evacuation Plan.   In case of fire, natural disasters, or other major emergencies, an evacuation plan should be prepared. This is a major topic and will be dealt with later in this chapter.

First Aid Kit. A first aid kit that is comprehensive enough for most emergencies should be available. The kit should be easy to access and at the same time should be out of reach of the children. It should include the items found in Table 8.4. The first aid kit should accompany the caregiver and children on any outings (walking) or any field trips (automobile). In addition to the kit, there should be ice or bags of frozen vegetables available for fast ice packs.

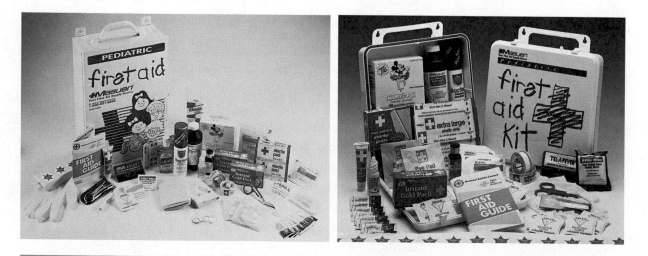

A first aid kit should accompany the caregiver and children on any outings or field trips. *(Courtesy of Masuen)*

TABLE **8.4**

First Aid Kit Checklist

Check for:

- ☐ Adhesive bandages (½″, ¾″, and 1″)
- ☐ Cotton balls
- ☐ Red Cross first-aid cards
- ☐ Adhesive bandage tape
- ☐ Sterile gauze pads
- ☐ Rolled flexible or stretch gauze
- ☐ Triangular bandages
- ☐ Eye pads or dressing
- ☐ Scissors
- ☐ Tweezers
- ☐ Thermometer
- ☐ Disposable latex gloves
- ☐ Flashlight with fresh batteries
- ☐ Syrup of ipecac
- ☐ Special items for children with liabilities such as a bee sting kit for allergic child or an inhaler for asthmatic child
- ☐ Antiseptic wipes in sealed packages
- ☐ Emergency phone numbers
- ☐ Change for pay phone
- ☐ Commercial cold pack or plastic bag for ice
- ☐ Clean cloth
- ☐ Liquid hand soap
- ☐ Rubber bulb syringe

Courtesy of American Red Cross.

Order of Response

The child care environment that is organized for possibilities of an emergency situation will be better prepared to respond to an emergency when it actually occurs. When an emergency does occur, the following responses are recommended by the National Association for the Education of Young Children for the caregiver to attend to the emergency:

1. Act immediately and remain calm!

2. Stay at the scene, giving help and reassurance to the victim and other children present. If another caregiver is present, assign him the task of keeping the other children calm.

3. Assess the child with a head-to-toe check as if using Figure 8.1 and the senses check in Table 8.1.

4. Do not move a seriously injured child unless in a life-threatening situation, such as immediate danger from fire.

5. If necessary, call for emergency help. In most areas of the country this is accessed by dialing 911. The emergency numbers will be posted by the phone. If for some reason the child care environment's phone is out, send someone to the nearest pay phone, car phone, or cellular phone. A portable or cellular phone serves as an extra precaution for emergencies in a child care environment.

6. Notify parents and agree on a plan of action. If the agreement is to meet at the emergency care site because it is closer, call for back-up help for the child care site. If the parent is unavailable call other emergency contacts and let the child's physician know what has happened. Call for back-up child caregiver.

Syrup of ipecac
a liquid substance used to
induce vomiting

7. Give medication only if authorized by the local poison control. This might be **syrup of ipecac** that will help the child vomit the poison. *This is used only in certain poisoning cases.*

8. Treat child for **shock,** if indicated. Cover with blanket and keep warm.

Shock
an imbalance of the
circulatory system as a
result of injury that includes
a decrease in blood
pressure, a rapid pulse, and
possible unconsciousness

9. Stay with the child until parents or emergency help arrives. Accompany child if parents are to meet the child at the emergency care site. Have back-up caregiver stay with children. If parents have not arrived and there is no other caregiver present and the back-up caregiver is unavailable, the caregiver must stay with the children who remain in child care. Try to reassure the child that he will be taken care of by the emergency technicians. If the caregiver knows that a parent or other emergency contact is going to be at the emergency care site let the child know that someone will be with her soon.

10. After the incident is over, fill out a report. Study it carefully to see if the incident could have been avoided through better safety practices or greater compliance with health practices.

These procedures are easy to follow if they have been reviewed frequently and are posted in several places throughout the child care site. Good planning and preparation will help the emergency situation go more smoothly.

KEY BASIC EMERGENCY RESPONSE PROCEDURES

CONCEPT

Knowledge of and training in basic emergency response procedures are essential for the child caregiver. All caregivers should have training in basic first aid and rescue breathing and at least one caregiver per site must be certified in CPR. The caregiver should organize for emergencies and plan accordingly. Emergency numbers and information should be posted and be easily accessible. Every child care situation should have a comprehensive first aid kit that travels with the group if they leave the site for an outing or field trip. Every child caregiver should have an understanding of the ten steps for emergency response and be able to respond in the right order.

BASIC CPR AND FIRST AID

Breathing emergencies are always life threatening. Regular breathing is effortless and comfortable. When breathing becomes an effort, causes pain, or makes unfamiliar noises these are indicators that a breathing emergency may be occurring. If a child is found unconscious it probably indicates a breathing problem. Every caregiver should be able to recognize the symptoms and be able to perform rescue breathing.

Basic CPR or Rescue Breathing

If a child is found unconscious, the caregiver should check the victim (Figure 8.3) and emergency assistance should be called. Figure 8.4 shows a caregiver administering rescue breathing.

FIGURE **8.3**
Check the victim.

FIGURE **8.4**
Give rescue breathing.

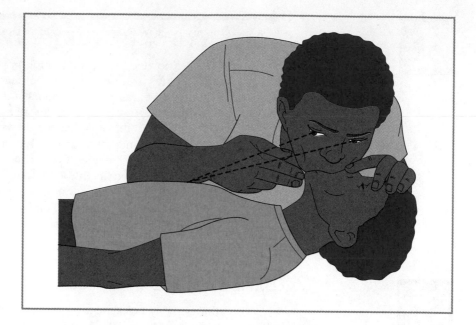

If a child appears to be choking, the airway for breathing may be partially or totally blocked. Choking in children can happen during eating or when a child puts an object in his mouth that is small enough to swallow and get caught. The usual recognized sign that a child is choking is when he grasps his throat with one or both hands. Another sign of a choking child is coughing. Forceful coughing usually indicates partial blockage. This means that the child still is able to get air in the lungs. The best procedure for the moment is to encourage the child to continue coughing and try to cough up the object. The child should be attended by a caregiver. If nothing comes out in a short time call for emergency assistance.

Weak coughing usually indicates the blockage is more complete. A choking child can stop breathing and lose consciousness rapidly. The caregiver should give abdominal thrusts until the object is coughed up or the child becomes unconscious (see Figure 8.5). Have someone call for emergency assistance.

If a breathing emergency exists and none of the other methods work, then the caregiver qualified in CPR should begin performing CPR (see Figure 8.6) while someone calls for emergency assistance.

First Aid Procedures

There are many minor emergencies such as scraping a knee or bumping a head that can be taken care of easily by first aid. Other emergencies such as a broken bone, a cut that needs stitches, or a burn that is beyond first degree, will need prompt first aid and then have the parent take the child to his own physician for further treatment. It is essential that the caregiver know how to perform basic pediatric first aid procedures. The American Red Cross and other organizations perform a service to the community by providing

FIGURE **8.5**
Give abdominal thrusts.

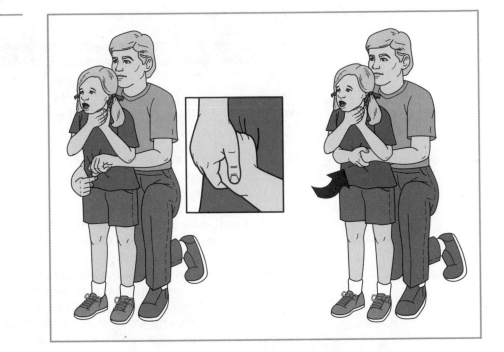

the training. The following are reminders for the caregiver of signs, symptoms, and responses.

Bites. There are a number of common ways that a child can suffer bites in a child care environment. These include bites from insects and other children or animals. Insects may bite or sting a child. These commonly come from bees, wasps, ants, and ticks. Some of these bites may cause an allergic reaction in some children. When the caregiver observes those signs, the emergency medical services should be called immediately. Table 8.5 reflects those signs.

FIGURE **8.6**
Give CPR.

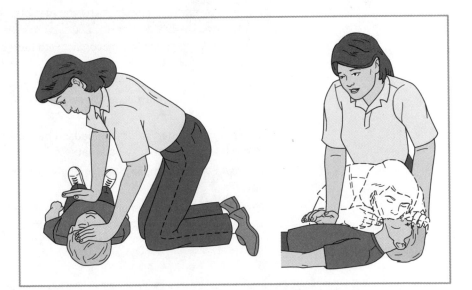

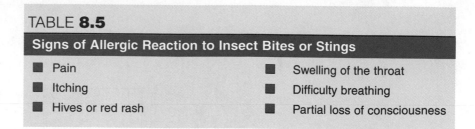

TABLE **8.5**

Signs of Allergic Reaction to Insect Bites or Stings

■ Pain	■ Swelling of the throat
■ Itching	■ Difficulty breathing
■ Hives or red rash	■ Partial loss of consciousness

If a child is stung and the stinger remains, the caregiver should try to remove it with tweezers. The area around the stinger must not be scraped or squeezed after removing the stinger, the caregiver must wash the area with soap and water and apply an ice pack. The same procedure is followed with an insect bite. If the child care is located in areas of the United States where ticks, scorpions, black widow spiders, and brown recluse spiders live, the caregiver should have first aid information regarding them.

For a bite from another child or an animal, the caregiver should wash the wound immediately with soap and water. If the bite breaks the skin, the child should be taken to his physician for a follow-up. The wound should be covered with a sterile gauze bandage. If heavy bleeding is caused by the wound, emergency assistance must be called.

Cuts and Other Injuries to the Skin. Cuts and other injuries to the skin occur often when children play, collide with objects, or take risks. The type of cut or degree of injury to the skin determines whether emergency assistance is necessary. If the cut is bleeding profusely or is jagged, torn, or deep, emergency assistance will be needed. Table 8.6 indicates the type of cut and the degree of injury.

TABLE **8.6**

Types of Cuts and Wounds

Abrasion. A scrape caused by contact with hard surface such as pavement or carpet. Common childhood cut.

Incision. A sharp, even cut caused by glass, knives, and other sharp objects. The depth or length of wound will determine the blood flow and the degree of seriousness.

Laceration. A jagged or torn cut caused by objects with uneven edges or by force. Tissue damage may be great.

Puncture. A hole in the skin caused by sharp objects such as a nail, thorn, or splinter.

Bruise. A discolored area of the skin caused by contact with an object, usually by force such as falling, or colliding with another object.

Adapted from American Red Cross.

Some cuts and wounds require stitches. *(Courtesy of the Mullen Family)*

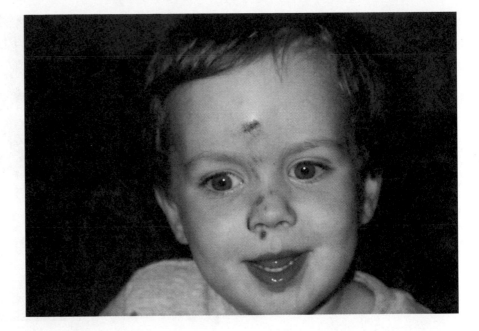

Cuts and wounds not needing emergency medical treatment should be washed with soap and water and covered with a bandage. Cuts that are over an inch long or involve a large or deep wound that may cause scarring may require stitches. If there is an indication for stitches, the child should be sent to his own physician as soon as possible.

Injuries Involving the Head, Mouth, and Nose.   Injuries involving the head are common in child care because of falls from outdoor equipment and collisions with objects or other children. Head injuries may be minor or they may be more serious. Sometimes it is difficult to tell immediately if the injury is serious when the child remains conscious. Table 8.7 lists the symptoms of a serious head injury.

For many children, the result of a fall will be a bruise and swelling where contact was made. Have the child lie down for a while with an ice pack. Carefully observe the child's behavior for at least one hour.

TABLE **8.7**

Symptoms of Serious Head Injury

■ Vomiting	■ Change in breathing rate
■ Shock	■ Change in pulse rate
■ Confused behavior	■ Cold, clammy skin
■ Unevenly dilated pupils	■ Loss of consciousness

Head injuries should be
carefully evaluated before
they are determined not
serious.

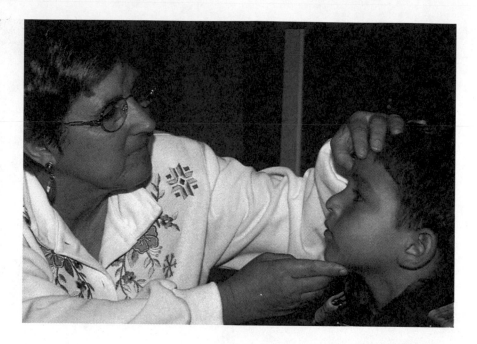

Injuries to the mouth and nose can happen easily. The injuries to the mouth can be to the gums, teeth, tongue, or lips. If there is unusually heavy bleeding, emergency assistance must be summoned. Otherwise bleeding is controlled by direct pressure by holding a sterile piece of gauze where the injury has occurred. Once the bleeding has stopped for a while have the child rinse out the mouth with water. If the injury is outside the mouth, wash with soap and water. In case of swelling, apply an ice pack. If a child loses a tooth, find the tooth and clean it off with water. Place the tooth in a jar of milk and have the parents take the child to his dentist immediately.

Nose injuries most commonly involve nosebleeds. This is usually handled by pinching the child's nostrils together between the caregiver's thumb and forefinger. Do not tilt the head back. Have the child sit quietly. Talk quietly to the child while this is being done. Explain the procedure and ask the child if he has any questions. It normally takes approximately ten minutes for a nosebleed to stop. If it does not stop after ten minutes, the child's physician should be consulted. Some children may have a history of nosebleeds and may take longer to stop. The physician can offer further advice.

Burns. Burns come from a number of sources, such as heat, steam, chemicals, or electrical sources. The different degrees of burns are listed in Figure 8.7.

If the burn is a third degree burn, emergency medical assistance must be called immediately. There are three basic steps to care for burns. First, the burning must stop, which may entail putting out a fire and removal from the area. Never pull off clothes that are stuck to the skin. Second, cool the burn by flushing it with water. Do not use ice unless it is a very minor burn, because it may damage the tissue. Flush the skin or layer cool, wet cloths on the burn. Third, when the burn has cooled down, cover with a dry, clean, and sterile dressing. If the burn appears to be more serious than a first degree burn, have the parents take the child to his physician.

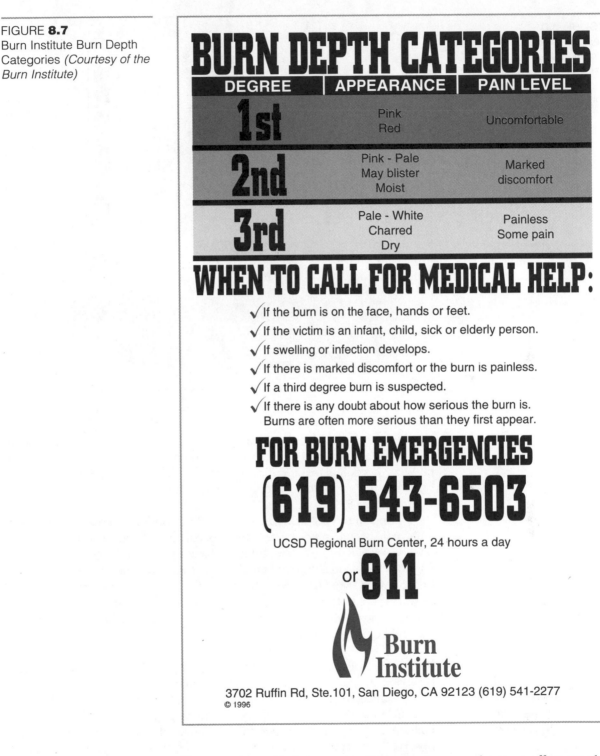

BURN DEPTH CATEGORIES

DEGREE	APPEARANCE	PAIN LEVEL
1st	Pink Red	Uncomfortable
2nd	Pink - Pale May blister Moist	Marked discomfort
3rd	Pale - White Charred Dry	Painless Some pain

WHEN TO CALL FOR MEDICAL HELP:

✓ If the burn is on the face, hands or feet.

✓ If the victim is an infant, child, sick or elderly person.

✓ If swelling or infection develops.

✓ If there is marked discomfort or the burn is painless.

✓ If a third degree burn is suspected.

✓ If there is any doubt about how serious the burn is.
Burns are often more serious than they first appear.

FOR BURN EMERGENCIES
(619) 543-6503

UCSD Regional Burn Center, 24 hours a day

or 911

**Burn
Institute**

3702 Ruffin Rd, Ste.101, San Diego, CA 92123 (619) 541-2277
© 1996

Temperature. Both extremes of temperature can have an effect on children in a child care environment. Children can get easily overheated. They may get cramps from the heat or heat exhaustion. The cramps occur in the leg muscles and the stomach. These are usually the first warning

FIGURE **8.8**
Heat exhaustion results
from fluid loss through
perspiration; heat stroke
results after sweating stops
and the body's temperature
continues to rise until vital
organs start to fail.

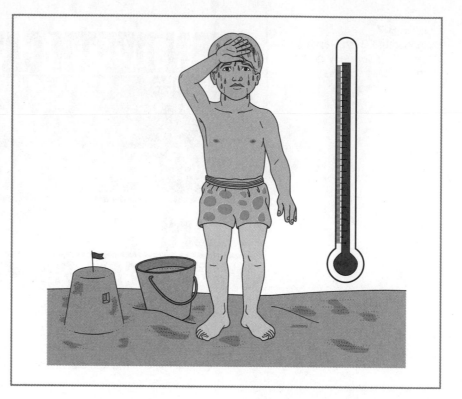

FIGURE **8.8**
Heat exhaustion results
from fluid loss through
perspiration; heat stroke
results after sweating stops
and the body's temperature
continues to rise until vital
organs start to fail.

signs of trouble with heat. Heat exhaustion involves nausea, headache, dizziness, and flushed skin. Both conditions are treated by placing the child in a cool place and having him drink lots of liquids. Sometimes applying a cool cloth to the face makes the child think he feels cooler (see Figure 8.8).

Exposure to cold may involve frostbite, but the normal conditions of child care would preclude this from occurring. However, if the caregiver observes the signs, he or she should act accordingly. Frostbite is indicated by a lack of feeling in an area where the skin is cold and may appear discolored or look waxy (see Figure 8.9). To render first aid, warm the area by soaking in warm (not hot) water. Keep in warm water until it appears red and feels warm. Bandage the area with a light sterile dressing. Have the parents take the child to her physician.

Poisoning.   Poisoning can occur in four ways: by ingestion, by inhalation, by absorption, and by injection such as snake venom. Under any poisoning circumstance, the first step in first aid is to call the **poison control center** in your area. Closely follow the instructions given. These instructions will include the age of child and the evidence of poisoning that has been observed. As indicated by poison control, call for emergency assistance where applicable. Table 8.7 indicates the symptoms of poisoning by ingestion, inhalation, and absorption. The symptoms in Table 8.5 are the same symptoms that may appear after injected poisoning.

Poison control center

a resource available through
a phone call in case of
poisoning

FIGURE **8.9**
Frostbite results when cold temperatures freeze body cells. Hypothermia results when, over time, the body's temperature drops.

The child must not have anything to eat or drink unless instructed. If the poison has been absorbed through the skin, flush the skin with water until help arrives. If the child appears to have inhaled a poison, provide fresh air or put the child in a well-ventilated room with an open window.

TABLE **8.8**

Symptoms of Poisoning	
Ingested	
■ Nausea and/or vomiting	■ Change in breathing
■ Diarrhea	■ Unconsciousness
Inhaled	
■ Headache	■ Difficulty breathing
■ Dizziness	■ Unconsciousness
Absorbed	
■ Irregular breathing	■ Abnormal pulse
■ Headache	■ Skin or eye irritations

DISASTER PREPAREDNESS

Disaster preparedness is an essential element in addressing emergency response procedures. No caregiver ever expects a disaster to occur. However, for the safety of the children in care, it should be planned for and the environment should be organized to cope with a disaster, should it occur.

Disasters have normally been associated with acts of nature such as tornadoes, floods, and earthquakes or fires. Fires may also be caused by human carelessness. Other potential disasters might include a gas leak or noxious fumes from a chemical spill. We have recently observed that child care may also be impacted by an intentional human act of violence, meant to harm. The bombing of the Federal Building in Oklahoma City involved a child care center and there was much loss of life, including children. Although not much could be done in that instance, most instances of disaster can be made more tolerable and have a lessened effect on the children if the caregiver is prepared.

The disaster most likely to occur is fire because it is more common than all of the other disasters combined. Fire can happen any time, any where, and under a number of circumstances. Because it is a common disaster, all child caregivers should prepare the environment to deal with a fire should it take place.

The location of the child care has an impact on the type of natural disaster that may occur. Tornadoes are more likely to occur in the mid-America sector, while hurricanes are more likely to occur on the southern coastal areas. Earthquakes are more apt to happen in California. Floods occur near rivers, lakes, dams, and other bodies of water. Snow, with blizzard potential, occurs throughout the country. Knowledge of the particular disasters that are likely to occur in the location of the child care is a good way to begin preparations.

Evacuation Procedures

Most disasters can be divided into two categories. The first is a disaster that requires **evacuation** and the second type of disaster calls for **survival procedures.** Many types of disaster such as fires, floods, tornadoes, and hurricanes may require evacuation. Evacuation procedures are basic. Since

Evacuation
removal of persons from a site where a disaster or emergency exists

Survival procedures
preparation and steps to follow to stay in place in case of disaster or weather emergency

evacuation may be necessary in the case of fire, all caregivers should be prepared with evacuation procedures and policies that help to reinforce them.

Every child care environment should have a written plan that includes a diagram about emergency evacuation. Figure 8.10 shows a diagram of a typical child care center. Included on the diagram are the exit doors and windows, location of first aid kit, daily attendance records and fire extinguishers, utility shutoff, and location of food, clothing, and tools. Each of these items may need to be accessed.

It is essential that there be an evacuation plan that everyone concerned with the child care understands. This includes caregivers, children, and their parents. Caregivers will need to know what emergency records might have to be accessed. It is a good idea to keep copies of all children's emergency information in a fireproof, portable file because this allows the caregiver access to information about emergency contacts, and so forth. If a child has a specific health challenge such as an allergy or other special needs, his records should be copied and placed in the portable file. A caregiver should be designated in charge of this file, including keeping the information current and updated.

A caregiver should be responsible for keeping daily attendance checklists for the children in care. The checklist should be frequently checked throughout the day for accuracy. This information may be needed if evacuation occurs and confusion ensues. Having a checklist will help to bring order. The child caregiver should also be familiar with emergency phone numbers and should follow the organization for emergencies.

The child caregiver should plan for emergency evacuation using several proactive strategies. These are included on Table 8.9.

The caregiver should discuss emergency procedures with parents so they are familiar with the practice and drills the children are performing. Inform parents of the emergency evacuation plans. The caregiver should let the families know where the children will be taken in case of an emergency.

FIGURE **8.10**
A diagram of the child care center is an important tool to have during emergencies, particularly if the center must be evacuated.

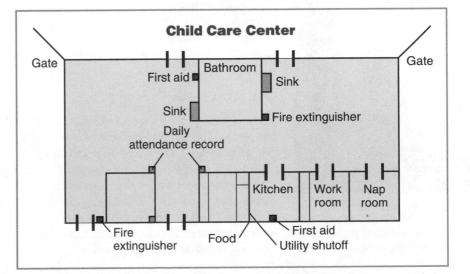

Child Care Center

TABLE **8.9**

Proactive Strategies for Evacuation

- ■ Plan two exit routes from the building. Post these throughout the building.
- ■ Test smoke and fire alarms once a month.
- ■ Plan a fire drill once per month.
- ■ Plan exit strategies for removing infants and toddlers. These may be using a wagon, crib, and so forth, that can carry several children at a time and will go through a door.
- ■ Be familiar with and post information concerning the shut-off switches for gas, water, electricity, and other utilities that may pose a safety risk.
- ■ Know how and when to use a fire extinguisher.
- ■ Prepare children to handle emergencies by drills, discussion, and use of diagram.
- ■ Teach children "Stop, Drop, and Roll" techniques and practice with them.
- ■ Keep a fireproof, portable file with emergency and health information for special needs of children in care.
- ■ Choose a safe emergency shelter spot and prearrange for its use during an emergency.

Caregivers and teachers should conduct practice fire drills once a month.

Having a safe emergency shelter is important and it is equally important that the parents know the location.

The caregiver should prepare the children for an evacuation emergency by having them practice fire drills, using and understanding exits. They should participate in group discussions about what to do and should understand about a meeting point outside if the building does have to be evacuated. These drills should be held once a month.

The caregiver should practice drills with infants and toddlers who may not walk or not walk well yet. These exit drills would take place in a wagon or crib, just as it would under emergency conditions. Children should also be taught the "Stop, Drop, and Roll" fire procedure (see Figure 8.11). They should practice it regularly on the day of a fire drill.

Survival Mode Procedures

Other disasters such as an earthquake or blizzard may call for everyone to remain in the child care environment. This isolation may last a few hours or several days. The survival mode may need to be applied in this instance. If the caregiver lives in a location that has potential for the need for survival, then he or she must be organized and properly prepared. Certo (1995) suggests that a "pretend" emergency day be held so that children and staff are prepared to function should that emergency occur. Table 8.10 shows a sample schedule explaining the functions that can take place when simulating an emergency due to an earthquake.

FIGURE **8.11**
Stop, Drop, and Roll
*(Courtesy of the Burn
Institute)*

Children should regularly
practice the "Stop, drop,
and roll" procedure.

TABLE **8.10**

Sample Schedule for an Earthquake Emergency

Time	Activity
8:15 A.M.	Pretend quake. Children get under tables. Staff supervises then gets in doorways. Staff then simulates damage and blocks off some areas. Staff tries to keep children calm and quiet.
8:25 A.M.	Go to center of room. Count children, check attendance list. Discuss plan and assign every child a partner. Give first aid with masking tape. Simulate shutoffs of gas, electricity, and water.
8:35 A.M.	Gather emergency survival kit (see Table 8.1) and emergency information. Pretend cleanup with children helping with smaller items.
8:45 A.M.	Try to resume normalcy by having children play in small groups away from windows. Simulate aftershock. Children go under tables, staff into doorways. Try to calm and quiet children again.
9:00 A.M.	Children wash up (simulate, using very little water). Have snack bar from emergency survival kit. Drink juice. Talk about quake and plans for further survival mode.
9:15 A.M.	End of drill.

Adapted from "Helping Children and Staff Cope with Earthquakes," by D. Certo, March 1995, Child Care Information Exchange.

Table 8.11 shows an emergency survival supplies list that should be kept on hand in case of a survival mode emergency.

In case of an earthquake, it may be safer if the caregiver carries out the survival mode outdoors. The supplies kept on hand might just be moved outside. It is important to have a designated area in which care will take place.

Helping Children Cope with Disaster

The first rule of any disaster is for the caregiver to behave in a calm manner. If the caregiver is in a total panic, the children's behavior will reflect this. Therefore, although the caregiver may feel upset or panicky, he or she should try not to show it. When disasters are planned for and practiced, physical safety is easier to cope with and handle.

Adults often tend to ignore the emotional needs of a child, once safety has been established. Children often have emotional consequences as a result of being in an emergency situation. Children are often very afraid and may not be able to verbalize it. This may be especially true in situations like earthquakes when aftershocks occur, or tornadoes, when the wind might still be blowing.

Fire extinguishers should be visible and all emergency exits should be clearly marked.

TABLE **8.11**

Emergency Survival Supplies Checklist

Check for:

- ☐ Fire extinguisher
- ☐ First aid kit
- ☐ Flashlights and extra batteries
- ☐ Crescent or pipe wrench to turn off gas/water, if needed
- ☐ Shovel, screw driver, 20′ length of rope
- ☐ 1 gallon of water per child, 2 gallons per adult, and iodine tablets
- ☐ Duct tape and one package plastic sheeting
- ☐ Portable radio and batteries for emergency broadcasts
- ☐ Three- to four-day supply of dry or canned food per person, hand (non-electric) can opener; include energy bars and juice boxes
- ☐ Paper plates, plastic utensils, paper cups, and paper towels
- ☐ Alternate cooking source, matches
- ☐ Blankets and extra clothing (Most child care sites already keep extra clothing for children.)
- ☐ Extra newspapers to wrap waste and trash
- ☐ Large plastic trash bags for trash and waste
- ☐ Three- to four-day supply of toilet paper
- ☐ Infant supplies—diapers, formula, food—for three to four days
- ☐ Three- to four-day supply of food and water for any pets present
- ☐ Essential medication needed for children with special needs (inhaler for asthmatic, and so forth)
- ☐ Safe alternate heat source (nonelectric) and fuel for it; this might be wood for a fireplace or kerosene for a room heater

Because children need reassurance, the caregiver must explain as clearly as possible what has occurred and the facts that are known about it. The caregiver should encourage the children to talk and express their concerns and fears. Listening to what they say about their fears and about how they feel and think about what has happened can help the children realize that this shared experience affected everyone. When things settle down, it is important for the caregiver to establish a routine. Routines give children a sense of comfort and some predictability.

Fire is just one of the destructive natural disasters that can occur in any region of the country. *(Courtesy of Palm Harbor Fire Dept.)*

Some children may act more clingy or revert to an earlier stage of behavior. Often children are afraid of being left alone, and this may be escalated because they are not with their families. Continued reassurance will help. In most disasters help arrives quickly and the children are likely to be reunited with families in a short period of time.

KEY DISASTER PREPAREDNESS

CONCEPT

Child caregivers should be prepared to handle a disaster. Although chances for disasters are slim, preparation will allow for the physical safety of the children to be carried out in an organized manner. Disasters come in many forms and may be natural, or man-made. Regardless of the source, disasters can be prepared for by defining what type of disaster might be likely to occur in the child care location. All child caregivers should prepare for evacuation, because fire is the most likely disaster to occur. Children should practice fire drills and know all exits. Caregivers in locations where the survival mode might be needed should be prepared to handle taking care of children for several days. Caregivers should also be prepared to help children with their emotions through the disaster as well as protect their physical safety.

IMPLICATIONS FOR **CAREGIVERS**

Providing prevention and protection should be a part of everyday child care. The caregivers should be prepared as best as possible to handle emergencies as they arise. In order to promote protection and prevention in the child care environment, the caregiver can act in several ways.

Education

The beginning step for the caregiver is training and education to be prepared to handle an emergency. All caregivers should know basic pediatric first aid and response breathing. At least one caregiver per child care site should have basic CPR training for infants and children. The caregiver should know how to organize for and respond to an emergency, including disasters.

The parents should be educated in prevention and emergency responses as well. The caregiver should provide written information to parents, explaining evacuation procedures, a safe place to meet, and basically how the child care environment will respond. Fire safety information can also be provided to parents. Families should create their own evacuation plans for their homes.

Children should be educated in evacuation procedures, should understand exit routes, and should know how to respond. The caregiver should arrange for the fire department to visit several times a year and explain about fires and the procedures to respond to them.

Fire drills should be given monthly to prepare and practice. The drill should be so routine that all children and caregivers are evacuated within two minutes. Children should also be taught about falls and collisions and how to avoid them. They can also be informed about how to avoid poisons in any environment. Children in areas where survival mode may be a possibility should be given practice drills in survival mode emergency situations.

Supervision

Supervision plays a major role in keeping the environment prepared to respond to emergency situations. The emergency forms should be accurate, current, copied, and ready for fast response by being in a fireproof file. Emergency information should be posted by each phone. The caregiver should make sure that everyone in the child care environment be prepared to make a call if necessary. Everyone should understand the information needed in an emergency. The caregiver should make sure that the back-up list for people to help in emergencies is updated and kept current. These back-up caregivers should be contacted on a monthly basis to maintain the currency of the list.

The first aid kit should be checked regularly to make sure that it is kept up-to-date. As items are used, they should be replaced. If there is a supervising caregiver, he or she should make sure all caregivers have the basic first aid and response breathing procedure training, and follow up to make sure everyone is kept current in their training. The caregiver should be prepared for evacuation or survival mode disasters. The evacuation plan should be regularly reviewed. The survival mode supplies should be periodically checked and replaced if needed.

Cultural Sensitivity

Emergencies are unsettling to everyone. Emergencies need understanding and adequate preparation. The caregiver should provide families of children whose first language is not English with all the written emergency information in their native language whenever possible. The caregiver may need to find someone who can translate by using resources such as the local chapter of the NAEYC or the National Family Child Care Association. Arming people with knowledge can prevent panic in emergency situations. The families can reinforce the information that the caregiver has given the children by discussing it at home.

If there are families who are recent immigrants or refugees, they may have left their home environments in emergency situations. Because of the trauma they suffered, these children may need extra support during emergencies.

KEY IMPLICATIONS FOR CAREGIVERS

CONCEPT

Caregivers need to be prepared to handle emergencies in the child care environment. This requires education, supervision, and cultural sensitivity. Education takes place by preparing the caregiver to be trained in basic first aid, response breathing, and organization for and response to emergencies. The caregiver needs to provide written information to families and to train children through fire drills and practice techniques for responding to emergencies. Supervision should be provided to keep updated and current the emergency information, the back-up caregiver list, the first aid kit, the evacuation plan, and the survival mode supplies. Cultural sensitivity should be practiced by having emergency information translated into native languages so that all families are prepared to help their children respond to emergencies.

CHAPTER **SUMMARY**

An important part of being a caregiver is knowing how to respond in an emergency. To be prepared to respond, the caregiver defines what constitutes an emergency and what injuries necessitate first aid. The steps for taking proper action and how they are performed are established. Basic CPR and first aid are summarized. The steps for disaster preparedness are given and the difference between evacuation procedures and survival mode procedures are defined. Strategies for supervision, observation, and education are discussed.

TO GO **BEYOND**

Questions for Review

1. Discuss the three factors that always indicate an emergency. Relate these to other indicators that an emergency is present.
2. Discuss the importance of preparing for an emergency.
3. Compare the evacuation and survival modes of disaster preparedness.

AS AN **INDIVIDUAL**

1. Assemble a list of emergency numbers for your area.
2. Create an emergency contact form for child care.
3. List the items you would have in an emergency survival mode kit for the type of emergency that might occur in your local area.

AS A **GROUP**

1. Discuss items that should be kept in child care to prepare for a disaster.
2. Role play different emergencies, taking turns being the injured and the teacher who finds them. Have the group evaluate the actions of the teacher during the exercise.
3. What might be done for a child care environment to help children and families that do not speak English prepare for emergencies?

CHAPTER **REFERENCES**

American Red Cross Community First Aid and Safety. (1993). St. Louis: Mosby Lifeline.

Certo, D. (1995, March). Helping children and staff cope with earthquakes. *Child Care Information Exchange.*

Chiara, S. (1995, February 2). American child care called unfit. *San Diego Union-Tribune,* A-1,10.

Copeland, M. (1996) Code blue! Establishing a child care emergency plan. *Child Care Information Exchange, 107,* 17–21.

Langlois, J., Wallen, B., Teret, S. Bailey, L., Hershey, H., & Peeler, M. (1991). The impact of specific toy warning labels. *Journal of the American Medical Association, 265*(21), 2848–2850.

Runyan, C., Gray, D., Kotch, J., & Kreuter, M. (1991). Analysis of U.S. child care safety regulations. *The American Journal of Public Health, 81*(8), 981–986.

SUGGESTIONS **FOR READING**

Aronson, S. (1993, September). Early childhood safety checklist #1: Emergency preparedness. *Child Care Information Exchange,* 73–74.

3

NUTRITION IN CHILD CARE

In this section we will discuss nutrition and how it impacts children:

9. Promoting Good Nutrition in Child Care

10. Providing Good Nutrition in Child Care

11. Menu Planning and Food Safety in Child Care

These topics will relate nutritional needs to health promotion and risk management tools that will enable the student to design nutritional policies that work well in child care settings.

CHAPTER NINE

PROMOTING GOOD NUTRITION IN CHILD CARE

Upon completion of this chapter, including a review of the summary, you should be able to:

NUTRITION POLICIES

Define and discuss nutrition policies and their use as tools for the nutritional well-being of children.

UNDERSTANDING NUTRITIONAL GUIDELINES

Describe the importance of the Dietary Guidelines for Americans, the USDA Food Guide Pyramid, the Recommended Daily Allowances, and other measures that provide guidelines for nutritional well-being.

BASIC NUTRIENTS

Define the six basic nutrients in the diet and discuss their importance to overall well-being.

CHILDHOOD NUTRITIONAL CHALLENGES

Discuss childhood nutrition in regard to the challenges of malnutrition, undernutrition, and overnutrition.

IMPLICATIONS FOR CAREGIVERS

Indicate the need for education, supervision, and role modeling for proper nutrition to promote health and well-being.

NUTRITION POLICIES

Policies that ensure proper nutrition for child care are important to the overall well-being and development of children in care. Children are at risk for poor nutrition under most circumstances. Indicators of the need for nutrition policies are:

- Child care facilities serve at least one meal a day to approximately 5 million young children. This figure is expected to increase by the year 2000 as more mothers join the workforce (Briley, Roberts-Gray, & Rowe, 1993).

- It is common practice in child care centers to restrict a child's food intake by portioning out food instead of allowing the child to self-select (Branen & Fletcher, 1994).

- Inadequate amounts of calories, niacin, iron, and zinc have been found in many child care menus. Iron deficiency is of special concern because it can make a child more prone to lead poisoning (Briley, Roberts-Gray, & Simpson, 1994).

- The low degree of staff nutritional knowledge has a direct effect on menu planning, food selection, and role modeling (Briley, Roberts-Gray, & Simpson, 1994).

- Excessive amounts of fats have been found in menus at child care centers and elementary school breakfast and lunch programs (Morris, 1991).

All caregivers should have a basic knowledge of nutrition. This information may be used to model proper food selection, create menus to serve the children, or teach nutrition to children and their parents. Food and nutrition should be an integral part of the promotion of health.

Child care centers or regulated family child care homes that participate in the Child and Adult Care Food Program (CACFP) are required to follow meal pattern guidelines, engage in some training, and utilize food and nutrition handbooks. In 1992, there were more than 24,000 child care centers and 160,000 family child care homes that were participating in CACFP. Investigations in 1989, 1991, and 1992 revealed that as many as 90 percent of observed participating centers fell short of the recommended standards used by CACFP (Briley, Roberts-Gray, & Rowe, 1993).

Caregivers need to create nutritional policies that will support the growth, health, and well-being of the children in their care. The four major goals for nutritional policies are similar to the policies for health and safety. They include:

1. Maximizing nutritional status
2. Minimizing nutritional risk
3. Using nutritional education as a tool
4. Recognizing the importance of nutritional guidelines

Nutritional policies may include menu planning guidelines, food selection, and preparation practices. These policies should be clearly written and should reflect nutrition as part of the promotion of health.

Nutritional policies should encompass the following:

■ *Nutritional Guidelines:* understanding nutritional guidelines for optimum nutritional well-being.

■ *Basic Nutrients:* understanding the basic **nutrients**, their sources, and the problems related to deficiencies.

■ *Nutritional Challenges:* awareness of specific nutritional challenges present in early childhood and how these challenges put children at risk.

■ *Implications for Caregivers:* methods and practices for promoting good nutrition through education, role modeling, and supervision to provide minimum nutritional risk and maximum health.

Nutrients
substances found in foods that provide for the growth, development, maintenance, and repair of the body

KEY NUTRITION POLICY

CONCEPT

Nutritional policies should be created for child care. These policies should use nutritional guidelines, apply basic nutrition, and address specific challenges of childhood nutrition. These policies should assist the caregiver with nutrition education, role modeling, supervision, and observation.

UNDERSTANDING NUTRITIONAL GUIDELINES

Adequate nutrition during childhood is necessary to maintain overall health and to provide for growth. A number of nutritional guidelines or strategies for good health have been established to help accomplish this task. In the past, the responsibility for following these recommendations fell to the parents because young children ate most of their meals at home. The past twenty years have presented major societal shifts in the number of working mothers and the number of single parent families. The resulting numbers of children in child care has risen dramatically. Approximately 15 million preschool children require child care (Splett & Story, 1991) and 34 million school aged children require after-school care.

Although some families of school aged children depend on the children caring for themselves, the majority of these children are in some form of care. It is essential that the caregiver understand nutrition regardless of whether the care is center based, school based, family child care, or nanny care. Since so many children are cared for by others, the transfer of responsibility for adequate nutrition has at least partially shifted from the home to child care. The more hours the child is in care, the greater the caregiver's responsibility for providing adequate nutrition for growth and maintenance of health. Established nutritional guidelines help the caregiver plan for adequate nutrition in menu selection. These guidelines and good nutritional practices can be shared with the children and their parents.

Dietary Guidelines for Americans

The U.S. Department of Health and Human Services in conjunction with the U.S. Department of Agriculture established dietary guidelines to maintain and improve the nutritional needs for health of Americans (U.S. Departments of Agriculture and Health and Human Services, 1990). The dietary guidelines are found in Table 9.1.

TABLE **9.1**

Dietary Guidelines for Americans

■ Eat a variety of foods.

■ Maintain a healthy weight.

■ Choose a diet low in fat, saturated fat, and cholesterol.

■ Choose a diet with plenty of vegetables, fruits, and grain products.

■ Use sugars only in moderation.

■ Use salt and sodium only in moderation.

■ If you drink alcoholic beverages do so in moderation.

The Food Guide Pyramid

The U.S. Department of Agriculture's Human Nutrition Information Service created a useful graphic dietary format called the Food Guide Pyramid. This pictorial format establishes good daily nutritional habits based on the dietary guidelines. The format is easy to remember and can be understood by most people, including young children (see Figure 9.1).

FIGURE **9.1**
Food Guide Pyramid

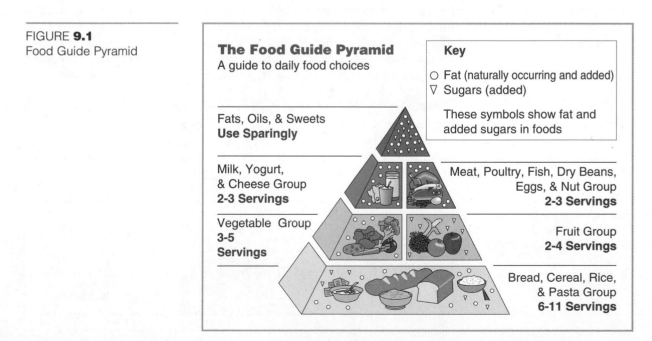

The Food Guide Pyramid
A guide to daily food choices

Key

○ Fat (naturally occurring and added)
▽ Sugars (added)

These symbols show fat and added sugars in foods

Fats, Oils, & Sweets
Use Sparingly

Milk, Yogurt,
& Cheese Group
2-3 Servings

Meat, Poultry, Fish, Dry Beans,
Eggs, & Nut Group
2-3 Servings

Vegetable Group
**3-5
Servings**

Fruit Group
2-4 Servings

Bread, Cereal, Rice,
& Pasta Group
6-11 Servings

Nutrition education includes teaching children about the basic food groups. Graphic representations of these groups using flannel boards or posters are good tools for teaching the importance of proper nutrition. What are some other ways to teach children about nutrition?

Overnutrition
excess intake of foods that provide more than adequate amounts of the substances needed for growth, development, maintenance, and repair of the body, often resulting in overweight

Undernutrition
less than adequate intake of foods that provide the substances needed for growth, development, maintenance, and repair of the body

Typical Level One Foods *(Courtesy of the U.S. Department of Agriculture)*

The Food Guide Pyramid focuses on the total diet and addresses the aspect of **overnutrition** as well as **undernutrition**. The Food Guide Pyramid supports the dietary guidelines by keying in on moderation of fats and sugars as well as supporting a varied diet consisting of a higher proportion of fruits, vegetables, and grains (Achterberg, McDonnell, & Bagby, 1994).

The information in the pyramid is organized by food choice levels from bottom to top. The levels of choices relate to the number of servings needed for adequate nutrition. The Food Guide Pyramid helps people of all ages and educational levels compare their food intake with the pyramid and make necessary changes at any level to improve their diet and nutritional well-being. This is probably the easiest overall guideline to proper nutrition.

Level One. The bread, cereal, rice, and pasta group includes whole grain breads, bagels, muffins, and cereals, as well as pastas, tortillas, pita, a variety of rice, and other ethnic breads and grains. This group is the major source of carbohydrates in our diet. Six to eleven servings should be consumed daily.

Bread, Cereal, Rice, & Pasta Group
6-11 Servings

Level Two. Level Two consists of two subgroups: the vegetable group and the fruit group. The vegetable group includes a wide variety of vegetable choices, from alfalfa sprouts to zucchini. Three to five servings per day are encouraged. Soups and stews can be counted as part of the daily vegetable servings.

Fruits, fruit juices, fruit leathers, and dried fruits such as banana chips and cranraisins comprise the fruit group. Fruits contain many of the vitamins and minerals we need in our diet.

Typical Level Two Foods
(Courtesy of the U.S. Department of Agriculture)

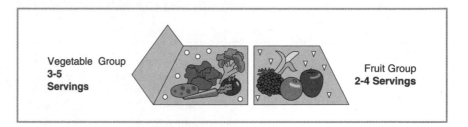

Level Three. Level Three consists of two subgroups: the milk, yogurt, and cheese group and the meat, poultry, fish, dry beans, eggs, and nuts group. The milk, yogurt, and cheese group is the major source of calcium in our diet. Selection of low-fat varieties of milk, yogurts, and cheeses is encouraged. Ice cream, custard, and pudding are included in the milk, yogurt, and cheese group.

The meat, poultry, fish, dry beans, eggs, and nuts group is the major source of protein in our diet. Low-fat selections of meat, poultry, and fish are encouraged. The number of eggs per week should be limited to four and dry beans and nuts should be used occasionally as an alternative to meats. Both subgroups at Level Four are also sources of fats in our diet.

Typical Level Three Foods
(Courtesy of the U.S. Department of Agriculture)

Level Four. Level Four consists of fats, oils, and sweets, including margarine, butter, and liquid oils; jams, jellies, and candy; and reduced fat candy bars. This group should be used in moderation to cut down on fats and sugar consumption that add nothing but empty calories to the diet.

Typical Level Four Foods
(Courtesy of the U.S. Department of Agriculture)

Recommended Dietary Allowances

The U.S. Recommended Dietary Allowances (U.S. RDA) are the suggested amounts of essential nutrients such as protein, vitamins, and minerals that should be consumed in foods daily to ensure good health. These recommendations are prepared by the National Academy of Sciences and are periodically revised. By following these recommendations, one should easily be able to meet daily nutritional needs.

RDAs are most commonly found on food labels (Figure 9.2) on packaged products where manufacturers are required to list nutrition facts. The

FIGURE **9.2**
Food Label *(Courtesy of U.S. Food and Drug Administration)*

Nutrition Facts

Serving Size 1/2 cup (114g)
Servings Per Container 4

Amount Per Serving

Calories 90	Calories from Fat 30

	% Daily Value
Total Fat 3g	**5%**
Saturated Fat 0g	**0%**
Cholesterol 0mg	**0%**
Sodium 300mg	**13%**
Total Carbohydrate 13g	**4%**
Dietary Fiber 3g	**12%**
Sugars 3g	
Protein 3g	

Vitamin A	80%	•	Vitamin C	60%
Calcium	4%	•	Iron	4%

• Percent Daily Values are based on a 2,000 calorie diet. Your daily values may be higher or lower depending on your calorie needs:

	Calories	2,000	2,500
Total Fat	Less than	65g	80g
Sat Fat	Less than	20g	25g
Cholesterol	Less than	300mg	300mg
Sodium	Less than	2,400mg	2,400mg
Total Carbohydrate		300g	375g
Fiber		25g	30g

Calories per gram:

Fat 9	•	Carbohydrate 4	•	Protein 4

information is broken down on a per serving basis. Calories and amounts of fat, cholesterol, carbohydrates, protein, vitamin A, vitamin B (thiamine, riboflavin, and niacin), vitamin C, vitamin D, sodium, and other essential minerals such as calcium and iron are listed.

Table 9.2 includes a suggested diet for children over the age of two years that closely parallels the food guide pyramid and is designed to meet the nutritional standards established in the recommended daily allowances. One caution is that these recommendations and guidelines apply to children over the age of two years. Infants and children under two years of age have other specific dietary needs and physical limitations that do not match with the guidelines.

TABLE **9.2**

A Healthy Diet for Children

■ Dairy Products: 2 servings; 1 serving = 1 cup milk or yogurt or 1.5 oz. cheese

■ Meats, Poultry, Fish, Dry Beans, Peas, Eggs, and Nuts: 2 servings; 1 serving = 6 oz. or 1 egg

■ Breads, Cereals, Rice, and Pasta: 6 servings; 1 serving = 1 slice bread, 1 bagel, ½ cup rice

■ Vegetables: 3 servings; 1 serving = 1 cup raw greens, ½ cup other vegetables

■ Fruits: 2 servings; 1 serving = 1 medium orange or apple, ½ cup diced fruit, or ¾ cup fruit juice

---

Healthy People 2000

Many of the objectives included in Healthy People 2000 are aimed at decreasing the prevalence of overweight, increasing fruit and vegetable intake, reducing intake of fat, sodium, and sugar, and reducing growth retardation and iron deficiency in children (Lewis, Crane, Moore, & Hubbard, 1994). These recommendations are consistent with Dietary Guidelines for Americans and support the Food Guide Pyramid and Recommended Daily Allowances.

Child and Adult Care Food Program

The Child and Adult Care Food Program (CACFP) of the U.S. Department of Agriculture enables family child care homes as well as nonprofit child care centers to be reimbursed for creating menus and serving meals that meet dietary guidelines established by this program. These dietary guidelines are based on the RDAs and the Dietary Guidelines for Americans. Recommended meal patterns are provided by CACFP.

Television has become a major challenge to healthy lifestyles. Television use in the preschool and home care setting should be kept to a minimum.

KEY NUTRITIONAL GUIDELINES

CONCEPT

An increasing number of children will rely on child care to provide a good portion of their nutritional needs. Caregivers should be knowledgeable about nutritional guidelines as they plan menus and provide food to the children in care. The Food Guide Pyramid is the easiest to understand and will help the child caregiver educate children and their parents about nutrition. Dietary Guidelines for Americans, the Recommended Daily Allowances, Healthy People 2000, and the Child and Adult Care Food Program also provide helpful information for the caregiver.

BASIC NUTRIENTS

The basic nutrients found in food perform all the functions needed to help the body grow, repair, regulate, and maintain itself. There are six sources of nutrients: carbohydrates, fats, protein, vitamins, minerals, and water. Each source of nutrients performs specific functions. The two major functions by which nutrients can be categorized are the energy nutrients and the supporting nutrients. Energy nutrients are fats, carbohydrates, and protein; supporting nutrients are vitamins, minerals, and water.

Energy Nutrients

Energy is needed to maintain life, support growth, regulate body processes, and perform voluntary activities. We measure the energy needs of our bodies in terms of **calories**. The number of calories each body needs

Calories
the unit of measurement for the energy found in foods

Basal metabolism
the amount of energy used by the body while at rest

Metabolism
chemical changes that take place as nutrients are taken into the blood, processed and absorbed by the blood, or eliminated from the body

Macronutrients
major nutrients needed for the body, such as fats, carbohydrates, and protein

Glucose
sugar found in blood

depends on the **basal metabolism**, **metabolism** of food, growth and physical activity, and age of that body. Calories are supplied to the body from three major nutrients:

■ Fats supply 9 calories per gram
■ Carbohydrates supply 4 calories per gram
■ Protein supplies 4 calories per gram

Carbohydrates, fats, and protein provide the energy needed to run the body and provide the materials to help the body grow and maintain its functions. These energy providers are often referred to as **macronutrients**

Carbohydrates.   Carbohydrates are the first source of energy the body uses and are the major source of energy for the central nervous system. Carbohydrates provide a slow, steady supply of energy necessary for utilization of other nutrients in the body. An example would be carbohydrates supplying energy so protein can be used for growth and maintenance of body cells. Carbohydrates also help digest fat, add roughage and fiber to promote elimination, and provide **glucose** to the liver to be stored as energy for later use.

The major sources of carbohydrates in the diet are from Level One and Level Two foods. According to the Dietary Guidelines for Americans, approximately 58 percent of our diet should come from these foods. Carbohydrates are also found in sugars in various forms, including lactose, which is found in milk. Lactose from breast milk or formula supplies the major source of carbohydrates for infants.

A diet with insufficient amounts of carbohydrates causes a body to use fats or proteins for the energy it needs, thus robbing it of the functions these two nutrients provide. Growth and maintenance of the body will be at risk.

Foods high in fat but low in nutritional value, such as fast food, should be limited in a child's diet. It is important to remember, however, that adequate amounts of fat are important for children's normal growth and development, particularly for infants and children under the age of two.

Cholesterol
a steroid or fatty alcohol
found in animal fats that is
produced by the liver of the
animal

Fats.   Fats are considered to be the body's second source of energy. Fat also supplies essential fatty acids that are critical for proper growth of children. Other functions of fat include cushioning of organs, maintaining body temperature, promoting healthy skin, and helping fat-soluble vitamins be carried throughout the body. Fats also help regulate the metabolism of **cholesterol** in the body.

The major source of fats comes from Level Three and Level Four foods. Sources are both plant and animal. Primary animal sources include red meats, fish, poultry, eggs, and milk products, which account for about 58 percent of the fat in our diets. Plant sources, such as corn, safflower, canola, palm, and coconut oils, provide the remaining 42 percent of the fat found in a typical diet. According to the RDA, only 30 percent or less of the total calories in our diet should come from fats. Table 9.3 lists the different types of fats.

TABLE **9.3**

Types of Fats

■ Polyunsaturated fats
Function: Lowers blood cholesterol, decreases tendency of blood to clot
Sources: Plants and plant oils (sunflower, corn, canola) and fish
RDA: 10 percent or less of total calories

■ Monounsaturated fats
Function: Neutral—neither raises nor lowers blood cholesterol
Sources: Olives, peanuts, nuts, avocado
RDA: 10 percent of total calories

■ Saturated fats
Function: Raises blood cholesterol, increases tendency of blood to clot
Sources: Animals, animal fats, butter, shortening, nuts, cheese, coconut, coconut and palm oil, ice cream
RDA: 10 percent or less of total calories

The recommended daily allowance for fat consumption in the diet takes into consideration the risk of excess fat. Saturated fats are of particular concern because they contribute to high blood cholesterol, which contributes to the development of coronary heart disease. All animal fats are saturated; most vegetable sources of fat are either polyunsaturated or monounsaturated. To help lower saturated fats in the diet, it is important to choose vegetable sources of fat more often than animal fats (see Figures 9.3 and 9.4).

Although the consumption of fat should be carefully monitored in order to meet the dietary guidelines, it is an important part of a child's diet. A diet that is inadequate in the amount of fat it provides could impair a child's normal growth and development.

Infants and children under the age of two years need greater amounts of fat for growth and development and should not be limited by the dietary guidelines recommended for those children over two years of age. The

FIGURE **9.3**
Chart of Fats (Comparison)
*(Data from Proctor &
Gamble and Reeves, J. B.,
& Weibrauch, J. L., (1979).*
Composition of foods,
agriculture handbook
no. 8-4. *Washington, DC:
U.S. Department of
Agriculture)*

Dietary Fat Comparison

| | Cholesterol mg/Tbsp | Saturated Fat |
| | Polyunsaturated Fat | Monounsaturated Fat |

	Cholesterol mg/Tbsp	Saturated Fat	Polyunsaturated Fat	Monounsaturated Fat
Canola oil	0	6%	32%	62%
Safflower oil	0	10%	77%	13%
Sunflower oil	0	11%	69%	20%
Corn oil	0	13%	62%	25%
Olive oil	0	14%	9%	77%
Soybean oil	0	15%	61%	24%
Peanut oil	0	18%	33%	49%
Margarine	0	19%	32%	49%
Vegetable shortening	0	28%	28%	44%
Lard	12	41%	12%	47%
Beef fat	14	52%	4%	44%
Butter	33	66%	4%	30%

FIGURE **9.4**
Saturated vs. Unsaturated
Fats *(From Hubbard, M., &
Robertson, C. [1989].*
Cholesterol countdown. *San
Diego, CA: Pegasus Press)*

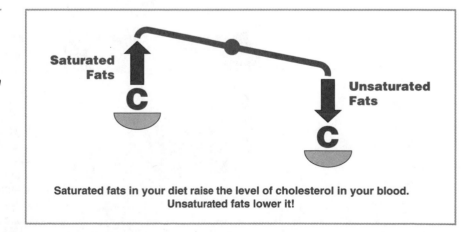

**Saturated
Fats**

**Unsaturated
Fats**

**Saturated fats in your diet raise the level of cholesterol in your blood.
Unsaturated fats lower it!**

American Academy of Pediatrics advises against restriction of fat in the diet for the first two years of life (Food Marketing Institute, 1991).

Protein. Protein, the third source of energy, is the major building block in our bodies. It is found in every cell of the body. Protein builds new cells, aids in the repair of damaged tissue, and is used to form enzymes that aid in digestion and to provide hormones and antibodies that increase resistance to infection.

Protein is made of **amino acids**, nine of which are essential for tissue growth, repair, and maintenance. A food containing protein that provides all nine essential amino acids is called a **complete protein**. Foods from animal sources are the only complete protein foods.

To obtain adequate protein with the essential amino acids in a vegetarian diet, foods can be combined to provide complete protein. For example, a grain food would be combined with a legume food. Additions of egg or milk products help to provide complete protein in a vegetarian diet. Vegetarian diets should be carefully monitored to ensure adequate intake of nutrients. The Food Guide Pyramid is a good source of information for this.

A diet that is deficient in protein causes stunted growth in children, and makes them easily fatigued and irritable. Lack of protein also makes children susceptible to infection and slow to recover or repair a wound.

Helper Nutrients

The energy nutrients depend on the helper nutrients, or **micronutrients**, to perform their functions and to regulate the body's metabolism. Micronutrients, which are classified as vitamins, minerals, and water, must be present in sufficient quantities for the energy nutrients to perform properly. Micronutrients do not contain calories. They each perform specific functions and are found in many foods.

Vitamins. Vitamins are categorized into two groups. Fat soluble vitamins attach to fats to travel throughout the body and can be stored in the body. Water soluble vitamins travel easily through the body with water and cannot be stored in the body, so they must be replaced daily (see Figure 9.5).

Amino acids
organic compounds containing carbon, hydrogen, oxygen, and nitrogen; the key components of proteins

---

Complete protein
protein that contains all essential amino acids

Micronutrients
supporting nutrients, such as vitamins, minerals, and water, needed by the body

---

FIGURE **9.5**
Fat and Water Soluble Vitamins

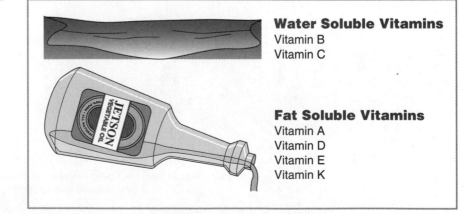

Water Soluble Vitamins
Vitamin B
Vitamin C

Fat Soluble Vitamins
Vitamin A
Vitamin D
Vitamin E
Vitamin K

The fat soluble vitamins are vitamin A, vitamin D, vitamin E, and vitamin K. Vitamin A promotes growth and is important for good vision, good skin, and strong bones. It also helps in wound healing. Lack of vitamin A can cause poor bone and tooth enamel growth, rough skin, and night blindness. It is found in yellow, orange, and green vegetables, yellow and orange fruits, and in the fat of animal products like fish, milk, eggs, and liver.

Vitamin D is needed to help calcium make strong bones and teeth. An insufficient amount of vitamin D can lead to rickets, a disease in children that stunts bone growth. Vitamin D is produced naturally in the skin when it gets sunshine. To ensure that vitamin D consumption is adequate in all parts of the country at all times of the year, vitamin D is added to most milk. It is also found in fatty fish, liver, eggs, and butter.

Vitamin E helps preserve cell tissues. There are no known effects of vitamin E deficiency. It is found in whole grain cereals, vegetable oils, and a wide variety of foods, so most people get enough.

Vitamin K is needed for normal blood clotting. Lack of vitamin K can cause hemorrhaging. It is found in dark green leafy vegetables and whole grains. Vitamin K is also made in our bodies.

Water soluble vitamins include the B vitamins and vitamin C. There are numerous B vitamins, but the most important for children are thiamin (B_1), riboflavin (B_2), niacin, and folacin (folic acid).

Thiamin is essential for carbohydrate metabolism and contributes to normal functioning of the nervous system. If there is not enough thiamin in the diet, fatigue and irritability may be present. Lean pork, nuts, grains, and green leafy vegetables are good sources of thiamin.

Riboflavin is essential for carbohydrate, protein, and fat metabolism. It also promotes healthy skin, eyes, and clear vision. Lack of riboflavin can cause skin and digestive disturbances, as well as sensitivity to light. Good sources of riboflavin include milk products, eggs, legumes, liver, and leafy vegetables.

Niacin is needed for carbohydrate metabolism as well as fat synthesis and tissue respiration. It helps promote healthy nerves and skin and aids in digestion. Niacin is known as the "Four D" vitamin because lack of it can cause dermatitis, diarrhea, dementia, and death. Meat, poultry, fish, peanuts, liver, whole grains, enriched cereals, and green leafy vegetables are good sources of niacin.

Folacin is required for normal growth, helps prevent anemia and is an important factor in reproduction. If there is an insufficient amount of folacin in the diet, anemia may result. Folacin is critical in the diet of a pregnant woman to help prevent neural tubal defects or damage to the fetus. Good sources of folacin include dark green leafy vegetables, legumes, liver, and nuts.

Minerals. Minerals help the metabolic process and regulate body fluids. There are twenty-five minerals that help the body to perform. The minerals especially important for children are calcium, phosphorous, iron, sodium, magnesium, potassium, and fluoride.

Calcium is the most important mineral because it is present in all bones and teeth. It helps to regulate the body systems, promotes normal nerve transmission, and functions in normal muscle contraction and relaxation. The major source of calcium is milk and milk products.

Milk is a primary source of calcium, an important mineral for bone and teeth development.

Encourage children to drink water when they are thirsty. This will make them more likely to turn to water instead of sugary fruit drinks.

Phosphorus is also present in bones and teeth. It helps to transport fat and provides enzymes for energy metabolism. Phosphorus is found in milk products, meat, poultry, fish, whole-grain cereals, and legumes.

Iron combines with protein to form red blood cells and carry oxygen in the blood. It also helps the immune system resist infection and helps enzymes to release energy to the body. A deficiency of iron causes anemia and fatigue. Anemia among children is one of the major health problems in the United States. Liver, green leafy vegetables, whole grains, legumes, meats, and dried fruits are good sources of iron.

Sodium is important for fluid balance in the body. It also contributes to the stimulation of nerves and muscle contractions. Sources are salt, baking powder, soda, celery, milk, eggs, meats, poultry, and fish.

Magnesium is present in bones and teeth. It helps transmit nerve impulses, aids enzymes for energy metabolism, and helps in muscle contraction. Magnesium is found in milk, meat, green leafy vegetables, whole-grain cereals, and legumes.

Potassium is important for protein and carbohydrate metabolism. It also helps in water balance in the body and transmits nerve impulses. Good sources of potassium are vegetables, fruit juices, and fruits, especially bananas and tomatoes. Potassium is also found in meats and cereals.

Fluoride helps promote strength of bone and teeth structure and is important in preventing tooth decay. It is found in fish and fluoridated water. Many water systems in the United States add fluoride to the water to help prevent tooth decay. Some fluoridated water is too high in fluoride for many young children. Overfluoridation can cause pitting and discoloration of teeth. It is recommended that caregivers use bottled water to avoid this condition.

Water. Water is necessary to sustain life. It comprises about 70 percent of the human body and must be replenished daily. Water is needed for the metabolic activities within cells, for transportation of nutrients and waste

products, and for regulation of body temperature. How much water a body needs on a daily basis depends on body metabolism, age, and outside temperature.

Most of the water loss in the body is due to urination or evaporation from the skin or respiratory tract. A small amount of water is lost through fecal elimination. If there is a problem with larger than normal losses such as may occur with increased sweating from exercise, the water must be replaced. This is especially important for infants and young children because loss of water from diarrhea, vomiting, or a high fever can occur quickly and cause the infant or young child to become dehydrated. It is important to keep track of water intake, and if the amount of water does not seem to replace the losses, a physician should be consulted.

Water is present in most foods found in nature. It is in fruits and vegetables in large amounts. Fruit juices can be a major source of water for older infants and young children, although children should be encouraged to drink water. Children who are encouraged to drink water at an early age are more likely to turn to water to quench their thirst instead of sugary drinks.

KEY BASIC NUTRIENTS

CONCEPT

Foods provide the basic nutrients needed by the body to grow, repair, regulate, and maintain itself. There are six sources of nutrients, which are divided into two categories. The energy nutrients—carbohydrates, fats, and protein—provide the calories needed to run the body and the materials needed for growth and maintenance. Protein is the major building block for the body. The helper nutrients—vitamins, minerals, and water—help the energy nutrients perform their functions and help regulate the body's metabolism. A diet that follows the Food Guide Pyramid and considers the RDA should provide all the basic nutrients in sufficient quantities.

CHILDHOOD NUTRITIONAL CHALLENGES

Malnutrition
inadequate nutrition as a result of improper diet or lack of food

Social changes such as increases in one-parent families, dual-career families, poverty, and homelessness have a negative impact on the food selection and nutrition of children in this country ("Position of the American Dietetic Association," 1993). Nutritional challenges that pose risks to children's health can be related to **malnutrition** or overnutrition. These risks may appear in the form of growth retardation, hunger, obesity, dental disease, and iron-deficiency anemia (Splett & Story, 1991). In addition, diets high in sodium and fat can lead to the development of hypertension and high levels of cholesterol later in life. Another risk factor is food allergies.

Starvation and malnutrition is not something that happens only in other parts of the world. Children in U.S. cities are especially at risk, as the number of single parent families below the poverty level continues to rise.

Some of the societal changes affecting the family relate to the lack of environmental support needed for proper growth. More than one-fourth of the children in the United States live in a single parent household. There are 500,000 children born to teenage mothers every year, of whom 70 percent are unmarried. More than half of the children in single parent families are living at the poverty level (Children's Defense Fund, 1996).

Other children may be at the poverty level or even homeless due to unemployment or underemployment. Families with children represent the fastest growing portion of the homeless population. It is estimated that more than 100,000 children are homeless every day. Half of these are reported to be under six years of age (Taylor & Koblinsky, 1994).

During the past two decades the number of working mothers has greatly increased. More than 11 million children under the age of six have mothers who work outside the home. These families are turning to child care for their children in increasing numbers. Child care often fails to meet the nutritional needs of children (Briley, Roberts-Gray, & Rowe, 1993).

Hunger and Growth Retardation

Hunger is defined as a chronic shortage of necessary nutrients. According to that definition, 12 million children in the United States are experiencing hunger (Brown, 1987). Hunger exists within all socioeconomic levels. The Community Childhood Hunger Identification Project estimates one in twenty-five families has children who are hungry. A close correlation between poverty and impaired growth exists. Growth retardation has been found to be as much as three times greater for poor children than children who are not poor ("Children's Nutrition and Learning," 1994).

Malnutrition may cause stunting and impaired brain function. This is especially true of children born to mothers who did not have a good diet during pregnancy. Nearly one-fourth of women who give birth in the United States each year do not have adequate nutrition, and as a result, they are three times as likely to deliver low birthweight infants (U.S. Department of Health and Human Services, 1990). These children have growth patterns that are already at risk.

Some parents or caregivers may lack the time, knowledge of nutrition, or ability to prepare nutritious meals. They may rely on fast foods and convenience foods to feed their children. These foods generally provide large amounts of fats, sugars, and sodium and lack adequate amounts of vegetables, fruits, and other sources of vitamins and minerals. Parents of children in middle and high income families may purchase more high-fat and high-sugar snacks, thus robbing their children of good nutritional choices for their diets.

Children with chronic health conditions, physical handicaps, and developmental delays may be at increased risk for hunger and growth retardation due to inadequate nutrition. These children may have physical feeding difficulties, alterations in bodily functions, or poor feeding behavior. Nutritional expectations and growth patterns must be carefully monitored for these children to prevent malnutrition.

Children who are poorly nourished are more vulnerable to infection and disease, including frequent colds, ear infections, anemia, tuberculosis, and environmental toxins such as lead poisoning.

Ruth, a nanny, went to work for a family when the child, Mark, was two months old. She had no problems with Mark's diet until he was eleven months old and ready to begin eating a regular diet without baby food. His parents ate all their meals away from home and were not used to keeping regular food at home. The only thing they normally had in the refrigerator were salad dressing, olives, and leftovers from their latest take-out meals.

Fortunately, Ruth was a trained nanny who had taken a child's nutrition class and was therefore aware of what Mark needed in his diet. She was able to educate the parents as to the importance of Mark's diet. They asked her to provide them with a shopping list and they bought the foods she requested. The nicest reward for Ruth was that the entire family began eating better and the parents started preparing family meals at home to share with Mark. They were grateful to Ruth for making them realize how their habits may have caused Mark problems.

Prevention strategies for malnutrition and undernutrition include nutrition education, a balanced diet with a selection of healthy foods, and healthy food preparation methods. Since many children eat twice a day in child care, the caregiver should examine the menus and compare them to the Food Guide Pyramid to see how the selections meet the standards. Children who eat well and see good food in care may change their outlook on food selection as well as influence their nutritional status. Children who understand that food is the fuel that makes their bodies work properly may make better food choices when offered the opportunity, especially if the food is enjoyable and appetizing.

REALITY CHECK

Hunger in America

Hunger in America is not a fantasy. Twelve million children in this country under twelve years of age suffer from hunger. Ten percent of the American population is on food stamps, and 82 percent of those on food stamps are families with children (SOS Online, 1996b). Food banks provide food to 25 million Americans. There has been a steady increase in the need for this type of assistance for the last fifteen years.

The reasons hunger exists in this country include unemployment, poverty, high cost of housing, high cost of living, substance abuse, and mental illness (SOS Online, 1996b). Lack of knowledge about nutrition and food purchasing also contributes to hunger in families where income is not an issue.

Hunger can disrupt the healthy development of children. It can lead to weight loss, stunted growth, weakened resistance to disease, and cognitive difficulties. Malnutrition can be especially harmful to children in the first years of life when their bodies and brains are developing rapidly.

continued

New findings have shown that malnutrition's effects on the brain development of young children can be reversed (Brown & Pollitt, 1996). These studies also found that healthy children over two years of age can be adversely affected if they become malnourished. This reverses the theory that malnourishment to children under two is always permanent and that these years are the only years to be concerned about.

Over the years studies have concentrated on which food provides the most adequate nutrition. The conclusion is that children need enough protein, calories, vitamins, and minerals for normal growth and development. Homeless children have been found to be lacking in the consumption of dairy products, fruits, vegetables, and lean meats (Derrickson, Widodo, & Jarosz, 1994). These are the items that would provide those things that children need for adequate growth.

A caregiver may be providing as much as two-thirds of the nutrition for the children in care. It is important that this food is adequate in basic nutrients that all children need. If money is an issue to the care situation, help from the Child and Adult Care Food Program (CACFP) should be sought. Other sources of help and information are local food programs, or an organization called Share Our Strength. This organization distributes food to people in need, provides meals through school breakfast and summer food programs, and provides access to healthy produce (SOS Online, 1996a). It also offers Operation Frontline, which helps people on limited incomes to shop smarter and eat better. This program currently operates in ten large cities throughout the country.

Caregivers have an opportunity to protect the children in their care by offering healthy, adequate food. They can also provide nutritional information and good food selection techniques for both children and parents. Caregivers have the ability to help reverse hunger in America for some children.

Obesity

Excess weight is basically a problem created by energy imbalance. The amount of energy taken in through foods is metabolized and then released through the body's work, including involuntary bodily functions such as breathing and voluntary functions such as movement and exercise. If more energy is taken in than is put out, then an imbalance results and that excess energy is stored in the body as fat.

A child who weighs more than 10 percent above the normal weight shown on the growth chart (see Appendix A) is considered overweight. A child who weighs more than 20 percent over the normal weight for the corresponding height on the growth chart is considered obese. Obesity appears to be on the increase in children from six to seventeen years of age (National Center for Health Statistics, 1995).

Obesity also appears to be ethnically linked. The Office of Maternal and Child Health reported that 12 percent of Hispanic boys and 19 percent of Hispanic girls were classified as obese. They also reported that 5 to 7 percent of both African American and Caucasian children were considered obese (Shapiro, 1990).

There are a number of reasons for obesity in children as shown in Table 9.4. It is likely that childhood obesity results from a combination of familial, nutritional, physical, and psychological factors.

Childhood obesity can cause pediatric hypertension and diabetes mellitus. Stress on the weight bearing joints is one of the physical problems that obesity may cause. Mentally and emotionally, obesity lowers self-esteem and has a powerful effect on peer relationships and social acceptance.

TABLE **9.4**

Common Reasons for Obesity in Children

- ■ Dietary excesses in foods containing fats, cholesterol, and sugar
- ■ Poor infant or child feeding practices
- ■ Lack of sufficient exercise
- ■ Watching too much television
- ■ Family genetic predisposition
- ■ Using food as a comforting device or for emotional support
- ■ Weight gain during critical developmental periods

The problem of childhood obesity can be improved by an increase in physical activity, diet management, and behavior modification. Physical activity alone does not seem to be effective, but the addition of diet and behavior modification contributes to successful weight loss in obese children.

Diet management should include both a doctor-recommended modified caloric intake and nutrition education. Modifying caloric intake reduces dietary fat intake and nutrition education encourages children to make better choices in food selection. Parents should be included in the behavior modification process, which should include problem-solving techniques. Early intervention that utilizes the whole child approach has been especially effective in helping obese children lose weight and increase their level of self-esteem. The best way to help prevent childhood obesity is good parent education.

Caregivers can help obese children by providing a well-balanced diet that is not high in fat. They can provide nutritional information for parents, including referrals for help if needed. Caregivers should provide children with plenty of activity and exercise throughout the day so they have adequate opportunities to burn calories.

Serving a balanced variety of child-size foods makes eating a pleasant and comfortable experience for young children. Color variety has also been shown to stimulate children's interest in food. What other ways can a caregiver make meals appealing to children?

Dental Caries

Dental caries, or cavities as they are commonly known, affect almost everyone in the population. Low-income African American and Hispanic mothers see dental caries as one of three major health problems affecting their children (Pestano-Binghay, Reis, & Walters, 1993).

Foods that are high in carbohydrates and sugar promote the formation of cavities. Carbohydrates in the form of starches break down as sugars, which change rapidly to acid when mixed with the microorganisms commonly found in the plaque present in the mouth. The acids produced break through the natural barrier and form cavities. When sugar is ingested, the acid formation process lasts for about 25 minutes. Sticky items that contain sugar, such as honey, soft drinks, raisins, and bananas, lengthen the acid formation process. This is also true of sugars found in milk and fruit juices.

Fluoride use is the most effective method of preventing dental caries. Fluoride is added to many water supplies in the United States. If the caregiver lives in an area that has fluoridated water, she should encourage children to drink the water. If fluoride is not in the water supply, then the family dentist should prescribe fluoride supplements. Many family doctors include fluoride in the vitamin and mineral supplements given to babies. Other prevention methods include brushing teeth after eating meals and using only water in a baby bottle at bedtime. When milk or juice is given in a bottle at bedtime, the fluid pools in the child's mouth and increases the incidence of cavities. If a baby needs a bottle to go to sleep, the baby should be fed a bottle of formula or should be nursed before going to bed, thus allowing for adequate nutrition.

Teeth brushing can be a fun and informative activity that caregivers can add to their nutrition education programs. Giving children the opportunity to brush after meals is another way to encourage good dental hygiene.

Caregivers can make sure that child care is using good practices to prevent dental caries by providing diets low in sugar and offering children the opportunity to brush their teeth.

Iron Deficiency Anemia

Iron deficiency anemia is the most prevalent nutritional problem in childhood ("Children's Nutrition," 1994). It is two times more likely to occur among poor children than among those whose families are not poor. Older infants and young children are more likely to become at risk for iron deficiency as the iron stored in their bodies when they were born diminishes over time. Anemia due to iron deficiency may cause a shortened attention span, irritability, and fatigue. Children with iron deficiency anemia may have trouble concentrating, which may later affect their IQ (Parker, 1989).

The only way to avoid iron deficiency and the anemia that results from it is to get adequate supplies of iron in the diet or to supplement the diet with a doctor-recommended vitamin compound containing iron.

Infants receive most of their nutrients from formulas or breast milk. Most formulas provide the necessary iron. Breast milk provides iron also, but after about four to five months of age, infants need more iron than their mothers can provide. Therefore, doctors recommend vitamin supplements that include iron to prevent iron deficiency. Baby cereals are fortified with iron to help provide the necessary iron in the diet.

Adequate supplies of iron must be provided in a growing child's diet but frequently are not. Caregivers should provide iron-rich meals to ensure that children get enough of this essential mineral.

As a child grows, more sources of iron, such as is in meats, fish, poultry, green leafy vegetables, and whole grains, are necessary to prevent iron deficiency. However, many children do not eat balanced diets. When quality of diets was investigated, Stanek, Abbott, and Cramer (1990) found that one-fourth of the children's diets studied were iron deficient. Menus at child care centers were found to be lacking in foods that could help children meet their need for iron (Briley, Roberts-Gray, & Rowe, 1993). Iron deficiency in poor children has been linked to poor compliance with feeding practices due possibly to inadequate funds or lack of parental understanding of the importance of diet.

The best way to prevent iron deficiency and the resulting anemia is through education of the parents, the caregivers, and the children themselves. Caregivers who are aware of the importance of iron can provide more balanced diets with better food selections. In cases where supplementation is necessary, iron-fortified breads and cereals should be used.

Cardiovascular Disease and Hypertension

The diet of many Americans contains too many calories, too much fat, and too much cholesterol. It is also high in sodium. The Bogalusa Heart Study is an ongoing research project focusing on **cardiovascular disease** risk factors present in children's lives (Graham, 1990). The National Cholesterol Education Program (NCEP) sponsored by the U.S. Department of Health and Human Services is also concerned with the issue of children's diet and cardiovascular risk.

Early elevated levels of cholesterol can lead to the development of early **coronary atherosclerosis**. The combination of diet and genetic risk factors can trigger a higher incidence of this disease than in the normal population. Higher blood cholesterol levels can also lead to **coronary heart disease (CHD)**, which is the number one cause of death in this country. Children who eat diets with excess calories and too much fat tend to be overweight. This is another risk factor in coronary heart disease (see Figure 9.6).

Excess weight and high sodium intake contribute to **hypertension**. The Bogalusa Heart Study found that nearly all children under ten years of age consume more than the RDA levels of sodium. High sodium intake can be linked to the later development of high blood pressure. Convenience foods and fast foods are high in sodium. Some of children's favorite foods contain too much salt, including chips, hot dogs, lunch meats, canned soups, and store bought breads. Menus found at child care centers used a large number of these foods and provided from 200 to 300 percent of the RDA for sodium (Briley, Roberts-Gray, & Rowe, 1993).

The best way to improve the risk factors for cardiovascular diseases and hypertension is to modify the diet. Following the recommendations of the Dietary Guidelines for Americans, children's fat intake should be decreased to no more than 30 percent of total calories, saturated fat should be decreased to less than 10 percent of total calories, and sodium intake should be decreased.

Children should also eat diets higher in carbohydrates, which means more fruits, vegetables, and grain products (U.S. Department of Health and Human Services, Public Health Service, & National Institutes of Health,

---

Cardiovascular disease
disease resulting from impaired function of the heart and/or surrounding arteries

Coronary atherosclerosis
disease of the heart resulting in the walls of arteries degenerating due to fat buildup

Coronary heart disease
disease of the arteries feeding the heart muscle

Hypertension
very high blood pressure

High cholesterol
Being male
Diabetes mellitus
High blood pressure
Obesity
Cigarette smoking
Vascular (blood
  vessel) disease
Family members with
  CHD before age 60

FIGURE **9.6**
Risk Factors for
Cardiovascular Disease

Children base their food interests on what tastes good, not nutritional value. Many of children's favorite foods contain too much salt and sugar.

1991). Helpful guidelines for following these recommendations are found in Table 9.5.

Child caregivers can help children decrease the amount of cholesterol, fat, and sodium intake by following Table 9.5.

TABLE **9.5**

Guidelines to Decrease Fat and Sodium Intake

■ Provide plenty of fresh fruits and vegetables.

■ Serve whole grain breads and cereals.

■ Use only lean meats, poultry, and fish.

■ Choose low-fat dairy products.

■ Choose fats from vegetable sources such as margarine and canola oil. Limit the intake of these fat products.

■ Select cooking methods that are lower fat alternatives to frying such as grilling or baking.

■ Avoid high-sodium foods such as hot dogs, lunch meats, and chips; if these foods are occasionally used, do so in moderation.

■ Carefully select menu items that are lower in fat and sodium at fast food restaurants.

■ Moderate the use of frozen, packaged, and canned foods.

■ Use margarine products made with unsaturated vegetable oils instead of saturated vegetable oils like coconut and palm kernel.

■ Set a good example by eating healthy foods.

Lactose intolerance is a common allergic reaction to lactose, the simple sugar found in milk. Good communication between caregivers and parents regarding a child's food allergies should be maintained.

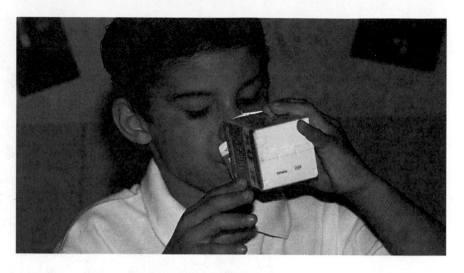

Lactose intolerance
inability of body to process lactose found in milk and milk products

Food Allergies

If a child cannot eat or properly metabolize a food with important nutrients, he may be at risk for malnutrition and undernutrition. The response to food allergies may range from skin rashes and difficulty breathing to gastrointestinal difficulties. Foods that commonly bring on allergic reactions are milk, peanuts, orange juice, wheat, pork, and eggs.

Allergic reaction to milk is most often apparent as **lactose intolerance**. Lactose is the simple sugar found in milk. When someone is unable to metabolize lactose properly, she experiences gastric distress such as diarrhea or vomiting. Infants who exhibit lactose intolerance are put on soy-based or other lactose-free formulas.

If a child is suspected to have an allergic reaction to a food, use of that food should be halted immediately and that child should be taken to a physician for diagnosis. The family and caregiver can use proper means prescribed to treat the allergy. Consulting a dietician for recommendations to compensate for any possible nutrient loss is also helpful. Parents should inform caregivers and caregivers should ask if a child suffers from a food allergy. It is necessary to post reminders of food allergies of the children in care on the refrigerator or other obvious places seen during food preparation.

KEY NUTRITIONAL CHALLENGE

Childhood nutritional challenges result from lack of balanced diets. Hunger, growth retardation, and iron deficiency anemia may result from undernutrition or malnutrition. Too many of the wrong kind of nutrients can result in dental caries, obesity, cardiovascular problems, and hypertension. Food allergies may result in a nutritional imbalance. Risk management measures such as monitoring children for growth, providing well-balanced diets with healthy food selections, and nutrition education will help prevent nutritional challenges for children.

IMPLICATIONS FOR **CAREGIVERS**

Nutrition education of children and their parents is one of the most powerful tools that a child caregiver has to promote and protect the health and well-being of children. Good nutrition can help a child maintain health and fight off infections, colds, and other communicable diseases. It allows children to grow adequately and develop to the best of their potential. Nutrition information shared with parents and other family members can lead to a healthier, more protective environment for the families.

Education

Many families are unaware of the importance of an adequate diet. Because of the pace of life in this country, regular family meal times are losing ground as part of a daily routine. Use of convenience foods, fast foods, and take-out meals is increasing and taking a toll on the general diet of Americans. Children in urban areas may obtain more than half of their calories outside the home ("Children's Nutrition," 1994).

Carol had a part-time job and did not rely much on child care for her daughter Jessamyn, age two-and one-half years. Carol had the opportunity to be promoted into the job of her dreams and she took it. Early every morning, she dropped Jessie off at the family child care home. In the evening when she returned to pick Jessie up, Carol was exhausted. Carol fell into the habit of feeding Jessie cold cereal almost every night, or picking up hamburgers, fries, and soft drinks. In the mornings, cold cereal was breakfast because it was easy and quick. Aleta, the family child caregiver, noticed how Jessie seemed to be coming down with more colds and seemed to lack the healthy glow she had had when she first arrived. Aleta spoke with Carol about Jessie's diet and Carol admitted that she knew it should be different but she didn't know what she should do and had very little time to figure it out. Aleta shared some nutritional information, gave Carol a few suggestions, and provided Carol with some tips that would improve the whole family's diet. Carol was willing to make changes because of Aleta's support and the nutritional information and tips for organizing food selection and menu planning. The entire family made it their project and it benefited the health of everyone in the family.

Parents play a major role in the prevention of inadequate nutrition or obesity in their children. If parents have the knowledge of some prevention methods, then children are more likely to follow good dietary practices. Some preventive practices for nutrition are listed in Table 9.6 and will help

TABLE **9.6**

Good Nutrition Practices for Parent Education

- ■ Monitor your child's growth in height and weight.
- ■ Help children understand the difference between hunger and other needs.
- ■ Provide only good, nutritious food choices that will lead to a well-balanced diet.
- ■ Observe the amount and type of food consumed.
- ■ Do not use food as a reward—choose other methods of rewarding a child.
- ■ Help children learn to interact with others.
- ■ Role model exercise and encourage children to exercise.
- ■ If a child's nutritional health seems to be at risk, seek nutritional counseling.

the caregiver educate parents about their role in providing children good nutrition.

Children can learn about nutrition and food selection early. Good role modeling, providing healthy food selections, and discussions about the Food Guide Pyramid can send children positive messages about good nutrition. Children can learn that they play a role in their nutritional well-being.

Children learn the most about nutrition from the adults in their life. Good role modeling by caregivers is therefore extremely important. This pregnant caregiver has an additional teaching opportunity, in that she can tell the children how good nutrition is helping the baby inside her grow.

Children may be bombarded by messages about food through visits to fast food restaurants, watching television ads, and looking at food labels in the supermarkets. The messages carried by these foods make it hard for children to understand that good nutrition is not present in all foods. Children may see poor food selections at home or in child care due to convenience and the time crush.

Role Modeling

Nutrition and food selection are integral to achieving good health and well-being. This is an area where many centers and family care homes fall short. Nutrition is often disregarded as an important part of child care. Recent studies have shown a majority of child care facilities do not meet the nutritional needs of the children they serve (Briley, Roberts-Gray, & Rowe, 1993; Briley, Roberts-Gray, & Simpson, 1994). Some common practices that role model poor nutrition and food selection are included in Table 9.7.

TABLE **9.7**

Observed Practices for Role Modeling Poor Nutrition

- There was little variety in the food presented; the same foods and menus were repeated often.
- Vegetables were generally ignored.
- Foods that were high in fats and low in fiber were served often.
- Sweets such as sugar, jelly, and honey were used moderately to liberally.
- Teachers encouraged children to eat, but rarely discussed the importance of a food and why the child should eat it.
- There was not enough food served to meet the RDA requirements for energy during the time the children were in child care.
- Menus did not reflect the cultural diversity of the groups they served.
- Food served did not provide adequate amounts of niacin, iron, zinc, and vitamin B_6 needed in a child's diet.
- Convenience seemed to drive menu planning and included using a majority of foods that were canned or frozen.
- Staff in some centers ordered fast food instead of eating the same foods prepared for the children.

These poor role modeling practices show a need for nutrition education and training in menu planning and food selection. A good background in basic nutrition and nutritional guidelines provides the knowledge for good role modeling strategies and practices. Some of the basic role modeling for good nutritional practice is included in Table 9.8.

TABLE **9.8**

Basic Practices for Role Modeling Good Nutrition

■ Provide menus and food selections that follow USDA, RDA, and CACFP guidelines, taking into consideration the number of meals and snacks a child will consume while in care. Match this consideration to the percentage of daily diet that the caregiver provides for the child. Plan the menus accordingly.

■ Select a variety of foods for snacks and meals while planning menus.

■ Use a large number of fresh fruits and vegetables to provide more vitamins, minerals, and fiber.

■ Select low-fat foods and preparations.

■ Eat with the children, eating the same foods and discussing the importance of individual foods in the children's diet. This is a good place to use the Food Guide Pyramid.

■ Plan menus that take into consideration the regional and cultural diversity of the population at the child care site. This includes children, teachers, and parents.

■ Establish good communication with parents about nutrition and why it is an integral part of overall health and well-being.

■ Promote and provide nutrition education for children, their parents, and staff.

■ Provide parents sack lunch guidelines for the children who bring their lunch from home. The guidelines should include acceptable food selections and suggestions for meeting the child's nutritional needs. Combined with healthy snacks provided by the caregiver, the child will have an adequate diet while in care.

Supervision

Supervision ensures that the process of parent education, child education, and role modeling occurs. It is also helpful in examining whether the child care facility, family child care home, or in-home site is practicing good nutrition habits and offering healthy food choices.

Marylou, a center director, has a basic knowledge of nutrition. When the center was small, Marylou planned the menus, but as it grew she got further away from menu planning and food selection. Several years ago the center became involved with the Child and Adult Care Food Program (CACFP), which allowed it to be reimbursed for providing meals that met CACFP program guidelines. CACFP provided training and technical assistance and gave the center a handbook to help in menu planning and food selection. With staff turnover, menus changed only gradually and the same foods appeared over and over—sometimes two or three times a week. When a local college dietetics class evaluating menus at several centers and family child care homes in the area asked Marylou's center to participate in their study, Marylou accepted because the staff felt they were doing an adequate job.

They were surprised to learn that not only was their menu not well-balanced, but it did not even comply with the directives of the CACFP. In addition, Marylou's staff had not considered the cultural diversity of the children now attending the center when planning menus. The staff looked carefully at the problems and decided to hold inservice nutrition workshops periodically and to put into practice the suggestions made by the college class. Marylou and her staff also took greater advantage of the CACFP handbook and technical assistance. The staff involved the parents in menu planning and asked for recipes that reflected the cultures present in their center.

When the center participated in the same college study the following year, the staff got a glowing report and the center was cited in the local press as being a good example of healthy nutritional practices in child care.

CHAPTER **SUMMARY**

An increasing number of children will rely on child care to provide a good portion of their nutritional needs. Nutritional policies that include the use of nutritional guidelines and that provide awareness of nutritional challenges should be created for child care. Caregivers should have an understanding of the basic nutrients and use the Food Guide Pyramid to plan menus. They can monitor children for growth and provide nutrition education to avoid nutritional challenges. Caregivers can use education, role modeling, and supervision to manage risk and practice good nutrition.

TO GO **BEYOND**

Questions for Review

1. Discuss the interrelationship between nutrition and health.
2. Discuss how nutritional challenges impact the caregiver.

AS AN **INDIVIDUAL**

1. Chart and record your diet for three days. Analyze it by comparing it to the Food Guide Pyramid. How do you rate?
2. Observe children eating in a fast food restaurant. How would you rate their diets?

AS A **GROUP**

1. Discuss practical ways to encourage children to try different kinds of foods.

2. Hold a class potluck, with students bringing foods from different cultures. Compare the tastes and share ideas for cultural foods for children.

3. Gather nutritional information available in your local community. Either pick up enough copies or photocopy enough copies for everyone in the class. Compile into nutritional files to use as reference.

CHAPTER **REFERENCES**

Achterberg, C., McDonnell, E., & Bagby, R. (1994). How to put the food pyramid into practice. *Journal of the American Dietetic Association, 94*(9), 1030–1035.

Barness, L. (Ed.). (1993). *Pediatric nutrition handbook*. Elk Grove, IL: American Academy of Pediatrics.

Branen, L., & Fletcher, J. (1994). Effects of restrictive and self-selected feeding on preschool children's food intake and waste at snacktime. *Journal of Nutrition Education, 26*(6), 273–277.

Briley, M., Roberts-Gray, C., & Rowe, S. (1993). What can children learn from the menu at the child care center? *Journal of Community Health, 18*(6), 363–377.

Briley, M., Roberts-Gray, C., & Simpson, D. (1994). Identification of factors that influence the menu at child care centers: A grounded theory approach. *Journal of the American Dietetic Association, 94*(3), 276–281.

Brown, L. (1987, February). Hunger in the U.S. *Scientific American*, 37–41.

Brown, L., & Pollitt, E. (1996, February). Malnutrition, poverty and intellectual development. *Scientific American*, 38–43.

Children's Defense Fund. (1996). *The state of America's children: Yearbook 1996*. Washington, DC: Author.

Children's nutrition and learning. (1994). Champaign, IL: ERIC Clearinghouse for Elementary and Early Childhood Education.

Derrickson, J., Widodo, M., & Jarosz, L. (1994). Providers of food to homeless and hungry people need more dairy, fruit, vegetable and lean meat items. *Journal of the American Dietetic Association, 94*(4), 445–446.

Food Marketing Institute. (1991). *Growing up healthy: Fat, cholesterol, and more.* [Brochure]. Washington, DC: Author.

Graham, J. (1990, February). Nutrition now: The hidden dangers in the food kids eat. *Redbook*, 114–120.

Lewis, C., Crane, N., Moore, B., & Hubbard, V. (1994). Healthy people 2000: Report on the 1994 nutrition progress review. *Nutrition Today, 29*(6), 6–13.

Morris, P. (1991). *Heading for a health crisis: Eating patterns of America's school children*. Washington, DC: Public Voice for Food and Health Policy.

National Center for Health Statistics. (1995). *National health and nutrition examination surveys—1988–1991*. Hyattsville, MD: Author.

Parker, L. (1989). *The relationship between nutrition and learning: A school employee's guide to information and action*. (Publication No. ED 309207). Washington, DC: National Education Association.

Pestano-Binghay, E., Reis, J., & Walters, M. (1993). Nutrition education issues for minority parents: A needs assessment. *Journal of Nutrition Education, 25*(3),144.

Position of the American Dietetic Association: Child nutrition services. (1993). *Journal of the American Dietetic Association, 93*(3), 334–336.

SOS Online. (1996a). Charge against hunger. *Share Our Strength Online.*

SOS Online. (1996b). Hunger in the United States. *Share Our Strength Online.*

Splett, P., & Story, M. (1991). Child nutrition: Objectives for the decade. *Journal of the American Dietetic Association, 91*(6), 665–668.

Stanek, K., Abbott, D., & Cramer, S. (1990). Diet quality and the eating environment of preschool children. *Journal of the American Dietetic Association, 90*(11), 1582–1584.

Taylor, M., & Koblinsky, S. (1994). Food consumption and eating behavior of homeless preschool children. *Journal of Nutrition Education, 26,* 20.

U.S. Department of Agriculture. (1992). *Food guide pyramid, A guide to daily food choices.* Hyattsville, MD: Human Nutrition Service.

U.S. Department of Health and Human Services. (1990). *Healthy people year 2000: National health promotion and disease prevention objectives* (Publication No. PHS 91-50213). Washington, DC: U.S. Government Printing Office.

U.S. Department of Health and Human Services, Public Health Service, & National Institutes of Health. (1991). *National Cholesterol Education Program Report of the expert panel on blood cholesterol levels in children and adolescents.* Washington, DC: National Institutes of Health.

U.S. Departments of Agriculture and Health and Human Services. (1990). *Nutrition and your health: Dietary guidelines for Americans* (Home and Garden Bulletin No. 232). Washington, DC: Authors.

SUGGESTIONS **FOR READING**

Basch, C., Zybert, P., & Shea, S. (1994). Five-a-day: Dietary behavior and the fruit and vegetable intake of Latino children. *The American Journal of Public Health, 84,* 814.

Danford, D., & Stephenson, M. (1991). Healthy people 2000: Development of nutrition objectives. *Journal of the American Dietetic Association, 91*(12), 1517–1519.

Dietz, W. (1994). Critical periods in childhood for the development of obesity. *American Journal of Clinical Nutrition, 59*(5), 955–959.

Gutfeld, G., & Munson, M. (1993, November). Weighty warning: Fat, not calories, plumps up kids. *Prevention, 45,* 24.

Hunter, B. T. (1994, March). The importance of breakfast. *Consumer's Research Magazine, 3,* 8.

Meltsner, S. (1996, September). The new skinny on overweight. *Parents Magazine,* 64–66.

Romero-Gwynn, E., Gwynn, D., Grivetti, L., McDonald, R., Stanford, G., Turner, B., West, E., & Williamson, E. (1993). Dietary acculturation among Latinos of Mexican descent. *Nutrition Today, 28*(8), 6.

Satter, E. (1987). *How to get your kid to eat . . . But not too much.* Palo Alto, CA: Bull Publishing Co.

Satter, E. (1989). *Feeding with love and good sense.* Palo Alto, CA: Bull Publishing Co.

Shapiro, S. (1990). *Nutrition resources for early childhood: A resource guide.* Washington, DC: National Center for Education in Maternal and Child Health.

The University of California. (1993, December). Kids and parents and food. *Berkeley Wellness Letter, 10,* 2.

Werner, P., Timms, S., & Almond, L. (1996). Health stops: Practical ideas for health related exercise in preschool and primary classrooms. *Young Children, 51*(6), 48–55.

CHAPTER TEN

Providing Good Nutrition in Child Care

Upon completion of this chapter, including a review of the summary, you should be able to:

Specific Nutritional Policies

Define and discuss the need for nutrition policies that address growth and development to prevent risk, provide protection, and promote nutritional well-being.

Early Feeding and the Infant in Care

Discuss breast feeding, bottle feeding, and the introduction of solids into the infant's diet including the developmental implications and practices for the caregiver.

Feeding the Toddler

Discuss the impact of development on the feeding behavior of the toddler and describe strategies for the caregiver to redirect that behavior.

Food and the Preschooler

Discuss the food behaviors of the preschooler and the strategies for the caregiver to guide the child to behaviors that foster well-being.

School-Age Nutrition

Discuss the nutritional needs of the school aged child and the strategies for the caregiver to meet these needs that may be compromised by outside influences.

Nutrition and the Child with Special Needs

Explain how special needs might affect the nutrition and feeding of a child and discuss specific strategies to meet the child's nutritional challenges.

Exercise as a Part of Diet

Discuss the impact of exercise on the diet and overall well-being of children and strategies to promote exercise.

Implications for Caregivers

Describe and discuss methods for education, supervision, and role modeling to ensure good nutrition for children in care.

SPECIFIC NUTRITIONAL POLICIES

The importance of providing good nutrition in child care cannot be stressed enough. Greater numbers of children are relying on their caregivers to provide a significant portion of their nutritional needs. Child caregivers play a significant role in the nutritional well-being of children. Creating policies to meet the changing nutritional needs of the children in care is a vital risk management tool that can affect the way children grow and learn. The following indicators reveal the need for those policies:

- 90 percent of the child care center menus evaluated in Texas fell short of the recommended standards for child day care nutrition (Briley, Roberts-Gray, & Rowe, 1993).
- Studies have shown that although child care providers say they are interested in nutrition, their menus do not provide adequate nutrition (Diriga, Olgesby, & Bassoff, 1991).
- Questions have been raised by the American Dietetic Association as to nutritional quality and lack of staff knowledge in child care in relation to meeting nutritional standards (Splett & Story, 1991).
- Children who were at child care centers for eight or more hours typically received less than 50 percent of their RDA (Briley, Roberts-Gray, & Simpson, 1994).
- Providing a pleasant eating environment helps set the stage for good nutritional habits (Kendrick, Kaufmann, & Messenger, 1995; Stanek, Cramer, & Abbott, 1990).

Many children are in child care for more than eight hours a day, yet their nutritional needs may not be met by the caregiver. The caregiver may be unaware of nutritional standards or may not know how to plan menus to meet those standards. The caregiver's perceptions about what a child will or will not eat may also influence food choices. For example, some caregivers may believe that children do not like vegetables and prefer foods that are like fast foods, so they may create menus that they think children will like and eat. These factors can have a negative effect on menu planning choices for food and the balance of the nutrition provided by that food.

Cost is always a factor when trying to balance care with the business of caregiving. Many caregivers watch for sales, buy in bulk, and look for other opportunities to cut back on cost. Saving should never be so important as to sacrifice the children's well-being. Child care centers and family child care homes may be eligible to participate in funded food programs that will help to defray the costs for children from low-income families.

Convenience may also be a factor in food selection in child care. Menus in child care have typically been in use a long time with few updates and are limited by lack of nutritional knowledge on the part of the staff (Briley, Roberts-Gray, & Simpson, 1994). If the effort is not made to change menus or to learn more about nutrition, then choices may be limited.

Culture may also affect food choices in child care. The caregiver may have a cultural background that influences cooking and menu selection and may even limit choices available. Children may or may not eat foods from cultural backgrounds that are different from their own. Children may have family cultural influences that may limit what they will eat. Television and fast food commercials may have an effect on what the caregiver fixes and what children will eat.

The caregiver who serves the family in their home may have an added difficulty providing proper nutrition. Many families who hire nannies are so busy and have their focus elsewhere that food for themselves and their children may be more of an irritant than an issue. Some parents may eat all of their meals away from home and only provide what they consider are the necessities for the child or what they think the child will eat, with no regard to nutritional value. Parents may have no knowledge about nutrition and how it can affect the growth and development of a child. This can make caring for the nutritional needs of a child a challenge to a nanny.

Another factor that should be considered is the purpose of the child care. Briley, Roberts-Gray, and Simpson (1994) pointed out that there were three perspectives on the purpose of child care: (1) to promote the well-being of the child, (2) to provide a service to the community, or (3) to pro-

Family style meals that allow children to serve themselves and be served by the caregiver work well in combination for feeding young children.

vide a living for the provider. If the child caregiver is focused on the second or third perspective, the nutritional well-being of the child may be at risk.

Children have specific nutritional needs at each stage of their growth and development. It is essential that the caregiver be aware of these nutritional needs and create policies that will help to meet the specific needs of the children as they grow and develop.

Nutritional policies that will help the caregiver meet the specific needs of the children in care are:

- *Early Feeding and the Infant:* understanding the changing need of infants including breast feeding, bottle feeding, and the introduction of solid foods.

- *Establishing the Feeding Behavior of the Toddler:* understanding the impact of development and changing needs on the behavior of the toddler regarding food and eating.

- *Food and the Preschool Child:* understanding the food behaviors and changing needs of the preschooler.

- *School-Age Nutrition:* understanding nutritional needs and how these needs are threatened by outside influence, including school food programs.

- *Nutrition and the Child with Special Needs:* understanding how special needs might affect the diet and feeding of a child.

- *Exercise as Part of Diet:* understanding the impact of exercise on the diet and well-being of children.

- *Implications for Caregivers:* understanding the need for education, supervision, support, and role modeling to ensure good nutrition.

KEY NUTRITIONAL POLICIES

CONCEPT

Every caregiver should practice good nutrition in child care. Many caregivers are not meeting the nutritional needs of children in their care. Nutrition for child care is approached by each caregiver with that person's own perspective based on background, food practices, culture, and what the children eat or will not eat. The caregiver should have nutritional policies that cover early infant feeding, food and the toddler, the preschool child, school-age children, special needs, and nutrition and exercise as part of nutrition. The implications for the child caregiver include education, role modeling, and supervision.

EARLY FEEDING AND THE INFANT IN CARE

The birthweight of a healthy baby will double in the first four months of life and nutritional needs will change as a child grows and develops. An

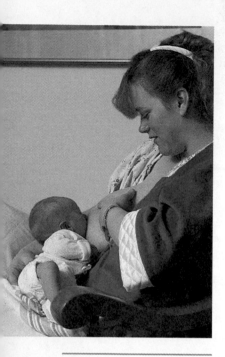

Breast milk contains all the nutrients that babies need during the first six months of life. Caregivers should work to accommodate the mother who wants to continue breast feeding while the child is in care.

infant grows faster during the first year than at any other time of her life. This growth rate is due to the growth patterns of all the internal organs. An infant's nutrition should be able to supply the nutrients including energy for this rapid growth.

The growth and development of an infant is directly related to nutrition. In the first four to six months of life, the only form of food an infant's body can accommodate is liquid breast milk or formula that provides the necessary nutrients. The changes in the organs provide the ability to digest and assimilate solid foods as the infant grows.

At birth, newborns cannot chew or use their tongues to push food. Their kidneys are too immature to handle the wastes of solid food. Digestive systems are not yet mature enough to handle the nutrients from solid foods. Allergic reactions, cramping, and crying are common results of introducing solid foods before the baby can assimilate it into the body.

Breast Feeding

Historically, infants were breast fed. This changed when technology was developed to provide sanitation for bottle feeding and formulas on which babies could survive and thrive were created for the bottle. Doctors saw bottle feeding as a way to measure the amount of milk a baby was drinking. The trend for bottle feeding infants increased until the early 1970s when research showed that breast feeding offered more nutrition and immunity than bottle feeding.

Current knowledge shows that breast feeding is the preferable form to provide infants proper nutrition, protection from bacteria, and give them immunity from diseases. See Table 10.1 for the benefits of breast feeding.

TABLE **10.1**

Benefits of Breast Feeding

- Protein is suited to baby's metabolism.
- Provides antibodies to combat bacteria.
- Provides immunological protection from illness and disease.
- Fat and iron in breast milk are easily absorbed and digested by the baby.
- Convenient—right temperature, sterile, and changes composition as baby's needs change.
- Psychological advantages—bonding with mother, tactile stimulation.

The caregiver may be called upon to help support the breast feeding mother (Morris, 1995). This offers advantages to everyone concerned. The baby will benefit as Table 10.1 indicates, and the mother and the caregiver will both benefit because a breastfed baby is less likely to become sick when left in care than a bottle fed baby (Jones & Matheny, 1993).

FIGURE **10.1**
Types of Nipples

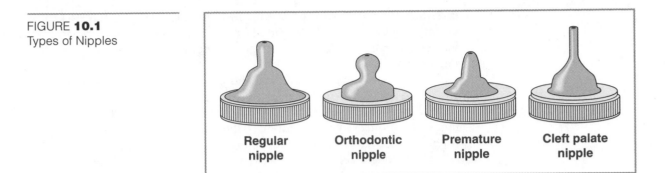

| Regular nipple | Orthodontic nipple | Premature nipple | Cleft palate nipple |

Mothers can help the caregiver by collecting and storing breast milk to use while they are not with the baby. Breast milk will last up to forty-eight hours in the refrigerator or can be frozen for two weeks. The caregiver can help the nursing mother by allowing the mother to nurse the baby at the child care site. This may occur as the baby is dropped off, picked up, and even at lunch time if the mother is close enough to visit her child during the lunch break. A mother should be discouraged from breast feeding if: (1) the mother has a communicable or chronic disease such as AIDS; (2) she is taking medication that is harmful to the baby; or (3) she is a drug or alcohol abuser.

Breastfed babies usually need to be fed every two to three hours. Breastfed babies may have more trouble accepting the bottle because they are used to sucking the breast. Using a breast-shaped nipple or a soft nipple may help the baby get more milk (see Figure 10.1). It may take several tries before the right nipple is found. The caregiver should not give up!

The caregiver should apply good sanitary practices and food safety procedures when using breast milk as listed in Table 10.2.

TABLE **10.2**

Safe and Sanitary Practices for Breast Feeding

■ Breast milk that has been stored unfrozen should be thrown away if not used within three days.

■ Expressed milk should be stored in single portion feedings.

■ Thaw frozen milk immediately before using and never heat in the microwave oven.

■ Shake refrigerator or thawed milk to mix cream into all the milk.

■ Do not refreeze thawed breast milk.

■ Dispose of any unused milk left in the bottle immediately after feeding.

Bottle Feeding

Although breast feeding is the preferable form, many children are fed formula from the beginning or are switched to formula for a variety of reasons. Mothers may find this is easier when they work, and it allows anyone, including fathers, to participate in the feeding of the baby. A child may also be on a combination of breast and bottle feeding; for example, breast milk may be fed in the morning and at night and bottled formula may be fed during the day.

Formulas are easy to prepare and come in several forms. Powdered and liquid concentrate formulas are meant to have sterile water added to the exact directions on the can. This is very important because when incorrectly mixed the formula may be harmful to the infant. The other kind of formula is ready-to-feed and merely needs to be put into the bottle.

Many manufacturers make soy-protein formulas for infants born with lactose intolerance. These infants may suffer from diarrhea, gas, and bloating. An infant may also be allergic to the soy formula, in which case there is a formula available with the proteins already broken down by enzyme action to prevent the allergic reaction.

Formulas try to copy breast milk as closely as possible. Formula manufacturers start with nonfat cow's milk as a base, then add vegetable oil, lactose, vitamins, and minerals to approximate energy and nutrients from human milk. Commercially prepared formulas are heavily regulated to keep infants safe from harm.

For proper food safety and sanitation, the measures in Table 10.3 should be commonly practiced in bottle preparation using formula.

TABLE **10.3**

Safe and Sanitary Practices for Bottle Feeding

- ■ Wash hands with liquid soap and hot water before beginning the sterilization process.
- ■ Wash bottles, nipples, and caps in hot, soapy water, using a bottle brush for hard-to-reach places. Rinse thoroughly in hot, clean water.
- ■ Sterilize all bottle parts in a pan of water. Boil for 5 to 6 minutes. Remove from pan with tongs and fill immediately.
- ■ Always buy cans of formula that are intact and have current use dates.
- ■ Wash the tops of formula cans before opening them.
- ■ Prepare formula exactly to manufacturers' instructions. If formula is diluted too much, malnutrition may result. If an insufficient amount of water is added, the child's digestive system may be strained.
- ■ Use clean, sterile bottled water rather than tap water because some tap water may cause digestive upsets in some infants.
- ■ Pour formula into sterilized bottles and top with nipples, caps, and rings if the bottle is being stored in the refrigerator. Use up all the prepared formula. Prepared bottles should be stored no longer than 24 hours.

Feeding Pattern. Whether the baby is being breastfed or bottle fed, there is an important factor to keep in mind. Even at this young age, the child should be able to control his own eating pattern. To accomplish this, the caregiver must be aware of the cues the baby gives when a break is needed

Babies should be held in a slightly elevated, reclined position when feeding to avoid choking and ear infections. These early feedings contribute significantly to the basis of the child's later eating habits.

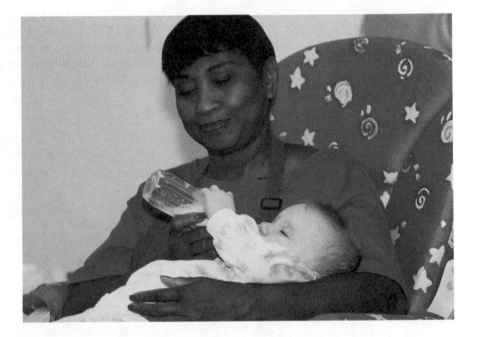

or when he is full. These cues include drawing the head away from the nipple, releasing it, spitting it out, or biting it. The infant may also stop sucking or shut his mouth tightly. Changing posture or being attentive to the surroundings and not the feeding are also cues that the child may not need any more breast or bottle feeding. A baby should be fed according to his own body's schedule of food energy needs instead of an imposed routine.

Infant controlled feeding requires the caregiver to be attentive to the infant's behavior and to allow the quantity eaten to vary depending on the infant's needs. The caregiver can identify the infant's cues by allowing time for pauses. This may be a good time to see if the baby needs to be held upright to pass a gas bubble. If the baby is fussy during a feeding, it is wise to find the source of the discomfort instead of interpreting the fussiness as a sign that the baby is done eating.

Introducing Solid Foods

Solid foods should not be introduced into a baby's diet until the baby is at least four months old and not until six months if she does not show signs of readiness. This is about the time it takes for the fine, gross, and oral motor skills to develop so that the child is ready to eat solid food. The normal pattern of development and ability of the body to accept solid food and the nutrients they supply are listed in Table 10.4.

Feeding Patterns.   When the infant is demonstrating developmental readiness, then solid foods should be introduced. Until this point, the protein needed for brain growth has been provided by the breast milk or formula. There is a common pattern for the introduction of this type of food and the pattern has been developed with good reasons. The caregiver should start

TABLE **10.4**

Pattern of Developmental Skills for Eating Solid Foods

- ■ Birth: Baby is only capable of sucking.
- ■ 6 weeks: Baby can smile and has the ability to extrude or push things out of the mouth with the tongue.
- ■ 8 weeks: Baby can use the tongue against the palate and can swallow semisoft food, but cannot digest the food itself.
- ■ 3 months: Baby's gastrointestinal system is sufficiently developed for digesting starch.
- ■ 4 months: Baby shows signs of being ready for solid foods: drinks 40 or more ounces of milk, can swallow instead of suck, and drools, indicating teeth will soon appear. Should be double his birthweight. If formula fed, iron stores may be depleted and baby will need iron from other food sources.
- ■ 4 to 6 months: Baby can control head movements and can keep food in the mouth instead of pushing it out with the tongue.
- ■ 5 months: Baby is a social creature and may be more interested in people and surroundings than in eating. May demonstrate interest in other people's food and open the mouth to show this interest.
- ■ 6 months: Baby can sit up in a high chair and can be easily spoon fed. If breastfed, iron stores may be depleted and baby will need iron from other food sources.
- ■ 8 months: Baby can grasp soft finger foods with hands and put them in the mouth.
- ■ 10 months: Baby should be able to grasp cup with both hands.
- ■ 12 months: Baby should be able to hold an age appropriate spoon.

the introduction of solid food slowly, serving only one or two servings of the food at the beginning. One new food is introduced at a time and the caregiver should wait five to seven days before introducing another new food. This waiting period allows the caregiver to identify if the food causes allergies or digestive complications such as diarrhea, gas, rashes, vomiting, or unusual fussiness. If this does not occur, move on to the next new food.

As the caregiver starts the solid food routine, there are several things to keep in mind that will help the baby learn how to eat in a safe way. Utensils used to feed the baby should be small and age appropriate. To begin with, only small amounts of food should be offered on the tip of the spoon. As the baby progresses, the amount should be increased to two or three tablespoons at a feeding. The food the caregiver serves should be placed in a small bowl or custard cup with only enough for one serving, and any unfinished food should be discarded. Returning food to the jar might contaminate the food remaining in the jar and make it unsafe for the baby to eat. Table 10.5 contains the introduction pattern for solid foods.

TABLE **10.5**

Solid Food Introduction Pattern

Age	Include	Exclude
0 to 4 months	Formula or breast milk	Solid foods, cow's milk
4 to 6 months	Add iron-fortified cereals	Honey, meat, eggs, sugar, powdered sweetened drink mix, cow's milk
6 to 9 months	Add vegetables, fruits, soft finger foods, yogurt, cheese, unsweetened fruit juices	Same as above plus soft drinks
9 to 12 months	Add meats, egg yolks, breads, crackers, cottage cheese, pasta, rice	Egg whites, all sugared products, honey, peanuts, popcorn, low- or nonfat milk, hot dogs, high sodium meat products

Cereals. The first food normally introduced is iron-fortified rice cereal. Rice is a good food to begin the introduction pattern because it is easily digested. The caregiver should mix the cereal with some formula until it is somewhat runny. It will be easier for infant to assimilate this experience if it is not totally dissimilar from her liquid diet. This food should be fed to the

Beginning around 4–6 months, babies can be fed a rice-fortified cereal. Remember to discard any uneaten food after the feeding, as the food may have been contaminated and should not be reused.

child on a spoon, not from a bottle. It is common practice among certain cultures, including Hispanics, to introduce this food mixed with formula in a bottle in which the nipple has been cut to allow the cereal to come out. Developmentally, this puts the child back to sucking and swallowing rather than using the developing oral skills that will be needed later.

Cereals are normally fed for the first month or two of the introduction of solid foods. The child should not be fed mixed cereals or wheat-based cereal because of possible allergic reactions. It is difficult to tell which ingredient in mixed cereal may be the culprit and wheat is often the basis for allergy among infants.

Vegetables.   The next food to introduce is vegetables, one at a time. Infants may show preference for flavors and may totally reject a food. This is one reason vegetables are introduced before fruits, since sweet flavors are preferred to savory flavors. This gives the child the opportunity to learn to enjoy vegetables before being introduced to fruits. It is a good idea to stick with dark green and yellow vegetables because they are good sources of vitamin A. Spinach and beets may cause allergic reactions, so the caregiver may want to avoid these in the beginning.

If the child rejects a food several days in a row, the caregiver should respect this dislike and discontinue it. The caregiver may try it again in a few months. Vegetables should be strained or pureed at this stage. The caregiver may use commercially prepared baby food or make it. Remember that infants do not need salt, spices, or other enhancements to make their food palatable. It is a good habit to get a child to accept food in its natural form so that the particular food will be acceptable later on in many forms. Infants cannot digest spices, and sweetening foods or adding salt may cause food preferences that may make it difficult for the child to follow the Food Guide Pyramid when he is older.

Fruits.   Fruits are introduced next, one at a time. Many fresh fruits can be easily mashed. This is a good time to introduce soft finger food such as bananas. Most infants respond well to the majority of fruits, but certain textures such as those in pears may cause the child to reject trying a particular food. If the child rejects a food, the caregiver can add the food to the list of things to try again later. Yellow fruits such as apricots and peaches are good sources of vitamin A. The caregiver must be watchful when introducing items such as fresh strawberries and citrus fruits, because although they are excellent sources of vitamin C, they also may cause allergic reactions. Fruit juices are another good source of vitamins, but the caregiver should use unsweetened juices. This is the perfect time to introduce a cup to a baby. It is preferable to feed a child juice from a cup, not from a bottle. Fruit juice in a bottle can lead to baby bottle tooth decay.

When choosing a cup, the caregiver should find one that is unbreakable and weighted at the bottom. It is better when first trying a cup to use one with at least one handle so the baby has something to grasp. These cups usually come with a lid, but if the baby seems to have difficulty with the sipping action, the lid may be removed. Try a sip at a time beginning with a small amount using a bib to protect baby from spills.

The toddler is ready to self-feed soft finger foods, such as cheese and cooked vegetables.

Other Foods. At this time most children will have enough teeth to be able to do some chewing. Soft finger foods such as cheese are good beginner foods to help the child learn to feed himself. Cheese and yogurt are good sources of calcium and protein and both are easily digestible by now.

At nine months meat such as chicken, beef, lamb, and fish can be added. Wait awhile for pork, because it may cause allergic reactions. If the child has enough teeth, the meat can be chopped into very small pieces so she can pick up the pieces and feed herself. Egg yolks can also be added now, but it is best to avoid egg whites and whole eggs until the child is at least one year old. Cottage cheese is another addition that will offer a good source of calcium and protein.

This is the time when other finger foods such as toast and crackers can be added. They are good sources of carbohydrates, as are rice and pasta. These items can be chewed and easily digested by now. The pasta and rice should be fairly plain, not highly seasoned. The caregiver should avoid serving finger foods that are not soft or will not soften in the mouth.

Caregiver Guidelines

There are some guidelines for infant feeding as shown in Table 10.6. As the caregiver helps to establish the eating behavior of an infant as he or she goes from breast or bottle feeding to solid foods these guidelines may assist in successful infant feeding.

TABLE **10.6**

Guidelines for Successful Infant Feeding

- ■ Use a small spoon and age-appropriate cup.
- ■ Watch for cues that baby is full.
- ■ Never use food as bribery, diversion, or reward.
- ■ Offer an assortment of healthy foods.
- ■ Try new foods at baby's best time of day.
- ■ Respect the child's food likes and dislikes.
- ■ Infants may not be able to eat a great deal at a time, so serve smaller meals throughout the day.
- ■ Make mealtime pleasant, not distracting.
- ■ Avoid serving foods that may choke an infant.
- ■ Only serve foods that are soft or will become soft in the mouth.

CONCEPT

KEY EARLY FEEDING AND THE INFANT IN CARE

Infancy is a critical time for forming the pattern to meet the nutritional needs of a child. Whether the baby is fed by breast milk or formula, a caregiver can manage health risk by using food safety behaviors. Being aware of the cues that an infant will give when he is full will help the caregiver allow the infant to gain control of his own feeding behavior. The introduction of solid foods brings nutritional challenges that can be easily met if the caregiver is knowledgeable about the pattern of introducing these foods. Understanding how to accommodate the infant's physical and psychological needs will allow the caregiver to encourage the infant to go at her own pace. The caregiver plays an important role in helping the infant and his family to establish good nutrition and providing the groundwork for good feeding behaviors.

FEEDING THE TODDLER

The transition from infant to toddler is most apparent in a child's eating behavior. This is the first place a child will begin to show his independence and need for autonomy. Good nutrition allows a child to grow, learn, and play. The challenge for this period is to maintain good nutrition while helping the child establish good food habits with her independence intact. Creating a framework for forming good food habits is one of the most important things the caregiver can do for a child to ensure good health and well-being. To help the child establish good eating behaviors, the caregiver must understand how growth patterns and developmental changes affect a toddler's actions (see Table 10.7).

The caregiver and the parent should work together in communicating the child's eating habits at school and at home, and decide how best to meet the child's nutritional needs.

TABLE **10.7**

Common Patterns of Toddler's Growth and Development That Affect Eating Actions

■ Child wants and needs to be independent; child wants to control his own eating.

■ Child learns to say "no" even to favorite foods.

■ Appetite is sporadic as growth slows.

■ Child learns by doing—wants to feed self.

■ Child has food likes and dislikes. Child may develop food jags for favorite foods.

■ Child is gaining more control over large motor skills, and can lift food to mouth. Because large muscle control is still developing, the child will sometimes drop or spill food.

■ Child is gaining more control over fine motor skills, and is able to use a spoon.

■ Child is learning to manipulate objects, and likes to touch and play with food.

■ Child may be teething and have difficulty chewing, and will spit out or remove food from mouth.

■ Child wants to master the job of eating and be successful, even if it means hiding food under plate or in a pocket to show he is done.

■ Child is learning to be a social creature, and may entertain others with food antics.

Food as an Issue of Control

Adults feel responsible for a child's eating habits. If the child is not eating right, we may cajole, coerce, bribe, or beg the child to eat. Without realizing it, adults have just drawn the line for the battle over food being used as an issue of control between a well-meaning adult and an independence seeking toddler. As a child recognizes the adult's concern over the consumption of food, the child may figure out creative ways to utilize food as a weapon in the quest for independence.

Ellyn Satter, dietitian and author of several books (1987,1989) on the subject of feeding behavior problems, has offered some specific guidelines to help alleviate the struggle for control between the adult and the child concerning food:

■ The adult is responsible for controlling what food comes into the house and how it is presented to the child.

■ The adult is also responsible for making sure the child is at a meal, keeping the child on task, making sure the child behaves well, and regulating the time for meals and snacks.

■ The child is responsible for how much he eats, whether he eats, and how his body turns out.

Careful examination of these areas of responsibility will change the battle into a cooperative venture.

The way that an adult treats a child at the table may very well be a reflection of how the adult treats the child elsewhere. The adult can help regulate the food consumption behavior in numerous ways. Training the child

Eating can often become a power struggle between the adult and child. Keeping the child on task and making mealtime enjoyable are ways that the adult can help to regulate the child's food consumption without causing undue stress.

to be on task in the eating of satisfying and well-prepared foods is a good first step. When a child realizes that food can be enjoyable he is more likely to be agreeable with the idea of eating and will be less likely to balk at the task at hand. If the child does not eat, the adult should learn to relax and stay calm. Erratic food intake is normal and it will support the child's growth because over time the proper balance will be achieved. Branen and Fletcher (1994) found that when children in child care were allowed select foods, the consumption pattern was not significantly different from being served pre-selected foods. The one difference they found is that children did not waste more food, but in some cases they tended to eat more because they were able to regulate their own intake. A conclusion of their study was that self-selection may help to regulate dietary intake in child care and may offer a more healthy alternative to preselection.

Another strategy for helping a child develop good eating habits is to make mealtimes significant for the child. Understanding the temperament of the child, his capabilities, and his tempo will help the caregiver prepare for mealtime. The caregiver should give the child time, attention, and awareness when meals are served. Sitting and talking with children while they are eating makes this time special. The caregiver should reinforce desirable behavior by paying attention, recognizing, and acknowledging good behavior.

Judith always sits with her two-year-old child care group at lunch time. Teresa, the cook, serves the food family-style in large bowls and helps each child select foods. During this process Judith keeps the children who have their food on task, and talks with the children who have not been served yet. When everyone is served, the group discusses the food and talks about how things taste. Judith also talks with the children about the morning activities and explains some of the things Roberta, the afternoon teacher, has planned for them. This helps the children prepare for the transition and helps them remember what they have done that day. Another significant thing Judith does daily is to eat the same food for lunch that the children are eating. She is role modeling that the food served is just as acceptable to her as it is for the children. Judith's pet peeve is teachers who bring in fast food to eat in front of children and who do not practice what they are trying to enforce—good eating habits.

The caregiver can contribute to regulating eating habits by managing the eating environment. Setting limits makes eating more important and worthwhile. When feeding a child a snack or a meal, the caregiver must make sure that is the only activity going on. The caregiver should also limit eating to one or two appropriate places. That may be in a kitchen or patio in a home situation, not in front of a television. In center-based care, eating may

The caregiver can promote good eating habits by managing the eating environment. The caregiver should also limit eating to one or two appropriate places.

occur in the classroom or on tables near the playground. The caregiver should spend some time getting the child ready to eat. The transition time from another activity should be quiet and calming to prepare children for eating time.

A child should come to the table at mealtime ready to eat. If the child is disinterested or not hungry, the caregiver should not force the issue, but should have the child stay at the table a few minutes before excusing him. This removes the temptation for the child to entertain or act out. If the child complains about being hungry a few minutes later, the caregiver can remind him that snack time is just a few hours away. The child made the choice not to participate and maybe next time will make a different choice. This reinforces the fact that the child made the decision and the caregiver supported it. The caregiver should not change the eating pattern for meals and snacks to accommodate whims.

The caregiver should keep food out of sight when eating is not the activity. Seeing food can make children think they need to eat when they are not really hungry. Age appropriate foods and utensils should be chosen. Finger foods and foods that are easy to eat should help toddlers to learn to manipulate more successfully. Foods such as popcorn, grapes, carrots, and celery that may cause the child to choke should be avoided. The caregiver must use utensils that a toddler can grasp easily, and small plates and cups that look as though they are full when the serving of food is placed on them.

Although it may be difficult to accommodate in some center schedules, child care homes and nannies can tailor the serving of food around when children need to eat. The caregiver should try to be as reliable and regular as possible in feeding the children, and not wait until they are really hungry and have behavior difficulties because of it. The caregiver should not feed children if they do not feel hungry at the moment.

These actions allow the caregiver to establish trust in relationship to food and children. Children will act more responsibly when they can trust their caregiver to provide the food and atmosphere that make them successful eaters.

Table 10.8 lists some key points about using food as nutrition and not as a battle ground.

Nutritional Considerations

Whether it is served as a meal or a snack, food should be satisfying and meet the children's nutritional needs. The ideal meal or snack would include a protein food, a carbohydrate food, and some fat. When planning meals or snacks, the caregiver must treat empty nutrient, high-calorie foods that have too much sugar or fat with respect. Snacks should be taken seriously and used as part of the day's nutrition. If someone has a birthday and brings cupcakes, enjoy them. The caregiver should model how the food should be savored and serve it with milk or some other nutritious food so all is not lost.

The caregiver should recognize that there will be a variation in food consumption. A child may refuse to eat foods from a particular food

TABLE **10.8**

Food as Nutrition, Not Control

■ The modeling of your actions and attitudes toward food will affect how the children feel about food.

■ Stay calm; do not react to negative behavior.

■ Realize pressure does not work—forcing or withholding are ineffective.

■ Do not use food as a punishment or as a reward.

■ Outside influences, including cultural influences, can affect your good intentions about children and their food behavior.

■ Respect cultural eating differences. Expose children to foods from many cultures.

■ Children learn from feeding, their first attempt at independence, what to expect from the world.

■ If they are successful, the world is a beautiful place. if they fail, they may withdraw or act out.

group or may eat only one food to the exclusion of others. This is referred to as a food jag and is common. If it continues for more than a short period of time, like a week, this food should be offered only at snack time and the caregiver must make sure other foods are served at regular mealtimes.

Milk is a food and should have its proper place. Children over the age of six months should not drink formula to the exclusion of other foods. Toddlers should not drink so much milk that they lose their appetite for other foods. Toddlers who use milk as the main source of energy and nutrients may have a condition called milk anemia, which is an iron deficiency due to lack of proper food and too much milk. A toddler should drink no more than 24 ounces of milk a day. Children over the age of one year can have cow's milk, but they should never be served nonfat milk, because they need the fat content for growth and development. Some children may not want to drink milk alone at this stage. The caregiver will need to substitute yogurt, cheese, and other dairy products to be sure the child receives the necessary amounts of calcium and other minerals.

According to a recent study, overconsumption of juice may cause a child to not keep pace with the growth and development of children of the same age ("Too Much," 1994). When juice was not served, all of the children observed began putting on weight again. As previously stated, the caregiver should serve juice only in a cup and should use it to enhance a meal but not to replace other foods. If a child is thirsty, water is the best alternative. Some guidelines for the caregiver to maximize the eating and nutritional needs of the toddler are listed in Table 10.9.

The caregiver should use whatever methods are available to encourage the toddlers in care to eat good food and be well-nourished.

TABLE **10.9**

Guidelines for Forming Good Food Habits for Toddlers

- ■ Make food easy to eat.
- ■ Cut finger food in bite-size pieces.
- ■ Make sure some of the foods served are soft and moist.
- ■ Serve food at room temperature. Toddlers shy away from foods that are too cold or too hot.
- ■ Toddlers are sensitive to texture and may not eat foods that are lumpy or stringy. Try these foods and if they will not eat them, try again later.
- ■ Toddlers like colorful foods and often prefer vegetables that are raw or undercooked because they are brighter in color and crisp.
- ■ A typical toddler may like his food in different or specific shapes. Carrots may need to be cut in coins before cooking so the toddler will eat them.
- ■ Toddlers like fun foods such as faces on pancakes or sandwiches or other foods cut into unusual shapes.

KEY FEEDING BEHAVIOR OF THE TODDLER

CONCEPT

The toddler is growing and developing in many ways. A number of these growth characteristics have an impact on the toddler's food behavior. If the caregiver understands this, food is less likely to be an issue of control. There are a number of strategies a caregiver can employ to help make mealtimes pleasant and encourage the child to eat, thus meeting the toddler's nutritional needs.

FOOD AND THE PRESCHOOLER

As children reach the preschool stage, a number of developmental changes have occurred that make feeding and nourishing a much easier task. A child of three knows that he is a separate person and understands acceptable and appropriate behavior. He is capable of being patient and can control impulses. If the preschooler whines, complains, or begs for food not on the table, he is capable of understanding that this behavior is unacceptable and he may be asked to get down from the table.

Outside Influences

Preschoolers are social beings who like eating with others. Children who have companionship at mealtimes have been observed to eat more servings of the basic food groups (Stanek, Abbott, & Cramer,

The toddler and preschooler are growing and developing, becoming more active and autonomous. The toddler's behavior at the table also reflects these changes and when identified can aid the caregiver in helping the child develop good eating habits.

1990). The preschooler learns much from observation and role play. She is likely to feel good about herself and enjoys cooperating. The preschooler probably has food preferences that may have been influenced by others. Messages children receive at home from their parents and television have a great deal of influence on their attitude about food (Gans et al., 1993).

Preschoolers can also be influenced by teachers and friends at school. They feel secure eating familiar foods, but if encouraged to explore, they

Encouraging children to accept new foods can be a difficult task. Serving new foods with familiar foods or having other children introduce the new foods are some methods for encouraging this exploration.

may try new foods. Often a preschooler may eat a food at school that she would not eat at home. This willingness to eat at school and not at home may be a result of negative messages or reinforcement about the particular food. A child whose parent says squash is "icky" or makes the comment, "Jerry won't eat squash," may be keeping that behavior a fact at home.

Children of this age are easily influenced by television advertising of food products that are poor nutritional choices (Kotz & Story, 1994). Over one-half of all the ads on television are for food products and the majority of these are for heavily sugared products. The cereal aisle of the grocery store contains an abundance of these foods. A parent may find it difficult to get through this aisle without a confrontation or without giving in to the child's demands. The cereal aisle is one of the best examples of **positive reinforcement** of negative behavior for young children. An adult who gives in to the demands for a certain sugared cereal seen on television allows the child to feel that television is right about the claims made. A better alternative for the adult, be it parent or caregiver, is to make positive use of the television ads and have the child help investigate the claim by reading the label.

Positive reinforcement
reward given in response to a particular behavior that increases the chance of that behavior occurring again

Dawn is a teacher of older four year olds in a community college preschool. The majority of children in her class have parents in the college. There is a real mixture of family types and income range. The children bring their lunches from home and Dawn spends time every day with each child investigating the lunches.

Kristin had a juice box that was full of sugar but not much juice. After reading the label with Dawn, Kristin informed her mother that it was not really juice and enlisted her help in finding a better drink for her lunch.

Zarli's dad was new to the lunch making business and the first few weeks were a struggle. But after Dawn helped Zarli investigate her lunches, Zarli became aware enough to encourage her dad to read the labels and learn about good food. Her lunches became more interesting and encouraged both child and parent to try to understand more about healthier eating. Her father often asked Dawn for advice on new ideas for lunches. He got to be very creative.

Rashid was from a different cultural background and often had foods that Dawn did not recognize. She did recognize the drink in his lunches as a highly advertised sugared drink and helped Rashid investigate the label. Dawn explained it to Rashid and he in turn helped explain it to his mother who spoke limited English. This exchange led to a wonderful dialogue between Rashid, his mother, and Dawn discussing the foods that Rashid brought. Dawn learned how the foods were prepared and what healthy ingredients they had in them. Rashid and his mother learned not to believe everything one sees on television.

REALITY CHECK

Television and its Effects on Children's Nutrition

Television has a great impact on the health and nutritional status of young children in this country. Hunger, obesity, dental cavities, iron deficiency anemia, cardiovascular diseases, and food allergies are the basic nutritional challenges facing children. All but food allergies may be affected by television viewing.

It has been estimated that children watch as many as three hours of television food commercials per week (American Academy of Pediatrics [AAP], 1992). The advertising industry spends at least $700 million on commercials that are directed to children (AAP, 1990). This is a concern to many health professionals and nutritionists. The food that is advertised is not healthy food. A recent study compiled information about children's television viewing and the ads that were run during this period (Kotz & Story, 1994). The study found that in the nearly 1,000 ads viewed, more than half were for food. Almost 50 percent of the foods advertised were high-fat, high-sugar, empty calorie snack foods. These included cookies, candy, soft drink, chips, pastries, and cakes. Another 37 percent of the advertisements were foods in the breads and grain group.

The majority of the ads in this group were for highly sugared cereals. Eleven percent of the ads were for fast food restaurants that touted hamburgers and pizza. Eaten alone, these may be high in fat. Accompanied by french fries and soft drinks, these meals are high in fat, sodium, and sugar.

Less than 5 percent of these paid ads promoted healthy foods. These ads were for milk and milk products ("T.V. Food Ads," 1995). About 14 percent of the public service announcements during this time were food related. These announcements encouraged healthy eating behaviors such as healthy snacking and cutting down on fat and salt. The regular ads promoted a very different food pyramid to the children (see Figure 10.2).

Advertising usually has a particular hook or appeal that makes people want to purchase a product. Children's ads viewed in this study showed an interesting array of appeals or messages.

- Taste—36 percent
- Fun—17 percent
- Free toys—17 percent
- Being cool or hip—7 percent
- Healthful or nutritious—2 percent
- Other

The ads implied the products were healthy or nutritious in 50 percent of the cases. Two-thirds of those ads referred to "part of a balanced breakfast" (Kotz & Story, 1994).

This is erroneous information, but young children do not have the knowledge or sophistication to put it in perspective. Six- to nine-year-old children were surveyed and they had a general knowledge of nutrition. They understood that the food ads were probably not for healthy foods (Kendall, 1994). However, one of four of these children always asked parents to buy the advertised foods.

Two-thirds of those surveyed related that they occasionally asked their parents to purchase these foods. Even though the children knew the food was not healthy, they still wanted it.

Another effect that television has on children's nutrition and health is that it discourages exercise as they become "couch potatoes." Children are watching television between 23 and 27 hours per week (Kendall, 1995). They are using less energy than they would if they were outdoors playing. There is speculation that television viewing is linked to obesity (Rice, 1992). Further, this may be a two-way link since it appears that children are eating more while watching television. High-sugar products may be a link to greater numbers of children with dental caries.

Caregivers can promote good nutrition by using the Food Guide Pyramid to help children make healthier choices. They can also talk about food advertisements and help children understand that while they are appealing, the food is not healthy and should be limited in their diets. Caregivers can help children by reading food labels so that they can become more discriminate in their food choices.

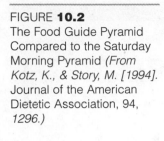

FIGURE **10.2**
The Food Guide Pyramid
Compared to the Saturday
Morning Pyramid *(From
Kotz, K., & Story, M. [1994].
Journal of the American
Dietetic Association, 94,
1296.)*

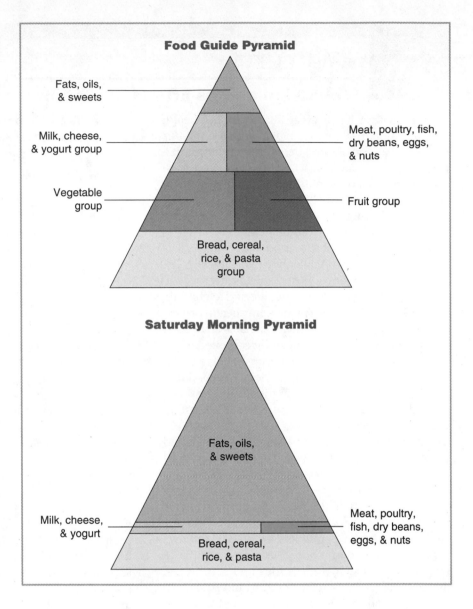

Participation

The caregiver can foster good nutrition by involving preschoolers with the selection of foods and helping with food preparation. Encouraging preschool children to be part of the process can empower them with the knowledge and awareness necessary to make better nutritional choices. Activities that are enjoyable give children confidence to try new foods and different ways of preparation. Children should have the opportunity to learn about food, nutrition, and food preparation and how they are linked to health. Reading books about new foods can pave the way for greater understanding. Letting preschoolers help prepare foods and experiment with new foods helps children develop skills that will widen their food horizons. Mealtime offers genuine opportunities for conversations about food and eating behavior. This is a good time to discuss, practice, and model good nutrition and correct eating behavior (Satter, 1989). These strategies will help the caregiver positively impact the preschooler's nutritional well-being.

KEY FOOD AND THE PRESCHOOLER

CONCEPT

A preschooler is likely to be influenced by others, including television, as to his or her food choices. These choices have a direct effect on the health and well-being of the preschooler. A caregiver can use participatory activities to bring an awareness to the preschooler about what the best nutritional choices are. Encouraging a child to be involved in food selection, preparation, and mealtime activities will give the child the confidence to make better choices.

SCHOOL-AGE NUTRITION

Caregivers from child care centers may not be involved with school-age care. Some centers do offer before and after school care to these children. Family child caregivers and nannies are commonly involved with school-aged children before and after school and during school vacations. The needs of school-aged children, ages five to eleven years, vary greatly from the infant, toddler, and preschooler.

Growth is slower during this period and is not as observable as the earlier infant-toddler growth spurt or the adolescent growth spurt that will occur later. However, the vigorous activity level that most school-aged children experience makes the need for adequate nutrition important. In addition, good nutrition will help the school-aged child maintain resistance to infection and help ensure adequate stores for the building materials and nutrition needed for the adolescent growth spurt.

Children of this age are not totally capable of planning a well-balanced diet each day. They may eat for social reasons, such as television viewing, when they are not really hungry. Children of this age may have fluctuating appetites and may become finicky in their eating habits. These changes may be attributed to the consumption of more and more foods that are low in nutrients and high in calories.

Snacking is easier because school-aged children are capable of preparing a variety of snacks. High-fat or sweetened foods or beverages are easy to prepare and serve. If these are available, children will probably eat them.

Fast food has a tremendous influence on the school-aged child. These children are more mobile and they may have their own money that allows these purchases. Many school lunch programs serve fast type foods in order to get the children to eat what is served and cut down on waste. Most fast foods are high in calories or low in nutrients.

Breakfast is a very important meal for children and has been proven to improve cognitive skills. Many schools and centers now provide this meal, which should be high in protein.

Good dietary habits should be focused on and practiced. Caregivers can perform a number of functions that will help school-aged children practice better nutritional habits. The first thing the caregiver can do is provide healthy, nutritious foods for the children to eat. If children have choices that are good foods, the choices will be limited and good nutrition will be more readily available.

Supervising school-aged children in planning their own menus and preparing good food will show children that they can affect their own nutritional well-being. If the child care includes breakfast, the caregiver can give children a good start by preparing a meal that includes some protein. Children who have a good breakfast are better at performing cognitive skills.

If the caregiver's job includes preparing or helping the child prepare a sack lunch, there are several important considerations. Children who help prepare their own lunches are more likely to eat the lunch. Typical brown bag lunches contain more sugar, sweets, and sweetened beverages and less meat, poultry, or fish than do school lunches prepared by cafeteria staff (Gordon & McKinney, 1995). Sack lunches usually do not contain enough fruits and vegetables and have too many convenience type foods. Packing good food may be a challenge, especially if food safety is taken into consideration. The caregiver should use imagination and safe food practices. Some suggestions are found in Table 10.10.

Snacks are likely to be the main foods that a caregiver will provide for most school-aged children. It is important that these foods are readily available when the child arrives at the site. Children are usually very hungry after a long school day. Offering foods prepared by the caregiver as well as items that are simple for the child to prepare will help the child appease hunger and build self-confidence.

TABLE **10.10**

Packing Healthy Foods for Brown Bag Lunches

■ Pre-cut fruits and vegetables can be stored in the refrigerator and packed in the morning.

■ Sandwiches can be prepared the afternoon before so they get thoroughly chilled in the refrigerator and will last longer in the lunches.

■ Choose low-fat cuts of meat. Cut the sandwiches into interesting shapes.

■ Leftovers can be frozen in small containers and packed in the morning.

■ Use only 100 percent fruit juices or have the parent provide money to purchase milk.

■ Forego chips and other high-calorie, low-nutrient foods; substitute pretzels or other low-fat snack foods.

■ Provide fruits that are in season and have the child select the fruit.

■ Use "blue ice" or other devices that will help keep the lunches cool.

KEY SCHOOL-AGE NUTRITION

CONCEPT

Many care situations do not have school-aged children. Those caregivers who do care for school-aged children face nutritional challenges that are different from infants, toddlers, or preschoolers. The caregiver needs to keep in mind the school-aged children's activity levels in order to provide them with adequate nutrition. The caregiver is practicing nutritional risk management by purchasing healthy foods, preparing them, and supervising the child in meal or snack preparation.

Developmental disabilities
physical or mental incapacities that interfere with normal progress of development

NUTRITION AND THE CHILD WITH SPECIAL NEEDS

Some caregivers care for children who have special needs. Many of these children have **developmental disabilities** or chronic illnesses that affect feeding skills, nutritional needs, or equipment needed. Some children require special feeding procedures and some require special foods or diets.

Children who have cerebral palsy, Down's syndrome, a cleft lip or palate, or other developmental abnormalities may have physical difficulties eating or feeding themselves. Children with metabolic disorders such as cystic fibrosis, diabetes, PKU, and maple syrup urine syndrome have special dietary limitations that prevent them from eating certain types of food that make the Food Guide Pyramid less useful. Some children may have conditions that require modifying their intake of sodium, protein, carbohydrates, or fats. Others may have allergies or food intolerances.

The Individuals with Disabilities Act (1990) requires certain child care centers and child care homes to accommodate children with special needs

Feeding practice may have to be altered for children with special needs. In this picture, the child is reclined in her chair instead of being cradled. Caregivers need to be accommodating and sensitive to these needs.

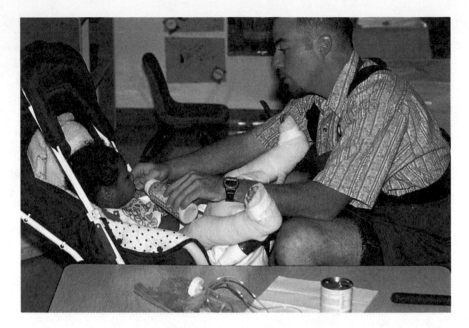

as best they can. That act also has a provision that requires states to provide early intervention services to infants and toddlers. Nutrition services were included in this early intervention (Yadrick & Sneed, 1994).

There are many children with special needs who can be accommodated easily and whose nutritional needs may not be difficult to meet. Chairs, tables, and eating utensils may need to be modified for some children. These accommodations can be made by the caregiver without great expense or effort.

Other children offer challenges that the caregiver really is not prepared or trained to accommodate. The nutritional needs of some children with chronic illness or developmental disabilities are complicated and may be compounded by eating difficulties. The average caregiver should not be expected to provide this type of accommodation without outside assessment, intervention, and help. The disabilities act provides the vehicle for the nutrition services the caregiver may need. Contacting the state child nutrition staff is a good place to begin. Local school districts may be involved in early intervention assessment, and local regional centers may also provide some of this assessment. The American Dietetic Association supports the participation of its members in providing nutrition services to child care programs that include children with disabilities and chronic illnesses. Parents of these children may be good sources of information and may be able to help the caregiver to link up with the community services needed to support the care of these children.

Access to these services may not provide a caregiver with the skills and special handling that some children with special needs require. A referral for the child to a special care program or regional center may be all that the child caregiver is able to do to help the families of these children.

KEY CHILDREN WITH SPECIAL NEEDS

CONCEPT

The Individuals with Disabilities Act may require that some child care programs and some family child care homes accommodate children with special needs as best they can. Some children with disabilities or chronic illnesses may be easily accommodated in their nutritional needs and feeding levels. Others may require special early intervention nutritional services. Those services may not be adequate to provide the level of care some children with special needs may require.

EXERCISE AS A PART OF DIET

Exercise should be a normal part of everyday activities for healthy young children. The balance between energy taken in through food and energy expended can be kept at a harmonious level through exercise and movement. A well-rounded nutrition program for children includes exercise as a key ingredient for success.

Children understand the importance of health. The majority of children understand that eating the right foods and exercising contribute to health (Singleton, Achterberg, & Shannon, 1992). Most children are physically active and large motor activities offer them the exercise that they need. Children expend energy in all of the following typical large motor activities:

- Running
- Throwing balls
- Climbing jungle gyms
- Swinging
- Digging in the sand
- Pulling wagons, pushing toys, riding tricycles
- Jumping
- Walking
- Dancing or moving to music

If the children in care are active, the caregiver should encourage them to remain that way. If some of the children in care are interested only in **sedentary** activities such as quiet play with dolls or puzzles, these children should be encouraged to be more active by providing interesting activities. Group activities like movement activities allow all children to participate in physical activity and have fun at the same time.

Encouraging children to take an active part in playground play is a good way for a caregiver to ensure children are getting good exercise. Taking a daily walk is another way to include exercise as a component of care. Caregivers should make both of these activities part of the daily routine. Exploring the environment around them is a good way for the children to

Sedentary
inactive or remaining in one location

A good amount of physical activity should be worked into every child care program. An evaluation of the general activity level of the class and of specific children, can help the caregiver identify what activities are best.

learn about their world. Nearby parks can be another source of vigorous outdoor play for the children. If the caregiver's neighborhood is not safe enough to walk in or play in the park she should try to access a local school or gym nearby. This will allow children to have a large indoor space to run in and use on a regular basis.

If the weather is inclement, indoor play should be planned for and used as a way for children to get exercise. Checking out a simple exercise video from the library and having the children try to perform the exercises on the video may be another fun way to exercise indoors on occasion (Brooks, 1996). If there are school-aged children in care, the caregiver can have them help lead the exercises. School-aged children might really enjoy demonstrating exercises they have learned in school.

The caregiver can also remove temptations to inactivity such as television. This may enhance greater exercise and movement for the children in care. Children who watch a lot of television are more likely to be less physically fit, more overweight, and have a distorted knowledge of nutrition. Use the television sparingly and only for educational viewing.

KEY EXERCISE AS PART OF DIET

CONCEPT

Daily large motor activities are a necessary component of a child care program. A caregiver who encourages exercise in the child care daily program provides a broad base for nutritional risk management. Encouraging all children to be physically active and providing daily large motor activities to ensure this allows the caregiver to promote good health and well-being.

IMPLICATIONS FOR **CAREGIVERS**

Nutrition education is an important tool for the caregiver to help parents and children better understand their role in proper nutrition for good health and well-being. Education can break down barriers, provide awareness of the effects of growth and development on feeding habits, and offer strategies to parents who want to make sure their children are getting a healthy start. Education can make children aware of their food selection and how their behavior has an effect on health and well-being. It can empower them to make better choices and participate in their own nutritional well-being. Role modeling can help the caregiver carry out educational strategies. Cultural sensitivity may be essential for the caregiver who has a diverse group in care. Supervision helps the caregiver to carry out good nutritional practices.

Education and Role Modeling

Caregivers and parents have a great influence on what children learn to eat. Modeling healthy eating to children of all ages can help children develop healthy eating habits themselves ("Infant Nutrition," 1994). The type and kinds of food that are provided for children help to determine how the child will eat and grow. Parents and caregivers model food selection and acceptability to the children in their lives. If these selections are healthy choices, a child will have a positive perspective about good foods. If the selections are poor choices, this sends a negative message about good nutrition.

For Parents. Parents and caregivers have the power to establish positive, supportive environments that allow children to develop good feeding behaviors and attitudes toward food. The caregiver can help the parent understand this by providing good role modeling and some positive nutrition information. The caregiver needs to be aware that there may be some barriers to accepting this information (Reicks, Randall, & Haynes, 1994). There may be environmental constraints to good nutrition for some of the families. Cost of food, access and availability of good food, and storage space are factors that may limit the family's ability to make a wide range of good food choices.

Poverty or low income may prohibit the selection of many foods including fresh fruits and vegetables and dairy products. These families may need help in accessing food programs that help families meet their food needs. The caregiver may also be able to provide the parents with information on food selections as well as recipes that use low-cost fresh foods. Consequently, the caregiver may find there is great interest on the part of the family to help improve their nutritional intake.

Another influence on food selection may be convenience of preparation of some foods. Some adults may find it easier to open a can or a box than to prepare fresh foods. Other adults might select fast foods as a further measure of convenience. These behaviors are an enormous barrier with middle and upper income families who can afford the convenience of packaged or fast foods. Having the children help prepare foods may help interest the parents in preparing more fresh food. Role modeling and providing recipes as well as activities for the families to do together may encourage this behavior.

Another perceived barrier may be related to the role the adult plays as a parent. The parent may not understand the stages and phases of growth and development as well as the caregiver does. This may make a parent unsure as to how to proceed. It may also influence the parent to feed the child as she was fed. Childhood food memories may influence selection or rejection of certain foods or food behaviors. A parent may model behaviors that are not productive to helping the child widen his food selections.

When four-year-old Amy came to Head Start, her mother reported that Amy did not like and would not eat most foods. Tanya, Amy's teacher, observed Amy at snack and lunch time for several weeks. She watched as Amy refused to try new things for the first two weeks. The foods that she was most vocal about were vegetables and fruits. Of the fruits and vegetables offered to her, Amy would eat only canned applesauce and corn. Other children were eating most of the foods that Amy was refusing. One day Joelle, another four-year-old, encouraged Amy to try some green beans. Amy tried them and ended up eating all of her beans and asked for more. Several days later the preschoolers picked some carrots and cherry tomatoes at a cooperative garden they toured near their school. The vegetables were brought back to school and the children helped wash them and prepare them for a snack. Amy ate both the carrots and tomatoes. She loved the carrots and was mildly interested in the tomatoes.

Tanya reported these breakthroughs to Amy's mother, who had a hard time believing Amy was eating vegetables. She explained that Amy's father, who was no longer living with them, had hated vegetables and did not even want them in the house. Amy's mother got used to serving only applesauce and canned corn. Her budget was also tight so this wasn't a sacrifice on her part. Tanya spent some time explaining the Food Guide Pyramid and why a balanced diet was important. She also pointed out that there were some plots available in the community garden, so it did not have to cost too much money to increase the variety of fresh produce in the families' diets. Once Amy's mother realized the importance of a balanced diet, she signed up for a plot in the nearby cooperative garden and she started trying to add more variety to the menu at home.

Adults may not realize that the social environment that is provided at mealtimes has a direct relationship to the dietary quality of their children. Children need a positive atmosphere, companionship, and the opportunity to view appropriate adult food-related behaviors to achieve good nutrition. The children in care may be the best educators for this barrier. The caregiver can help parents by explaining the different stages of growth and development and encouraging parents to observe their child's behavior. Parents may then try different ways to support their children's eating behavior.

Children learn many of their behaviors by watching the adults in their lives. For this reason, one of the most effective ways to teach children about good eating habits is for the caregiver to model these behaviors by sitting with the children and eating with them. In what other ways can caregivers model good nutrition habits?

The results of companionship at mealtimes and the positive social atmosphere that can be created will be apparent through food selections and observation of behavior. Modeling these behaviors with the children in care will help the caregiver provide this information to the families.

The level of written nutritional information may be another barrier for the caregiver and the parent. Not all adults are literate. Approximately 60 million adults in the United States have not completed high school. Those who have completed high school may not read at the 12th grade level. In order to be effective, the nutritional information provided to the parent should be at the level that he is capable of understanding (Busselman & Holcomb, 1994).

With Children.   One of the greatest contributors to good health is good food habits. A child is capable of learning this through practice and observation from a very young age. Children are strongly influenced by what they see and hear. Parents and caregivers are sources of behavior and information that children model and remember. Children have an influence on the shopping habits of parents. One study found that as much as 14 percent of the food purchasing dollar was influenced by children and over half of those purchases were for high-calorie, low-nutrient food products. (Dewalt et al., 1990).

The child caregiver should take time out, on a regular basis, to go over the Food Guide Pyramid with the children in care. The nutritional information about what each person should be eating in a day can be assimilated over time. Regular intervals of repetition help the children to understand and remember. This practice also helps the caregiver keep good nutritional information in action.

This caregiver uses a flannel board story to discuss with children the benefits of good eating habits and the risks of making poor food choices.

Enlisting children's help with food selection and preparation encourages them to try new foods and new ways of food preparation. Preparing children to help can be accomplished in several ways. The educational experience can be enhanced by reading books on certain foods, watching a video about foods, having circle time about what is going to be prepared, or telling a flannel board story about the food or activity.

Cultural Sensitivity

Cultural influences may present an obstacle to proper nutritional balance. The caregiver may face a challenge in helping parents select good food choices.

Understanding the cultural influence on food is important if the caregiver is going to help the families provide optimum nutrition for their children when they are not in care. Asking parents to share their culture's foods and food habits with the children in care is a good way for the caregiver to find out the extent of this obstacle. Adapting food selections to cultural influences may help increase the selection of foods available to the family. As the caregiver understands the dietary or food limitations of a family, he may need to call on outside help, such as a nutritionist.

Another issue in cultural sensitivity may be the caregiver's own cultural perspective on the selection of foods. Not all children like foods that are different from the ones they are used to eating. These differences may be in the manner in which the foods are prepared or in the way they are seasoned. It is important for the caregiver to be sensitive to the needs of the children. The caregiver needs to present a balance of foods that represent the food selections of children from a number of other cultures.

Supervision

A caregiver is likely to serve one or more meals per day to the children in care. Supervision of mealtime requires a number of skills. If the caregiver provides meals to the children, the first area of supervision needed will be for the selection of healthy food choices. Regardless of whether the food is prepared by the caregiver or someone else, planning the meals should focus on healthy food choices and preparation forms. Food safety and sanitary practices should be used.

If the child brings meals from home, the caregiver may have to supervise what are acceptable food selections and what are not. Sending a sheet of acceptable food choices for the child care situation may help remind the parents that the caregiver is there to provide optimum care for their children. If a child brings unacceptable foods, these foods can be set aside to eat only after the good choices have been finished. Reading labels with children can help make them aware of what foods contain. This can be a powerful tool to help influence the parents to make better food selections.

Direction or redirection of mealtime behaviors helps to establish good eating habits and feeding behaviors. Observing the behaviors of children will be made easier when growth and developmental levels are understood. Good role modeling of mealtime practices is essential. The caregiver has a great deal of influence on how the children in her care behave. Understanding the caregiver's level of responsibility and the child's responsibility about eating will help alleviate any issue of control over food. This helps the caregiver to provide a foundation of good feeding behaviors and eating practices.

C 10.8

CONCEPT

KEY IMPLICATIONS FOR CAREGIVERS

The caregiver has an opportunity to provide positive food practices, good food selections, and an atmosphere conducive to eating. Application of information, strategies, and practices found in this chapter and the previous chapter enables the caregiver to do this. Opportunities to educate the children about nutrition will occur on a daily basis. Every time there is a meal or snack, the caregiver can sit with the children and role model good eating practices and have a dialogue about the food. Practicing cultural sensitivity can help remove any barriers about food selection and choices. Acknowledging diverse food habits and preparing foods to reflect this can help break down barriers. Supervision provides the caregiver with the tools needed to make sure that proper nutritional habits are being formed and practiced in the child care environment.

CHAPTER **SUMMARY**

Every caregiver should practice good nutrition in child care. Many caregivers are not meeting the nutritional needs of children in their care. Caregivers may approach nutrition with their own perspective based on background, food practices, culture, and what the children eat or will not eat. Caregivers should have nutritional policies that cover early infant feeding, food and the toddler, the preschool child, school-aged children, special needs, and nutrition and exercise as part of nutrition.

The caregiver who understands how to accommodate the infant's physical and psychological needs will encourage the infant to go at his own pace. A caregiver who understands that the developmental characteristics of a toddler influences how she deals with food is less likely to make food an issue of control. A caregiver should use participatory activities to help the preschooler develop an awareness about the best nutritional choices. The caregiver can provide adequate nutrition for school-aged children by keeping in mind their activity levels.

Some children with disabilities or chronic illnesses may be easily accommodated in their nutritional needs and feeding levels. Others may require special early intervention nutritional services or may not be able to be in the child care situation. Including exercise in the child care daily program helps the caregiver provide a broad base for nutritional risk management.

The implications for the child caregiver include education, role modeling, and supervision. Opportunities to educate and role model good nutrition to the children and adults occur on a daily basis. Cultural sensitivity can break down barriers to food selection. Supervision provides the caregiver with the tools needed to make sure that proper nutritional habits are being formed and practiced in the child care environment.

TO GO **BEYOND**

Questions for Review

1. Discuss how developmental levels relate to nutritional needs of children of different ages. How do the developmental levels affect the eating process for children?
2. Discuss the benefits of breast feeding vs. bottle feeding.
3. Describe how you would introduce solid food to infants.
4. Discuss how food is used as an issue of control by toddlers and their parents.

AS AN **INDIVIDUAL**

1. Using "Rate Your Plate" found in Appendix C, rate your own diet. How does this differ from the three-day charting of your diet? Compare and contrast the two.

2. Observe children and their parents in the grocery store. How do they act in the cereal aisle? How do these interactions reflect positive rewards for negative behaviors? How do you see food as an issue of control is these interactions.

AS A **GROUP**

1. Observe various patterns of children eating, including cultural patterns. Discuss this in class. List these observations. How would you use this information to talk to children about eating and food?

2. Collect menus from child care centers, family care homes, and elementary schools. Do these menus meet the nutritional needs of children? How would you change them to meet the Food Guide Pyramid?

CHAPTER **REFERENCES**

American Academy of Pediatrics (AAP). (1990). *Television and the family* [Brochure]. Elk Grove, IL: Author.

American Academy of Pediatrics (AAP). (1992). Statement on cholesterol. *Pediatrics, 90,* 469–472.

Branen, L., & Fletcher, J. (1994). Effects of restrictive and self-selected feeding on preschool children's food intake and waste at snacktime. *Journal of Nutrition Education, 26*(6), 273–277.

Briley, M., Roberts-Gray, C., & Rowe, S. (1993). What can children learn from the menu at the child care center? *Journal of Community Health, 18*(6), 363–377.

Briley, M., Roberts-Gray, C., & Simpson, D. (1994). Identification of factors that influence the menu at child care centers: A grounded theory approach. *Journal of the American Dietetic Association, 94*(3), 276–281.

Brooks, M. (1996, January 6). Get a move on: Teaching kids to exercise should be a family affair—one that's fun. *San Diego Union Tribune,* E-1,4.

Busselman, D., & Holcomb, C. (1994). Reading skill and comprehension of the Dietary Guidelines by WIC participants. *Journal of the American Dietetics Association, 94*(6), 622–625.

Dewalt, K., D'Angelo, S., McFadden, M., Danner, F., Noland, M., & Kochen, A. (1990). *Journal of the American Dietetic Association, 90*(4).

Diriga, O., Olgesby, A., & Bassoff, B. (1991). Assessment of the nutrition education needs of day care providers. *Journal of the American Dietetics Association, 91*(6), 714–715.

Gans, K., Sundaram, S., McPhillips, J., Hixson, M., Linnan, L., & Carleton, R. (1993). Rate your plate: An eating pattern assessment and educational tool used at cholesterol screening and education program. *Journal of Nutrition Education, 25*(1), 29–35.

Gordon, A., & McKinney, R. (1995). Sources of nutrients for students. *Journal of Clinical Nutrition, 61*(1), 232–240.

Infant nutrition: Drinking from a cup, eating with a spoon. (1994, Fall). *Texas Child Care,* 8–14.

Jones, E. & Matheny, R. (1993). Relationship between infant feeding and exclusion from child care. *Journal of the American Dietetic Association. 93*(7), 809–811.

Kendall, P. (1994). *The good news, bad news on kids, t.v., nutrition and fitness.* Colorado State Cooperative Extension via Penn State Nutrition Center. Path: http://countrystore.org:80/webpages/health/direct175.htm. Internet document number: 12101640.

Kendrick, A., Kaufman, R., & Messenger, K. (1995). *Healthy young children.* Washington, DC: NAEYC.

Kotz, K., & Story, M. (1994). Food advertisements during children's Saturday morning television programming: Are they consistent with dietary recommendations? *Journal of the American Dietetic Association, 94*(11), 1296–1300.

Morris, P. (1991). *Heading for a health crisis: eating patterns of America's school children.* Washington, DC: Public Voice for Food and Health Policy.

Oesterreich, L. (1995). *Iowa family care handbook.* Ames, IA: Iowa State University.

Reicks, M., Randall, J., & Haynes, B. (1994). Factors affecting consumption of fruits and vegetables by low-income families. *Journal of the American Dietetic Association, 94*(11), 1309.

Rice, B. (1992, September). Mixed signals: T.V.'s effect on children continue to stir debate. *American Health,* 58–62.

Satter, E. (1987). *How to get your kid to eat . . . But not too much.* Palo Alto, CA: Bull Publishing Co.

Satter, E. (1989). *Feeding with love and good sense.* Palo Alto, CA: Bull Publishing Co.

Singleton, J., Achterberg, C., & Shannon, B. (1992). Role of food and nutrition in the health perceptions of young children. *Journal of the American Dietetic Association, 92*(1), 67–70.

Splett, P., & Story, M. (1991). Child nutrition: Objectives for the decade. *Journal of the American Dietetic Association, 91*(6), 665–668.

Stanek, K. , Abbott, D., & Cramer, S. (1990). Diet quality and the eating environment of preschool children. *Journal of the American Dietetic Association, 90(11),* 1582–1584.

Too much of a good thing. (1994). *Tufts University Diet and Nutrition Letter, 12*(5), 1.

T.V. food ads feed kids the wrong message. (1995, January). *Tufts University Diet and Nutrition Letter, 12*(11) 7–8.

Yadrick, K., & Sneed, J. (1994). Nutrition services for children with developmental disabilities and chronic illness in education program. *Journal of the American Dietetic Association 94*(10), 1122–1128.

SUGGESTIONS **FOR READING**

American Academy of Pediatrics (AAP). (1993). *Pediatrics nutrition handbook.* Elk Grove, IL: Author.

Kendall, P. (1995). *Health impacts of Saturday morning t.v.* Colorado State University Cooperative Extension via Penn State Nutrition Center. Path:http://countrystore.org:80/webpages/health/direct175.htm. Internet document number: 121011628.

Nicklas, T., Bao, W., Webber, L., & Berenson, G. (1993). Breakfast consumption affects adequacy of total daily intake in children. *Journal of the American Dietetic Association, 93*(8), 886–891.

T.V. may be a factor in girl's obesity: Study. *The Toronto Star.* (1992, March 30).

CHAPTER ELEVEN

Menu Planning and Food Safety in Child Care

Upon completion of this chapter, including a review of the summary, you should be able to:

Nutritional Policies

Define and discuss nutritional policies in relation to menu planning and food safety in the child care environment.

Guidelines for Food Programs

Discuss the guidelines for subsidized food programs available for child care environments.

Menu Planning for Child Care

Indicate the importance of proper menu planning for children's well-being including strategies for planning healthy breakfasts, snacks, and lunches.

Food Safety in Child Care

Summarize the need for food sanitation and safety and practice strategies for providing it in the child care environment.

Implications for Caregivers

Relate the strategies for providing safe and healthy meals in child care through education, observation, cultural sensitivity, and supervision.

NUTRITIONAL POLICIES

An increasing number of children are being cared for in a child care environment. Child care appears to be the place where many children are learning their food habits since they are spending much of their day in care. In order to meet the nutritional needs of the children in care, caregivers must be prepared to plan healthy menus that children will enjoy and eat. Caregivers must also be prepared to protect the children from disease by practicing food safety. The following are indicators of the need for sound nutritional policies for menu planning and food safety:

■ More than five million children eat a meal in child care every day, and this number is expected to increase (Briley, Roberts-Gray, & Rowe, l993). Children in child care do not consume adequate amounts of most nutrients (Drake, 1992).

■ Ninety-three percent of Latino children consume less than the recommended five servings of fruits and vegetables. Low intakes can put these children at risk for poor nutrition (Basch, Zybert, & Shea, 1994).

■ Concerns have been raised about child care programs not meeting the iron and zinc needs of children (Drake, 1992). These needs are associated with growth and learning (Troccoli, 1993).

■ It is recommended that caregivers provide two-thirds of the recommended daily allowances for children who are in care for long hours (Oesterreich, 1995).

■ Only 34 percent of child care food preparers had any training in nutrition or food sanitation and safety (Pond-Smith, Richarz, & Gonzales, 1992).

Many family child caregivers and in-home caregivers are also responsible for menu planning and food preparation in addition to child care responsibilities.

Child care centers have a number of caregivers on staff. In some centers one of these may double as the food preparer and menu planner. The director may plan the menus, while a food preparation person is hired specifically for the job of cooking. In some cases, there may be a centrally located kitchen or food is catered and pre-prepared food is distributed to several child care centers. These menus may be provided by a dietician hired exclusively for that task.

The family child caregiver and the in-home caregiver are probably the menu planner and food preparer. This task, in addition to caring for children, may appear to be burdensome. With proper training in menu planning and food safety, the caregiver may find that awareness and knowledge often make a job easier to perform.

Recently, child care has been examined for its ability to provide good nutritional practices and safe food handling techniques. This can be improved through a more thorough understanding of the meals provided in care and the necessity for good menu planning as well as proper food sanitation and safety practices. Caregivers will need to use education, cultural sensitivity, observation, and supervision to carry out this task.

It is recommended that policies be created for the following areas:

Proper nutrition needs to be taught and reinforced at all levels.

■ *Guidelines for Food Programs:* understanding how the subsidized food programs guidelines should impact the food selection in child care.

■ *Menu Planning:* understanding how to plan menus that meet children's tastes and nutritional needs, as well as being cost effective and easy to prepare.

■ *Food Sanitation and Safety:* understanding the methods and practices for food sanitation and safety in child care.

■ *Implications for Caregivers:* understanding how education, cultural sensitivity, and supervision can help the caregiver plan for adequate nutrition and food safety in child care.

KEY NUTRITIONAL POLICIES

CONCEPT

More than five million children are eating meals in child care on a daily basis. Nutrition and food safety have been found to be inadequate in many child care environments. It is up to the caregiver who plans and/or prepares meals for children to be adequately trained. The caregiver needs to have an understanding of how breakfast, snacks, and lunches impact a child's nutritional needs. The caregiver should know how to select healthy foods, plan adequate menus, and prepare food that is safe. By using education, cultural sensitivity, observation, and supervision the caregiver ensures a child care environment that is providing for the nutritional needs of the children in care.

GUIDELINES FOR FOOD PROGRAMS

There are a number of food programs that caregivers and families can use to meet the nutritional needs of children. Several of these impact the child care program directly. The Child and Adult Care Food Program (CACFP), the Food Distribution Program, and the Summer Food Service Program for Children (SFSPC) help to provide foods for child care environments that meet the criteria. The CACFP, the Nutrition Education and Training Program (NET), and the Expanded Food and Nutrition Education Program (EFNEP) all provide nutrition information and training for teachers, food service personnel, and children.

Programs that help families include the Special Supplemental Food Program for Women, Infants, and Children (WIC), the USDA's Food Stamp Program, the National School Lunch Program, and the School Breakfast program. WIC provides formula and other foods to families with children under age three. The Food Stamp Program provides more food to children and their families than any other source. Eighty-three percent of the people who receive food stamp monies are families with children (Greenstein, 1992). Child caregivers should be informed about these resources should they need to make referrals to families to help them provide adequate nutrition to their children when not in care.

The main goal of organized food programs is to provide nutritious foods for children in need.

The Child and Adult Care Food Program

The Child and Adult Care Food Program provides funding for children to age twelve years. To be eligible to participate in this program and receive funds, the child care center or home must be a

1. Nonprofit licensed or approved public or private child care center
2. Family child care home that belongs to a sponsoring agency
3. For-profit private program that receives funding for more than one-fourth of the children present in care through Title Twenty (Title XX) of the Social Security Act

Approximately 25,000 child care centers and 160,000 family child care homes were participating in this program in 1992. There were 1.9 million children participating in these programs daily (Briley, Roberts-Gray, & Simpson, 1994).

Funding for the CACFP is made possible through the United States Department of Agriculture's Food and Nutrition Service. Eligible child care sites may be funded for up to two meals and one snack per day or two snacks and one meal. A sliding scale is applied at the child care site that indicates how much to charge a family for meals depending upon their income. Many children receive free meals as a result of the application of the scale.

The family child care home must have a sponsoring agency that administers the program. This may be a local child care resource and referral agency, a public agency such as a USDA cooperative extension service, or other local agencies willing to provide financial administration. The state child care licensing agency can provide the caregiver with this information.

The CACFP provides funding for meals and nutritional training and menu planning for the child caregivers. In return, the child caregiver must meet the nutritional guidelines set by the CACFP. These are included in Table 11.1.

TABLE **11.1**

CACFP Nutritional Guidelines

Infants

Birth to three months
Breakfast, Lunch, and Snack
4–6 oz. formula

Four to Seven Months
Breakfast, Lunch, and Snack
4–6 oz. formula
0–3 Tbs. iron-fortified infant cereal (not snack)
0–3 Tbs. vegetables or fruits (not snack)

Eight to Eleven Months
Breakfast and Lunch
6–8 oz. formula
2–4 Tbs. iron-fortified infant cereal
1–4 Tbs. fruit or vegetables

CACFP Nutritional Guidelines *continued*

Infants *continued*

Lunch

1–4 Tbs. meat, fish, poultry, egg yolk, or dried beans *or*

1–4 oz. cottage cheese, cheese spread, or cheese food *or*

½–2 oz. cheese

Snack

2–4 oz. formula or milk or full strength fruit juice

2 crackers or ½ slice bread

Children

One to Two Years

Breakfast

½ cup milk

¼ cup fruit juice, fruit, or vegetable

Bread and/or cereal (¼ cup cereal, ½ slice bread)

Lunch

½ cup milk

Meat or meat alternate (1 oz. meat or cheese, 1 egg, 2 Tbs. peanut butter, or ¼ cup cooked dry beans or peas)

¼ cup (total) vegetables and/or fruits (more than one choice)

½ slice bread

Snack (Select two)

½ cup milk

½ oz. meat or meat alternate *or*

2 oz. plain yogurt or ¼ cup flavored yogurt *(do not serve yogurt and milk at same snack)*

Three to Five Years

Breakfast

¾ cup milk

½ cup fruit juice, fruit, or vegetable

½ slice bread *or*

⅓ cup cold cereal *or*

¼ cup hot cereal

Lunch

¾ cup milk

Meat or Meat Alternate (1½ oz. meat, poultry, cheese, *or* 1 egg, *or*

⅜ cup cooked dry beans or peas *or* 3 Tbs. peanut butter *or*

¾ oz. nuts or seeds)

½ cup (total) vegetables and/or fruits (more than one choice)

½ slice bread

Snack (Select two)

½ cup milk

½ oz. meat or meat alternate *or*

2 oz. plain yogurt or ¼ cup flavored yogurt

½ cup fruit juice or fruit or vegetable

Bread and/or cereal (½ slice bread, ⅓ cup cold cereal, ¼ cup hot cereal)

These teachers are receiving nutrition education to help them teach children about nutrition.

Other Programs

The other program that may be of help to child care environments in supplying food is the USDA Food Distribution Program. It is organized to distribute surplus foods such as cheese, grains, and canned goods. A child care site that participates in the CACFP program will automatically receive an application to participate in this program as well. Other licensed child care programs are also eligible to apply. If the child care is selected to participate it can receive commodity foods or cash supplements for the surplus food.

The Summer Food Service Program for Children supplies children from low-income families nutritious foods when their regular schools are on summer vacation. Child care programs and family child care that provide care to school aged children while on summer break may be eligible for these funds.

The Nutrition Education and Training Program provides education to teachers to help them teach children about nutrition. Funds can be used for instructional materials and instruction. The Expanded Food and Nutrition Education Program is run by cooperative extension. Extension professionals train others to teach food and nutrition to children and their families as well as food purchasing, safety, sanitation, and menu planning for child care. The National Food Service Management Institute at the University of Mississippi has a resource center for child care nutrition.

KEY GUIDELINES FOR FOOD PROGRAMS

There are a number of nutritional programs that offer assistance to child care centers or sites by providing funding or educational information. Other programs help children and their families access nutritional foods at no or low cost. The program that helps many child care sites is the Child and Adult Care Food Program. It provides specific guidelines for the food to be served, and it offers menu planning and nutritional information to caregivers. In return, caregivers agree to follow the guidelines and provide nutritious meals to children in care. Other programs that offer education support, training, and instructional materials are the Nutrition Education and Training Program, the Expanded Food and Nutrition Education Program, and the National Food Service Management Institute.

MENU PLANNING FOR CHILD CARE

The American Dietetic Association has set recommended standards for child care programs; that is the child care should provide 67 percent of the nutritional needs for all children present for a full day ("Position of the American Dietetic Association," 1994). The Food and Nutrition Service suggests that child nutrition programs should offer meals low in fats and cholesterol; plenty of fruits, vegetables, grains, and milk products; sugar and salt only in moderation; and a variety of foods (U.S. Department of Agriculture [USDA], 1992). These guidelines follow the Dietary Guidelines for Americans.

This lunch menu in a child care center reflects the recommended standards for child care programs.

Lunch Menu

Mon: Peanut butter + Jelly on whole wheat bread, watermelon, and apple slices.

Tue: Split Pea Soup, crackers, fruit cocktail, and banana.

Wed: Refried beans, flour tortilla, green beans, and oranges.

Thur: Fish Fillet, noodles, carrots, and apple sauce.

Fri: Cheese ravioli, green salad, and corn.

Building a Menu

There are a number of considerations in menu planning and food preparation (see Figure 11.1). The best base for good menu planning is knowledge of nutrition and children's nutritional needs and developmental stages (see Table 11.2).

This first level of menu planning also includes understanding the Food Guide Pyramid, the Dietary Guidelines for Americans, and any regulations that may accompany a food program in which the child care may participate. It should be prepared to meet state licensing procedures. This level should also consider appetizing presentations. The child caregiver will need to be able to apply this information to help create menus that are healthy and meet the children's nutritional needs as well as fit their developmental level.

The second level involved in menu planning is based on accessibility to healthy food choices. A number of factors influence this level. The cost of food and the economics of providing adequate nutrition heavily influence the food that is purchased or the subsidized food programs that the child care may access.

Another consideration at this level is the culinary skills of the caregiver or the food preparer who will cook the meals planned in the menu. Someone with limited skills will have fewer choices and may rely on more convenience type foods that may be less nutritional and more expensive.

Convenience itself may be a factor. Time is often limited, especially if there is only one caregiver present in the child care environment. This convenience factor may limit accessibility to the healthiest choices.

Convenience foods do not have to be unhealthy as these caregivers show with cereal and bananas.

Access to healthy food is also affected by seasons. Foods that are in season are much more moderate in price and are more readily available. Fruits, vegetables, and occasionally meats are affected by seasonal availability.

The last factor at this level is the amount of storage available for foods. This includes both room in a refrigerator and room in a pantry or kitchen cabinet. Child care environments with good storage facilities are able to buy in bulk and save money. These child care environments can also purchase more fresh foods at one time and plan for more frequent use of these foods.

The third level of influence on menu planning is the environment, including the goal of child care. The goal will affect food selection. The menu in a setting where the goal is the well-being of children will be different from the menu in a setting where goal is to provide an income for the staff.

The cultural diversity of the child care environment often has an influence on menu planning. The diversity may be reflected in the caregiver's cultural background and may limit choices in the menu items for planning. A positive process occurs when the menu selection is influenced by the diversity of the children in care.

Another influence at this level is the personal history of the caregiver, menu planner, or food purchaser, which in many cases will be the same person. The person who creates the menu and/or prepares the food is going to be influenced by her own food memories, prejudices, and preferences. If she hated lima beans as a child, they will probably never appear on the menu.

Some caregivers have a perception of what foods children will or will not eat. Many menus are planned and are limited by the choices that a caregiver "knows" are the only things a child will eat.

FIGURE **11.1**
Factors Involved in Menu
Planning in Child Care

Factors Involved in Menu Planning in Child Care

Level One
Knowledge of Nutrition
Children's Nutritional Needs
A Child's Developmental Stages
Dietary Guidelines for Americans
Food Guide Pyramid

Level Two
Accessibility
for Health Choices
Cost   Convenience   Storage
Culinary Skills   Economy
Seasonal Food Considerations

Level Three
Environment
Goal of Child Care
Personal History
Cultural Diversity
Perceptions of
Child Food Choices

Considering the influences at every level, the child caregiver can begin planning a menu. Care should be taken to remove all prejudices, preferences, and perceptions or any other factor that may be a barrier to good menu planning. The caregiver should also remove any barriers to the accessibility of the healthiest food selections. This may involve applying for subsidized food programs, taking cooking lessons, and looking for easier ways to cook nutritious fresh foods.

The caregiver should be equipped with the necessary nutritional knowledge and influences of the developmental stages by reading and referencing this text. If the caregiver feels more information would be helpful, further training and education in nutrition may be the next step.

Menu planning should be done on a regular basis, such as every two weeks or once per month. The menu should be reviewed and revised on a regular basis. Some child care centers have had the same menu for fifteen years (Briley, Roberts-Gray, & Rowe, 1993). It is important to keep the menu updated and to change it so a variety of foods can be offered and seasonal availability can be accessed.

By applying the meal guidelines found in Table 11.1, or following specific meal guidelines supplied by a child care licensing agency, the caregiver can create menus that meet the needs of the children. Using the "Rate Your Plate" pyramid found in Figure 11.2 is a good beginning point. Several other considerations should be kept in mind.

Many child care menus fail to meet the energy needs of the young child. They also fail to provide enough fresh fruits and vegetables and often do not meet the daily requirements for iron and niacin. Child care menus have often been found to provide too much fat, sugar, and salt.

FIGURE **11.2**
Rate Your Plate *(1993 Pyramid Packet, Penn State Nutrition Center, 417 East Calder Way, University Park, PA 16801-5663; 814-865-6323)*

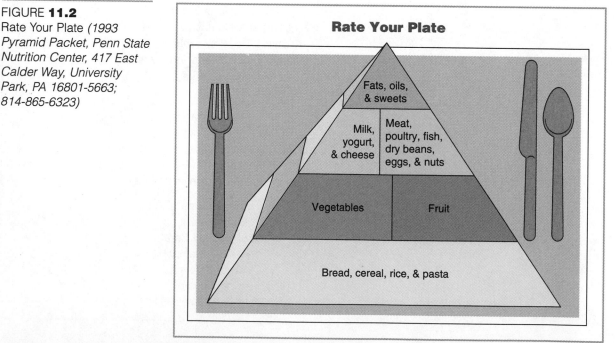

REALITY CHECK

Children of the Fast Food Generation

Children are consuming fast foods with more frequency. It is often a part of school lunch programs and some caregivers are providing fast foods or similar foods to the children in care. It is estimated that one dollar of every ten dollars spent on food is for fast food (American Academy of Pediatrics [AAP], 1993). Fast food restaurant eating captures 83 percent of the market for children under the age of eighteen years. Fast food is noted for its oversupply of fat, cholesterol, sodium, and sugar. A typical fast food meal for children can provide as much as 36 percent of their caloric needs for a day, but fall short of basic nutrients.

The most popular meals for children at fast food restaurants include soft drinks, hamburgers, french fries, pizza, and fried chicken. The most typical meal a child eats at a fast food restaurant is the kid's meal that includes a main item, fries, and a drink. Occasionally these meals include a dessert, and they almost always include a toy that draws many children to this type of meal. Following are some typical kids meals with nutritional breakdown.

Fast Food Kids Meals Nutritional Breakdown

	Calories	Fats (g)	Protein (g)	Sodium (mg)	Carbohydrates (g)
Daily Total	**2000**	**65**	**24**	**2400**	**300**
Burger King (Source: Burger King Corporation)					
Hamburger	275	11	15	510	28
French Fries	227	13	3	161	24
Cola	190	0	0	20	16
Total	**692**	**24**	**18**	**691**	**68**
McDonald's (Source: McDonald's Corporation)					
Cheeseburger	305	13	15	725	30
French Fries	220	12	3	110	30
Orange Drink	230	0	0	30	59
Total	**755**	**18**	**18**	**865**	**119**
Taco Bell (Source: Taco Bell Corporation)					
Taco	183	11	10	276	11
Cinn. Twists	231	11	3	316	32
Lemon-lime	190	0	0	90	48
Total	**604**	**22**	**13**	**682**	**91**
Kentucky Fried Chicken (Source: Kentucky Fried Chicken Corporation)					
Nuggets	276	17	17	840	13
Kentucky Fries	377	18	5	215	18
Root Beer	244	0	0	45	16
Total	**897**	**35**	**22**	**1100**	**46**

As this table reflects, children are getting an overabundance of fat and sodium and a large number of calories for the nutrients present in these meals.

Because children are eating out so often, it is even more important for the caregiver to provide nutritious meals during child care. It is important to refrain from getting caught in the fast food habit. Children prefer these highly flavored, high-fat meals, so this may be a challenge. However, caregivers can discuss this with children and help them select better choices when they do go out.

Another method of making sure the menu is planned properly is to use a checklist (Table 11.2).

A sample menu is found in Table 11.3. Further sample menu plans may be found in Appendix C.

TABLE **11.2**

Menu Planning Checklist

Check for:

☐ Menu fits budget.

☐ Food is seasonally available.

☐ Culinary skills are available to prepare foods selected.

☐ There is adequate time and labor to prepare food.

☐ Personal history barriers are removed.

☐ Different methods of preparation are used.

☐ There is adequate storage for the food.

☐ Cultural and ethnic diversity are considered.

☐ Meal pattern meets CAFCP guidelines or the Food Guide Pyramid guidelines.

☐ A few new foods are tried every menu planning period.

☐ Few foods are offered that have high fat, high sodium, or high sugar content.

☐ A source of vitamin C is served daily.

☐ A source of vitamin A is served 3 to 4 times per week.

☐ Whole grain breads and grains are offered.

☐ Raw vegetables and fruits are served often.

Breakfast

Breakfast may well be the most critical meal of the day. Studies reflect that eating breakfast affects cognition, strength, attitude, and endurance (Food Insight, 1992). Children who skip breakfast do not make up for the nutritional loss over the period of the rest of the day (Nicklaus, Bao, Webber, & Berenson, 1993). People who eat breakfast are less likely to be obese because their nutritional needs are spread throughout the day. Poor nutrition among children in the United States is in part a result of skipping breakfast. ("Nutrition Programs," 1994).

As reflected in Table 11.1 (page 344), breakfast should consist of milk, bread/cereal, and fruit. Breakfasts can be built around traditional breakfast

TABLE **11.3**

Sample Menu for Child Care

	Breakfast	Snack	Lunch	Snack
Monday	Cheerios Banana Milk	Rye crisp Cheese Apple juice	Spaghetti with meat sauce Salad & fruit Milk	Quesadillas Orange juice
Tuesday	French toast Applesauce Milk	Carrot sticks Saltine crackers Fruit juice	Chicken and vegetable soup Grilled cheese sandwich Melon slice Milk	Corn muffins Milk
Wednesday	Cinnamon whole wheat tortillas Peaches Milk	Popcorn Apple juice	Fettucini with cheese sauce Carrot rounds Fruit cup Milk	Banana bread with cream cheese Grape juice
Thursday	Yogurt Strawberries Wheat toast	Rice cakes with peanut butter Fruit juice	Chicken chow mein over crisp noodles Orange wedge Milk	Cranberry muffins Apple juice
Friday	Granola Pears Milk Water	Yogurt dip with vegetable sticks & tomato Milk	Beef tostado with beans, rice, lettuce Milk	Bread sticks Orange Water

foods such as cereal, toast, fruit, milk, and so forth. These food choices can be enhanced by making them more attractive. Fruits or nuts can be put on hot or cold cereals. A bagel can have cream cheese or cottage cheese and fruit on it. The child caregiver will have to understand the food habits of the children in care. Some children do not like mixing foods. Other children may be affected by cultural tradition or practices regarding breakfast choices.

Other nontraditional food choices for breakfast are available, such as dried fruits, peanut butter, burritos, pizza, fruit salad, and fruit smoothies, which all offer good nutrition and might encourage children to eat better at breakfast. Foods from other cultures such as stir fried rice may be served as an alternative to the traditional choices.

Snacks

Snacks are an essential part of a child's nutritional day. Snacks should provide adequate nutrition, and should be served at a sufficient time between meals for the children to be hungry but not too hungry. Snacks are a good time to begin to reflect the cultural diversity of the children in care. It is also the best time to introduce new foods. If children do not like the food, their nutritional needs for the day will be less at risk.

A nutritious breakfast consisting of milk, bread/cereal, and fruit is just one way to provide a healthy start for children.

As shown in Table 11.1, snacks should consist of a milk or meat/meat alternate choice, such as yogurt and a bread/grain or fruit choice. Some licensing standards dictate that there be pure fruit juice served at one snack and milk at the other snack. Ideally, there should always be a protein source either from milk, a meat, or a meat alternate. An example of this is peanut butter on celery or crackers. Protein should be spread throughout the day for optimum benefit. The fat in the meat or milk will offer satiety and help to fill up the child. Using a bread, grain, or fruit will provide bulk, flavor, and help the children meet the food pyramid guidelines.

Typical snacks might include bagels, tortillas, crackers, milk, yogurt, string cheese, and fresh fruit such as apples, bananas or oranges, or applesauce. Snacks may occasionally be more unusual such as a vegetable soup, a yogurt sundae, a cheese crisp, a bread pudding, a fruit smoothie, or a frozen banana pop with peanut butter and coconut. The type of snack may be impacted by food preparation time and cost.

Lunches

Lunches in child care help provide the greatest amount of nutrition in the child's day. The child's lunch should consist of milk, a meat, or meat alternate, fruits and/or vegetables (minimum of two), and a bread or grain. School lunches contain more than the average amount of fats and saturated fats (Bushweller, 1993). It is important to address this issue when planning menus.

Some child caregivers limit the lunches they prepare to those things children are familiar with or those things that may resemble fast food that children will eat. Menu items such as peanut butter sandwiches, burritos, pizza, hamburgers, spaghetti, fish sticks, tacos, macaroni and cheese, and hot dogs may appear often and in some cases may be the rotating menu. Several of these items may contribute more fat at one meal than may be desired. This is a practice that should be examined and changed to better meet the nutritional needs of the children.

Caregivers who provide lunches for children should keep a menu in mind that offers less fat and a greater variety of food over time. Children who are involved in helping prepare lunches may be more likely to eat a wider variety of foods. Foods such as stir fries, baked chicken or fish, hearty soups, pita pockets, quesadillas, and different pastas can add variety and flavor to the menu. Most children will eat these foods.

Pasta is a favorite nutritious food for children.

Lunches from Home.   Lunches may present a unique problem if they are not prepared at the child care site. When children bring their own lunches to school they are more likely to consume sugar, sweets, and sweetened beverages. They are also less likely to eat vegetables, drink milk, or have adequate amounts of meat or meat alternatives (Gordon & McKinney, 1995). Many licensed programs prohibit the presence of these less desirable foods. Caregivers should have a parent handout of unacceptable food choices such as high-density fat, sugar, and calorie-laden foods that offer little food value.

KEY MENU PLANNING

Menu planning begins with building a foundation of knowledge and eliminating barriers to accessing healthy food choices and background influences. Guidelines for meeting nutritional needs should be followed and a variety of foods, including fresh vegetables and fruits, should be provided. Child caregivers can look at each area of menu planning and relate it to the entire day's menu choices. They should use a checklist to examine if all criteria for food menu planning are met. A caregiver who understands the importance of breakfast, snacks, and lunch will plan more carefully to meet the needs of the children in care.

FOOD SAFETY IN CHILD CARE

Preventing foodborne illness should be a primary task of the caregiver who is planning and preparing meals for children in care. Food safety involves proper food purchasing, food storage, handling, and cooking. These practices and strategies for providing protection from risk and prevention of foodborne illnesses should be carefully monitored. It is recommended that the child caregiver responsible for food purchasing, storage, handling, and cooking use the Food Safety Checklists (Tables 11.4–11.7) to periodically monitor the child care environment for food safety.

Food Purchasing

Food purchasing is the starting point of making sure the food in the environment is safe. Food should be of good quality, fresh, and undamaged. To ensure quality, the purchases should be made from reputable wholesalers, markets, butchers, and others who provide food to the child care environment. These businesses should meet proper local and state health and sanitation codes as well as keep up with any federal regulations that may apply to them.

Buy fresh products before the "sell by" or "use by" dates. Any products that should be refrigerated, should be stored in that section of the store. Do not purchase foods that require refrigeration but are not. Avoid fresh products such as fish and poultry that have the label "frozen, defrosted." It is difficult to tell how long these items have been frozen or how long they have been sitting defrosted, or the manner in which they were defrosted.

When buying poultry and other meats, keep them away from fresh fruits, vegetables, and other foods that will not be cooked. This will avoid cross contamination. Always purchase perishable and fresh foods last. When having food packed, store fresh and frozen foods together to keep them cold.

Do not buy canned goods that are dented or otherwise compromised. The few cents that may be saved could be very costly later. Only buy prepackaged foods if the package is intact. A tear or a rip can allow the food to be contaminated. Table 11.4 lists some guidelines to ensure food safety when purchasing food.

TABLE **11.4**

Food Safety Purchasing Checklist

Check for:

- [ ] Buy from sources that are inspected for health and sanitation.
- [ ] Buy only good quality, fresh, and undamaged foods.
- [ ] Buy perishable food before "sell by" date.
- [ ] Perishable foods are refrigerated.
- [ ] Do not purchase "frozen, defrosted" foods.
- [ ] Purchase fresh foods last.
- [ ] Keep poultry and meats away from other foods.
- [ ] Do not buy damaged canned or packaged goods.

Food Storage

Proper food storage is a key to keeping food safe. This involves proper wrapping, proper labeling, temperature, and arrangement of the food that has been purchased.

Foods need to be protected from contamination by insects, rodents, dust, coughing, sneezing, dirty utensils, and improper temperature while being stored. Proper temperature maintenance is primary. Germs multiply rapidly in lukewarm foods.

Refrigerated Foods. Meats, poultry, and fish should be well wrapped so they do not contaminate other foods in the refrigerator. Placing the store package in a waterproof plastic bag works well. If these foods are being frozen, freezer bags or aluminum foil will help protect them from freezer burn and quality loss. It is essential that all food in child care be labeled by date of purchase to prevent waste and avoid risk.

All refrigerated products should be refrigerated immediately. Quickly freeze all frozen foods. If they have thawed, they must be used within 24 hours. This avoids any contamination. Eggs should be stored in the refrigerator, preferably in their cartons.

Clean utensils must always be used if storing the food. Food must be refrigerated or stored in covered, shallow containers within two hours after cooking. Containers should be less than 2 inches high. If the food is planned for later use, they should be put immediately in the refrigerator. *Never store food in its cooking container!* There is a short period of time to cool the food to avoid contamination.

Cooked food should always be dated, so it will be used while still good and not be wasted or present risk. The caregiver should always reheat cooked foods to a minimum of 160°F and make sure runny foods like soups have come to a full rolling boil before serving.

The refrigerator should be maintained at a temperature of less than 40°F and the freezer should be maintained at less than 0°F. This inhibits growth of bacteria that can cause foodborne illnesses. There is a danger zone for contamination of foods above 40°F. Bacteria multiplies rapidly between 40° and 125°F.

The refrigerator should be arranged so that there is adequate circulation of cold air. A refrigerator that is too full may not keep the proper temperature and foods may be at risk for contamination.

Unrefrigerated Foods.   All unrefrigerated products should be stored in clean, rodent-free areas, preferably with doors to cover the storage area. These areas should also be a minimum of 8 inches above the floor. Foods should be stored so that those items that were purchased first, will be used first. First in storage, first out of storage is the recommendation. This avoids waste and risk. Nonperishable items such as flour, sugar, and so forth, should be stored in airtight containers once the package is opened. A food safety storage checklist can be found in Table 11.5.

Food Handling

Anyone who has any signs of illness or infectious skin sores that cannot be covered should not be handling food. It is also preferable that the food handler not change diapers. This is more practical in a center situation where there are a number of caregivers. In a family child care home or in the child's own home the single caregiver must perform many roles. In these cases, extra care should be taken, including the use of disposable gloves.

Caregivers can avoid many risks for foodborne illnesses by handling food properly. Using sanitary practices and healthy habits for handling food (see Table 11.6) can avoid food contamination and growth of bacteria. Food may be handled in its raw form, or it may be frozen or cooked. *Never* thaw any food at room temperature. Thawing should take place in the refrigerator, the microwave oven, or by placing the item in a waterproof plastic bag and submerging it in cold water. Change the water every 30 minutes. When handling cooked foods, always wash hands.

Proper food handling is essential to avoiding risks for foodborne illnesses. Using sanitary practices and developing healthy habits for handling food can prevent food contamination and growth of bacteria.

TABLE **11.5**

Food Safety Storage Checklist

Check for:

- ☐ Meat, fish, and poultry wrapped in waterproof bags for refrigeration and in foil or freezer bags for freezer.
- ☐ Refrigerator set for 40°F or less. Freezer set at 0°F or less. Use special thermometers to measure the maintenance of these temperatures.
- ☐ Refrigerator has adequate circulation.
- ☐ All refrigerated foods placed in refrigerator immediately upon arrival at child care, including lunches brought from home until lunch time.
- ☐ All frozen foods immediately in freezer. Use thawed foods within one day.
- ☐ Label and date all foods. Use leftovers within two days after first use.
- ☐ Eggs stored in refrigerator.
- ☐ All food stored in clean, airtight containers.
- ☐ Hot foods placed in shallow containers (less than 2 inches) to promote rapid boiling.
- ☐ Nonperishable food stored in clean, rodent and insect proof containers, 8 inches from the ground, away from cleaning supplies or poisonous materials.
- ☐ First food in storage, first food out of storage.
- ☐ Nonperishable items stored in airtight containers.

The food handler's clothing should be clean and using a clean apron will help maintain a higher cleanliness standard. Other food handling safety measures are included in Table 11.6.

An excellent way to ensure that food is handled properly is to have the person who is preparing and serving food take a food handler's course that is offered in most communities.

Cooking Foods

Safe, sanitary, and healthy practices should always be used when preparing foods for cooking. As the foods are being cooked, other measures help to provide further protection. Poultry and meats should always be cooked to an internal temperature of 160° to 180°F. The minimum temperature of 160°F protects the food from causing foodborne illnesses. This is especially important for children. Recent outbreaks of E. coli bacteria have caused concern about the internal temperature of meats meeting the minimum degree criteria.

TABLE **11.6**

Healthy Food Handling Tips

■ Always wash hands.

■ Always prepare food handling environment using sanitary practices. This includes counter tops, bread boards, and can openers.

■ Keep nails well-trimmed and clean.

■ Keep hair tied back, in a hat, or in a net.

■ Wash all fruits, vegetables, and tops of cans prior to use.

■ Do not thaw frozen foods at room temperature.

■ After cutting poultry, meat, or fish follow sanitary cleaning procedures for cutting boards and hands.

■ Never let meat, poultry, or fish juices get on other foods.

■ Check internal temperatures of meats using a meat thermometer before serving. This is extremely important to prevent E. coli or salmonella bacteria from contaminating food. Follow temperature gauge for proper meat temperatures.

■ Always reheat food to a minimum of 160°F, or if runny food like soup, bring to a full rolling boil.

■ Refrigerate all cooked foods within two hours or foods for freezing immediately.

■ Never reuse a spoon that has been used for tasting.

■ Never reuse leftover food from serving bowls used on the table, except when the food is packaged and will not spoil.

■ Never prepare food when you are ill.

■ Do not help children with toileting, diapering, or blowing noses while preparing food.

■ Keep cloth for wiping up food for that purpose only, or use disposable cloths.

■ Wash dishes and preparation tools in hot, soapy water. Rinse. Dip for one minute in bleach solution that is at least 75°F. Let air dry. Do not use a dish towel to dry.

■ If using a dishwasher, thoroughly rinse dishes first, then utilize hottest, sanitizing cycle. Allow to dry before removing.

If a crockpot or slow cooker is used for cooking foods in child care several precautions should be taken to provide protection. The cooker should never be more than two-thirds full with plenty of liquid. If using meat, the pieces should be small and uniform and the internal temperature must be checked before serving to make sure it meets the 160°F requirement.

REALITY CHECK

E. coli and Children

In January, 1993, there was a serious outbreak of the E. coli bacteria because of contaminated hamburger meat. Three children died and many more suffered life-long disabling conditions (Evans, 1995). Since that time we have learned much about this bacteria and the conditions that harbor its presence. It is estimated that as many as 20,000 cases of E. coli infection appear each year, and as many as 500 people die from it every year (Cooper, 1995).

E. coli stands for *Escherichia coli* and is one of the most abundant species of bacteria in our environment. It lives in the intestines of humans and animals. E. coli is common and works with other bacteria within our intestines to enable us to function properly and remain healthy. The problem occurs when the E. coli bacteria that are present in animal intestines produce different strains that can be harmful to humans. The rare strain that has occurred recently is referred to as E. coli 0157:H7, and causes hemorrhaging, blood loss, and dehydration (Brown, 1996).

The E. coli 0157:H7 bacteria has been infected with a strain of virus producing toxins. The toxin appears as a protein that causes severe damage to the lining of the intestines. Salt and water are lost in the intestines and blood vessels are damaged (Brown, 1996). It can also result in hemolytic uremic syndrome that can cause acute kidney failure. Young children and elderly persons are the most susceptible to these toxins because dehydration, blood loss, and kidney failure can easily progress to lethal conditions.

Harmful E. coli bacteria can be found in a number of places, the most common of which is ground beef. E. coli is commonly found in cattle feces and can be spread by animals and people. This harmful strain is also found in roast beef, unpasteurized milk, apple cider, and municipal water.

The meat inspection system has undergone some radical changes recently, because the most common source of this bacteria is related to hamburger. On July 6, 1996, the U.S. Department of Agriculture announced its new four step program to revamp the inspection system and to try to reduce the E. coli bacteria found in meat products (White House Press Briefing, 1996). The new system of inspection is referred to as "hazard analysis critical control point" or HACCP, and should greatly reduce the harmful E. coli bacteria. E. coli testing is also occurring and will further reduce any contaminated meat products from being marketed.

Other measures have been taken to protect the public from the harmful E. coli bacteria. The state of Rhode Island passed a law in 1995 to prohibit children under twelve from ordering rare meat in public facilities (Simpson, 1995). The organization called S.T.O.P. (Safe Tables Our Priority) provides information on the E. coli bacteria and how safeguards can be practiced to prevent food-borne illnesses (Gaines, 1995).

Symptoms for the disease related to the E. coli bacteria may appear from several hours to several days. In young children, the time period is more likely to be short. In a healthy adult, symptoms may appear and be gone in about a week. In young children this disease is far more serious and should be reported to the physician immediately if blood is noticed in the diarrhea or if the stools appear watery.

It has been noted that the E. coli infection can easily spread from one person to another in nursing homes, hospitals, and child care centers (Cooper, 1995). There are specific safeguards that the caregiver can use to prevent the spread of the E. coli bacteria. These include:

■ All meat should be cooked to a temperature of 155°F. The juices should run clear and should not be pink.

■ Always clean any surface that has had raw meat on it, including utensils, before another item touches that surface.

■ Do not use the plate or tray that the raw meat was on to place the cooked meat on.

■ Always wash hands thoroughly before and after handling meat.

■ Do not serve unfiltered apple cider or unpasteurized milk.

■ Always handle diarrhea under strict universal hygiene conditions.

If cooking foods in the microwave, the caregiver should make sure the foods are cooked through and allowed to sit for a short period so the cooking process may finish. Using a microwave probe or a meat thermometer ensures all meats are at an internal temperature of 160°F. Table 11.7 contains a checklist for food safety.

TABLE **11.7**

Food Safety When Cooking

Check for:

- [ ] Always cook meats to an internal temperature of 160 to 180°F.
- [ ] If using a crockpot, never fill more than two-thirds and always use plenty of liquids.
- [ ] For a crockpot, cut meat pieces small and uniform.
- [ ] Before serving foods from a crockpot, always make sure internal temperature is a minimum of 160°F.
- [ ] Let microwave foods sit for a short time to finish the cooking cycle.
- [ ] Check microwave foods for thorough cooking.
- [ ] Always check internal temperature of meats cooked in microwave to meet the 160°F criterion.

KEY FOOD SAFETY

CONCEPT

Food safety in child care is essential to prevent the spread of foodborne illnesses. Protecting the child care environment by using safe food practices and strategies will prevent risk. The caregiver can use safe, sanitary food handling practices to better manage food preparation activities to evade bacteria and food spoilage. Using good food purchasing behaviors helps elliminate foods that may pose risk. The child caregiver can avoid contamination of foods by understanding how to store foods. The caregiver can offer protection from bacteria growth by cooking foods to a minimum of 160°F and checking all cooking methods to meet this temperature criterion.

IMPLICATIONS FOR **CAREGIVERS**

As more children in this country enter child care, caregivers should understand that they are the people who will be meeting the majority of the nutritional needs for many of these children. The child caregiver will need to prepare to meet those needs.

Education

Familiarity with food programs such as Child and Adult Care Food Program will help the caregiver to access available funds to provide better nutrition for children from low- and limited-income families. The caregiver can plan nutritious meals by using CACFP guidelines. Other programs provide nutritional training and instructional materials for the children and their parents.

Training for food safety and sanitation is essential for child caregivers (Briley, Roberts-Gray, & Simpson, 1994). Knowledge is the basis of menu planning. The child caregiver should know the basics of nutrition, what children's nutritional needs are, and how to use the Food Guide Pyramid and the Dietary Guidelines for Americans to apply that knowledge to create menus that meet those needs. The caregiver also should understand the child's developmental stages and how it affects the eating abilities and habits of children.

The person in charge of menu planning should have an understanding of accessibility for healthy choices. This understanding allows access to be maximized. Any barriers should be removed. The caregiver who plans menus should also do a personal checkup of practices, prejudices, and perceptions that may limit food selection.

The child caregiver should have knowledge of food safety practices and strategies that protect the food environment in child care. The caregiver can prevent waste and risk to health and safety by using good food purchasing, storage, handling, and cooking measures.

With Children. The caregiver can teach the children better nutritional practices by getting them to try new foods, eat a variety of foods, and consume more fruits and vegetables. Meeting a child's nutritional needs may take more than providing the food and the information. Information about foods is more meaningful, when the actual foods are involved. One of the easiest ways a caregiver can help to educate children to eat the foods found

With all the appropriate information the caregiver can plan menus considering the child's nutritional needs as well as developmental level/stage.

Children enjoy cooking experiences and feel they have contributed in a small way.

on the menu is to cook it with them. Having a cooking experience for new foods, culturally diverse foods, and fruits and vegetables is a good way to get children to participate in eating them. Children are likely to eat foods that they helped to prepare. Having at least one cooking experience per week will encourage participation and variety.

Snacks are a fast meal for the children to help prepare. Some children may be able to make their own snacks. Simple items such as rice cakes and peanut butter are a way to begin. Children are capable of this from toddlerhood. More complicated dishes and meals can be made in stages. To prepare soups, for example, vegetables can be cut one day, and the rest of the ingredients prepared and cooked the next.

Another way to educate children is to take them on field trips to the market, vegetable stands, and even farms to see how and where food is grown. There are also excellent videos that provide this information if funding, time, and access prove to be constraints.

There are a number of books that feature foods, many of which involve fruits and vegetables. Having those fruits and vegetables for a snack or meal the same day may encourage children to try new things.

For Parents.   Education for the parent is also essential. Good menu planning is not as effective if the parents are not involved at some level. Many parents would like more information on nutrition. Pestano-Binghay, Reis, & Walters (1993) found that parents of minority groups want more nutritional information in the form of written handouts, once or twice monthly. Cooking and tasting demonstrations and videos were other choices for education by these parents. When the parents are more educated they are more willing to participate in planning and encouraging their children to try more variety and new foods.

Another form of education that the caregiver may provide to the parents is how to access supplemental foods. Many families have limited or low incomes and food selections may be limited because of cost. Helping these families access food programs in order to provide them with better food at home may have a positive effect on the child care environment. Children who have well-balanced meals all the time are healthier and more ready to learn.

Information on food safety should also be provided to parents. This information may help the parent avoid foodborne illnesses and prevent the spread of infectious disease in the child care environment. Modeling these food safety behaviors is a good way to educate the parents. Handouts and workshops are another way.

Cultural Sensitivity

Cultural sensitivity needs to be practiced in menu planning. The caregiver should understand the daily and special event eating patterns of the diverse children in their care. Often the foods themselves are not different from the ones used in child care. However, the names, recipes, method of preparation, and condiments used may make the food appear very different (Block, Norris, Mandel, & Disogra, 1995).

The caregiver can ask families to share their recipes, and talk to them about food. This may be a way to discover the daily and special event choices. Another way to break any barriers to food selection is to have a potluck several times a year, so families can bring a favorite dish that represents their culture. Using their recipes for menu selections is another way to have the children try new foods and have parents feel respected.

Hispanic children and other ethnic groups have a difficult time meeting their Food Pyramid Guidelines for fruits and vegetables. Only 7 percent of a study group ate the adequate amount of fruits and vegetables (Basch, Zybert, & Shea, 1994). Using a variety of fruits and vegetables may help. One reason for lacking fruits and vegetables may be the access to food purchasing due to a lack of funds. The caregiver may want to make sure these families get the food program information so that they may have more selections to choose from to meet their children's needs.

Supervision

If the child care is involved in a food program, it is up to the designated caregiver to make sure that all rules, regulations, and guidelines are met. If training or instructional materials are supplied by food programs, it is up to this person to make sure this information is used properly and dispensed to the caregiver, the children, and the parents.

Supervision plays a key role in menu planning and food safety. Being able to make sure that these items are handled correctly and are properly supported is important. If the caregiver is also the menu planner, this offers checking and balance to the processes. Using the checklists for menu planning and food safety can ensure these processes are carried out properly.

It is up to the caregiver to supervise the children's reaction to the menu and observe whether or not they are eating what was prepared. This supervision may lead to more frequent review and revision. It is important that the guidelines and nutritional needs of the children are being met.

KEY IMPLICATIONS FOR CAREGIVERS

CONCEPT

The child caregiver needs to meet the nutritional and developmental needs of the child. Using guidelines and information from supplemental food programs may help. The caregiver needs to be educated in how to apply this knowledge to menu planning and breaking down any barriers that may prevent healthy food choices. Education also helps the caregiver to plan for safe food practices. Educating children through cooking and other methods can help them eat a greater variety of foods and try new foods. Parents can learn more about nutrition and better food selection at home. Cultural sensitivity provides information as well as help to remove barriers to both food selection and trying new foods. Supervision provides the method to ensure that proper menu planning and food safety are carried out.

CHAPTER **SUMMARY**

More than 5 million children are eating meals in child care on a daily basis. The nutrition and food safety have been found to be inadequate in many child care environments. It is up to the caregiver who plans, and/or prepares meals for children to be adequately trained. There are a number of nutritional programs that offer assistance to child care environments by providing funding or educational information.

The caregiver should know how to select healthy foods, plan adequate menus, and prepare food that is safe. Understanding the importance of breakfast, snacks, and lunch helps the caregiver to plan more carefully to meet the needs of the children in care. Protecting the child care environment by using safe food practices and strategies will prevent risk.

The caregiver can use education, cultural sensitivity, observation, and supervision to ensure the child care environment is providing for the nutritional needs of the children in care.

TO GO **BEYOND**

Questions for Review

1. Discuss the importance of menu planning in child care. What are the components a caregiver must consider?
2. Discuss how a caregiver would access help with nutrition and foods and menu planning.

AS AN **INDIVIDUAL**

1. Go to a fast food restaurant and observe the foods that children are ordering. How much of that food do they appear to be eating? Record your observations.
2. What food safety and storage practices have you observed in child care? In a fast food restaurant? Compare the two.
3. Observe parents and their children at the check-out line of the grocery store. What types of food are they buying? Please record your findings.
4. Plan one week's menu for a child care center. Be sure it is balanced nutritionally and is culturally diverse.

AS A **GROUP**

1. Divide up in groups and assign each group three or four fast food restaurants to obtain nutritional information. Was it easy to get? Are

there lighter food choices offered? How would you help children select better menu items for nutrition?

2. Survey the community for information about food programs that have help for child care. Compile the information and distribute to the class.

CHAPTER **REFERENCES**

American Academy of Pediatrics. (1993). *Pediatric nutrition handbook*. Elk Grove, IL: Author.

Basch, C., Zybert, P., & Shea, S. (1994). Dietary behavior and the fruit and vegetable intake of Latino children. *American Journal of Public Health, 94*(5), 914–918.

Block, G., Norris, J., Mandel, R., & Disogra, C. (1995). *Sources of energy and six nutrients in diets of low-income Hispanic-American women and their children: Quantitative data fro HHANES, 1982–1984.*

Briefing on meat and poultry. (1996, July 6). White House Press Briefing, Path: daemonAai.mit.edu or PDI://OMA.EOP.GOV.US/1996/7/6/2.TEXT.1.

Briley, M., Roberts-Gray, C., & Rowe, S. (1993). What can children learn from the menu at the child care center? *Journal of Community Health, 18*(6), 363–377.

Briley, M. Roberts-Gray, C., & Simpson, D. (1994). Identification of factors that influence the menu at child care centers: A grounded theory approach. *Journal of the American Dietetic Association, 94*(3), 276–281.

Brown, J. C. (1996, July 4). *What the heck is E. coli?* My home page, KU Microbiology. Path:http://falcon.cc.ukans.edu:80/%7EJBROWN/Ecoli.html.

Bushweller, K. (1993). Is school nutrition out to lunch? *Education Digest, 59*(3)54–57.

Cooper, J. R. (1995). *Like your burgers on the raw side? E. coli may give you a raw deal: Death*. Internet: The Medical Reporter. Path:email:jcooper@medreport.com.

Drake, M. A. (1992). Menu evaluation nutrient intake of young children and nutrition knowledge of menu planners in child care centers in Missouri. *Journal of Nutrition Education, 24*, 145–148.

Evans, E. (1995, January 17). U.S. moves to update meat inspect tests two years after fatal E. coli outbreak. *San Diego Union-Tribune*, C-3.

Food Insight. (1992). *Breakfast: Waking up to a healthy start*. Washington, DC: International Food Information Council.

Gaines, J. (1995, Febrary 9). Her crusade for safer meat keeps heat on. *San Diego Union Tribune*, B1,3.

Gordon, A., & McKinney, R. (1995). Sources of nutrients for students. *Journal of Clinical Nutrition, 61*(1), 232–240.

Greenstein, R. (1992). *Improving the health of the poor: Strategies for prevention*. Menlo Park, CA: Henry J. Kaiser Foundation.

Nicklaus, T., Bao, W., Webber, L., & Berenson, G. (1993). Breakfast consumption affects adequacy of total daily intake of children. *Journal of the American Dietetic Association, 93*(8), 886–891.

Nutrition programs for children. (1994). Champaign, IL: ERIC Clearinghouse for Elementary and Early Childhood Education.

Oesterreich, L. (1995). *Iowa family car handbook*. Iowa State University.

Pestano-Binghay, E., Reis, J., & Walters, M. (1993). Nutrition education issues for minority parents: A needs assessment. *Journal of Nutrition Education, 25*(3), 144.

Pond-Smith, D., Richarz, S., & Gonzalez, N. (1992). A survey of food service operation in child care centers in Washington, DC. *Journal of the American Dietetic Association, 92*(5), 483–484.

Position of the American Dietetic Association: Child nutrition services. (1994). *Journal of the American Dietetic Association, 93*(3), 334–336.

Simpson, K. (1995, April 12). Rare meat pulled from kids' menu. *San Diego Union-Tribune,* A-7.

Troccoli, K. (1993). *Eat to learn, learn to eat: The link between nutrition and learning in children.* Washington, DC: National Health Education Consortium.

U.S. Department of Agriculture, Food and Nutrition Services (1992). *Child nutrition program operations student, second year report: Executive Summary.* Alexandria, VA: Author.

SUGGESTIONS **FOR READING**

Bomba, A., Oakley, C., & Knight, K (1996). Planning the menu in the child care center. *Young Children, 51*(6), 62–67.

Luckhardt, W., & Diana, S. (1991). Factors affecting child care program menu planning. *Food Service Research Review, 15,* 105–110.

Nicklaus, T., Farris, R., Meyers, L., & Berenson, G. (1995). Dietary fiber intake of children and young adults: The Bogalusa Heart Study. *Journal of the American Dietetic Association, 95*(2), 209–214.

Position of the American Dietetic Association: Nutrition standards for child care programs. (1994) *Journal of the American Dietetic Association, 94,* 323: Author.

U.S. Department of Agriculture, Food and Nutrition Services (1994). *Quantity recipes for child care centers.* FNS-86. Washington, DC: Author.

U.S. Department of Health and Human Services (1993). *Learning readiness: Promising strategies.* Washington, DC: Author.

Wolfe, W., and Campbell, C. (1994). Food pattern, diet quality, and related characteristics of school children in New York State. *Journal of the American Dietetic Association, 93*(11), 1280-1284.

Wotecki, C. (1992). Nutrition in childhood and adolescence, I and II. *Contemporary Nutrition, 17* (I,II). [Brochures]. Minneapolis, MN: General Mills Nutrition Department.

CURRENT ISSUES IN CHILD CARE SAFETY, HEALTH, AND NUTRITION

In this section we will discuss four areas that deal with current issues:

12. **Child Abuse**

13. **Special Topics in Safety, Health, and Nutrition**

14. **Creating Linkages**

15. **Building Curriculum for Safety, Health, and Nutrition**

These topics will prepare the caregiver to deal with sensitive issues, create linkages with children, families, and the community, and develop curriculum for safety, health, and nutrition in child care.

CHAPTER TWELVE

CHILD ABUSE

Upon completion of this chapter, including a review of the summary, you should be able to:

POLICIES FOR CHILD ABUSE

Define and discuss policies for child abuse that may affect the child care setting.

PREVENTIVE MEASURES

Describe and discuss measures for preventing child abuse.

PROTECTIVE MEASURES

Describe and discuss how to recognize, document, and report child abuse, and methods for caring for an abused child.

IMPLICATIONS FOR CAREGIVERS

Describe and discuss the importance of education, observation, role-modeling, and supervision in dealing with special topics issues.

POLICIES FOR CHILD ABUSE

A child caregiver may encounter child abuse that involves a child in care. Child abuse is becoming a serious threat to the health, safety, and well-being of the children in this country. It is up to the caregiver to offer preventive and protective measures to all children in care. The following issues show the need to create policies that deal with child abuse (see Figure 12.1).

■ Child abuse and neglect have become a major threat to children four and younger. Every year 2,000 die, 18,000 are permanently disabled, and 142,000 are seriously injured (Dixon, 1995).

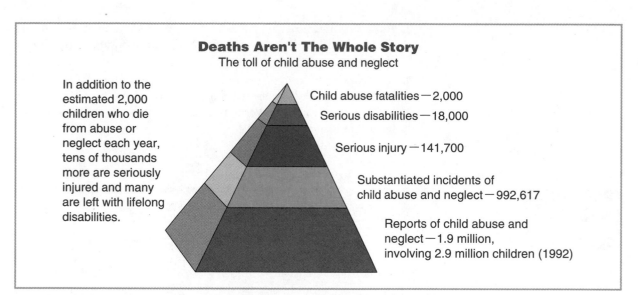

Deaths Aren't The Whole Story
The toll of child abuse and neglect

In addition to the estimated 2,000 children who die from abuse or neglect each year, tens of thousands more are seriously injured and many are left with lifelong disabilities.

Child abuse fatalities—2,000

Serious disabilities—18,000

Serious injury—141,700

Substantiated incidents of child abuse and neglect—992,617

Reports of child abuse and neglect—1.9 million, involving 2.9 million children (1992)

FIGURE **12.1** Abuse Statistics. *(From U.S. Department of Health and Human Services, Report of U.S. Advisory Board on Child Abuse and Neglect, April 1995)*

■ Child abuse affected 3.1 million children in 1994. This figure was double that of ten years prior (Children's Defense Fund [CDF], 1996).

■ Fifty-three percent of children who die of abuse and neglect are less than one year old ("The Quiet Crisis," 1994).

■ Helping parents recognize behaviors that may develop into abusive behaviors can produce positive parent-child relationships instead of the cycle of abuse (Daro, 1993).

■ A supportive adult can make a difference in the life of a child who is in an abusive family (Bennetts, 1994).

The child caregiver should provide a child care environment that supports the children's well-being. The environment and the actions of the caregivers must be beyond reproach. Methods of practices for preventing accusations must be used.

The child caregiver should learn to recognize any indicators that a family may be at risk for abusing the children. Intervention methods and strategies should be used when necessary. The child caregiver is mandated to report any abuse that may be observed. She should learn to recognize the signs and symptoms of abuse. The caregiver needs to know how to document and report any indicators of abuse that have been observed (Gootman, 1993). Caregivers should know the methods and strategies used to provide for the well-being of a child in care who has been abused.

The following are areas in which policies should be created for child abuse prevention and protection:

1. *Preventive Measures*: understanding how to prevent accusations and how to intervene to protect children in care from abuse.

2. *Protective Measures:* practices to recognize, document, and report all forms of child abuse and methods for working with abused children.

3. *Implications for Caregivers:* practices that use the tools of education, cultural sensitivity, observation, and supervision to provide children with protection and prevention from harm and to offer an environment that fosters well-being.

KEY POLICIES FOR CHILD ABUSE

Child abuse affects over 3 million children annually. Caregivers should learn preventive, protective, and promotional measures that will help provide for the well-being of children. Policies should be created to help the caregiver provide intervention and prevent accusation. These policies should offer the caregiver methods and practices needed for recognition, documentation, and reporting of child abuse. The caregiver should understand protective strategies to provide the child who has been abused with an atmosphere of support and a sense of trust in the caregiver.

PREVENTIVE MEASURES FOR CHILD ABUSE

Child abuse is a very sensitive issue that needs to be carefully handled. Child abuse can be complex when it surfaces as an issue in child care. The caregiver has a number of responsibilities for handling this issue. Prevention, protection, and promotion of child safety are essential. Prevention of child maltreatment can be effective and is less costly in terms of human suffering as well as financial cost needed to remedy it (Donnelly, 1992).

Caregivers can offer preventive measures by cooperating with their state licensing agency. Many states will screen caregivers for a history of abuse. The caregiver who employs others can make sure all prospective employees are screened for child abuse and neglect and conform to the licensing regulations.

In addition to the licensing process, each prospective employee should be carefully interviewed and all referrals for previous employment should be checked. Table 12.1 lists a sample of questions the caregiver may ask prospective employees. If there are any doubts about the person after the interview, the caregiver should listen to his intuition. There is no room for doubt when it comes to the safety of children in care. New employees should go through a probationary period so that the employing caregiver may carefully observe them as they relate to the children.

A good policy for hiring of new child care providers is to carefully screen them, including an in-depth interview and checking all references.

Another preventive measure is to set up the child care environment so that children and caregivers are never isolated from view of others. Restrooms should have an open door policy that require the door to remain open so that there is no opportunity for privacy. Supervision should be provided to support this.

TABLE **12.1**

Sample Interview Questions to Screen for Abuse Potential

- Why do you want to work with children?
- How would you describe your own childhood?
- What is your viewpoint on discipline?
- Do you believe in corporal punishment (hitting a child)?
- Does child behavior ever make you angry?
- How do you express your anger?
- A series of "What would you do if?" questions that relate to anger, discipline, etc.
- What are some coping skills you have to alleviate stress?

Caregivers are in a good position to identify possible abuse. In most states, they are mandated to report suspected abuse.

Mandate
an order by law

Preventing Accusations

Caregivers should inform parents who sign their children up for care that there is a policy that covers child abuse. The caregiver needs the parent to understand that any suspected abuse must be reported. Most states **mandate** that caregivers report any suspected child abuse. The parents should also be informed of the steps the caregiver uses to prevent abuse from occurring in the care situation. The caregiver should make sure the parents understand the philosophy of discipline, guidance, and child care.

Use "ouch" reports for any time an accident or injury occurs in your care. Discuss these daily with the parents as they pick up the children. Save a copy of the report in the child's file to document each accident or injury. If the child comes to care with an unexplained bruise or physical injury, the caregiver should ask the parent about it. The report of the bruise and the explanation should be recorded and added to the child's file. Any "ouch" report should include the date, time, nature of the injury, and any comments by the parent. Documentation is the caregiver's best defense (see Figure 12.2).

Intervention

Intervention strategies such as observation, discussion, and action may prevent abuse. The caregiver should learn to identify when parents or their children are under stress. The caregiver should work closely with parents to establish a good, communicative relationship. Developing trust and respect keeps the line of communication open between caregiver and parent. The caregiver may observe a parent or child under stress over a period of time. Talking with the parent may help to relieve the stress or open up other avenues to relieve stress. The caregiver can inform the parent that there may be coping skills or outside help for this stress. This may provide the action needed to impede the progress of abuse.

"Ouch" Report

Child's name:_____

Date: _____ Time: _____

Where did the incident take place? _____

Description of incident: _____

_____

_____

_____

Caregiver initials:_____

Action taken by caregiver: _____

_____

_____

_____

Observations of behavior changes, if any: _____

_____

_____

_____

Parent notified: _____

Caregiver initials: _____

Caregiver signature _____ Parent signature _____

FIGURE **12.2** Ouch Report

Table 12.2 relates some factors that may exhibit potential for abuse. These behaviors may be exhibited to greater extent when a parent is under stress.

A child's behavior may not always be consistent, due to temperament and developmental changes. The caregiver will, however, probably be able

Stress is a major factor in abusive situations involving parents and children. Training is available for caregivers that teaches sensitivity to these areas and provides resources that can be provided to parents.

to find a pattern of behavior for most children. When a child begins to exhibit increases in poor behavior or appears sad or withdrawn, he may be experiencing stress in his life. The caregiver can talk with the child about his feelings, and alert a parent to these changes. Children can also use coping skills to relieve stress.

TABLE **12.2**

Factors That May Lead to Abusive Behaviors

■ Significant changes in lifestyle: death of family member, divorce, unemployment, marital difficulties, or a recent move.

■ Poor knowledge of child development and unrealistic expectations of the child's capabilities; e.g., the child is a little adult.

■ Isolation from support; little or no contact with extended family, neighbors, and friends.

■ Low self-esteem.

■ Few coping abilities.

■ Poor impulse control. Gets angry for even minor things.

■ Questionable communication behaviors. May appear to feel threatened or defensive when ordinary questions are asked concerning the child or children.

■ Lack of bonding or attachment to a child or children.

■ Appears to be under the influence of alcohol or drugs.

KEY PREVENTIVE MEASURE

CONCEPT

Preventive measures such as screening caregivers and having an open door policy can help prevent undue accusations against responsible caregivers. Caregivers should always document an accident, injury, or illness that a child may have while in care. The caregiver should be aware of the indicators of social circumstances and behaviors of children and parents that could escalate into child abuse. Intervention may help prevent abuse from occurring.

PROTECTIVE MEASURES FOR CHILD ABUSE

It is imperative that every caregiver be aware of the physical and behavioral indicators of abuse. Child abuse can be defined as "harm or neglect of a child by a parent, relative, babysitter, caregiver, or any other adult" (Seattle-King County Department of Public Health, 1991).

Recognition

A child caregiver needs to know how to recognize the indicators of child abuse. Child abuse is divided into four categories: physical, emotional, sexual, and neglect. Each type of abuse has signs and symptoms that may indicate that child abuse has taken place. A child may suffer from abuse in one or more areas.

It is essential that the caregiver have an awareness of the indicators of abuse. All states mandate that people who care for children are to report

Each type of abuse has signs and symptoms that a caregiver should be on the lookout for.

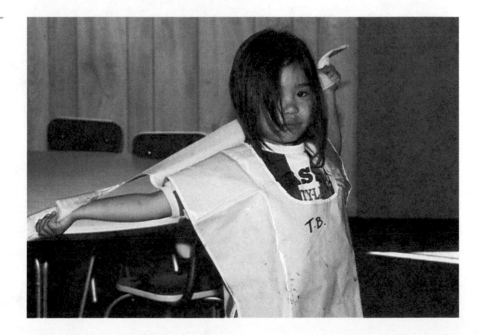

suspected abuse. In most states, failure to report abuse brings penalties, including a monetary fine. Some caregivers may feel reluctant to report because they feel that the parents may retaliate or that their relationship with the parents may be compromised. In some states, the only follow-up to the abuse report may have to come from the child care center unless the children were removed from parental custody. This places the child caregiver in an awkward situation. All states protect the caregiver from criminal or civil liability due to reporting of abuse.

Physical Abuse. Physical abuse is any act that results in a nonaccidental physical injury. This type of abuse may be a result of severe corporal punishment or intentional injury by deliberate assault. Table 12.3 includes many physical and behavioral indicators of physical abuse.

TABLE **12.3**

Indicators of Physical Abuse

Physical

■ Bruises—in linear markings, clusters, on several different areas at a time, and at various stages of healing. May appear after absence, weekend, or vacation.

■ Burns—cigarette or cigar, immersion burns (on buttocks and genitalia), patterns (iron, grid) rope or infected burns for which treatment may have been delayed.

■ Unexplained bite marks.

■ Lacerations or abrasions—typically around mouth, eyes, and external genitalia and may be in various stages of healing.

■ Internal injuries.

■ Head injury or whiplash—from shaking the child, known as shaken infant syndrome.

Behavioral

■ Tells you parents or other adult hurt him.

■ Over-compliant.

■ Poor self-concept.

■ Wary of adult contact, may be frightened of parent or parents or other adults.

■ Does not want to leave child care.

■ Extremes in behavior.

■ Feels deserving of punishment.

■ Vacant, withdrawn, or detached.

■ Indiscriminately seeks affection.

■ Chronic ailments—stomachaches, headaches, vomiting.

Emotional Abuse.   Emotional abuse includes placing unrealistic demands, excessive yelling, or unnecessary criticism that results in emotional harm or mental suffering. It is perhaps the most difficult to prove, but it may be observed when the interaction between a child and parent is seen. See Table 12.4 for a list of indicators of this type of abuse.

Sexual Abuse.   Child sexual abuse can be sexual exploitation as well as sexual assault upon the child by an adult or older child. Sexual exploitation includes fondling, mouth to genital contact, exhibition, and showing or using the child for obscene materials. The offender is known to the child in 80 percent of the cases. Sexual abuse is a reality in the United States. As many as one in five adult women were abused as children (ERIC Digest, 1990). Table 12.5 includes indicators of sexual abuse.

Neglect.   Neglect causes death more frequently than abuse does (California Child Care Resource and Referral Network [CCRRN] 1987). Neglect of a child includes depriving the child of food, shelter, medical care, supervision, or education. Negligence occurs in both actions and failure to act on behalf of the child. Severe neglect includes intentional failure to provide and allowing danger to the child's person or health. Table 12.6 includes the indicators of neglect.

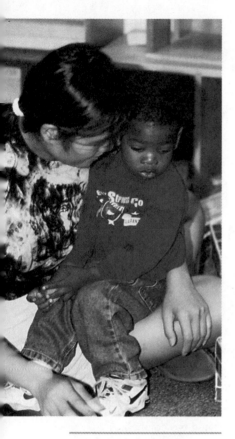

A consistently vacant, withdrawn, or detached child may be a victim of emotional abuse.

TABLE **12.4**

Indicators of Emotional Abuse

Physical

- Failure to thrive.
- Withdrawn or depressed.
- Disruptive or hyperactive.
- Speech or language disorders.
- Repetitive rhythmic movements.
- Little facial effect—no signs of emotional response.
- Bedwetting or toileting accidents for older children.

Behavioral

- Rigid in conformity to authority.
- Parent is demanding and unrealistic about the capabilities of the child.
- Destructive or antisocial.
- Sleep disorders.
- Unusual fears.
- Behind in mental or emotional development.
- Aggressive or compliant behavioral extremes.

TABLE **12.5**

Indicators of Sexual Abuse

Physical

- ■ Torn, stained, or bloody underclothing.
- ■ Pain, itching, or swelling in genital area.
- ■ Bruises, lacerations, or bleeding in genital, vaginal, or anal area.
- ■ Discharge in vaginal/genital area.
- ■ Venereal disease.
- ■ Difficulty in walking or sitting.
- ■ Pain when urinating or defecating.

Behavioral

- ■ Withdrawn, fantasy, or infantile.
- ■ Poor self-esteem and self-image.
- ■ Poor peer relationships.
- ■ Depression.
- ■ Abrupt changes in behavior such as eating, sleeping, or school performance.
- ■ Excessively clingy or inappropriate attachment.
- ■ Exceptional fear of a person or place.
- ■ Draws scary pictures that include plenty of black and red coloring.
- ■ Inappropriate sexual knowledge or behavior.

A child who is unsupervised for long periods of time (a sign of neglect) is at a higher risk for death than physical abuse.

TABLE 12.6

Indicators of Neglect

Physical

- Always hungry, dirty, or inappropriately dressed.
- Unsupervised for long periods of time.
- Lacks medical or dental care.
- Lack of supervision, especially for long periods of time.
- Unsanitary home.
- Abandonment.
- Underweight, poor growth.
- Consistently absent from school.

Behavioral

- Stealing or begging for food or money for food.
- Parent brings child early and picks up late.
- Inappropriate attachment or affection.
- Shows or expresses no emotions.
- Parent abusing drugs or alcohol.
- Overly responsible; assumes adult role.

REALITY CHECK

Domestic Violence and Its Effect on Children's Lives

The home can be a more dangerous place than the streets. Women are nine times more likely to get hurt at home than they are on the streets ("Too Often," 1994). Two million women were battered and more than three million children were abused or neglected in 1991 (Velsor-Friedrich, 1994). Interpersonal violence is a major health problem in this country (Kroll, 1993). Fourteen percent of children in this country experience family violence such as watching their mothers being abused by fathers, stepfathers, and boyfriends (Velsor-Friedrich, 1994).

Changes that have occurred in family systems in recent years have led to greater stress in families (Holmes, 1992). "Poverty, social isolation, marital problems, lack of education; all can increase the chances of babies and children suffering from child abuse and neglect" (Healthy Families California, p. 3). Families are no longer like the typical families portrayed on television in the 1950s and 1960s like *Ozzie and Harriet* or *Leave it to Beaver*. Divorce affects almost one of two families, and more than one in four families are headed by a single parent. Families may move more frequently. Mothers may no longer be able to stay at home due to economic stresses so some children may be cared for in nonparental child care, while others may be latchkey children. More families with children live in poverty today than ever before. There is a greater degree of drug and

continued

alcohol abuse than we have previously seen in this country. All of these factors contribute to stress that manifests domestic violence.

Domestic violence occurs at every socioeconomic level and in every racial, cultural, religious, and ethnic group. There may be a correlation between the battering of women and the abuse of children. It is estimated that between 30 percent and 40 percent of children of battered women are being physically or sexually abused. Men are more likely than women to commit domestic violence. Women who commit domestic violence usually do so in self-defense or reprisal for abuse.

Even if children themselves are not abused, witnessing abuse can have traumatic effects on them. Witnessing violence may lead to discipline problems, fear, depression, poor social interaction, and drug abuse among children (Bennetts, 1994). Long-term effects may be post-traumatic stress disorder, personality disorders, and physical disorders (Elders, 1994). Witnessing violence may lead to the child performing violent acts as they get older. It has been reported that 79 percent of children in institu-tions for violent behaviors have witnessed violence. Boys who witness violence are more likely than girls to act out. They are three times more likely to become abusive to their domestic partners later in life (Velsor-Friedrich, 1994). Girls are much more likely to allow abuse to occur as women. Both behaviors perpetuate domestic violence.

Children who have been abused or have witnessed violence often feel isolated with nowhere to turn. Children who have an adult they can trust in their lives are more likely to cope better (Bennetts, 1994). Child caregivers can provide this trust to the children in their care. A model program for caregivers and other child care professionals has been created to help them foster resiliency in children and learn how to teach conflict resolution (Texas Child Care, 1994).

Caregivers can model prosocial behaviors and help children have a greater sense of acceptance. Children can be praised and recognized for good behaviors and redirected away from aggressive behaviors. Caregivers can also provide a safe haven from a difficult home life for a few hours a day.

Documentation

If the caregiver suspects or has reason to believe that abuse is occurring, then it must be reported. The caregiver does not have to personally witness the abuse or have positive proof that it occurred. Caregivers need to understand how to document suspected abuse and how to report it.

Observing children is one of the major jobs of a caregiver. The caregiver needs to be aware of the indicators of abuse to observe in order to notice a problem. The caregiver should observe the child at different times of day and in different settings and record the observation in note form.

The caregiver should record behavior, conversation, and physical signs. This type of anecdotal record may signify a pattern that indicates abuse may be present. It may also indicate that there is no pattern present and what the caregiver noticed about a bruise and limp might have been a result of a fall. The records should be kept for a while in case there is need to refer to them again.

Reporting

If the caregiver needs to report child abuse, the reporting process should be clear. In most states there is a Child Welfare Office or Child Protective Services. If the caregiver is unsure then he should contact the local Department of Social Services or law enforcement agency. This should be done before any suspected abuse. There may be forms that the caregiver should keep on hand. The caregiver should also inquire if there is a 24 hour hotline so the number may be posted.

When a report is filed, the child's name, address, and age must be included. The parents' names and address or addresses should be given if they have separate homes. The caregiver should provide her name and address. Anonymity for the caregiver will be provided. The caregiver must realize that the parents might be able to tell who reported the abuse, because it is likely she will have more information about the child than anyone else.

The caregiver may want to talk to the parent before reporting the abuse. Some parents may be relieved that help is available, although anger and hostility are another common reaction and may result in the parents removing the child from child care. If the caregiver decides to tell the parents before the report, once again, she should explain the requirement to report any suspected abuse. As difficult as it may be to tell the parents before reporting the suspected abuse, it may be better that they still have trust in the caregiver for her honesty. The best course is for the caregiver to plan to help the parents through the process. Supporting the family after reporting abuse is often a center-based responsibility and includes referrals to meet the needs of the family.

Caring for the Abused Child

If abuse is blatant and puts the child in real danger, the child may be removed from the family. If this is the case, the courts, foster families, or other family members who gain custody of the child may wish to continue to keep the child in the care situation to maintain some consistency in the child's life.

Caregivers need to understand how to support a child and his family or custodian once the abuse has been established. The first step in this process is for the caregiver to examine her confidence level, her knowledge of human development, and how she feels about the abuse. How the caregiver feels about herself will affect whether or not she can offer support. If the caregiver has a low confidence level, it will be difficult to help the child raise his.

The caregiver needs to determine her level of understanding about what is normal behavior. She needs to understand what behaviors need to be redirected. These factors will determine the skill level the caregiver has to do the job. The child may need to address factors of his social and emotional development process. Can the caregiver help a child learn to trust and live within safe boundaries? Judging the abuse can impede the caregiver's ability to perform. Placing blame and being angry will not help the caregiver perform her job.

It is estimated that one out of five women was sexually abused as a child (ERIC Digest, 1990). If the caregiver has personally suffered from abuse in some form as a child there may be unresolved feelings. Will these feelings hinder the relationship with the child or parent?

If the caregiver determines that she is capable of helping and supporting an abused child, there are several critical things that she can provide the child:

■ Trust

■ Predictable routines

When dealing with an abused child, caregivers must first identify their own feelings about abuse and determine if they are ready emotionally to support the child.

- Consistent behavior
- Safe boundaries
- Confidence
- Good communication skills

These will offer the child the sense of well-being needed to progress beyond the abuse.

KEY PROTECTIVE MEASURE FOR CHILD ABUSE

CONCEPT

Protective measures such as recognition of abuse, documentation, and reporting give the caregivers the tools needed to protect children from abuse. The caregiver should be able to recognize the physical and behavioral indicators of physical abuse, emotional abuse, sexual abuse, and neglect. The caregiver should understand the procedures for documenting and reporting abuse, and know the practices and strategies that will offer care to an abused child.

IMPLICATIONS FOR **CAREGIVERS**

Caregivers need to see that there is a policy created for child abuse. The policy should include the processes needed to help prevent child abuse and protect the children in child care. These methods and strategies should include education, cultural sensitivity, observation, and supervision. Education for the caregivers, as well as the parents and children offers prevention and protection. Cultural sensitivity is crucial because in some cultures child abuse may not be seen as a problem, but may be a parental right. Observation helps the caregiver to recognize and document. Supervision maintains a set of checks and balances to provide the protection of the children in child care and prevent some abuse from occurring.

Education

It is essential that the child caregiver understand what child abuse is and how to recognize it. Awareness and familiarity with the indicators of abuse of the four areas—physical, emotional, sexual, and neglect—can help a caregiver observe for them. Caregivers need to understand the process to report abuse because they are the mandated reporters of child abuse. The child caregiver must know how to report abuse, and in order to do so the caregiver must know how to document for accuracy and support.

For the Parents. Education can also help the caregiver help to prevent abuse. Having methods and strategies for working with children and parents

Cultural sensitivity and good communication skills will assist a caregiver in dealing with children and their families to help prevent child abuse and protect the children in their care.

can help the caregiver offer greater protection for the children. The child caregiver can educate the parents and children to help prevent abuse. Parents can be educated about normal child development and the behaviors that can be expected at that point of development. Parents who have an understanding of the capabilities of their children may have more realistic expectations. The caregiver should keep an open line of communication with the parent. They can share common concerns about the child or about stress in the family environment. This can help to form a partnership. The caregiver can also support the parent during times of stress or other difficulties by providing referrals or resources.

With Children.   The caregiver can help to educate the child about what is and what is not acceptable behavior between the child and an adult. The caregiver can promote safety from sexual abuse from an early stage. At eighteen months children can learn about body parts. From three to five years of age they can learn about the body parts and what parts are unacceptable for others to touch. A child who learns to use the word "no" will be empowered to help protect himself.

A child who learns to achieve mastery in her life by making choices may be more prepared to act if she is abused. A caregiver can provide opportunities that allow the child choices.

A caregiver can model self-control, verbalize feelings and fears, and provide a predictable, stable environment. These actions will offer the child a protective environment where he feels safe enough to talk. A child who experiences this environment may be more willing to share difficulties in his life.

Cultural Sensitivity

Cultural sensitivity is a preventive measure. The process of childrearing may be culturally defined. What is normal and acceptable in one culture may not be considered normal or acceptable in another. The United States has a large **immigrant** and **migrant** population that is ever increasing. A caregiver who cares for children from a culture other than her own should try to learn about the childrearing practices and behavior of that culture.

The family's view on discipline and punishment may be in conflict with the laws of this country. Some cultures believe in corporal punishment as a consequence for unquestioning obedience and unrealistic expectations. The caregiver can ask a family about their cultural customs. This is a good way to understand if this is the case. If it is the case, the caregiver may need to begin a dialogue with the family. The caregiver should show respect about differing cultural beliefs of the family, but should also clearly inform them about the law (Gonzalez-Mena, 1997).

Families who recently immigrated or migrated may have experienced a great deal of stress (CCRRN, 1987). Stressful events related to the relocation of families may affect their psychological well-being. Strange customs, lack of support networks, and inability to speak English may all contribute to the stress of a child and family.

Observation

Observation is the most important tool that a child caregiver has to protect a child from abuse. The observation for signs and symptoms of child abuse can make the caregiver aware of the possibility that the child's safety and well-being are in jeopardy. Observation is also the key tool for documentation of suspected abuse. A good observer will use the tools of the sense to report what was seen, heard, felt, and smelled.

Observation also plays a part in preventing abuse. It is important to observe the caregiving environment for practices that offer prevention from abuse. The caregiver may also observe for the stressors and behaviors of families, because the caregiver can intervene before abuse takes place.

Supervision

Everyone in the caregiver's employ must be trained to recognize, document, and report abuse. Employees should learn to recognize their own stress. The caregiver should supervise the child care environment to prevent any situation or practice that does not offer protection from, and prevention of child abuse. Discipline should be supervised to make sure it is correct and that all child caregivers offer good guidance and discipline and do not cross the line into punishment.

The caregiver should supervise to make sure all protective measures such as recognition, documentation, and reporting of child abuse are done when necessary, in the right way, and in a timely manner. It is important for the caregiver to supervise the care of an abused child and to make sure the child is being offered a supportive environment. The caregiver should make sure the child's health, safety, and well-being are promoted by healthy interactions.

Immigrant
one who leaves a country to settle in another

Migrant
a transient who travels from place to place to find work

C 12.4

CONCEPT

KEY IMPLICATIONS FOR CAREGIVERS

The caregiver can promote a safe environment by using tools that prevent and protect children from child abuse. The tools of education, cultural sensitivity, observation, and supervision can help the caregiver to offer a safe environment for the well-being of the children in care. Education helps the caregiver recognize the signs and symptoms of behaviors prior to abuse and the four types of abuse. It helps the caregiver understand how to document and report abuse. Education gives the caregiver strategies to help the abused child. Cultural sensitivity may offer an intervening measure to prevent children from being abused. Observation is the major tool used to recognize, document, and report abuse. Supervision provides the necessary checks to make sure the environment is offering protection and prevention of abuse.

CHAPTER **SUMMARY**

Considering the large number of children abused or neglected each year, caregivers should learn preventive, protective, and promotional measures that will help provide for children's well-being. Policies should be created that will help the caregiver ensure preventive measures such as freedom from accusation and the ability to intervene. Protective measures such as recognizing abuse, documentation, and reporting give caregivers the tools needed to protect children from abuse. The caregiver should know the practices and strategies that will offer care to an abused child. The tools of education, cultural sensitivity, observation, and supervision can help the caregiver to offer an environment that offers safety and well-being to the children in care.

TO GO **BEYOND**

Questions for Review

1. Discuss the different forms of child abuse. Describe some of the factors involved in child abuse.
2. Discuss how child abuse is recognized.
3. Describe how a caregiver would report child abuse.

AS AN **INDIVIDUAL**

1. Collect information in the community about the child abuse services available.

AS A **GROUP**

1. Watch a film or video that describes child abuse. Do you feel it was realistic?

2. List some factors in today's society that might lead to child abuse. Especially discuss domestic violence and its effect on the family.

CHAPTER **REFERENCES**

Bennetts, L. (1994, November). How domestic abuse hurts kids. *Parent's Magazine*, 44–46.

California Child Care Resource and Referral Network (CCRRN). (1987). *Making a difference: Handbook for child care providers.* San Francisco, CA: Author.

Children's Defense Fund (CDF). (1996). *The state of America's children: Yearbook 1996.* Washington, DC: Author.

Daro, D. (1993). *Reducing child abuse through support program for new parents* [Factsheet #3]. Chicago, IL: National Committee for the Prevention of Child Abuse.

Dixon, J. (1995, April 27). Child abuse, parental neglect blamed in 200 deaths per year. *San Diego Union-Tribune*, A-7.

Donnelly, A. (1992). Healthy families America. *Children Today, 21*(2), 25–26.

Elders, J. (1994). Violence as a public health issue. *Childhood Education, 70*(5), 260–262.

ERIC Digest. (1990). *Child sexual abuse, what it is and how to prevent it.* Champaign, IL: Eric Clearinghouse for Elementary and Early Childhood Education.

Gonzalez-Mena, J. (1997). *Multicultural issues in child care.* Mountain View, CA: Mayfield Publishing.

Gootman, M. (1993). Reaching and teaching abused children. *Childhood Education, 70*(1), 15–19.

Holmes, R. (1992). *Reducing violence.* Minnesota Extension Service INFO-U script. University of Minnesota Extension Service.

Kroll, L. (1993). The American Medical Association's family violence campaign. *Journal of the American Medical Association, 269*(40), 1875.

The quiet crisis. (1994). *Young Children, 49,* 60.

Seattle King County Department of Public Health. (1991). *Child care health handbook.* Seattle, WA: Washington State Department of Social and Health Services.

Texas Child Care. (1994, Fall). Child violence. *Texas Child Care Magazine,* 29.

Too often these days, home is where the hurt is. (1994, July 10). *San Diego Union Tribune,* pp. A-1, A-22.

Velsor-Friedrich, B. (1994). Family violence: A growing epidemic. *Journal of Pediatric Nursing, 9*(4), 272–274.

SUGGESTIONS **FOR READING**

Chernofsky, B. (1992). *Child abuse awareness and prevention program: A home study course for family day care providers.* La Mesa, CA: Advocates for Better Childcare.

Crittenden, P. (1992). Children's strategies for coping with adverse home environments: An interpretation using attachment theory. *Child Abuse and Neglect, 16,* 329–343.

Elrod, J., & Rubine, R. (1993). Parental involvement in sexual abuse prevention education. *Child Abuse and Neglect, 17*, 527–538.

Good, L. (1996). When a child has been sexually abused: Several resources for parents and early childhood professionals. *Young Children, 51*(5), 84–85.

Haberman, M. (1994). Gentle teaching in a violent society. *Educational Horizons, 73*(3), 131–135.

Jordan, N. (1993). Sexual abuse prevention programs in early childhood education: A caveat. *Young Children, 48*(6), 76–79.

Spaccarelli, S., Sandler, I., & Roosa, M. (1994). History of spouse violence against mother: Correlated risk and unique effects in child mental health. *Journal of Family Violence, 9J*(1), 79–98.

Wright, R. (1994, April). Child abuse is a tragedy: It takes many forms. *San Diego Family Press*, 66–67.

CHAPTER THIRTEEN

SPECIAL TOPICS IN SAFETY, HEALTH, AND NUTRITION

Upon completion of this chapter, including a review of the summary, you should be able to:

POLICIES FOR SPECIAL TOPICS

Define and discuss policies for special topics that may affect the child care setting.

SPECIAL NEEDS

Describe and discuss the process of including children with special needs into your child care setting.

CHILDREN WITH CHRONIC ILLNESSES

Describe and discuss special considerations for caring for children with chronic illnesses.

CHILDREN AND STRESS

Describe and discuss common stressors and their impact on children.

CHILDREN FROM DRUG ABUSING FAMILIES

Describe and discuss the common problems and their solutions that may arise in child care when working with children from drug abusing families.

IMPLICATIONS FOR CAREGIVERS

Describe and discuss the importance of education, observation, role modeling, and supervision in dealing with special topics issues.

POLICIES FOR SPECIAL TOPICS

Policies need to be developed for special topics that may appear in child care. The caregiver may deal with some of these issues often, while other issues may never emerge. These issues should be examined in order to provide protection and prevention in the child care environment. The following are reasons for the development of policies on special issues:

■ Children who have disabilities and are in care with nondisabled children show more advanced play than if they were in special care for disabled children alone (Diamond, Hestenes, & O'Connor, 1994).

■ The Americans with Disabilities Act requires that all public accommodations, including family child care homes and day care programs, must provide access to children with disabilities (Surr, 1992).

■ Children who experience stressful life events may externalize them by exhibiting overactivity, discipline problems, and inattention (Campbell, March, Pierce, Ewing, & Szumowski, 1991).

■ Seven and one-half million children under eighteen years of age are chronically ill (Frieman & Settle, 1994).

■ According to the National Association of Perinatal Addiction Research and Education approximately 11 percent of all children born in the United States have been prenatally exposed to drugs and/or alcohol (Robertson, 1993).

Some children may come to child care with no issues that affect their health, safety, and well-being. Preventive measures can help these children

All children can benefit from play in an inclusive environment.

remain risk-free in care. Other children may have special needs, chronic illness, stress, or are in families with drug histories that will affect them and their care. In order to provide the most protective and healthy environment, policies need to be created to deal with some of these special issues.

The special issues that are most likely to emerge as the caregiver performs child care are:

1. *Inclusion of Children with Special Needs*: understanding the effects of accommodation on child care and strategies to offer the optimum environment for the child with special needs.

2. *Children with Chronic Illnesses*: understanding coping skills and strategies needed to provide the most protective and preventive environment for these children in child care.

3. *Children with Stress*: practices for recognizing and supporting children with stress to protect them and promote their well-being.

4. *Children from Drug Abusing Families*: strategies and practices for working with children from drug abusing families.

KEY POLICIES FOR SPECIAL NEEDS

CONCEPT

Many children in care have no special issues in their lives that will affect caregiving. Others may have one or more that the caregiver must help them deal with while they are in care. Three child care issues that are the most likely to affect the caregiver and the care site are: inclusion of children with special needs, children with chronic illnesses, and children who are suffering from stress in their lives.

INCLUSION OF CHILDREN WITH SPECIAL NEEDS INTO CHILD CARE

The Americans with Disabilities Act (ADA) of 1990 is federal legislation enacted to protect people with physical or mental disabilities from discrimination. The ADA defines disability as "a physical or mental impairment that substantially limits a major life activity." Title III of this act states that public accommodations must make reasonable modification to accommodate people with disabilities. Under the law, privately operated child care is considered a public accommodation. Title II of the ADA applies to child care programs that are operated by state or local government agencies such as school districts or municipalities.

The ADA basically applies to all child care situations except for a nanny caring for children in their home and church-operated programs. A caregiver cannot discriminate against a child because of a disability. This nondiscrimination policy might be included on any promotional literature the caregiver offers and should be included in the caregiver's health care policies. A caregiver should be willing to make reasonable adjustments or adaptations in order to accept a child with special needs into care.

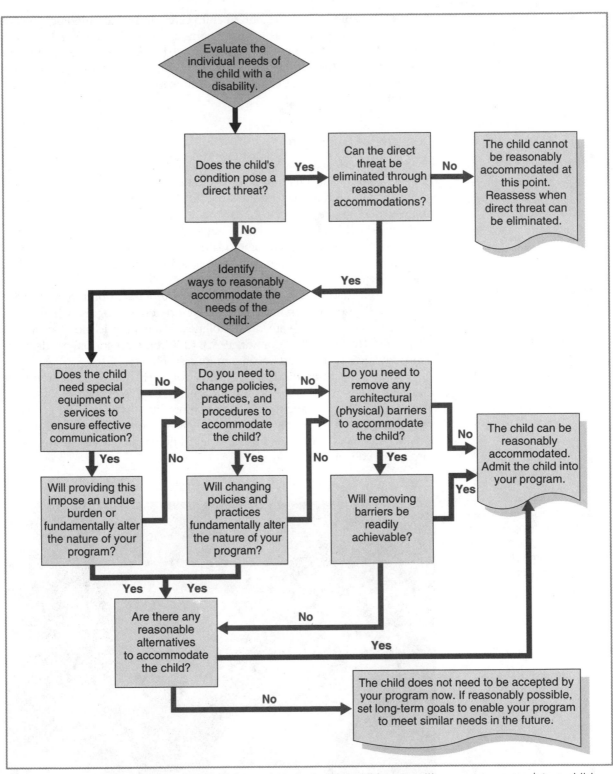

FIGURE **13.1** Use the flowchart to help determine whether the child care setting can accommodate a child with special needs. *(Courtesy of Child Care Law Center. © 1994 Child Care Law Center. Not to be reproduced without permission; 415-495-5498. Revised January 1994.)*

Reasonable accommodation in child care can include modifications in toys, equipment, policies, activities or some easily changeable architectural barriers. The ADA does not require any "undue burden" (significant difficulty or expense) on the part of the accommodator. See Figures 13.1 (p. 393) and 13.2 for directions in determining the effects of this law on the child care situation.

Benefits of Inclusion

The ADA legislation was created to encourage acceptance and lessen discrimination. Some children with disabilities can easily be accommodated into care, while others may require some adaptation. Some children with disabilities may be beyond the caregiver's abilities to accommodate. These decisions should never be made automatically. Rather, a decision of whether a child can be reasonably accommodated needs to be made on a case-by-case basis. Including children with special needs in regular care settings has many benefits.

For the child with special needs, child care offers opportunities to play and grow. These children make better developmental progress when main-streamed with children with no disabilities. Their play is more advanced (Diamond, Hestenes, & O'Connor, 1994). Children with special needs learn better interaction skills and become more self-reliant.

Children with no disabilities benefit from being around children with disabilities. They can learn empathy and can see that diversity is not so scary. Those children who have disabilities are more like those who do not have disabilities than they are different (Woolery & Wilbers, 1994). Opportunities for interaction between children with special needs and other children reinforces this concept.

By offering a setting where children with special needs are included with children without impairments, children learn acceptance and self-esteem.

FIGURE **13.2**
Accommodating the child
with special needs

ADA Goal

To *reasonably accommodate* individuals with disabilities in order to *integrate* them into the program to the extent feasible, given *each individual's* limitations.

ADA Principles

INDIVIDUALITY
the limitations and needs of *each* individual;

REASONABLENESS
of the accommodation to the *program* and to the *individual;*

INTEGRATION
of the individual *with others* in the program.

Types of Accommodations

AUXILIARY AIDS AND SERVICES
special equipment and services to ensure effective communication;

CHANGES IN POLICIES, PRACTICES, AND PROCEDURES;

REMOVAL OF BARRIERS
architectural, arrangement of furniture and equipment, vehicular.

Reason to Deny Care

ACCOMMODATION IS UNREASONABLE, and there are no reasonable alternatives.

- For **auxiliary aids and services,** if accommodations pose an **UNDUE BURDEN** (will result in a significant difficulty or expense to the program);

- For **auxiliary aids and services,** or **changes in policies, practices, or procedures,** if accommodations **FUNDAMENTALLY ALTER** the nature of the program;

- For **removal of barriers,** if accommodations are **NOT READILY ACHIEVABLE** (cannot be done without much difficulty or expense to the program).

DIRECT THREAT
The individual's condition will pose or does pose a significant threat to the health or safety of other children or staff in the program, and there are no reasonable means of removing the threat.

(Courtesy of Child Care Law Center. © 1994 Child Care Law Center. Not to be reproduced without permission; 415-495-5498. Revised January 1994.)

Caregivers can also benefit by realizing that all children are more alike than different. The caregiver working with a child with special needs will learn patience and self-confidence in his ability to care for the child. Children have the same basic needs, and every caregiver skill that is strengthened is shared with all the children in care.

The parents may learn that the child with special needs is more like other children than they expected, and this awareness may allow them a comfort they had not experienced before. The parents of children with special needs will receive support from the caregiver to carry on everyday life.

The Team Approach

Caring for a child with special needs should not be done without help and support. The parents who approach a caregiver about providing care for their special child should provide contact to a number of professionals who are dealing with the child. Some typical members of this group might be a physician, an audiologist, an occupational therapist, a nutritional consultant, a speech pathologist, and a counselor. Each child has unique needs and the people who will help the child are selected to meet those needs. In the classroom additional assistance may be needed depending on the particular needs of the child. For example, a child with hearing impairment may need a sign language translator; or a child with cerebral palsy may need an occupational therapy technician to visit regularly to help the child reach his maximum potential for physical movement and coordination.

The Individuals with Disabilities Education Act was passed in 1990. This act provides special education and other services related to disabilities or developmental delay in children. It provides the means to create a team for each child with special needs. This team approach supports the child and offers everyone involved a common sense of purpose. Everyone on the team works together to help the child reach his maximum potential developmental growth level. It is essential that those involved participate in the team on an equal level.

Each professional may have ownership in part of the process, and may tend to see that part as the most significant. All parts of the team have the key ingredient to help the child. Each player on the team must contribute his unique ingredient and cooperate to make this holistic approach work.

Individualized family service plan

plan that coordinates services to meet the needs of the child with special needs and his family

The Individualized Family Service Plan. The team should work together to prepare what is called an **individualized family service plan** (IFSP). The IFSP provides for an organized goal and delivery of services to the child and the family. The plan should be made up of measurable outcome objectives, which help guide the team to provide what the child needs. It is much easier to assess the success of the plan based on whether the objectives have been met or not.

Usually one person is designated the coordinator of the service plan. This is often the representative of the group that has financial responsibility. It can be a professional who represents the Department of Health or the Department of Education and varies from state to state.

There should be one contact person who would designate the coordinating of the care of the child with special needs in the child care situation.

The cooperative team should work together, each bringing to the system their unique expertise to benefit the child.

For a center, it might be the director or the child's primary teacher. In a family day care home it would most likely be the caregiver. In an in-home care situation, it would be the nanny who has agreed to care for the child with special needs.

If a child with special needs is accepted into child care, the caregiver should be prepared to accept the responsibilities that go along with caring for that child. The team effort continues at the child care site. All people involved in the care of the child should be privy to what is planned for the child. The IFSP should be shared and the objectives should be reviewed to identify the progress of the child. If any training is needed to provide care for the child, all members of the caregiving team should receive it. The child care that accepts a special needs team should provide the skills necessary to help the child reach maximum potential.

Supporting the Child with Special Needs

Each child with special needs has his or her own particular needs for support. Support can be offered to all children with special needs in some general ways. The caregiver and the special needs team should develop goals that match the needs and abilities of the child. The caregiver is the one who will carry out these goals on a daily basis and should be involved in the process.

The Environment. Adjusting the physical environment to adapt to whatever special needs are present is a good starting point. Removing obstacles assist children who are visually impaired or who have physical disabilities that may require a walker or a wheelchair. For children with emotional disabilities the caregiver may need to provide a quiet corner. The area needed for adaptive equipment should be a place that does not interfere with other activities.

The toys that are present in the environment should be safe and durable for the sake of all children. They should provide opportunities for learning, interaction, exploration, and engagement. Modifying toys as needed may help the child with special needs use the toy for its intended purpose. As an example, the ring in a ring toss game may need to be cut larger for the child with special needs to feel successful. After a child with special needs has been in care for a while, the caregiver may notice what types of toys that child is most likely to choose and use. Selecting new toys that have similarities will offer new challenges or things to explore. Table 13.1 includes strategies for the successful inclusion of children with differing abilities in the child care environment.

Intervention.   If the caregiver observes the child having difficulty playing with certain toys, games, and other materials, she may need to intervene. The caregiver may help the child learn how to play with a toy or adapt the toy to play. She may have to show the child how to use or adapt for use other play materials. Modeling appropriate play behavior may help the child learn how to be a player.

The caregiver may also encourage other children to assist the child. The children who are not disabled may need help in learning how to understand and accept the child with a disability. The caregiver may teach specific skills such as eye contact or appropriate language. The children in the group can learn to help the child with a disability to accomplish tasks on her own when capable and learn specific helping behaviors when appropriate. The caregiver can also model acceptance and show understanding. Her actions and words with the child with special needs are the most effective tools she

A least restrictive environment should be provided for all children with special needs.

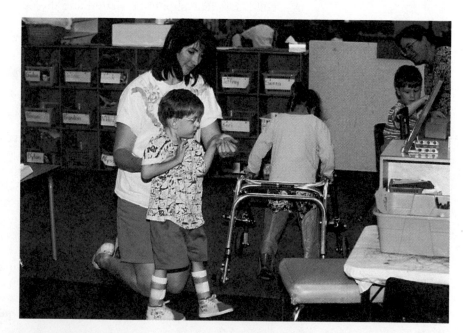

TABLE **13.1**

Strategies for Successfully Including Children with Differing Abilities

Language delay	Expand on what child says; talk about what you are doing; model the correct usage and pronunciation instead of correcting.
	Provide frequent visual or concrete reinforcement.
	Keep directions simple; encourage child to repeat them for reinforcement.
	Explain new concepts or vocabulary.
Attention problems	Start with short group sessions and activities.
	Provide visual clues (e.g., define floor space with tape).
	Offer a limited number of choices.
	Provide positive reinforcement for sustained attention.
	Help child quiet down after vigorous play.
	Plan for transition times, including arrival and departure.
Developmental delays and learning disabilities	Allow for extra demonstrations and practice sessions.
	Keep all directions simple, sequenced, and organized.
	Offer extra help in developing fine and gross motor skills, if needed.
Emotional/social problems	Provide extra structure by limiting toys and defining physical space for activities.
	Allow shy child to observe group activities until ready to participate.
	Help aggressive child control behavior through consistent enforcement of rules.
	Observe dramatic play for important clues about feelings and concerns.
	Help child learn how to express feelings in appropriate ways.
Mental retardation	Establish realistic goals for each child.
	Provide frequent positive feedback.
	Sequence learning activities into small steps.
	Allow adequate time for performance and learning.
	Encourage cooperative play and help the child move from independent to parallel to group interaction.
Impaired hearing	Obtain child's attention when speaking; seat child close to voice or music.
	Repeat, rephrase as needed; alert other children to use same technique.
	Learn some sign language and teach signing to the entire class.
	Provide visual clues (e.g., pictures or . . — . . — to represent rhythm).
	Demonstrate new activities or tasks.
Impaired vision	Ensure child's safety at all times without being overprotective.
	Provide verbal clues for activities.
	Introduce child to equipment and space verbally and through touch.
	Use a "buddy" system.
Physical disability or poor coordination	*Accessibility*
	Organize physical space to accommodate child in wheelchair.
	Use tables that accommodate wheelchairs or provide trays on wheelchairs.
	Use bolsters or other supports for floor activities.
	Provide adaptive equipment for standing.
	Learn about the availability of assistive technology and devices.
	Manual dexterity
	Use magnetic toys to facilitate small muscle activities.
	Attach bells to wrist or ankles for musical activities.
	Use adaptive scissors or spoons as needed.

Reprinted from The Creative Curriculum® for Early Childhood (3rd Ed.) Washington, DC: © 1992, Teaching Strategies, Inc.

Activity based
activities that promote adaptive behavior

Functional skills
skills that allow children to adapt to their environment

Generalizable skills
common skills that can be practiced and used in different settings

has to teach the other children about interaction. The nondisabled child can role model and provide opportunities for positive interaction with the child with special needs.

Caregiver intervention should be **activity based** and occur in a natural manner. Opportunities for this type of intervention occur in everyday activities. The objective of activity-based intervention is to help develop two different skills for the child with special needs (Bracer & Cripe, 1992). The first skill is referred to as **functional skill** and offers the child the opportunities to adapt to the physical and social environments in care. The child receives personal satisfaction and a sense of accomplishment that helps the child gain confidence.

The other type of skill is referred to as **generalizable skill** and transfers from one setting to another. An example of this would be a child with a speech or language disorder learning how to name a particular object. A ball is a ball whether it is at child care, at home, or in the park.

Tamara, an autistic child, was acquiring some sign language capabilities. She spent part of her morning in a special school and then went to Kate's family day care before lunch. Her favorite food was watermelon, and whenever Kate served Tamara watermelon she could sign the word *more*.

Kate felt that there was an opportunity for learning here, so she went to the special education teacher at Tamara's school and learned how to sign the word *watermelon*. She used it every opportunity she could when she gave Tamara watermelon for lunch or snack. Eventually, Tamara learned how to sign the word. Her mother was so excited when she informed Kate several days later that Tamara had asked through signing for watermelon for dinner. It was a real milestone in Tamara's limited language.

The caregiver should recognize the strengths in all children in care. The holistic approach to child care focuses on the whole child. Activities and opportunities that focus on strengths, support, and minimize difficulties should be provided. All children want to feel capable, successful, and confident. A caregiver who is aware of this can easily provide the environment a child needs.

Intervention may also include the caregiver being able to identify a child who is already in care. Some children may have special needs that have not been detected and need to be addressed. The caregiver should look for help to identify the behaviors or characteristics that appear to be a special need. Local regional centers, maternal and child health services, and other resources are helpful sources for this information.

A child centered approach focuses on the child's individual needs.

KEY CHILDREN WITH SPECIAL NEEDS

CONCEPT

Children with special needs may be included in child care. The American Disabilities Act discusses public accommodations. This act may affect a child care site. If children with disabilities are included, the caregiver should work as part of a team and help to support the child with special needs. The caregiver should provide a safe, protective environment and should also do whatever possible to help challenge the child. When intervention is necessary, the caregiver should provide it or have another child help. Children with disabilities generally thrive in an environment that includes children from all backgrounds and capabilities.

Chronic illnesses
medical conditions requiring continuous treatment

CHILDREN WITH CHRONIC ILLNESSES

Chronic illnesses or conditions may affect more than 30 percent of the population under the age of eighteen years (Newacheck & Taylor, 1992). A chronic illness requires continued treatment. The range of the condition can be from mild to severe. Caregivers are most likely to be confronted with children who have a mild or moderate form of a chronic illness.

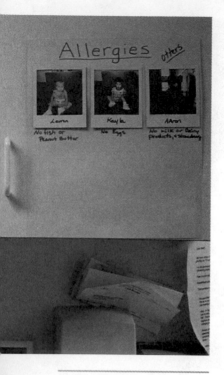

Caregivers need to be aware of any or potential allergies for all children in their care.

Triggers
substances or conditions that activate a response

Each chronic illness has its own unique causes, indicators, and medical responses. Most chronic illnesses have organizations that can provide the caregiver with a wealth of resources. These following chronic illnesses are covered in this text: allergies, asthma, diabetes mellitus, HIV, seizure disorders, and sickle cell anemia. These are the most common chronic illnesses that may be found in child care.

The following information should help a caregiver provide care for a child in care who has one of the chronic illnesses. Each chronic illness description provides the definition, significance, and how the disease occurs. This information gives the caregiver a background in order to understand the rest of the table. The remaining information gives the caregiver some triggers, identifiers, and strategies for care of the child who may have the chronic illness. It is important to note that some states do not allow child caregivers the ability to administer medication. If this is the case, a health professional should be close by if help is needed, or the family of a child with chronic illness should make provisions for emergencies, if needed.

Allergies

Definition.   An allergy is a heightened response to a substance.

Significance.   Some children have known allergies; many others may have undiagnosed allergies.

How Does It Occur?   The person who is allergic to a substance is exposed to it by ingestion, touch, or breathing.

When Does It Occur?   It occurs when the person is exposed to a substance that causes the response. Common allergy **triggers** are:

- Foods such as peanut butter, nuts, wheat, chocolate, milk, fish, and citrus
- Pollen from flowers, grasses, hay, weeds, or trees
- Mold spores
- Dust
- Animal fur, feathers, or dander; this may be on a live animal, feathers in a comforter, or an animal skin on a wall
- Insects including stings or parts from dead insects like cockroaches

Identifiers of Reaction.   Allergic reaction may take the form of sneezing, hay fever, asthma, swelling/hives, eczema, or cold-like symptoms.

Child Care Support.   Be alert to the signs of allergic reactions of children in care. Discuss any allergies with parents and avoid those triggers that are observed to cause a response. For more serious allergic reactions, the child may have medication that will need to be administered.

Asthma

Definition.   Asthma occurs when there is a narrowing of the small airways in the lungs called bronchi and bronchioles. Muscles around the airways tighten and when mucus clogs these airways, breathing difficulty results.

Significance. Approximately 12 million people have asthma, more than half of whom are children (Frieman & Settle, 1994).

How Does It Occur? Most asthmatics have persistent bronchial irritation. Environmental irritants trigger reactions that lead to an attack or episode.

When Does It Occur? The asthma episode or attack may occur if the child is exposed to one or more of the following triggers:

- The same items found on the allergy list
- Household products—vapors, deodorants, sprays, cleaning solvents, paints
- Dust from clothes, broom, furniture, or filters on furnaces and air conditioners
- Weather—humidity, cold, wind
- Exercise—overexertion
- Infections such as colds, bronchitis, or other viruses
- Smoke—cigarette, pipe, or cigar
- Strong emotions—fear, laughing, crying, anger
- Aspirin
- At the end of the day when tired, lying down and mucus accumulates

Identifiers of Reaction. Tightening of airways and muscles cause difficulty breathing. Wheezing, coughing, and spitting up mucus may also occur.

Child Care Support. Be aware of asthmatic reactions especially after exercise, emotional display, or exposure to allergens. The caregiver should keep the child free from infection by providing a healthy, safe environment. If an episode does occur, the caregiver should make sure the child is sitting up, the child is calm, and encourage the child to focus on slow, deep breathing. Follow procedures if medication should be given.

Diabetes Mellitus

Definition. Diabetes mellitus occurs when insulin is not produced in the pancreas at the rate the body needs it. Insulin is involved in the process that stores and uses glucose for energy. There are two types of diabetes: type I, which is insulin dependent, and type II, which is noninsulin dependent.

Significance. Type I diabetes is often referred to as juvenile onset diabetes and is the most common type for children. This type of diabetes requires insulin injections at least twice daily. Food and exercise levels must be controlled, and blood sugar needs to be tested several times throughout the day.

How Does It Occur?   Since adequate insulin is missing, the amount of glucose produced by the body cannot absorb the excess glucose. Glucose levels: (1) build in the blood and spill into the urine; (2) sugar not used for energy is stored in fats and when broken down the resulting chemicals, ketones, can poison the blood if they are allowed to accumulate.

When Does It Occur?   Diabetes reaction is triggered when there is:

- Too much exercise
- Not enough food
- Too much sugar
- Too much insulin

Identifiers of Reaction.   Lack of insulin can cause numerous reactions. Among them are:

- Disorientation, confusion, blurred vision
- Excessive sweating
- Dizziness, poor coordination
- Irritability, behavior change
- Excessive thirst or sudden hunger
- Coma

Child Care Support.   The caregiver will need to be educated in what to watch for when caring for a diabetic child. Glucose levels are affected by food and exercise so those activities should be monitored. If several of the preceding indicators are present, the caregiver may need to provide glucose in the form of sugar, such as ½ cup orange juice or soda, 1 graham cracker, or several sugar cubes. Follow the procedures the caregiver has worked out with the parent. If there is no improvement in the condition the caregiver should call the parent or physician.

HIV/AIDS

Definition.   Human immunodeficiency virus is a viral infection that threatens the immune system's ability to fight off infection. It can lead to acquired immunodeficiency syndrome (AIDS), which is a combination of illnesses that may become life threatening.

Significance.   By the year 2000, AIDS may rank among the top five causes of death for children under five years of age (U.S. News and World Report, 1993).

How Does It Occur?   The method of transmission that affects children are: *in utero*, blood from their mothers who have HIV, sexual abuse by a person with AIDS, and exposure to blood or blood products from an infected person through a cut or sore.

When Does It Occur?   Exposure to infection or normal childhood diseases can trigger an immunosuppressed response. Chicken pox is especially dangerous.

Identifiers of Reaction. Some symptoms found in children with HIV/AIDS are:

■ Multiple bacterial infections
■ Enlarged spleen and liver
■ Abnormal growth patterns
■ Frequent illnesses

REALITY CHECK

Children with HIV/AIDS in Child Care

Approximately 1,800 children are born with HIV each year in the United States (Gorman, 1994). Worldwide, there are 1,000 children born with HIV each day (Health Gate, 1996). AIDS is listed as one of the top ten causes of death of children in the United States (Jessee, Nagy, & Poteet-Johnson, 1993). AIDS is expected to rise to one of the top five causes of childhood deaths by the year 2000 ("Outlook," 1993). Minority children represent a disproportionate number of the children who have HIV/AIDS (National Pediatric HIV Resource Center, 1992).

It is estimated that at a point in every teacher's career he or she will have a child with AIDS in the classroom (Jessee, Nagy, & Poteet-Johnson, 1993). Caregivers must realize that children with HIV/AIDS may be present in a number of child care situations. These children need special care, as well as special consideration. There is a great deal of controversy, fear, and lack of understanding about children who may be infected with HIV/AIDS (Osborn, Kistner, and Helgemo, 1995). A number of people are not educated about how the virus spreads (see HIV/AIDS in this chapter). Some people feel casual contact is a way for children with this disease to spread their disease. Others may be rightfully concerned about child biting in a child care environment. Regardless of the confusion and concern, a number of these children will filter into child care. Children with HIV infection or the AIDS virus may exhibit some developmental factors that may need special considerations from child caregivers. A resource manual for Head Start (National Pediatric HIV Resource Center,

1992) caregivers relates the following changes that may be noted:

Social—increased activity, irritability, and confusion.

Cognitive—decrease in intelligence, memory, or academic skills. Children may also exhibit decrease in previously displayed motor skills, such as the ability to hold a crayon or assemble puzzles.

Physical—clumsiness, staggering walk, and inability to perform usual physical tasks. Illness or infection may appear without warning.

Black (1994) reports that children need help coping with stressful events due to chronic illness, and problems with role transitions due to changes in their condition. Children with HIV/AIDS may also exhibit problems with appetite and difficulty with eating.

Caregivers need to adapt to the HIV/AIDS of children in care taking into consideration the stress and coping mechanisms that will be needed. Caregivers will need to view the situation from the ecological perspective (Lasar & Maldonado, 1994). They should remember to always use universal sanitary precautions associated with this disease. Caregivers should apply strategies used with children with chronic illnesses as well as those for special needs. If a caregiver finds herself caring for a child with AIDS, extra reading and education on the subject might be helpful.

Child Care Support. There are two areas of support that a caregiver needs to give. The first area is protecting the child with HIV/AIDS from exposure to childhood diseases, especially chicken pox. To protect all other children and caregivers from HIV/AIDS, universal precautions should be followed. These include hand washing and sanitary procedures, and wearing gloves when in contact with blood or other bodily fluids. Everyone with sores, scratches, or lesions should keep them covered. The caregiver should also attempt to prevent and handle immediately any biting by any child in care.

Seizure Disorders

Definition. Seizure disorders is another term for epilepsy. Twenty types of seizure disorders may occur when there is temporary overactivity in the electrical impulses in the brain.

Significance. One in every 100 persons has some form of seizure disorder on the continuum from rare to frequent displays.

How Does It Occur? Seizure disorder can result from head injuries, infections, high fevers, lead poisoning, or may be hereditary.

When Does It Happen? Possible triggers include:

- Fast rising fevers
- Fatigue
- Disorientation from outside source such as flashing lights or rapid movement

Identifiers of Reaction. Because there are twenty different types of seizure disorders the reaction range is wide. The following demonstrates the range:

- Dazed behavior
- Unusual sleepiness and irritability
- Unexplained clumsiness, falls
- Feeling strange, disoriented
- Rapid eye movements, eyes rolling up
- Head appears to move involuntarily
- Involuntary, unnatural movements of body
- Unconsciousness, drooling at the mouth

Child Care Support. The first thing a caregiver should do is to become familiar with the type of disorder the child has and how to handle the reaction of that disorder. When the reaction occurs remain calm. If a child is having a seizure that includes unconsciousness place the child on the floor and turn him on the side. Place something soft under the child's head. Patiently wait until the seizure has finished and help the child in the transition to normal activity. If the seizure lasts more than 10 minutes, call the parents or physician.

Sickle Cell Anemia

Definition. Sickle cell anemia is a hereditary disease that affects the red blood cells. It is most often found in African American children and young adults.

Significance. Sickle cell anemia occurs in one out of 400 African Americans.

How Does It Occur? An abnormality in the red blood cells causes them to change shape and decrease the oxygen that they deliver to all parts of the body. When this causes blockage to tissues of an organ or joint, this leads to pain and may be damaging to the tissues in that location.

When Does It Happen? Sickle cell anemia can be triggered by:

■ Fatigue
■ Overexertion from exercise
■ Stress

Identifiers of Reaction. There may be no apparent triggers. When it happens there may be intense pain in arms, legs, back, and chest.

Child Care Support. A caregiver should be aware of the disease and watch the child for shortness of breath and fatigue. If a crisis occurs, the caregiver should remain calm, call the parents, and support the child until he is picked up. A preventive measure would be to protect the child from infection by offering a sanitary environment.

Working as a Team

Many of the issues that occur when caring for a child with a chronic illness are similar to those of a child with special needs. Some children with a chronic illness qualify as children with special needs under the ADA. Regardless of whether or not the child qualifies, using the strategies developed for children with special needs will help the caregiver meet most of the needs of the chronically ill child.

The team for a chronically ill child may only consist of the parent, the physician, and the caregiver. The caregiver needs to ask questions and access any other resources available to help support the care for the child. The caregiver should have a plan for care of each child with a chronic illness if a reactive or crisis episode should occur. It is vital that the caregiver learn to recognize and identify reactions that may lead to crisis. She must also understand what to do in terms of a crisis situation. This includes understanding what constitutes an emergency needing outside help. The caregiver who possesses the knowledge of how to handle a crisis can remain calm and do what needs to be done.

KEY CHRONICALLY ILL CHILDREN

CONCEPT

Many caregivers will find themselves caring for one or more children with a chronic illness. A caregiver needs general knowledge of the chronic illness—especially the reactions leading to a crisis episode. She should also have understanding of what to do should this occur. Many of the strategies used for the child with special needs can be applied to the child with a chronic illness.

CHILDREN WITH STRESS

Children today are dealing with many stressful events and life changes. Losses, events, or lifestyles that make the child feel she has no control may cause stress. One or more of the events or lifestyles that may produce stress in a child are listed in Table 13.2.

TABLE **13.2**

Stressors in a Child's Life

■ Divorce/single parent family/stepfamily adjustments

■ Birth of a sibling

■ Separation anxiety

■ Loss (death) of a loved one or pet

■ Too many scheduled activities

■ A new care situation or being placed in care for the first time

■ A friend leaves child care

■ Lack of bonding or attachment

■ Financial problems at home

■ Fears, real or imagined

■ Special needs or chronic illness

■ Victim of child abuse

■ Drug abuse in the home

■ Frequent relocation

■ Cultural considerations, including language and immigration

■ Observing violence in the home, neighborhood, or other real situation

■ Poverty

■ Homelessness

This child may react differently to stress in her life than other children.

Children's reaction to stress may be visible in physical, emotional, or behavioral reactions. Children have a limited understanding and a good imagination. When life feels out of control the child may magnify the significance of the stressor. Children do not have the same coping skills as an adult, so their reaction to stress may be somewhat different.

Children who react physically to stress may have headaches, stomachaches, or bouts of diarrhea. They may not have their regular appetites and may either not eat, or constantly be eating. Children who have normal language may have some language difficulties, such as rapid speech or stuttering. Children with allergies or asthma may have reactions that appear more often.

The emotional reaction to stress can be expressed in a number of ways. The spectra of behaviors range from regressive to aggressive. Children may show regressive behaviors in forms such as withdrawing or having toileting accidents. Children may become clingy, and too dependent. They may be unable to make simple decisions such as with what and whom to play. Children who are stressed may not laugh or smile and may cry more than usual. They may appear to escape into fantasy by constantly daydreaming or watching television. Children may appear fearful and nervous.

Aggressive emotional behaviors are exhibited by acting out. This might range from throwing a tantrum to more violent behavior. Stressed children may bite or hit other children or adults. Children who use aggression to cope with stress may vandalize toys, equipment, or art of their own or others. They might have difficulty with social interactions. Children under stress may become easily frustrated and use colorful language to express their anger.

Stress may exhibit itself in aggressive behavior.

Regardless of how it is expressed, caregivers need to be alert to the fact that stress can be an important factor in children's behavior. If a child abruptly changes behavior, or is a constant source of regressive or aggressive behavior, stress may be a factor. The best way for the caregiver to help the child is to structure the environment so it supports the child. The environment should be protective and prevent more stress to the child. Robinson and Rotter (1991) proposed three coping skills for adults to provide to children. These include giving the child security, a sense of control, and the feeling of self-worth to help prepare the child to cope with stress and fears.

Providing structure through a predictable routine allows the child the comfort of understanding what comes next. The caregiver can improve the quality of interaction with children by being consistent and reliable. The caregiver who forms an attachment to children helps them learn to trust the caregiver and the care environment. This gives some children a feeling of safety and stability that they may not otherwise have.

The caregiver can provide children under stress a sense of security in other ways. Some children under stress may need a quiet place to go to be free of stimulation. Providing a corner of a room that is not decorated and has a comfortable place to sit helps achieve this. Sometimes going from one activity to another can cause a child more stress. The caregiver can help children in their transition from one activity to another to reduce stress.

The caregiver also needs to help children under stress learn to identify and express their emotions. Role modeling, dramatic play, reading books, and discussions with the child help. A caregiver can support children by redirecting their anger, frustration, and aggression. Activities such as rocking horses, swings, and punching bags can alleviate anger. Water play and sand play are soothing and may help dissipate anger. A withdrawn child can be

The caregiver and parent should always work together for the benefit of the child.

stimulated to act out emotions through play. A child who feels more in control will be able to cope with stress under other situations.

A caregiver who listens to children and responds with positive action and words allows them the opportunity to express problems and get in touch with feelings. The caregiver should reinforce positive behaviors and reward them at least with a positive comment. A caregiver who allows children choices where appropriate can help teach decision making and problem solving skills. Those actions show children that the caregiver respects them, because children who feel respected have a sense of self-worth.

The team approach of the caregiver and a parent working together can also be helpful with stress. A parent may be a source of stress for the child and may choose not to participate, although most parents will be cooperative. Some parents who are under stress themselves may welcome the caregiver's help. The caregiver can set up times with the parent to discuss the child. The caregiver should show the family respect and acknowledge their feelings. Being consistent and predictable in all dealings with the parent can build trust. The caregiver can also provide opportunities for the parent under stress to find additional help through counseling.

KEY CHILDREN WITH STRESS

CONCEPT

Stress can have an effect on a child. It can cause physical, emotional, and behavioral difficulties. The caregiver needs to acknowledge stressors in a child's life and identify the reactions. Coping skills can be taught by the caregiver to provide a sense of security, control, and self-worth. The caregiver and parent can team up to help alleviate the child's stress.

WORKING WITH CHILDREN FROM DRUG ABUSING FAMILIES

It is estimated that 6 million women of childbearing age abuse drugs on a regular basis (Kelley, 1992). A minimum of 11 percent of all children born in this country have been exposed to substances prenatally. Prenatal exposure to drugs can cause developmental difficulties in several areas:

- Children may be unable to organize their own play.
- Sporadic mastery is common.
- Learning strategies and problem solving may be hindered by a lack of organization of inner states.
- Communication and language development may be impaired by delayed acquisition of words and gestures, inability to express feelings, and speech difficulties.
- Difficulty with motor skills may be exhibited in both gross and fine motor skills.
- Acquiring a sense of self may be hampered by lack of attachment, inconsistent or negligent care.

All of these vulnerabilities can be assessed through observation and the use of assessment tools. A child who has any one of these difficulties can be very challenging for the caregiver. It would be helpful for the caregiver to work with the family. However, these families may present an even greater challenge. The families may be represented in several ways:

- The recovering family, who may be feeling vulnerable
- The addicted family living in chaos, who may be emotionally unavailable or negligent
- The foster family or relative caregiver, who may feel overwhelmed

The Recovering Family

The recovering family may be in or out of a recovery program. The parent or parents may have few coping skills. The parents may be developmentally "frozen" at the stage they were in their own development when they began abusing drugs. They may be emotionally unavailable and struggling with attachment issues. They may be struggling to remain clean. The environment may be chaotic.

The Actively Abusing Family

The addictive family brings a whole series of problems. As people who abuse drugs go through the cycle of abuse, there is a tendency to get hostile when dealing with people in authority. Figure 13.3 shows the feelings that the downward spiral of addiction can cause in an active drug-using family.

Drug abusing families live in an extremely chaotic environment. Children from this environment may have difficulty getting their physical needs met. There may not be food or clean clothes available for them. They may

Distrust

Unhappiness

Denial

Irritability

Loss of interest

Self-defense

Depression

Self-neglect

Loss of self-respect

Dishonesty

Isolation

Indefinable fears

Hostility

Blames others

Escape

Chronic depression

Increased drug use

Suicide attempts or admits defeat

Bottoming out and into recovery or death

FIGURE 13.3
Downward Spiral of Addiction

suffer great stress from negligent or inconsistent care at home. It is estimated that 675,000 children per year are maltreated or neglected by a drug abusive family caretaker (Kelley, 1992).

It is very difficult for a child to be able to count on a drug abusing parent to meet the child's needs. An active substance abuser may have sudden mood swings that display the person as being either really up or really down and depressed. It is difficult to predict if the person will show up when expected to for appointments, including bringing the child to care. An addict may lose track of time or suffer from a hang over. Another common characteristic of an active abuser is the avoidance of contact with concerned persons. "Isolation is the core of addiction" ("The Battlefield," 1993, p. 37). A mother who is actively abusing drugs may have difficulty forming a bond of trust with anyone and may be emotionally unavailable to the child or the caregiver. Abusing families put their children at risk. They may fear that if help is sought, the child may be removed from the home. The family addictive system may discourage any behavior changes.

The Foster Family

Foster families or families where the caretaker is a relative may have their own difficulties. Legal custody of the child may be in flux. The parents may still have legal custody. The circumstances that led the child to this caretaker situation may have an effect on the caretakers. They may be sad, angry, depressed, or overwhelmed. If the parent of the children is around and wants to participate in the child's life, that can cause difficulties. There may be legal boundaries that have been or need to be mandated. The caregiver will need to be aware of this or any other legal custody issues. Caregivers can also assist these families by recognizing that extra help may be needed both at the center and in the home. Caregivers can help access social services to support them through the difficulties they may encounter.

Establishing a Relationship with the Family

Establishing a relationship with the family is a crucial step in the intervention process to help a child from a drug abusing family. Providing a safe and secure environment for the parent and family is almost as critical as providing that type of care for the child. As difficult as it may be, the caregiver should try to establish communication with the parent concerning the child. The caregiver should be consistent and predictable in this relationship, and use cultural sensitivity if applicable. The caregiver who tries to show respect to the family is more likely to be accepted by them.

Many caregivers try to avoid difficult situations involving parents. They may also avoid difficult parents (Boutte, Keepler, Tyler, & Terry, 1992). Children in this situation need the support of the caregiver. The caregiver should avoid arguing with the parent, getting angry, being taken in by the parents defensiveness and becoming an enabler. The caregiver should model good coping skills, be flexible, remain calm and nonjudgmental, and be culturally sensitive. It might help the caregiver to practice possible parent responses and be prepared to answer them.

Working with the Children

The caregiver needs to provide a safe and protective environment. Good child development techniques are essential. A child at risk can be a challenge. The caregiver may need to add some protective and facilitative factors to her skills. The best thing that the caregiver can do is to provide consistent, predictable, and reliable care. These measures can improve the quality of interaction with the child and help to form an attachment bond.

The child at risk may need to be protected from overstimulation. The caregiver can help the child by creating a quiet, safe place to retreat. Transition times may stress the child at risk. The caregiver can provide structure and clear limits to help make the transition more manageable. These measures also allow the child to understand boundaries and acceptable behaviors. Recent studies have shown that if the child at risk is able to find someone with whom to develop a secure attachment, that child is likely to be able to overcome nonmedical, behavioral, and developmental difficulties (Wallach, 1994). A child at risk from a drug environment will have to find reliable bonds with other people. The caregiver who helps a child in this way may give the child the tools needed to find other adults to rely on.

If the situation at home is intolerable, the caregiver may have to report the situation to the local Child Protective Services (CPS) office. If the child or children are removed from the drug environment, it is possible that CPS will work with the foster family or relative caring for the children to continue in the child care situation. The consistency of the caregiver and the caregiving situation will be a very important source of support to the child.

CONCEPT ### KEY CHILDREN FROM DRUG ABUSING FAMILIES

Many caregivers may find themselves working with children from drug abusing families. They should learn to recognize the indicators for this condition. Caregivers who understand the family situation are more likely to be able to help. Families may be in recovery, may be active abusers, or may be a foster family that has complex issues to address. Caregivers can work more productively by developing good communication and trust with these families and their children.

IMPLICATIONS FOR **CAREGIVERS**

The caregiver needs to understand that some children in care may have special circumstances that may be challenging. Children with special needs or chronic illnesses may be included in care. Some children may be suffering from a great deal of stress in their lives. Children may come from drug abusing families with chaotic conditions in their lives. The caregiver needs to use tools such as education, supervision, and cultural sensitivity to help these children and their families by providing an environment that will support the health, safety, and nutrition of these children.

Education

When children with special needs are included in care some modifications may need to be made in the child care environment. These may include toys, equipment, or nutritional requirements. Caregiver intervention may be needed to help the child interact and engage in exploration of the environment. The caregiver may need to use natural situations for activity based learning. All of these situations require caregiver knowledge and awareness. The caregiver may need special training by the other IFSP team members in order to be fully able to support the child.

Children who are not disabled may need some instruction on how to act with a disabled child. Encouraging interaction may provide the best education. Parents of nondisabled children may also need education to help them understand the benefits of inclusion. Cultural sensitivity is important with this issue because other cultures have different reactions to disabilities.

Katy went to special school that mainstreamed healthy children with children with chronic diseases. Both she and her friend, Paul, had diabetes that required urine testing and shots of insulin as needed. Many of the other children watched as Katy and Paul and their caregiver, Charles, tested the urine to find out the condition of each of their systems for insulin. This process evolved into an activity for all the children. They would all gather around and most could identify what the insulin test result was. They often watched Katy and Paul get shots. Everyone was involved so there was nothing really "different" about Katy and Paul that the other children considered to be a problem.

Many of the same strategies used for child abuse and children with special needs can be applied to children with chronic illnesses. Recognition of reactions that bring on crisis episodes may help to prevent them, and preparation for crisis episodes can help to minimize them. Teaching all children about the chronic disease(s) present in care can offer even more protection and prevention. This also provides understanding and the appreciation of diversity. Parents can be encouraged to appreciate how similar the chronically ill child is to the other children in care rather than to focus on the child's differences from other children.

The caregiver can use similar strategies when dealing with children who are experiencing stress in their lives. Recognizing stressors and identifying behaviors help the caregiver establish the presence of stress. Offering the child with stress skills that will help him to cope can alleviate stress and promote well-being. Teaching children about stress and helping them learn

Reversed mainstreaming

to communicate offer a measure of protection. Providing resources for the parents may be stress reducing for the whole family.

Those same skills can be applied to children who come from drug abusing families, although the caregiver may need more coping skills to work with these families. Knowledge of the family situation, such as whether drug abuse is active or the family is in recovery will help the caregiver understand which skills to employ.

Cultural Sensitivity

If the child with special needs is from a different cultural background, the caregiver may need an additional tool, which is cultural sensitivity. Many cultures have the tendency to either ignore or deny that a child has a problem. Other cultures may focus on the problem to such a degree that it becomes an obsession. Values, childrearing practices, family roles, and outside support may all have an effect on how the disability is perceived (Anderson & Fenichel, 1989). State departments of maternal and child health, departments of social services, and regional centers may be good resources for this information. The reactions and tendencies on the part of families may be equally true of chronically ill children.

Cultural sensitivity may also be necessary for children with stress and their families. For some children, the stress may be a direct result of cultural differences and adjustment to a new environment. This may cause the parents more stress than the child. The caregiver who offers the culturally diverse family an opportunity to discuss the child's stress may help the parents reduce their own. The caregiver may help reduce family stress by providing resources for information on the difficulties they may be experiencing.

Drug abusing families from different cultural backgrounds may look at the drug abuse differently than the caregiver. In some cultures drug abuse has less social stigma attached to it. Caregivers may need extra sensitivity when approaching these families.

Supervision

The caregiver who cares for a child with special needs, a chronically ill child, a child under a great deal of stress, or a child from drug abusing families must supervise the child care environment, because these children are more at risk for health and safety issues as well as nutritional well-being. It is up to the caregiver to observe these children with a holistic approach.

The caregiver may need to observe more often and make certain that the special needs are met, that the health of the chronically ill child is assessed, and that a child under stress or from a chaotic family environment is offered relief through supportive behaviors.

Medication and nutritional needs must be maintained through careful supervision. Timing and frequency of medication for a child with special needs or a chronically ill child may be critical. These needs may have to be met by an outside source if the caregiver lives in a state where she is not allowed to offer medication. Nutritional needs may also be significant. In addition, the caregiver will need to supervise any team created for a child from the child care viewpoint in order to reinforce that child's goals.

KEY IMPLICATIONS FOR CAREGIVERS

CONCEPT

A caregiver may take care of children who have special needs, chronic illness, significant stress, or come from chaotic environments. These children need a holistic approach to their care. The tools that the child caregiver will use are education, cultural sensitivity, and supervision. The caregiver needs a knowledge base for these. Children who do not have these conditions may need to be taught to understand and support the other children who do. Cultural sensitivity needs to be practiced because of the actions and reactions of other cultures to children who are disabled or ill. Supervision will provide an environment that offers maximum well-being for the children.

CHAPTER **SUMMARY**

Some children in care have special issues in their lives that will affect caregiving. Four issues that are the most likely to affect the caregiver and the child care site are inclusion of children with special needs, children with chronic illnesses, children who are suffering from stress in their lives, and children who come from drug abusing families.

If children with disabilities are included the caregiver should work as part of a team and help support the child with special needs. Children with disabilities generally thrive in an environment that includes children from all backgrounds and capabilities.

Many caregivers will find themselves caring for one or more children with a chronic illness. A caregiver needs general knowledge of the chronic illness, the reactions leading to crisis episodes, and how to deal with the crisis.

Stress can cause physical, emotional, and behavioral difficulties in children. The caregiver needs to acknowledge stressors in children's lives, identify common reactions, and provide coping skills.

Caregivers need to be prepared to offer stability and support to children who may come from chaotic environments due to drug abuse. It is essential that they understand how to work with the families as well as the children. Caregivers are most effective in meeting children's needs when they use a holistic approach, including education, cultural sensitivity, and supervision.

TO GO **BEYOND**

Questions for Review

1. How does the ADA impact child care? Describe the process of accommodating children with disabilities.

2. Discuss the presence of children with chronic illnesses in child care. Should a child caregiver have more qualifications to work with these children?

3. Discuss children's stresses and the situations that cause the stress. What supportive measures can caregivers provide to help alleviate some stress?

AS AN **INDIVIDUAL**

1. Have each student research children's books that deal with the issues in this chapter. Create a list of ten "special subject" books, and report to the class on one of the books. Collate the lists, duplicate them, and distribute them in class.

2. Have students research how individualized family service plans (IFSP) are handled in your community. What agencies might handle the IFSP and deliver the services needed for the family and the child with special needs? What type of support do these agencies offer to child caregivers?

AS A **GROUP**

1. Divide the class into small groups. Send these groups into the community to gather information on what help is available for children with special needs. Collate the information and distribute it to the entire class.

2. Discuss the downward spiral of addiction that might affect some families. List several scenarios where each behavior (from top to bottom) might be found. Break up into smaller groups and role-play several of the scenarios that the class discussed. Did the exercise help the students to better understand these behaviors?

CHAPTER **REFERENCES**

Anderson, P., & Fenichel, E. (1989). *Serving culturally diverse families of infants and toddlers with disabilities.* Arlington, VA: National Center for Clinical Infant Programs.

The Battlefield of addiction. (1993, July 19). *Maclean's.* Special report. 36–39.

Black, S. (1994). *Providing psychoeducational support for children affected by AIDS.* Florida: Nova University.

Boutte, G., Keepler, D., Tyler, V., & Terry, B. (1992). Effective techniques for involving "difficult" parents. *Young Children, 47*(3), 19–23.

Bracer, D., & Cripe, J. (1992). *An activity based approach to early intervention.* Baltimore: Paul H. Brooks.

Campbell, S., March, C., Pierce, E., Ewing, L., & Szumowksi, L. (1991). Hard to manage preschool boys: Family context and the stability of externalizing behavior. *Journal of Abnormal Psychology, 19*(3), 301–318.

Diamond, K., Hestenes, L., & O'Connor, C. (1994). Integrating children with disability in preschool: Problems and promise. *Young Children, 49,* 68–79.

Frieman, B., & Settle, J. (1994). What the classroom teacher needs to know about children with chronic medical problems. *Childhood Education, 70*(4), 196–201.

Gorman, C. (1994, July 4). Moms, kids and AIDS. *Time Magazine,* 60.

HealthGate. (1996). Women, children focus of AIDS conference. Reuters Limited, Health Gate Internet Access, July 14, 1996. Path:http://www.healthgate.com:80/.

Jessee, P., Nagy, M., & Poteet-Johnson, D. (1993). Children with AIDS. *Childhood Education, 70*(1), 10–14.

Kelley, S. (1992). Parenting stress and child maltreatment in drug-exposed children. *Child Abuse and Neglect, 16,* 317–328.

Lasar, S., & Maldonado, Y. (1994). Infants and young children with HIV infection: Service delivery considerations for family support. *Infants and Young Children, 49*(4), 70–81.

National Pediatric HIV Resource Center. (1992). Getting a head start on HIV. New York: National Pediatric HIV Resource Center in cooperation with Region ll Head Start Resource Center.

Newacheck, P., & Taylor, W. (1992). Childhood illness: Prevalence, severity and impact. *American Journal of Public Health, 82*(3), 364–371.

Osborn, M., Kistner, J., & Helgemo, B. (1995). Parental knowledge and attitudes toward children with AIDS: Influences on educational policies and children's attitudes. *Journal of Pediatric Psychology, 20*(1), 79–90.

Outlook. (1993, February 22) *U.S. News and World Report,* 8.

Robertson, C. (1993). *Working with prenatally substance exposed children and their families. California Community College curriculum and resource guide.* Sacramento, CA: California Community Colleges Chancellor's Office.

Robinson, E., & Rotter, J. (1991). *Coping with fears and stress.* (Eric Digest). Champaign, IL: Eric Clearinghouse on Elementary and Early Childhood Education.

Surr, J. (1992). Early childhood programs and the Americans with Disabilities Act. *Young Children, 47*(5), 18–21.

Wallach, L. (1994). Helping children cope with violence. *Young Children, 48*(4), 4–11.

Woolery, M., & Wilburs, J. (Eds.) (1994). *Including children with special needs in early childhood programs.* Washington, DC: NAEYC.

SUGGESTIONS **FOR READING**

Daniels, J. (1995). New beginnings: Transitions for difficult children. *Young Children, 50*(3), 17–23.

Furman, R. (1995). Helping children cope with stress and deal with feeling. *Young Children, 50*(2), 33–41.

Goldberg, E. (1994). Including children with chronic health conditions: Nebulizers in the classroom. *Young Children, 49*(1), 34–39.

Malick, M., Holder, G., & Walthers, V. (1994). Coping with childhood asthma: Caretakers view. *Health and Social Work, 19*(2), 103–110.

Needlman, R., & Needlman, G. (1996, March). HIV: Facts and myths. *Scholastic Early Childhood Today,* 8–10.

Oesterreich, L. (1995). *Iowa family child care handbook.* Amass, IA: Iowa State University Extension.

Paasche, C., Gorril, L., & Strom, B. (1990) *Children with special needs in early childhood settings.* Menlo Park, CA: Addison-Wesley.

Putnam, F., & Trickett, P. (1993). Child sexual abuse: A model of chronic trauma. *Psychiatry: Interpersonal and Biological Process, 56*(1), 82–95.

Schwartz, S., & Heller-Miller, J. (1988). *The language of toys: Teaching communication skills to special needs children.* Bethesda, MD: Woodbine House.

Siegler, A. (1996, February). Preventing burnout: Why children need some unscheduled time. *Child Magazine,* 45–47.

Solit, G. (1993, September). A place for Marie. *Child Care Information Exchange,* 49–53.

Terr, I. (1983). Trauma aftermath: The young hostages of Chowchilla. *Psychology Today, 15*(4), 29–30.

CHAPTER FOURTEEN

CREATING LINKAGES

Upon completion of this chapter, including a review of the summary, you should be able to:

POLICIES FOR CREATING LINKAGES

Describe and discuss policies for creating linkages for better health and well-being within the child care environment and the community.

TOWARD BETTER COMMUNICATION SKILLS

Describe and discuss how to develop good communication skills for working with parents and coworkers.

MANAGING DIVERSITY

Describe and discuss the importance of understanding issues regarding diversity and how they may affect health, safety, and nutrition in child care.

ACCESSING COMMUNITY RESOURCES

Describe and discuss the importance of assessing and developing community health, safety, and nutrition resources for helping the caregiver, the child, and the parents.

DEVELOPING EFFECTIVE ADVOCACY

Describe and discuss the advocacy role the child caregiver plays in linking the child, the family, the community, and beyond.

CREATING A TEAM APPROACH

Describe and discuss how to create a team that provides the maximum protection for a child's health and well-being.

Linkages
connections that unify the caregiver, child, family, and community

POLICIES FOR CREATING LINKAGES

Linkages should be formed within and without the child care environment in order to offer the maximum in protection and prevention for issues dealing with children's health, safety, and nutrition. The caregiver needs to secure the cooperation of coworkers, parents, and community resources to create these linkages. The following indicators reflect reasons for linkages to offer support to the child care environment:

■ Strategies should be initiated to break down cultural bias or racial attitudes and recognize diversity as positive (Carter, 1996).

■ Professionals must be prepared to be agents of change as well as competent practitioners (Whitebook, 1994).

■ Leadership empowers people to effect change (Bloom, 1994).

■ Child caregivers should acknowledge community resources and use them for consultation and other services (American Public Health Association [APHA] & American Academy of Pediatrics [AAP], 1992).

■ Caregivers and parents who work together as a team can improve the quality of child care (Herr, 1991).

Synergy
combined effort or action

Synergy or combined effort is much more effective than individual effort. This is especially true in child care. Policies should be in force to help develop approaches using synergy as often as possible. The holistic approach to child care allows the caregiver to understand that one person would be less effective than a combined effort. A child caregiver is called upon to be many things to the child. The physical, emotional, and cognitive care and education of a child is a very large task. Most caregivers are involved in this task on a daily basis for a number of children.

Communicating with the child is the first step toward learning how to communicate with parents, coworkers, and directors regarding a child's health, safety, and nutritional needs.

The director posts available community resources for parents and caregivers to access.

The caregiver can help make this job easier. The caregiver who learns to communicate about the child's health, safety, and nutritional needs can be more proactive in the care of children. This effort will involve communicating to the parent as well as all those present in the child care environment. Coworkers, directors, assistants, and food preparers should all be involved in the effort to promote and protect the health and well-being of children in care.

The communication effort helps the transition from child care to the home environment so the child might feel the sense of well-being as a constant. Many parents do not realize how they can actively affect their own environment. A child caregiver who passes on knowledge about health, safety, and nutrition can help parents create a better environment at home.

A caregiver who is sensitive about diversity is more effective in preventing problems and protecting the well-being of the child. The many cultures, races, and other diverse conditions of people in this country are rapidly causing change and this diversity should be understood instead of ignored. The caregiver who learns to celebrate the differences and understand the similarities will be more effective in offering the children in care the maximum environment. The caregiver who approaches situations from a diverse viewpoint will be more likely to pick nuances of how families approach health, safety, and nutrition.

In addition to the parents and families, the caregiver also needs to seek help from outside the child care environment. A child caregiver is rarely a qualified health or nutritional professional. There will probably be instances where the caregiver will need to call on outside resources and professionals to deal with a situation that presents a challenge.

It is getting more difficult to remain in the child care environment without acknowledging that the caregiver be an advocate for the health, safety, and well-being of children. This not only occurs within the environment and to the parents, but in the greater community. The difficulties that communities are seeing with violence, poverty, homelessness, child abuse, and other family situations may have a residual effect in the child care environment. The caregiver may feel the need to take a leadership role to help improve the community or the situation.

A team effort is the best way to use the synergistic approach. A team can be created in working with people within the child care, with parents, and the greater community. A child caregiver who makes the most of the people and the resources available will offer the children in child care the best environment possible.

In order to provide the maximum benefit to the child, there should be policies that include:

1. *Communication Skills:* practices for supporting better communications between caregivers, parents, and others.

2. *Managing Diversity:* understanding diverse cultures, race, and health conditions in order to recognize differences and similarities that will help maintain the well-being of children.

3. *Accessing Community Resources:* understanding how to recognize and access community resources that will help the caregiver be more effective in providing for health, safety, and nutrition.

4. *Developing Effective Advocacy:* understanding the importance of advocacy and how to perform it.
5. *Creating a Team Approach:* understanding how to create a team for providing for the health and well-being of children in care.

KEY POLICIES FOR LINKAGES

CONCEPT

Child care is an important part of many children's lives. Child care quality is greatly improved if there is good communication with parents and if cultural sensitivity is practiced. The quality of care is promoted by accessing and using community resources. The caregiver who is an advocate for the child with the parents, others, and the greater community is offering maximum protection and prevention. A team approach combines efforts to provide for better health, safety, and nutrition.

TOWARD BETTER COMMUNICATION SKILLS

Development of good communication is critical for the child care environment. Families come in many different forms. There may be two parents present, or only a single parent. There may be two parents present where one of them is a stepparent. Grandparents, aunts, uncles, and foster parents are becoming increasingly responsible for raising children. Mutual communication with the parent or guardian concerning the child should show respect and acknowledge feelings about certain situations. This helps both parties feel more comfortable.

A bond of trust between caregiver, parent, and child can be formed by consistency and respect.

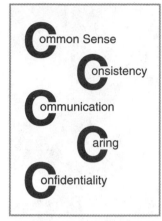

FIGURE **14.1**
Five Cs of Parent Relations

Developing Trust and Respect

The child caregiver who is consistent and predictable in the relationship with parents helps develop a bond of trust. If the caregiver shows the child and the family respect, they are much more likely to be responsive to participate actively in the health, safety, and nutrition of the child (see Figure 14.1).

The caregiver should be supportive and responsive to concerns about a child. This should be established at the beginning of the relationship with the child and parent or guardian and should be continued on a daily basis. Establishing and continuing the communication relationship is often a matter of common sense as listed in Table 14.1.

TABLE **14.1**
A Dozen Ways For a Child Caregiver to Successfully Communicate

- Show a genuine interest in the child and ask the parent to share feelings and concerns about the child.

- Encourage the parent to ask questions, visit the child care, and participate whenever possible. Seek input whenever possible.

- Be an active listener. Focus on the parent or guardian, not on how to respond. Assume nothing. Clarify any confusion or misunderstanding by repeating what was heard.

- Provide parents with verbal and written information about the child and the concerns or information that will help address the health, safety, and nutritional needs of the child.

- Think before speaking. What is it that needs to be communicated? What is the best way to do it? Practice through role play if you need to.

- Any concern about the child should be dealt with immediately and not be allowed to go unchecked. Never discuss a child in front of other children or adults.

- Be positive and discuss good behaviors and accomplishments as well as problems.

- Be flexible. Each family is unique and has different needs. Be aware of the family situation, the cultural background, and the child's home environment.

- Be a good observer. Often it is what is not said or done that may be significant. Learn to read nonverbal cues such as body tension, avoidance of contact, a sense of chaos, or other vulnerabilities.

- Never compare the child or situations with others. This never accomplishes anything and can cause resentment and guilt.

- Always keep whatever is communicated in confidence. Use the information to help the child and family find resources or get any help necessary.

- Remain calm, do not argue or be defensive. Model good coping skills.

Face to face verbal communication between caregivers and supervisors is the most effective way to monitor situations and identify problem areas and training possibilities.

Developing a System of Communication in Child Care

Good communication skills are necessary for the child care staff. During a day the same child may have more than one caregiver. These caregivers need to communicate with each other as to the child's health, safety, and nutritional needs. The quality of any interactions concerning the child affect the care of the child. Children need to feel that their environment is constant and that the care is consistent. The degree of communication between staff can affect the morale of the child care environment. There can be problems if any one person feels that he is not being heard or his opinion is not respected. When the communication within a child care environment is consistent the children can also learn to communicate at a greater level.

Communication is most effective when it is verbal and face to face. However, the nature of child care may not always offer the opportunity. A system of communication through notes, after hours telephone conversations, and regular staff meetings can help to maintain an open line of communication about concerns and issues concerning the well-being of the children in care. If the child care environment includes a director, he or she should be modeling good communication and help others on the staff to resolve any conflicts that may be present.

KEY GOOD COMMUNICATION SKILLS

CONCEPT

Communication is a key factor in the success of a child care environment's effort to provide for the health, safety, and nutrition of the children present. Communication with the families of the children is vitally important and should be a priority. Asking for input and listening to parents is a key to consistency and optimum care. Communicating with others who participate in the child care environment allow protection and prevention to be at the highest level.

Diversity
differences; variety often
related to culture

MANAGING DIVERSITY

Culture is defined as parameters of behavior. Regardless of the culture of a home environment, when one steps into the outside world, **diversity** is everywhere. The increasing population of different cultural groups has had an impact on the United States (Loeb, Friedman, Lord, Guttman, & Kukula, 1993; O'Hare, 1992). The society that we live in is multicultural and multifaceted.

Everyone should learn how to handle this diversity, but that is especially true for people who care for children. The child caregiver has the opportunity to teach children positive values about gender, race, ethnicity, class, and disabling conditions. The child caregiver will also be dealing with families of children who may represent differing cultures, social class, ethnicity, and other variations of background and experiences.

Preparing for Diversity

Preparation for dealing with diversity begins with the child caregiver. The caregiver should examine her own cultural background, attitudes, beliefs, and guidelines for behavior. People can break down barriers to accept those who are different if they understand their own biases and ways of operating. If a child caregiver becomes aware that he has a strong prejudice that cannot be overcome, he should consider seriously whether or not he should be working with children.

Each person should appreciate his own uniqueness as well as the similarities to others (Gonzalez-Mena, 1997). This is the first step that enables the child caregiver to create an environment where all children are able to accept who they are and value their backgrounds. In order to do this, there are several techniques that will help the caregiver learn about the diversity of the children and families in the child care.

Diverse classrooms present the immediate need of understanding and nurturing diversity. Caregivers play an important role in creating an anti-bias environment in which children can grow and learn about their own and others' uniqueness.

The child caregiver can gain insight into diversity issues by talking with parents individually or in groups.

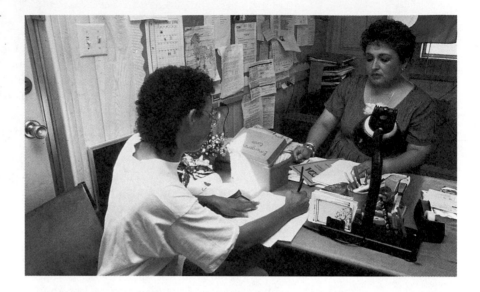

This approach should cover more than just how different cultures celebrate holidays or the foods they eat. A caregiver who is trying to understand diversity should learn how families behave on an ongoing and every day basis (see Table 14.2). Values and beliefs regarding items such as family

TABLE **14.2**

Techniques for Understanding Diversity

- ■ Develop a dialogue with parents about their own cultures. Invite them to share their culture with others in child care. This might include having them help plan curriculum and participate in activities.

- ■ If language barriers exist, try to find someone who can help translate and break down any barriers to caregiver-parent communication.

- ■ Have family evening potlucks where families bring dishes representing their backgrounds and share some of their histories with other families.

- ■ Research games, songs, and so forth, from other cultures in books on child care curriculum and histories. If there are children in care who have disabilities, this can also be researched.

- ■ Attend cultural fairs to get a greater understanding about the cultures represented in the child care.

- ■ Create a support group with other caregivers. This collaborative effort can share information, resources, and open discussion. This is a good way to remove barriers that the caregiver may have.

- ■ Observe children who are from diverse cultures, socioeconomic levels, or who may be disabled. Watch the child with the parents and family members.

- ■ Talk to others in the community who represent the diverse group to find out about the group.

- ■ In larger child care situations, encourage the hiring of diverse staff.

roles, child-rearing practices, gender differences, and communication are reflected in how families live their lives on a daily basis (Ahmann, 1994).

Personal Interactions

Personal interactions are the best way to adapt to the issues of cultural diversity (Smith, 1992). As diversity is explored and understood it allows the caregiver to be more able to communicate, be more sensitive, and be more willing to change and adapt.

Differences in backgrounds may elicit necessary responses in order to maintain the health, safety, and nutritional well-being of the children in care. Parents develop their philosophy of how to parent based on their own culture, socioeconomic background, personality, and family experiences.

An understanding of different cultural backgrounds provides a deeper understanding of parenting strategies. Socioeconomic differences are also an important factor.

Recent studies have shown that even though parents may come from diverse cultural backgrounds, it is the socioeconomic level that most greatly affects parenting styles (Julian, McKenry, & McKelvey, 1994; Brooks, 1991). These and other studies have found that there were few differences in parenting based on culture alone. Low income status may bring with it emotional stress and decreased abilities of parents and families to provide the necessary support for the children. Social conditions such as large households, lack of access to health care, and unemployment were found to have an effect on the health of children of Mexican immigrants (Guendelman, English, & Chavez, 1995).

As the caregiver realizes that families are more alike than different, it breaks down further barriers to providing care. The effects of low income may be more easily understood than a cultural difference. As the child caregiver recognizes the similarities to families of other cultures, the ability to discern differences may increase.

Understanding Family Actions

Acculturated
adopting attitudes and beliefs

There may be cultural differences that account for the actions of families. These are most likely to occur in families who are less **acculturated** to the social values commonly accepted by American society. Families who perceived difficulties in adapting to the patterns of social integration were more likely to place greater demands on children and were found to practice more strict control over them (Julian, McKenry, & McKelvey, 1994). The families that operate from the viewpoint of their own culture alone are more likely to have bicultural conflicts. These conflicts may include how children are expected to behave, how health is perceived, whether or not safety is seen as an issue, and how children are fed.

Diversity can be incorporated into any type of activity simply by presenting different types of people, food, or landscapes that encourage discussion of those differences.

Integrating Diversity into Child Care

The best way to manage diversity is on an ongoing basis. The child caregiver should continually interact with children and other adults with diversity in mind. The child care environment should integrate diversity into all aspects of providing for the health, safety, and nutrition of children. Children who learn about diversity in a positive manner are more likely not to develop any biases as adults (Derman-Sparks, 1993, 1995). Children learn from what the people around them think, say, and do. Table 14.3 offers some suggestions to help integrate diversity into the curriculum for health, safety, and nutrition.

TABLE **14.3**

Activities That Integrate Diversity

■ Provide materials that depict diverse images. This might include pictures on the walls of children from all backgrounds, toys that are nonsexist, and dolls that are anatomically correct.

■ Include staff from diverse backgrounds at all levels of responsibility.

■ Encourage participation by community helpers from diverse backgrounds for special circle times or programs that deal with health, safety, and nutritional issues. A visiting nurse may be Filipino, a police officer may be African American, and a dietician may be a male in a wheelchair.

■ Initiate activities that help provide self-esteem and well-being of mental health. Help the children learn to value the differences and similarities among themselves. This will help break down stereotypical viewpoints that may impair how a child feels about himself and others.

■ Respond positively to children's questions about issues concerning diversity. A child who asks about a disabled person should be answered instead of having the question ignored or sidestepped. What is not discussed becomes the foundation for bias. These are times for the teachable moment.

■ Provide books and opportunities for storytelling that reflect many issues of diversity.

KEY MANAGING DIVERSITY

CONCEPT

A child caregiver needs to manage diversity on an ongoing basis. Children in care represent a wide array of different family structures, ethnic and cultural backgrounds, and experiences. The child caregiver who employs techniques that help understand diversity is better prepared to interact with children and their parents. This is essential for the caregiver who wants to offer an environment that provides the best in health, safety, and nutrition for the child. The caregiver can initiate activities that promote the integration of diversity into the child care environment.

ACCESSING COMMUNITY RESOURCES

The child caregiver may need to access a host of resources to help in meeting the health, safety, and nutritional needs of the children in care. The number of resources available may depend on the type of community where the care is provided.

Surveying the Community for Resources

Larger urban communities such as major cities are more likely to have a number of resources that the caregiver may access. Smaller urban or suburban communities may offer a more limited number of resources, while rural communities may have even fewer. This is only one determining factor. The caregiver will have to attempt access to resources to determine the number available in the local community.

Another factor is the degree of commitment that the local governments have to the well-being of children. Some cities, counties, and states have a higher degree of commitment and therefore have more resources available for the caregiver. An example would be those cities that have a child care specialist on staff to help the area organize for child care. However, other states and counties and cities may have less commitment or fewer resources themselves that limits the information that they might otherwise provide.

Many states, counties, and cities have community child care resource and referral agencies. These agencies provide the much needed information that the child caregiver should attempt to access.

Child care resource and referral agencies are a good source for parents to find quality, licensed childcare that meets their individual needs.

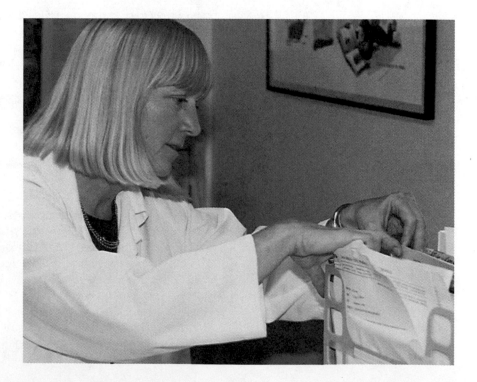

REALITY CHECK

Bananas—A Few People Can Make a Difference

In 1973 in Berkeley, California, three women organized a support group for other mothers who did not have extended families in their area. Originally, they wanted to exchange care, information, form a play group, and relate their childrearing concerns. They called themselves "Bananas," which referred to how they were feeling as well as what was present in their lives at this point—children who were at the banana eating and squishing stage. They felt that this name would make them more accessible and would be easy to remember. Some mothers in the group were looking for nonparental child care so they could work outside the home. At about the same time, the state government was wondering if public monies for child care was really necessary. These women were afraid that the already scarce care available would become nonexistent, so they became politically active. They organized a survey and found that money for care was needed, especially for the care of infants. These women began a campaign to change the situation. They motivated legislators to introduce and pass the legislation that created the first resource and referral network in the nation.

Bananas found themselves in business as they became the first resource and referral agency in the country. They worked as volunteers for the first year or so and later found that there was enough money coming in that there could be some paid positions. They began offering caregiver workshops, classes, and organizing support groups for parents and caregivers.

Today, Bananas has evolved into one of the most effective linkages in the nation. They employ a staff of twenty-six people, with volunteers still donating their time and effort. Their mission is to help parents in any way that they can. They help find child care of all types. From experience in their area, they know that the preferred care for infants is an in-home caregiver who is shared by two families. They help create these family-family links through interviews and questionnaires. Bananas also helps families access needed resources and gives workshops for parents.

For fifteen years they employed a nurse to handle health and safety issues. She not only interacted with the parents, but also created informational handouts on health and safety issues. Bananas entered new territory when an out-of-state move turned one woman from an employee to a health consultant who writes a column for their newsletter.

Bananas offers caregivers a place where they can link with families that need care, find information they need, and participate in caregiver training workshops. Bananas offers classes and workshops on site and they have created a linkage with the Peralta Community College District. They teach classes at Merritt College and the college gives credit for some of the classes held at Bananas.

Bananas is still actively involved in affecting legislation. One of its major achievements is the creation of TRUSTLINE, an 800 hot line number for parents to check the backgrounds of license exempt caregivers, such as nannies. This hot line has found a number of individuals with criminal backgrounds or who have been registered as sex offenders and are trying to care for children.

Bananas has formed another organization that shares their space, and deals with children with special needs. This organization offers services to families, caregivers, and children. It organizes teams that include the family, the caregiver, and health and nutritional professionals, and offers support and access to resources and referrals.

None of the original founders of Bananas remain involved. Arlyce Curry joined Bananas when it was six months old and at the volunteer stage. For many years she has led Bananas to bigger and greater goals. Bananas is a shining example of what a few people can do to make a difference in the care of children.

A parent bulletin board is an excellent way to provide parents with information on different types of resource and support organizations in the community.

The federal government provides many resources that the caregiver can access. Government agencies such as the U.S. Department of Health and Human Services and the U.S. Department of Agriculture provide a great deal of information to promote health, safety, and nutrition. The information is readily available to all consumers and is easy to access through mail or the Internet. Some information may be available locally at government offices or through local programs such as the Women, Infants, and Children program (WIC) and Head Start.

Many national organizations have offices that provide information to promote the health and well-being of children. All the organizations have a national office and some have state and local affiliates that provide easier access to information. Examples of these are the American Red Cross and the American Cancer Society.

Colleges and universities are resources for information. The departments most likely to have important information are child development, nutrition, human services, family studies, nursing, and schools of medicine. Both public and private institutions of higher learning are usually happy to share their information. Some might even be willing to share expertise, if time permits. Many child care health consultants come from this resource. Some universities offer extension services that are excellent sources of all types of information concerning children, families, nutrition, and health. Pennsylvania State University and Iowa State University are good examples of this type of support.

Hospitals, clinics and health centers, and poison control centers may also be good resources. They may have information readily available that concerns the health, safety, and well-being of children. These types of facilities may also offer speakers for specific information such as immunizations. These speakers can be utilized for special topic programs that the caregiver may provide for the families. These people are also likely resources for seeking a health consultant for the child care environment.

Many common local resources exist for caregivers regardless of their location. These resources are included in Table 14.4.

TABLE **14.4**

Common Local Resources for Health, Safety, or Nutritional Information or Assistance

- Department of Public Health
- Hospitals, children's hospitals
- Health centers and clinics
- Fire and police departments
- Child care licensing/foster care licensing
- Child care resource and referral agencies
- Children's protective services
- Gas and electric companies
- Colleges and universities
- Medical societies (e.g., American Academy of Pediatrics)
- Local chapters of national organizations such as American Red Cross, American Dietetic Association, Girl Scouts, American Cancer Society, American Heart Association, and the March of Dimes
- Poison control centers
- Libraries
- Head Start
- Department of Social Services
- Dental societies
- Family day dare associations
- State and local affiliates of the National Association for the Education of Young Children (NAEYC)
- Schools and school districts (for screening, school nurses, and special education resources)
- Humane societies
- County extension services
- WIC
- Visiting Nurses Associations
- Department of Parks and Recreation
- Pharmacies and pharmacists
- Department of Environmental Protection
- Associations for cultural and ethnic affiliations

Prominent health organizations recommend that child caregivers create a community resource file that includes written information on different topics dealing with health, safety, and nutrition.

Organizing and Using the Resources

It is vitally important that the child caregiver have resources organized should need for access occur. The American Public Health Association and the American Academy of Pediatrics recommend that a child caregiver create a community resource file that includes written information on a number of topics dealing with health, safety, and nutrition. These resources are for the caregiver and the parents of children in care. If the information is available in the parent's native language, it should be provided or as an alternative, a translator should be used, whenever possible. These organizations also recommend that the child caregiver use consultants from local available resources. Consultants might include people from the fields of health care, nutrition, safety, mental health, or child abuse prevention. Since the child caregiver's time is often taken up with the business of care, the consultants can offer the caregiver an invaluable service.

KEY ACCESSING COMMUNITY RESOURCES

CONCEPT

Access to community resources is very important for the child caregiver. The caregiver should be prepared with a number of local resources for the health, safety, and nutritional well-being of the children in care. These resources include written information and people who might consult. Resources should be surveyed and organized so the caregiver is prepared to use them if the need arises.

Advocate
to support or speak on behalf of another

DEVELOPING EFFECTIVE ADVOCACY

The majority of people who become child caregivers do so because of care and concern for children and their welfare. Regardless of the type of child care the caregiver is supplying, opportunity may present itself to **advocate** on behalf of a child. It is an inherent part of the job of a caregiver to make sure the children in care are supported for the optimum health, safety, and well-being. This may require the caregiver to talk to parents, health professionals, and other sources of community resource and support.

For the Child Care Center

Center-based care may already anticipate this need. It may even be part of a director's job description. Teachers in center care may need to advocate to the director about problems or issues about children or the environment of care. In turn, directors may represent the child care to the parents and others. Directors should be prepared for this through their education, training, and experience. They should help the teachers in their facilities to learn to

Child caregivers by nature of their profession also become child advocates to make sure that children in care are supported for the optimum health, safety, and well-being.

do the same. Staff meetings, daily consultation, and mentoring will help teachers learn to best represent the children in care. Education and training will provide added support for teachers.

For the Family Child Caregiver

New family child caregivers may not anticipate the need to intercede on behalf of a child. Veteran family child caregivers will report a great deal

Family caregivers can benefit from contact with other family caregivers. This promotes the sharing of information and support that are inherent in a center.

Nannies may find themselves in the awkward position of not being able to communicate effectively with parents about the child because of employer-employee relationship. Nanny support groups are a good way for nannies to get together and share solutions to these and other common problems.

of advocacy on behalf of the children in care. Approaching parents is usually the first line of communication. However, community resources and support may be necessary to help the caregiver approach a situation with the parents.

Support from others in the same profession might prove to be very valuable to the family day caregiver. National organizations have local chapters that may provide this support. Local child care resource and referrals may also help the family caregiver to find others to share concerns and solutions. Local licensing may also be a source of connecting with other family day caregivers. Education and training facilities are also a source of support and learning to advocate on behalf of children.

For the Nanny

The in-home care provided for by a nanny may appear to be an ideal caregiving situation. With lower caregiver-child ratio one might think there are few problems. Very few people performing the job of a nanny are trained and may be surprised to find difficulties are present here too. Two issues raised by many nannies are home safety and nutritional needs. The families that employ nannies are not always aware of what is safe or healthy for children. It may be awkward for the nanny to approach the family because of the employer-employee relationship. Nannies need to understand the importance of advocacy for the children in care. Community resources and support can provide the foundations needed.

Nanny support groups are good sources of resources and solutions for advocacy. Local placement agencies may know of support groups in the area. Placing an ad in the local family press or newspaper to start a nanny support group has been effective in many parts of this country and in

The American Public Health Association and American Academy of Pediatrics recommends that child care centers designate a "health advocate" to receive additional training in the areas of health, safety, and nutrition.

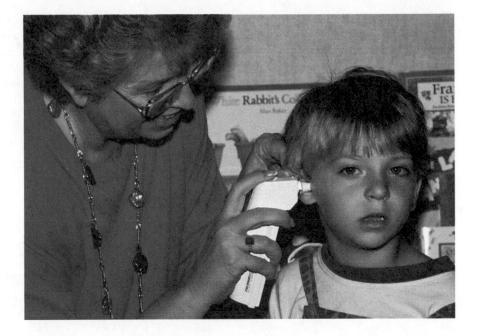

Canada. A national organization, NANI, may provide other nanny solutions and help the nanny learn to advocate for the children.

The Health Advocate

The American Public Health Association and the American Academy of Pediatrics would like to see health advocacy in child care taken one step further. They recommend that child care facilities or large family child care homes should have one person who is designated as the health advocate. In most cases this would be an assigned caregiver. This designated caregiver would receive more training in issues concerning health, safety, and nutrition. In cases of small family child care homes and in-home caregivers, the health advocate is usually the caregiver. The designated health advocate could also be an outside community resource such as a health professional who is in the facility on a frequent basis and knows the children well.

Leadership

Leadership may go beyond advocating for the children in care to the parents and others. Some issues may be of real concern and the caregiver may want to pursue the issue at another level. This may be involvement to make changes at the local level or even more sweeping changes at the state or national level.

Grassroots advocacy or leadership begins at the local level. Local affiliates of national organizations that represent child care or children may be a good starting point. The national office can provide the local contact. Some cities and counties have a child care coordinator. This office may be able to provide good information and may be willing to help change local ordinances, laws, and other matters affecting the care of children.

Another source of help, support, and need for change may be the local health department. Other local places of support for advocacy may be children's hospitals, school districts, and medical societies.

Some states and local areas have child law advocacy groups, and some have a child care lobbyist who may provide valuable information and assistance. These can be found by contacting the local or statewide legal societies.

The caregiver may have to take a greater leadership role if the preceding support for advocacy is not available. Pursuing the issue may call for directly working with townships, city councils, county board of supervisors, or aldermen. If the issue goes beyond local assistance, the caregiver may need to contact state legislators, the governor, the house representative or senators who represent the area in state or national matters.

Whatever the reason for advocacy or leadership, many caregivers feel it is their responsibility to go beyond just providing daily care. The issues involved in health, safety, and nutrition for children have a tremendous impact on the well-being of children and their future.

KEY ADVOCACY FOR CHILDREN

CONCEPT

Caregivers may need to advocate for the children in care on issues concerning health, safety, and nutrition. The caregiver can do this in all areas of child care. Child care centers, family child care homes, and nannies may all need advocacy at a point in time. The advocacy contact may be with parents, community resources, or other sources of support. Some issues may cause the caregiver to seek local, state, or national assistance to make changes.

CREATING A TEAM APPROACH

Although the caregiver might want to be able to provide everything the children and their families need, no one caregiver is prepared to do it all. The best answer to providing the maximum protection and prevention for health, safety, and nutritional issues is to work as a part of a team.

The Team Members

The team includes the caregiver, the family, and the community resources and services (see Figure 14.2).

As a team member, the caregiver represents the issues dealing with health, safety, and nutrition that concern child care. The caregiver may have solutions to some of these issues. It is important for the caregiver to determine the areas in which she is well-informed, has had experience, and has

FIGURE **14.2**
The Team Approach to
Childcare

Periodic measurements of a child's height is one example of the type of information that might go in a child's health, safety, and nutrition file.

received specialized training. This will allow the caregiver to form the base from which to seek help from outside sources.

Creating a file of health, safety, and nutritional information will allow the caregiver to have a great deal of necessary information available as it is needed. Keeping a current list of community resources will also help the caregiver function as a team member. Networking with other child caregivers will also help provide information.

The health records, daily observation, and assessments of a child will help the caregiver establish whether the child has an issue or problem that may affect the child's health or well-being. If a problem does exist and the parent denies it, then creating a team may be more difficult. Issues or problems that affect the health, safety, or nutrition of a child should not be ignored. The sooner a problem or issue is identified and dealt with, the greater the opportunity for preventing the problem from having a lifelong effect. Parents want to be able to feel a sense of control. If the issue is approached in a manner where assistance to empower the parent is offered, the parent may be more responsive to intervention.

Providing an Atmosphere for Teamwork

The caregiver can provide an atmosphere for teamwork that will encourage the parents to participate. Responsiveness to parental concerns, trust, modeling respect, and good communication skills provide the basis for a parent-caregiver relationship. Parents appreciate warmth, positive attitudes, and accessibility of the caregiver. When this type of climate is available to parents they are more likely to participate (Comer & Haynes, 1991).

Schwick (1992) noted that particular strategies are helpful to creating the family-school team. The needs and interests of the parents are important. These may be examined through surveys, conferences, parent information centers, parental involvement in the program, and home visits.

The caregiver should survey the parents and other adults in the child care environment on a regular basis to find out where help is needed on issues concerning health, safety, and nutrition of the children. Parents often respond to the call for information solicited from the caregiver. The survey might form the basis of special topics for newsletters, parent handouts, speakers, videos, or even field trips including both parents and children.

The survey could begin a dialogue between a parent and the caregiver relating to a specific issue with a child. Caregiver and parent conferences may help to continue this dialogue. Parents may recognize a problem but may be unwilling to admit that it exists if the caregiver approaches them first. Asking the parents for input may put the parent at ease and may help the parent to acknowledge the problem. If this approach does not work, soliciting the help of a community resource may be necessary.

Annie was a family child caregiver who was very organized and really tried to help the parents of the children in her care. She printed a weekly newsletter telling parents what the children did that week and reminding them of future events. She included any new health, safety, or nutrition information she received from the local agencies that she was linked to.

One day, a mother came to her, worried and stressed. Lisa, a first generation Vietnamese American, was concerned that her extended family wanted to "coin" her son Vu when he was sick. Coining involves placing a hot coin on the child's neck that causes red streaks in this area. Normally, Lisa would have gone along with tradition, but she had read in the paper that this practice was dangerous. She wanted Annie to help her with this problem. Annie called several local health care agencies and confirmed that "coining" was indeed dangerous. The agencies mailed information to her that she gave to Lisa. Lisa was able to go to her family and tell them that although she appreciated their traditions, she could not allow her son to be put in danger with that particular tradition. She told them whenever Vu was ill, she would take him to the physician for care.

Parents may also feel the need for specific help dealing with parenting issues that could affect the health and well-being of children. Posting a list of topics to be considered may help parents decide which issues are more pressing to them, so they can request information. Creating a parent center, even if it is just a tabletop or rack for providing information may help engage the parent in a mutual effort. A parent who is used to accessing information may be better prepared to participate as a team member. If there are a significant number of non-English speaking families in care, the caregiver should attempt to provide information in the language of the family. Community support may be needed to accomplish this.

Home visits allow the caregiver to view the child in a more holistic manner, with all the environments considered. Some parents and families are more than happy to encourage the caregiver to visit their homes, but this may not be possible due to time constraints. However, if an issue is creating difficulties, a home visit may provide a better picture or elicit more cooperation from the parents involved. A home visit should be handled carefully and it might be a good idea to consult with community resource professionals before visiting the family. Some families may refuse to participate in this strategy. The in-home caregiver may have an advantage in creating a partnership based on this aspect, because the care is provided in the family's own home and the caregiver is privy to most of what is occurring.

Providing Linkages to the Community

All of the strategies used to create a parent/caregiver network may also help to promote the partnership of the third party, the community resource. Caregivers should have access to a number of people who are resources for community support. These people may include health professionals, nutritionists, and those employed in safety professions such as police and firemen. Social workers, occupational therapists, family counselors, speech therapists, and child abuse prevention specialists are all good sources of community support. Team members may also be secured from organizations such as the American Red Cross, Head Start, community health services, resource and referral agencies, and special interest groups like the March of Dimes.

The "team" of childcare provider/worker and parent can also be expanded to include a resource and referral worker.

Prevention is one of the primary goals of the caregiver to protect the children's health, safety, and well-being. Providing linkages for families to many of the community resources can help prevent problems concerning these issues. These linkages may occur by simply providing brochures and access information, and can occur by inviting these community resources to speak at special programs the caregiver provides for parents. Linkages may also occur through referrals to specific professionals to provide extra help or care to children who may need it. A parent must participate for this linkage to be successful.

KEY CREATING A TEAM

CONCEPT

Child caregivers need the help of parents and community resources in order to provide the optimum environment for good health, safety, and nutrition for children. Providing an atmosphere for teamwork can engage parents and create a linkage between the child care environment and the home environment. Providing families a linkage to community resources can help the caregiver to create a team that will help protect and provide the best for the children's health, safety, and well-being in and out of the child care environment.

CHAPTER **SUMMARY**

A child caregiver should provide an environment that meets the health, safety, and nutritional needs for the children while in care. Communication with the families of the children is vitally important and should be a priority.

The caregiver should access and use community resources that will help provide a greater degree of health and well-being for the child. The child caregiver should manage diversity on an ongoing basis. Children in care represent a wide array of different family structures, ethnic and cultural backgrounds, and experiences. The caregiver can initiate activities that promote the integration of diversity into the child care environment.

Caregivers may need to advocate for the children in care on issues concerning health, safety, and nutrition. Child caregivers need the help of parents and community resources in order to provide the optimum environment for good health, safety, and nutrition for children.

TO GO **BEYOND**

Questions for Review

1. Discuss the importance of communication in the child care environment.

2. How does diversity impact child care? What steps should a caregiver take to manage diversity?

3. How would you go about accessing resources in your local community?

AS AN **INDIVIDUAL**

1. List the resources in your area. Which ones might a caregiver utilize?

2. Survey the community for culturally diverse health and safety practices. Make a list and share with the group.

AS A **GROUP**

1. Working in groups of four or five, create a list of resources for a child caregiver that is a compilation of what the individuals collected. Do any of these deal with diversity or advocacy?

2. These same groups will work together to create a team of caregivers, parents, and resources. Role-play these different roles.

CHAPTER **REFERENCES**

Ahmann, E. (1994). "Chunky stew": Appreciating cultural diversity while providing health care for children. *Pediatric Nursing, 20*(3), 320–324.

American Public Health Association (APHA), & American Academy of Pediatrics (AAP). (1992). *Caring for our children: National health and safety performance standards: Guidelines for out-of-home child care programs.* Washington, DC: APHA.

Bloom, P. (1994). Building a sense of community: A broader view. *Childcare Information Exchange, 101,* 47–50.

Carter, M. (1996). Building community in cross cultural work environments. *Child Care Information Exchange, 107,* 74–75.

Comer, J., & Haynes, M. (1991). Parent involvement in schools: An ecological approach. *Elementary School Journal, 91,* 271–278.

Derman-Sparks, L. (1993). Empowering children to create a caring culture in a world of differences. *Childhood Education, 70*(2), 66–71.

Derman-Sparks, L. (1995, November/December). Children and diversity. *Scholastic Early Childhood Today,* 42–45.

Gonzalez-Mena, J. (1997). *Multicultural Issues in Child Care.* Menlo Park, CA: Mayfield Publishing.

Guendelman S., English, P., & Chavez, G. (1995). Infants of Mexican immigrants: Health status of an emerging population. *Med Care, 33*(1), 41–52.

Herr, J. (1991). Child care providers and parents: Let's work together for America's young children. *Personnel, 68*(9), 15.

Julian, T., McKenry, P., & McKelvey, M. (1994). Cultural variations in parenting: Perceptions of Caucasian, African-American, Hispanic-American and Asian-American families. *Family Relations, 43*(1), 30–38.

Loeb, P., Friedman, D., Lord, M., Guttman, M., Kukula, G. (1993, October 4). To make a nation: How immigrants are changing America for better or worse. *U.S. News and World Report,* 47–52.

O'Hare, W. (1992). America's minorities: The demographics of diversity. *Population Bulletin, 47*(4), 82–125.

Schwick, K. (1992). *Teacher parent partnerships.* [ERIC Digest]. Champaign, IL: Eric Clearinghouse for Elementary and Early Childhood Education.

Smith, D. (1992). Changing U.S. demographics: Implications for professional preparation. *Journal of Home Economics, 84*(1), 19–23.

Whitebook, M. (1994). Finding the support you need. *Scholastic Early Childhood Today, 8,* 14–15.

SUGGESTIONS **FOR READING**

Allen, J., McNeill, E., & Schmidt, V. (1992). *Cultural awareness for children.* Menlo Park, CA: Addison-Wesley.

Bassett, M. M. (1998). *The professional nanny.* Albany, NY: Delmar Publishers.

Brand, S. (1996). Making parent involvement a reality: Helping teachers develop partnerships with parents. *Young Children, 51*(1), 76–81.

Carter, M. (1996, July). Communicating with parents. *Child Care Information Exchange,* 80–83.

Copeland, M., & McCreedy, B. (1997). Creating family friendly policies. *Child Care Information Exchange, 113,* 7–12.

Copeland, T. (1997). How to help your staff cope with conflict—Using the three choice model. *Child Care Information Exchange, 113,* 83–84.

Derman-Sparks, L., Gutierrez, M., & Phillips, C. (1990). *Teaching young children to resist bias: What parents can do.* [Brochure]. Washington, DC: NAEYC.

Fuchs, V. (1991). Are Americans underinvesting in their children? *Society, 26*(8), 14–22.

Gonzalez-Mena (1996, March). When values collide. *Child Care Information Exchange, 108,* 30–32.

Hohensee, J., & Derman-Sparks, L. (1992). *Implementing an anti-bias curriculum in early childhood classrooms.* [ERIC Digest]. Champaign, IL: Eric Clearinghouse on Elementary and Early Childhood Education.

Kellaghan, R. (Ed.) (1993). *The home environment and school learning: Promoting parent involvement in the education of children.* New York: MacMillan.

Knitzer, J., & Page, S. (1996). Public policy report: Young children and families: The view from the states. *Young Children, 51*(5), 51–55.

Maddux, R. (1988). *Team building: An exercise in leadership.* Los Altos, CA: Crisp.

Morrison, J., & Rodgers, L. (1996) Being responsive to the needs of children from dual heritage backgrounds. *Young Children, 51*(1), 29–33.

Pestano-Binghay, E., Reis, J., & Walthers, M. (1993). Nutrition education issues for minority parents: A needs assessment. *Journal of Nutrition Education, 25*(3), 144–146.

Sontag, D. (1993, June 29). A fervent "no" to assimilation in new American children of immigrants: Rewriting an axiom. *New York Times,* A-6,10.

Sparrow, J. (1996). Speaking parents language. *Scholoastic Early Childhood Today, 11,* 17–18.

Stanley, D. (1996). How to defuse an angry parent. *Child Care Information Exchange, 108,* 34–35.

Sturm, C. (1997). Creating a parent-teacher dialogue: Intercultural communication in child care. *Young Children, 52*(5), 34–38.

Sung, B. (1987). *Chinese immigrant children in New York City: The experience of adjustment.* New York: Center for Migration Studies.

Surr, J. (1992). Early childhood programs and the Americans with Disabilities Act. *Young Children, 47*(5), 18–21.

Vilchez, K., & Tinsley, F. (1993, March). *Latino familial childhood health socialization: Theoretical and applied issues.* Paper presented at biennial meeting of the Society for Research in Child Development, New Orleans, LA.

CHAPTER FIFTEEN

BUILDING CURRICULUM FOR SAFETY, HEALTH, AND NUTRITION

Upon completion of this chapter, including a review of the summary, you should be able to:

CURRICULUM

Describe and discuss the elements needed to design curriculum for health, safety, and nutrition.

LESSON PLANNING

Summarize the steps in planning lessons for presenting health, safety, and nutrition concepts to children.

SAMPLE LESSON PLANS FOR HEALTH, SAFETY, AND NUTRITION

Indicate an understanding of the application of concepts through lessons on health, safety, and nutrition.

Curriculum
course of study that relates to the subject being examined

CURRICULUM

Curriculum provides the mechanism for teaching children about health, safety, and nutrition. Caregivers teach children every day by role modeling behaviors and actions. However, role modeling does not provide enough information for children so that they may understand, change their actions, and practice healthy and safe behaviors. Caregivers need to use other methods to properly inform children.

Curriculum can be presented in a number of ways (see Table 15.1). Group or circle time is the perfect opportunity to introduce a subject, discuss it, and plan for further experiences. Those experiences may include field trips or having a resource person visit the child care. Social studies may apply the information to other areas. Experiences can include tapes and videos that offer either individual or group learning time. Songs may reinforce the subject. Large muscle activities and manipulative activities offer

447

opportunity for physical expression or practicing of the information. Dramatic play allows the children opportunity to act out and practice information to gain a greater understanding. Cooking experiences can help children understand nutrition, health, and safety, if properly presented.

Bulletin boards offer constant reminders of the subject being discussed. Books may deal directly with the subject or may reinforce the subject from a different direction. Stories, flannel boards, and finger plays can apply the subject information in a specific way for the children to whom it is presented. Arts, crafts, and sensory experiences may reinforce information already presented.

TABLE **15.1**

Ways to Present Curriculum

- Group or circle time
- Field trips
- Dramatic play
- Resource people visiting child care
- Social studies
- Large muscle and manipulative experiences
- Cooking
- Books
- Bulletin boards
- Sensory experiences
- Tapes
- Videos
- Stories
- Finger plays
- Arts and crafts

Curriculum Design

Curriculum must include a number of elements in order for it to be effective. It should provide a holistic approach to the subject for the children, and should also address the children with a holistic approach. The abilities of the children should be taken into consideration, which include the cognitive, physical, and social abilities. The caregiver needs to be aware of these abilities in order to begin curriculum design.

Curriculum should be developmentally appropriate. The National Association for the Education of Young Children (NAEYC) offers this information for caregivers. Sue Bredekamp (1987) edited *Developmentally Appropriate Practice in Early Childhood Programs Serving Children from Birth to Age 8*, which helps teacher understand what positive practices apply to certain age groups. Infants, toddlers, preschoolers, and school aged children have different abilities. They also have different interests that should be reflected in the curriculum. What is appropriate for a toddler may be boring to a preschooler.

Curriculum should offer children several important qualities, and should be flexible. Curriculum needs to allow for flow that may involve children's interest and attention span. Any curriculum that is used should promote positive feelings for children. It should help children to feel better about themselves. Curriculum also needs to offer children choice. If only one activity is planned and it does not interest a child, then the objective is lost for that child. If several choices are offered, one is bound to appeal to some of the children.

A variety of activities allows the children different ways to explore the subject. This may reinforce the information so that children grasp the idea that is being presented. Using different methods for presentation will also help reinforce the information. Some methods such as dramatic play and field trips allow children opportunities to explore and interact. Children may be able to retain the information better if these types of opportunities are available.

Another consideration should be the diversity of the audience. Curriculum should be **anti-bias**. Regardless of the method that the material is presented, all material should be checked for bias. The caregiver should be aware of any prejudice or limiting feelings that may prevent this from being done. Table 15.2 includes considerations when designing a curriculum.

Anti-bias

an approach to curriculum that removes all inequities due to race, gender, and abilities

TABLE **15.2**

Curriculum Design Considerations

- Is it developmentally appropriate?
- Does it provide for a holistic approach?
- Do children have choices?
- Does it promote positive feelings?
- Is it flexible?
- Can children explore and interact?
- Are there a variety of activities?
- Does it use a number of methods for presentation?
- Is the information presented in an anti-biased manner?

Designing curriculum for the child care environment is an ongoing task. For new caregivers, this may seem an overwhelming task. Some caregivers find that designing curriculum for other areas is easier or more interesting than in the subjects of health, safety, or nutrition. This chapter addresses the subjects in order to help the caregiver make this task easier.

There is a process that will help the caregiver to develop a lesson plan. First, the curriculum unit must be decided. The appropriate units that come from this text include:

Unit One—Children's Environment (Introduction)
Unit Two—Health Education (Chapters One through Four)
Unit Three—Safety Education (Chapters Five through Eight)
Unit Four—Nutrition Education (Chapters Nine through Eleven)
Unit Five—Special Topic Education (Chapters Twelve and Thirteen)

LESSON PLANNING

Lesson plans are the daily substance of curriculum. For some beginning caretakers, learning how to develop a lesson plan may help them develop an entire curriculum. Five lesson plans might equate to a week's curriculum unit on a particular subject. More experienced caregivers may design a week's curriculum first, then proceed to create lesson plans to match it. Both methods work if the information being presented is accepted and practiced by the children.

The **theme** or purpose for each lesson plan must be selected. Each unit may have a number of themes to help the caregiver address the subject. The theme should emphasize the point that is being made. The **objectives** or expected outcomes should be clearly connected to the theme. The objectives allow the caregiver a way to measure the success of the lesson.

This is time for a curriculum design check (see Table 15.2). The questions posed should be applied to the theme and the objectives. If the theme or objectives are not feasible or are not appropriate, try again.

The caregiver should select materials to use based on the theme, the developmental level of the children, and what is available. Materials may help to present the subject or reinforce what has been presented. Supportive materials may be available in the environment to emphasize and reinforce the theme.

Before the lesson plan is presented to the children, it helps to survey the children for their level of understanding on the subject. For example, hand washing is the theme and the plan is to present basic information to four year olds. The caregiver surveys the children and finds out that they all know the process. They may not be clear as to why they should wash their hands or when they should wash their hands. The caregiver may keep the theme, but may emphasize germs being the reason for hand washing and focus on the times to wash so that germs can be removed.

The caregiver also should have a tentative schedule for presenting the lesson plan. The schedule should offer a parameter for time or focus. The schedule should allow for flexibility and the teachable moment. The teachable moment occurs as a question is asked or a thought is expressed and the children are very receptive. This moment offers the caregiver the opportunity to focus on the subject in a way that is easily understood by the children.

After the lesson is presented, an evaluation process should take place. How did the children receive the information? Was it at the appropriate level for the children? Are they showing behavioral changes due to the lesson? If

Theme
subject being emphasized

Objectives
goals; expected outcomes

changes need to be made, the changes should be written down and added to the plan for future presentation.

Another part of the process of lesson planning is to pass on to the parents the relevant information that has been given to children. This could happen in several ways:

■ There may be a notice on the bulletin board about the day's events.

■ A weekly newsletter may be sent to the parents about the next week's daily schedule.

■ A parent information sheet or learning card might be handed out to the parent concerning a particular lesson.

Whatever method is used, it is important for the parents to receive the information. They can help the caregiver reinforce the lessons and perhaps change practices at home.

An example of a lesson plan follows.

LESSON PLAN	**Unit:**	**Safety**
■■	**Theme:**	Using Traffic Signs and Signals to be Safe
EXAMPLE	**Objectives:**	Children will learn how signs and signals help them to be safe.
S	**Materials:**	A standing pretend stoplight. A flannel board and flannel cutouts. A hand-held stop sign. A whistle. A bulletin board about traffic safety. Block area set up for street, street signs, and cars.
	Lesson:	Tell a flannel board story about Bobby and the traffic signs to children in group time. Ask children when they see these signs in their environment.

Lesson:

Practice what red lights, green lights, and yellow lights mean, using the standing stoplight. Repeat several times. Show the stop sign and ask them what it means. Demonstrate the whistle and talk about traffic guards and how they help children. Ask the children what signs are around when they cross the street. Talk about crossing safety.

■ Always cross the street in a crosswalk.

■ Stay on the curb and look both ways.

■ When there is no traffic or the traffic is stopped, it is safe to cross.

■ Look both ways again and then cross.

Discuss how this would be different in the case of a stoplight. Practice traffic light crossing safety by playing "Red Light, Green Light" for several minutes to reinforce the idea.

Follow-Up: Have traffic lines drawn outside on playground surface. Take out the traffic signal and traffic sign. Children can get on trikes and wagons and practice traffic safety. Whistles are available for guiding traffic. A handout to parents requesting they practice the traffic safety procedures that are included.

Age-Appropriate: This may be presented to mixed age or preschoolers only. Toddlers may not grasp idea by themselves, but may model behaviors of older children.

SAMPLE LESSON PLANS FOR HEALTH, SAFETY, AND NUTRITION

Sample lesson plans for every chapter of this text are provided for the caregiver to help reinforce the information that is being learned. In addition to the information provided, there is a list of resources available at the conclusion of this chapter. These resources include children's books and sources for further help. For example, there are a number of songs or finger plays that can be looked up in the Suggested Readings section. For that reason, we will not include many of these in the lesson plans. Caregivers can help design their own curriculum by adding to the lesson plans provided.

Unit: **Children's Environment**

Suggested Themes: My Neighborhood, My Family, Where Do You Live?

Theme: Where Do You Live?

Objectives: Helping children become familiar with their physical environment.

Materials: Books about different lifestyles; living in the country, the city, and the suburbs. Dramatic play materials to play house or farm. Bulletin board with pictures depicting different lifestyles. Magazines for children to cut out pictures.

Lesson: Talk about different lifestyles and read book *A Crack in the Wall.* Discuss how the boy who lived in the city brought happiness to his environment by changing how he viewed the crack in the wall. Talk about what life is or might be like to live in a city. Ask how living in the country would be different.

Follow-Up: Provide dress-up materials for playing house in the city or the country. Have children cut out pictures of houses, apartments, and so forth, in cities and in the country. Have them circle those places that represent their own lifestyles. Put a note on bulletin board about what was discussed today. Read *Come Home With Us* later in the day. Talk about how people in different places in the city live. Discuss different ways families do things. Compare differences and similarities.

Age-Appropriate: Preschoolers.

LESSON PLAN

CHAPTER I

Unit: Health

Suggested Themes: My Family, Myself, Being a Friend, Showing and Sharing My Feelings.

Theme: Showing and Sharing My Feelings.

Objectives: Children will develop an understanding of the feelings they experience. They will learn ways to express their feelings.

Materials: Marking pens and paper. Books. Magazines. Finger paints and paper. Paints and paper. Play dough. Cut out cardstock circles 3 to 4 inches in diameter.

Lesson: Talk with children about feelings. Read book *Feelings Inside and Outloud Too!* Discuss book. Have children practice feelings on their faces as you read the book. Talk about ways to verbalize feelings like singing, yelling, and so forth.

Talk about positive ways that children might express anger (punching bag, play dough, painting, and so forth). Talk about inappropriate ways to express emotions (biting, kicking, hitting, and so forth). Show pictures from magazines or books and have children identify feelings. Let children have free time to express a feeling they have had. This can be done by drawing a happy picture, drawing or painting faces to match moods, picking out a magazine picture, or making a finger paint to match a mood. Some children may have difficulty with this concept, while others will easily be able to do it.

Follow-Up: Provide more books on feelings for children to read. When reading any book and a feeling is shown, note that feeling and the expression or ask children to tell you what it is. Have materials available for children to make a mobile with circles that they can draw or cut out faces with feelings that express a range of emotions. Learning card given to parents to explain the importance of encouraging children to express their feelings in socially accepted ways.

Age-Appropriate: Preschoolers. If handled correctly even toddlers can benefit.

Unit:	**Health**
Suggested Themes:	Hearing, Smelling, Seeing, Tasting, Doctor Check-ups, A Visit to the Dentist, My Body and Its Parts, How Tall Am I and What Do I Weigh?
Theme:	A Visit to the Dentist.
Objectives:	Children should understand the importance of healthy teeth and who can help them keep healthy.
Materials:	A new toothbrush for each child (supplied by dentist). Clothing for the dramatic play area to emulate dentist uniform. Books. Bulletin board on dental health.
Lesson:	Have a dentist come visit children. A toothbrush is given to teach child. Dentist explains how to brush teeth. Children do a "dry" run with toothbrushes. Dentist talks about what he/she does when children visit. After dentist leaves, children brush teeth with water in bathroom. Reinforce proper tooth brushing techniques. Put each toothbrush in baggy and place in each child's cubby.
Follow-Up:	Read *Doctor De Soto* about a mouse who is the dentist to a number of different animals. Talk about how different the teeth are. Talk about how they would brush teeth. Discuss other ways to help keep teeth healthy such as good diet. Watch dramatic play for reinforcement. Give parents information sheet provided by dentist or create one on proper brushing. Play the song "Brush Your Teeth" by Raffi.
Age-Appropriate:	Toddlers and preschoolers.

LESSON PLAN

CHAPTER 3

Unit:	Health
Suggested Themes:	What is a Germ? Wash Those Germs Right Off of Your Hands! Keeping Food Safe. What Is an Immunization?
Theme:	Wash Those Germs Right Off of Your Hands!
Objectives:	Children should know how and when to wash their hands.
Materials:	Plaster of Paris. Magazines. Books. Sink, liquid soap. Bulletin board on hand washing procedures with pictures of when to wash.
Lesson:	In circle or group time. Discuss germs. Read *Germs Make Me Sick!* Discuss the importance of hand washing and the occasions that hands should be washed. Demonstrate how to wash hands. Have children show you how to wash hands. Move into bathroom area with sinks. Show children how you wash your hands. Sing "This is the Way We Wash our Hands" (All Around the Mulberry Bush tune) as children show the caregiver how hands should be washed. Correct if needed. Query as to when hands should be washed.
Follow-Up:	Make plaster of Paris hand prints for children to take home. Wash hands at appropriate times. Have children wash hands at appropriate times. Do several finger plays including "My Hands" (Herr, J. & Libby, Y. 1995). This makes children more aware of their hands. See if they can add a line to the finger play that indicates hand washing and the importance of it. Hand out parent information sheet or learning card so parents are aware of correct procedures and times for children to wash their hands.
Age-Appropriate:	Toddlers and preschoolers. Toddlers may not understand but they are sensory and will wash hands properly with encouragement and reinforcement.

Unit:	**Health**
Suggested Themes:	Keeping My Body Healthy, Getting Enough Sleep, Taking Care of Myself When I Am Sick, How Do I Feel?
Theme:	Taking Care of Myself When I Am Sick.
Objectives:	Children should be able to help themselves get well.
Materials:	Blankets and pillows, doctor kit, and so forth, for dramatic play area. Books. Paints, pens, and paper.
Lesson:	Have a nurse visit to explain what a child needs when she is sick. Talk about rest, drinking liquids, and taking the medicines the doctor gives. Discuss ways to rest, what drinks might be appealing, and how you never take medicine unless the doctor says you should. Also talk about preventing other people from getting sick by washing hands, not sharing cups.
Follow-Up:	Read *Sick in Bed*. Let children play patient and nurse or doctor. Have children draw picture of things they could do for themselves to make them well. Put a note on the bulletin board to parents on what was discussed today.
Age-Appropriate:	Preschoolers.

LESSON PLAN

CHAPTER 5

S

Unit:	Safety
Suggested Themes:	Injury Prevention, Practicing Safe Behaviors, Hazards in My Environment.
Theme:	Practicing Safe Behaviors.
Objectives:	Children should be able to understand and practice safe behaviors.
Materials:	Books. Pictures from magazines. Paper in the shape of a badge and crayons. Police officer badges and hats. Stop sign, stop light. Box of items to sort for safety.
Lesson:	Talk about safe behaviors to practice on a daily basis like crossing the street, staying away from medicines or poisons, using seat belts, staying away from strangers, not playing with matches or guns, and so forth. Talk about people who help keep us safe, like police officers, firefighters, and so on. Have a box of items. Show them one at a time and have children sort those items that promote safety, such as a stop sign, from those that may cause problems, such as a cigarette lighter. Sort them into two boxes. Talk about things that may keep young children safe in child care. Take a safety walk around the indoor and outdoor environment. Point out the things that help keep the children safe.
Follow-Up:	Have safety books available in the library. Read *Dinosaurs Beware: A Safety Guide*. Observe dramatic area for play with props such as police badges, uniforms. Offer badge shaped paper to color on. Hand out parent information sheet about safe practices.
Age-Appropriate:	Preschoolers.

Unit:	**Safety**
Suggested Themes:	Fire Safety/Stop, Drop, and Roll, Poison Safety, Indoor Water Safety, Toy Safety, Electrical Safety.
Theme:	Fire Safety.
Objectives:	Children should be able to protect themselves by understanding fire safety and fire safety strategies.
Materials:	Fire hats, uniforms, and other props for dramatic play area. Books. Cut shapes of a smoke alarm to color. Bulletin board featuring STOP! DROP! and ROLL!
Lesson:	Visit a fire station or fire house. A firefighter will show a uniform, including full gear. Talk about how important it is to listen to firefighters if they are trying to rescue us. Have a firefighter show the fire engine and other equipment and how it works. If the children are not allowed in the fire station, have the firefighter come to you. This varies from area to area.
	Have a firefighter demonstrate stop, drop, and roll. If possible, have children practice now. Otherwise, practice when children have returned to care.
Follow-Up:	A great number of books available in library. Read *Fire Diary*. Observe dramatic play area for firefighter/fire station play. Talk about safe behaviors that help support firefighters. Talk about smoke alarms and how they work. Listen to one. Put out smoke alarm cutouts for coloring.
	Talk about how to get out of fires. Talk about fire drills. Hand out information sheets for parents. Include a request to have them diagram home and create a fire drill for evacuation, then practice it. Several days later, have a fire drill.
Age-Appropriate:	Preschoolers.

Unit:	**Safety**
Suggested Themes:	Poisonous Plants, Car Travel Safety, Bicycle or Riding Toy Safety, Water Safety, Playground Safety, Neighborhood Safety. Choose only those that are appropriate to care site.
Theme:	Car Travel Safety/Buckle Up.
Objectives:	Children should understand how to be safe when in a car, truck, or bus.
Materials:	Chairs set up in dramatic play area to simulate a four- or six-passenger car with a steering wheel for the driver. Books. Bulletin board on travel safety. Toy cars to paint on paper. Toy cars, buses, and trucks. Outside, a gas station set up for trikes and wagons. Magazines for pictures of vehicles.
Lesson:	During group time, read *When I Ride in a Car*. Talk about safety in the car. Always buckle up, no hands out the windows, speak with indoor voices, and so forth. Talk about how safety might be different in a bus or in a truck. Compare behaviors.
Follow-Up:	Go on a field trip in a car or bus. Practice what children learned. Observe children in dramatic play area playing car or bus. Put books about vehicles in library. Encourage children to play gas station in outdoor area and have them practice safe behaviors while on their "vehicles."
	Have children use toy cars for painting. Have children cut pictures of vehicles out of magazine. Discuss safety while they are doing the task. Give parents an information sheet on travel safety. It might be nice to include a few tips on how to survive travel with children.
Age-Appropriate:	Preschoolers.

Unit:	**Safety**
Suggested Themes:	First Aid, Disaster Preparedness, Fire Drills, Earthquake, Tornado, Hurricane.
Theme:	Fire Drills.
Objectives:	Children will learn the importance of fire drills and how to protect themselves in case of fire.
Materials:	A fire drill bell or buzzer. Clearly marked exits. Sign or poster that shows stop, drop, roll concept. A bulletin board with fire safety, fire drill information. A safe place outdoors to meet during the fire drill.
Lesson:	Invite a firefighter to talk about fires and how they destroy things and hurt people. Talk about how things can be replaced, but that people cannot. Discuss the importance of getting out of a fire. Have students practice a fire drill. Have fireman demonstrate stop, drop, and roll. Children will practice stop, drop, and roll. At one point during the day, have a random fire drill so children can practice while the ideas are fresh in their minds.
Follow-Up:	Read the book *When There is a Fire, Go Outside*. Give parents information about home fire drills and ask them to practice at home. Once a month conduct a random fire drill in child care.
Age-Appropriate:	Toddlers, preschoolers, and school-aged children are all capable of understanding this information at some level. Toddlers may model the behavior without understanding it, but that modeling could save their lives.

Unit:	Nutrition
Suggested Themes:	Food Guide Pyramid, Fruits and Vegetables, Milk and Milk Products, Strong Bones and Teeth, How Food Helps Us Grow, Where Do Foods Come From, and Bread and Grains.
Theme:	Breads and Grains.
Objectives:	Children will understand how breads and grains fit into the Food Guide Pyramid and how they help them grow and have energy. They will be able to identify foods that fit into this category.
Materials:	Examples of fresh bread, bagels, rice, cereals, and pasta and other products that belong in this category of the pyramid. Poster of the Food Guide Pyramid. Magazine pictures of foods including numerous breads and grains, an empty poster board, and glue or paste.
Lesson:	Read the book *Bread, Bread, Bread*. Have children name all the different kinds of breads they can think of. Talk about how bread helps children grow and have energy. Show children examples of other foods that fit into the breads and grains categories. Have them select and cut out pictures of this category from magazine pictures of foods. Using glue sticks, have all children glue their pictures of these foods on a large poster board, creating a collage of breads and grains.
Follow-Up:	Snack and lunch items will feature bread and cereal group foods such as cereal, spaghetti, tortillas, pancakes, and rice cakes. Read the book *On Top of Spaghetti*, *Pancakes for Breakfast*, or *Strega Nona*. If children bring their lunches, have all children participate in identifying the bread or grain food group items.
Age-Appropriate:	Preschool age children will be able to identify these foods.

Unit:	**Nutrition**
Suggested Themes:	Junk Foods, Television Ads Influence Food Choices. Learning to Feed Ourselves (for Toddlers), and Exercise Our Bodies.
Themes:	Exercise Our Bodies.
Objectives:	Children will understand how exercise makes their bodies strong and healthy.
Materials:	A flannel board and flannel cutouts. An exercise video. Balls, trikes, and a whistle.
Lesson:	Explain the importance of exercise to children. Have them give examples of what they think is exercise, clarifying as you go. Tell a flannel board story about a little boy who didn't exercise and how it made him unhealthy and how he felt after he started exercising. Put on an exercise video and have everyone participate. Take a walk and walk at different speeds from slow to fast. Read the book *Willie Takes a Hike*.
Follow-Up:	Plan some organized exercises for the rest of the week. Include foot races and trike races; play Red Light, Green Light, and Simon Says. Use exercise video for kids again. Read books like *Too Much Junk Food, Too Much T.V.*, and *I Went Walking,* and discuss how these might affect children and their exercise effort and time.
Age-Appropriate:	Preschoolers will enjoy using their energies in this lesson.

LESSON PLAN

CHAPTER II

N

Unit:	**Nutrition**
Suggested Themes:	Breakfast Starts My Day, Lunch Helps Me Grow, Snacks are Important, and Good Fast Food Selections.
Theme:	Lunch Helps Me Grow.
Objectives:	Children will learn how to make good selections for lunch box meals.
Materials:	Labels from typical convenience foods such as Lunchables and snack items often packed in lunches. Lunch sacks, breads, condiments, meats, cheese, peanut butter and jelly, chips, veggies, juices, sodas, junk food selections. Magazine pictures of foods, paper, scissors, and glue or paste.
Lesson:	Show children labels from typical lunch and snack foods. Help them learn how to look at the labels to see what is healthy and what is not. Talk about good selections for a lunch box. Read *Lunch Boxes*. Have children discuss how many different items from different cultures are healthy lunch selections. Have children practice good selections by choosing lunch items from magazine pictures and pasting them on paper. Have children select their own lunch items and make their own lunches. Talk about their selections, and help them make better choices, if necessary.
Follow-Up:	Send home a handout of good lunch box selections and those foods you do not want to see in child care (such as candy and soda). Read *What's on My Plate?*, *Lunch*, and *Gregory, the Terrible Eater*. During lunch time for the rest of the week, read labels from children's lunch box selections. Have children discuss their food choices.
Age-Appropriate:	Preschoolers and school-aged children are most likely to be receptive to this information.

Unit:	**Special Topics—Child Abuse Prevention**
Suggested Themes:	I Know My Body, Stranger Safety, Good Touches and Bad Touches.
Theme:	Stranger Safety.
Objectives:	To be safe, children are made aware of some of the lures that a stranger may use.
Materials:	Puppets—an adult and several children. Pictures of child lures strangers use such as candy, emergencies, open car doors, and so forth.
Lesson:	Using the puppets, depict some of the lures that strangers use that put children's safety at risk. Show children pictures of some of the items or conditions that may occur during a child lure situation. Discuss the use of candy, asking for directions, and the open car door. Talk about safe people to go to for help. Discuss having a password for an emergency lure.
Follow-Up:	Reminders on the bulletin board. Parent handout on child lures. Have a parent meeting to discuss the importance of training children about child lures.
Age-Appropriate:	Older preschoolers and school-aged children are able to assimilate this information.

Unit:	**Special Topics—Inclusion, Chronically Ill Children, Children in Stress**
Suggested Themes:	Being Different/Being Alike, How to Help Our Friends, Sometimes I Feel Sad, Sometimes I Feel Angry, Sometimes I Feel Lonely.
Theme:	Being Different/Being Alike.
Objectives:	Children learn to recognize that they are more alike children with disabilities than different. They also learn to accept differences.
Materials:	Pictures of children with disabilities. Dolls with disabilities.
Lesson:	Read *My Buddy* and *In Other Words*. Have a discussion comparing the two themes. Talk about how both boys might feel. Ask children to recognize how both boys are the same, then ask the children to recognize how they are similar to both boys. Have children who are willing to wear a patch over one eye during snack time. Discuss how it felt. Ask them to tell you in what ways they felt similar to when they did not wear a patch. How did the two compare?
Follow-Up:	Read *Teacher's in a Wheelchair*. Ask the children if being the different/same changes when someone is grownup. Place pictures in room of children with different disabilities. Have dolls with disabilities available to play with in dramatic play area.
Age-Appropriate:	Preschoolers can discern the same and different.

RESOURCES BUILDING CURRICULUM

Children's Environment

Aliki. (1992). *I'm Growing*. New York, NY: Harper Collins Publishers.
Aliki. (1984). *My Five Senses*.
Berenstain, S., & Berenstain J., (1994). *The New Neighbors*. New York: Random House.
Bertrand, L. (1994). *Who Sleeps in the City?* Shelburne, Vermont: Chapters.
Bliss, C. D. (1994). *The Shortest Kid in the World*. New York: Random House.
Boyd, L. (1987). *The Not-so-Wicked Stepmother*. New York: Viking Press.
Bridwell, N. (1985). *Clifford and the Grouchy Neighbors*.
de Paola, T. (1996). *The Baby Sister*. New York: G.S. Putnam and Son.
Haggerty, M. E. (1993). *A Crack in the Wall*. New York: Lee and Low Books. A new home in a poverty situation and the fears that it brings.
Kadish, S. (1994). *Discovering Friendship*. Austin, TX: Steck-Vaughn.
Kubler, A., & Formby, C. (1995). *Come Home with Us*. Swindon, England: Child's Play. Multicultural homes.
Kubler, A., & Formby, C. (1995). *Come Play with Us*. Multicultural play.
Meyer, M. (1988). *Just My Friend and Me*. New York: Golden Book.
Meyer, M. (1983). *All by Myself*.
Raffi. (1988). *One Light, One Son*. New York, NY: Crown Publishing. We are all the same.
Shelby, A. (1995). *Homeplace*. Orchard Books. Living in the country, history of an old house and the people in it, including today.
Simon, N. (1975). *All Kinds of Families*. Niles, IL.: A. Whitman.
Spier, P. (1980). *People*. New York: Doubleday.
Williams, V. B. (1986). *Cherries and Cherry Pitts*. New York: William Morrow and Co. Life in the city.

Health Subjects

Aliki. (1992). *I'm Growing*. New York, NY: Harper Collins Publishers.
Aliki. (1984). *My Five Senses*.
Allington, R., & Kriell, K. (1985). *Hearing*. Milwaukee, WI: Raintree.
Berenstain, S., & Berestain, J. (1988). *The Bad Dream*. New York: Random House.
Berenstain, S., & Berestain, J. (1988). *Ready, Set, Go*. Exercise.
Berenstain, S., & Berestain, J. (1983). *The Messy Room*.
Berenstain, S., & Berestain, J. (1981). *Visit to the Dentist*.
Brandenburg, F. (1979). *I Wish I Was Sick, Too!* New York: Mulberry Books.
Bridwell, N. (1996). *Clifford's Sports Day*. New York: Scholastic Books. About exercise during a sports day.
Cole, J. (1994). *You Can Smell Forever with Your Ear*. New York, NY: Grosset and Dunlap. Five senses.
Creative Group at PSS! (1996). *The Boo Boo Book*. New York: Putnam and Grosset.
Dunn, S. (1994). *Keeping Fit*. Chicago: Good Year Books.
Fowler, A. (1991). *Feeling Things*. Chicago, IL: Children's Press.
Fowler, A. (1991). *Hearing Things*.
Fowler, A. (1991). *Seeing Things*.
Fowler, A. (1991). *Smelling Things*.
Frandsen, K. (1987). *I'd Rather Get a Spanking Than Go to the Doctor*. Chicago: Children's Press.
Leonard, M. (1988). *Getting Dressed*. New York: Bantam Books.
Leonard, M. (1988). *Taking a Bath*.

Numeroff, L. (1995). *Chimps Don't Wear Glasses.* New York: Simon and Schuster.

Oremerod, J. (1983). *Be Brave Billy.* London: J.M. Dent and Sons Ltd. Being brave about going to doctor and dentist.

Oxenbury, H. (1983). *The Check-up.* New York: Penguin Books.

Payne, L. M. (1994). *Just Because I Am.* MN: Free Spirit Publishing Inc.

Polland, B. K. (1975) *Feelings: Inside and Outloud Too.* Berkeley, CA: Celestial Arts.

Reasoner, C. (1995). *Little Box Book's First Aid Kit.* New York: Putnam and Grosset. Four small books including Stethoscope, Cough Syrup, Adhesive Tape, and First Aid Kits.

Rey, H. A. *Curious George Goes to the Hospital.* Boston, MA: Houghton Mifflin.

Rockwell, A. (1982). *Sick in Bed.* New York: Macmillan.

Rogers, F. (1989). *Going to the Dentist.* New York, NY: G.P. Putman and Sons.

Rogers, F. (1986). *Going to the Doctor.*

Sesame Street. (1985). *Sign Language ABC with Linda Bove.* New York: Children's Television Workshop, Random House.

Simon, N. (1974). *I Was So Mad.* Morton Grove, IL: A. Whitman.

Steig, W. (1982). *Doctor De Soto.* New York: Farrar, Strauss and Giroux. Mouse dentist works on all kinds of animals.

Wells, R. (1995). *Edward's Overwhelming Overnight.* New York: Penguin Books. Edward the unready bear has fears about spending the night with a friend.

Ziefert, H., & Smith, M. (1988). *What Do I Hear?* New York: Bantam Books.

Ziefert, H., & Smith, M. (1988). *What Do I See?*

Ziefert, H., & Smith, M. (1988). *What Do I Smell?*

Ziefert, H., & Smith, M. (1988). *What Do I Taste?*

Ziefert, H., & Smith, M. (1988). *What Do I Touch?*

Safety Subjects

Bingham, C. (1995). *Mighty Machines: Fire Truck.* New York: Dorling Kendersly Publishing.

Branley, F. M. (1985). *Flash, Crash, Rumble, and Roll.* New York: Harper Collins Publishers.

Bridwell, N. (1994). *Clifford the Firehouse Dog.* New York: Scholastic Books.

Brown, M., & Krensky, S. (1982). *Dinosaurs Beware: A Safety Guide.* Boston: Little, Brown and Company.

Chlad, D. (1984). *Bicycles Are Fun to Ride.* Chicago, IL: Children's.

Chlad, D. (1983). *When I Ride in a Car.*

Chlad, D. (1982). *When There Is a Fire, Go Outside.*

Cole, J. (1995). *The Magic School Bus: Inside a Hurricane.* New York: Scholastic Books.

Hankin, R. (1985). *I Can Be a Firefighter.* Chicago: Children's.

Hopping, L. (1994). *Tornadoes!* New York: Scholastic Books.

Keats, E. J. (1987). *The Trip.* New York: Morrow.

Kubler, A., & Formby, C. (1995). *Come Ride with Us.* Swindon, England: Child's Play.

Leaf, M. (1988). *Safety Can Be Fun.* New York: Harper and Row.

Packard, M. (1995). *I Am a Firefighter.* New York: Scholastic Books.

Polacco, P. (1990). *Thunder Cake.* New York: Philomel Books. Cake must go in oven before storm hits.

Polacco, P. (1987). *Meteor.* Funny book about what happens when a meteor lands.

Raffi, (1988). *Wheels on the Bus.* New York: Crown Publishing. With song.

Rey, H. A. (1973). *Curious George Rides a Bike.* Boston, MA: Houghton Mifflin Company.

Rey, M., & Rey, H.A. (1985) *Curious George at the Fire Station.* Boston, MA: Houghton Mifflin Company.

Rosenblatt, L. (1994). *Fire Diary.* Morton Grove, IL: A. Whitman.

Seuling, B. (1985). *Stay Safe, Play Safe*. New York: Western Publishing, Golden Books.

Stater, T. (1991). *All About Fire Trucks*. New York: Grosset and Dunlap.

Stoltz, M. (1988). *Storm in the Night*. New York: Harper Collins. Story about a thunderstorm where electricity goes off.

Wells, R. (1995). *Edward in Deep Water*. New York: Penguin Books. Edward the unready bear is afraid of the water.

Nutrition Subjects

Berenstain, S., & Berenstain, J. (1985). *Too Much Junk Food*. New York: Random House.

Berenstain, S., & Berenstain, J. (1984). *Too Much T.V.*

Brown, M. (1986). *Stone Soup*. New York: Macmillan.

Carle, E. (1987). *The Very Hungry Caterpillar*. New York: Philomel Books.

Coplans, P. (1993). *Spaghetti for Suzy*. New York: Houghton Mifflin.

de Paola, T. (1989). *Tony's Bread*. New York: Putnam.

de Paola, T. (1988). *Strega Nona*. New York: Simon and Schuster.

de Paola, T. (1978). *Pancakes for Breakfast*. San Diego, CA: Harcourt Brace Jovanovich.

Ehlert, L. (1989). *Eating the Alphabet from A to Z*. San Diego, CA: Harcourt Brace Jovanovich. Fruits and vegetables from A to Z.

Ehlert, L. (1987). *Growing Vegetable Soup*.

Erlich, F. (1991). *Lunch Boxes*. New York: Puffin Books.

Fleming, D. (1992). *Lunch*. New York: Holt.

Fowler, A. (1995). *Corn On and Off the Cob*. Chicago, IL: Children's Press.

Glazer, T. (1995). *On Top of Spaghetti*. Chicago: Good Year Books.

Gomi, T. (1991). *Who Ate It?* Brookfield, CT: Millbrook Press.

Gross, R. (1990). *What's on My Plate?* New York: MacMillan.

Hoban, R. (1964). *Bread and Jam for Francis*. New York: Harper and Row.

Krauss, R. (1944). *The Carrot Seed*. New York: Harper and Row.

Kubler, A., & Formby, C. (1995). *Come Eat with Us*. Swindon, England: Child's Play. Multicultural foods and eating methods.

Lord, J. (1987). *The Giant Jam Sandwich*. Boston: Houghton Mifflin.

Lottridge, C. (1986). *One Watermelon Seed*. London: Oxford University Press.

McCloskey, R. (1976). *Blueberries for Sal*. New York: Penguin.

Morris, A. (1989). *Bread, Bread, Bread*. New York: William Morrow.

Numeroff, L. (1985). *If You Give a Mouse a Cookie*. New York: Harper Collins.

Oda, M. (1984). *Happy Veggies*. Boston: Houghton Mifflin.

Passen, L. (1991). *Fat, Fat Rose Marie*. New York: Holt.

Preiss, L. *The Pig's Alphabet*. Boston: David R. Goding.

Pruemin, M. (1994). *How to Make an Apple Pie and See the World*. New York: Alfred Knopf.

Rand, G. (1996). *Willie Takes a Hike*. San Diego, CA: Harcourt Brace Jovanovich.

Seuss, Dr. (1960). *Green Eggs and Ham*. New York: Random House.

Sharmat, M. (1987). *Gregory, the Terrible Eater*. New York: Macmillan.

Sinykin, S. C. (1990). *Come Out, Come Out, Wherever You Are*. Hazeldon, Minnesota: Hazeldon Educational Materials. Story about an overweight girl and her changing perception of herself.

Smalls-Hector, I. (1992). *Apple Picking Time*. New York: Crown Publishing. American tradition of picking apples.

Williams, B. (1978). *Jeremy Isn't Hungry*. New York: Penguin Books. Older brother tries to feed Jeremy, but he wants to feed himself.

Williams, S. (1989). *I Went Walking*. San Diego, CA: Harcourt Brace Jovanovich.

Wood, D., & Wood, A. (1984). *The Little Mouse, The Red Ripe Strawberry, and the Big Hungry Bear*. Swindon, England: Child's Play.

Special Topics Subjects

Arthur, C. (1979). *My Sisters Silent World*. Chicago, IL. Children's.

Charlip, R. (1979). *Handtalk: An ABC of Finger Spelling and Sign Language*. New York: MacMillan.

Cohn, J. (1994). *Why Did It Happen?: Helping Children Cope in a Violent World*. New York: Morrow.

Hoban, T, (1987). *I Read Signs*. New York: Morrow.

Mayer, M. (1983), *I Was So Mad*. New York: Golden Books.

Ofosky, A. (1992). *My Buddy*. New York: Henry Holt and Company. About a boy's disabilities.

Peterson, J. W. (1977). *I Have a Sister and My Sister Is Deaf*. New York, NY: Harper-Collins Publishers.

Polland, B. K. (1975). *Feelings: Inside and Outloud Too*. Berkeley, CA: Celestial Arts.

Powers, M. E. (1986). *Our Teacher's in a Wheelchair*. Niles, IL: A. Whitman.

Simon, N. (1974). *I Was So Mad*. Morton Grove, IL: A. Whitman.

Walker, J. (1993). *In Other Words*. Toronto, Canada: Annick Press. A handicapped boy imagines what it would be like to be whole.

Watson, E. (1996). *Talking to Angels*. San Diego: Harcourt Brace Jovanovich. Girl who talks to her sister who is autistic.

Suggested Readings

Anderson, L. (1996). *Early Childhood Health and Curriculum*. Grand Rapids, MI: T.S. Denison.

Berman, C., & Fromer, J. (1991). *Teach Children About Food: A Teaching and Activities Guide*. Palo Alto, CA: Bull Publishing Company.

Bickert, G. (1994). *Food to Grow and Learn On*. Nashville, TN: Incentive Publications.

Cook, D. (1995). *The Kids Multi-Cultural Cookbook-Food and Fun Around the World*. Charlotte VT: Williamson Publishing Co.

Greene, K. (1987). *Once Upon a Recipe*. New York: Putnam.

Harms, T. (1981). *Learning from Cooking Experiences*. Menlo Park, CA: Addison-Wesley and Co.

Jacobson, M., & Hill, L. (1991). *Kitchen Fun for Kids*. New York: Henry Holt and Company.

Knox, G. (Ed.) (1989). *Better Homes and Gardens New Junior Cookbook*. Des Moines, IA: Meredith Corporation.

M'Guinness, J. (Illustrator). (1987). *Kids Cooking: A Very Slightly Messy Manual*. Palo Alto, CA: Klutz Press.

Ralph, J., & Gompf, R. (1995). *The Peanut Butter Cookbook for Kids*. New York: Hyperion Paperbacks for Children.

Veitch, B., & Harms, T. (1981). *Cook and Learn: Nutritious Foods from Various Cultures*. Menlo Park, CA: Addison-Wesley Publishing Co.

Winget, M. (Ed.) (1992). *Vegetarian Cooking Around the World*. Minneapolis, MN: Lerner Publications, Co.

CHAPTER **REFERENCES**

Bredekamp, S. (1987). Developmentally appropriate practice in early childhood programs serving children from birth through age eight. Washington, DC: NAEYC.

Herr, J., & Libby, Y. (1995). *Creative resources for the early childhood classroom*. Albany, NY: Delmar Publishers.

SUGGESTIONS **FOR READING**

Allen, J., McNeill, E., & Schmidt, V. (1992). *Cultural awareness for children*. Menlo Park, CA: Addison-Wesley.

Allen, K. (1992). *The exceptional child: Mainstreaming in early childhood education*. Albany, NY: Delmar Publishers.

Bassett, M. M. (1998). *The professional nanny*. Albany, NY: Delmar Publisher.

Berman, C., & Fromer, J. (1991). *Teaching children about food. A teachers and activities guide*. Palo Alto, CA: Bull Publishing Co.

Cook, R., Tessier, A., & Klein, M. (1992). *Adapting early childhood curricula for children with special needs*. New York: Macmillan.

Gestwicki, C. (1995). *Developmentally appropriate practice: Curriculum and development in early education*. Albany, NY: Delmar Publishers.

Hendrick, J. (1995). *Total learning*. Englewood Cliffs, NJ: Merrill.

Moore, C., Kerr, M., & Shulman, R. (1990). *Young chef's nutrition guide and cookbook*. New York: Barron's.

Nutrition and wellness for the young child: A curriculum for adults. (1984). Pleasant Hills, CA: Diablo Valley College.

Taylor, B. (1995). *A child goes forth: A curriculum guide for preschool children*. Englewood Cliffs, NJ: Prentice Hall.

APPENDIX A

FORMS

- Child's Health History

- Developmental Health History

- Caregiver Health History

- Immunization Schedule for Children Not Immunized in Early Infancy

- Content for Medical Treatment

- Physician's Report

- Physician to be Called in Emergency

- Identification and Emergency Information for Day Care Centers

- Consent for Child Care Provider Access to Physician Records

- Authorization for Emergency Medical Care

- Symptom Record

- Sample Letter to Parents about Exposure to Communicable Disease

- Incident Report Form

- Evacuation Procedure

- Stop, Drop, and Roll

CHILD'S HEALTH HISTORY
(Sample)

Child's Name _____ Nickname _____

Date of Birth _____ Telephone No. _____

Address _____

Parents' Names

1. _____ 2. _____

    Employed at _____ Employed at _____

    Telephone No. _____ Telephone No. _____

Emergency Numbers

If the above cannot be reached, call

1. _____

    Relationship to Child _____ Telephone No. _____

2. _____

    Relationship to Child _____ Telephone No. _____

State of Child's Health

Please put N/A if not applicable.

Any recent health problems? _____

Does the child have any dietary restrictions, including food allergies? _____

Does the child have any allergies? _____

Does the child have any condition that would warrant special consideration or attention in our care?

Please explain. _____

Any special problems or fears? _____

Is the child under treatment of a doctor or dentist for previous illness or injury? Please explain.

_____

If yes, please give name of doctor or dentist.

Name _____ Telephone No. _____

Is the child taking medication? If yes, what? _____

Name of prescribing physician

Name _____ Telephone No. _____

DEVELOPMENTAL HEALTH HISTORY

Child's Name _____   Nickname _____

Date of Birth _____   Telephone No. _____

Address _____

Parents' Names

1. _____   2. _____

    Employed at _____   Employed at _____

    Telephone No. _____   Telephone No. _____

Physical

Does your child have any problems

    1. with speech or language? _____

    2. seeing? _____

    3. running, walking, or moving? _____

    4. hearing? _____

    5. using their hands? _____

If so, please explain. _____

    6. What is the child's favorite food? _____

    7. What foods does the child dislike? _____

    8. How does the child indicate the need to use the bathroom? _____

    9. Any special words for bodily functions or body parts? _____

    10. What are the regular bowel and bladder patterns? _____

    11. Does the child take naps regularly? _____

    12. What help does the child need in getting dressed? _____

Social/Emotional

    1. Describe the child's personality. _____

    2. What are the child's favorite toys? _____

    3. What ages are the children that the child frequently plays with? _____

    4. Does the child play happily alone? _____

    5. Describe the child's home environment. _____

    6. Does anything frighten your child? _____

    7. Does the child have a special comforting article (blanket, etc.)? _____

CAREGIVER HEALTH HISTORY
(Sample)

Your Facility Name _____

Address _____

Name _____

Address _____ Telephone No. _____

Date of Birth _____ Social Security No. _____

Position Title _____

Duty Statement _____

_____

Authorization for Release of Medical Information

I hereby authorize the release of medical information contained in this report.

_____   _____   _____
Signature of Applicant   Address   Date

Physician Fills Out

Evaluation of general health

_____

_____

Evaluation of physical ability to perform duties

_____

_____

Note Any Condition That May Create a Hazard to Children or Staff

_____

_____

TB Test   Positive _____   If positive, what action taken? _____

             Negative _____   _____

Date of Test _____

Vision _____

Hearing _____

	Chickenpox	Measles	Mumps	Rubella	DPT	Polio
History of Childhood Diseases (Date)	_____	_____	_____	_____	_____	_____
Immunization Status	_____	_____	_____	_____	_____	_____

Any special medications? _____

_____

Name of Physician _____

Address _____ Telephone No. _____

Physician's Signature _____

IMMUNIZATION SCHEDULE FOR CHILDREN
NOT IMMUNIZED IN EARLY INFANCY

Schedule	Immunization
First Visit	DPT-1, Polio-1, MMR*, HBCV
2 Months Later	DPT-2, Polio-2, HBCV
4 Months Later	DPT-3
6–12 Months Later	DPT-4, Polio 3
Kindergarten Entry	DPT-5, Polio 4

*MMR to be given if 15 months of age or older

NOTE: Children who are in the process of immunization and in the specified waiting period may be admitted to or remain in care until next dose is due. Those children who exceed the specified waiting period must be excluded. Immunization requirements vary with each state. Be sure to check your state's requirements before admitting a child to care.

STATE OF CALIFORNIA HEALTH AND WELFARE AGENCY

DEPARTMENT OF SOCIAL SERVICES
COMMUNITY CARE LICENSING

CONSENT FOR MEDICAL TREATMENT

As the parent, agency representative, or legal guardian, I hereby give consent to

_____ to provide all emergency dental or medical care
Facility Name

prescribed by a duly licensed physician (MD) or dentist (DDS) for _____.
Name

This care may be given under whatever conditions are necessary to preserve the life, limb, or well-being of my dependent.

Child has the following medication allergies:

_____   _____
Date   Parent/Agency Representative/Guardian Signature

Home Address _____

Home Telephone (___) _____   Work Telephone (___) _____

UC 627 (10/88) (Confidential)   89 51494

*This form is required by California Law for all Day Care Centers and Family Daycare Centers.

Sample consent for medical treatment form. Different states may have different requirements; check with your state agency for the correct form. *(Courtesy of the State of California Health and Welfare Agency)*

PHYSICIAN'S REPORT

Facility name _____

Address _____ Telephone _____

Dear _____:

_____ is in child care. We have observed

_____ and would like your diagnosis of the condi-

tion so that we can best protect the health of all the children in care.

Results of Examination

_____ No illness found

_____ Noncommunicable disease (Specify) _____

Describe any treatment required at the child care setting. _____

_____

_____

_____ Communicable disease (Specify) _____

Describe any treatment required before this child can be readmitted. _____

_____

_____

_____ Describe any actions required for this child's contacts. _____

_____

_____

List Medications Prescribed

Name _____

Dosage _____ From _____ Until _____

Date child can return to care _____

Physician's Signature _____

I, _____, give permission for Dr. _____
        Parent's Name

to release information about _____ to _____.
                                    Child's Name   Facility Name

_____
          Parent's Signature

When to Use: This form allows you to share information with the child's physician. It can help
        reduce misunderstandings when information is related verbally.

PHYSICIAN TO BE CALLED IN EMERGENCY

Name _____   Telephone No. _____

Medical Plan No. _____

If physician cannot be reached, what action should be taken? _____

_____

Allergies or Other Medical Limitations

_____

Permission for Medical Treatment

Administrative procedures vary among medical personnel and medical facilities with regard to provision of medical care for a child in the absence of the parent. The exact procedure required by the physician or hospital to be used in emergencies should be verified in advance.

In case of an accident or an emergency, I authorize a staff member of Grossmont College Child Development Center to take my child to the above-named physician or to the nearest emergency hospital for such emergency treatment and measures as are deemed necessary for the safety and protection of the child, at my expense.

This authorization is given pursuant to the provisions of Section 25.8 of the Civil Code of California.

Parent's Signature _____   Date _____

Policies

I hereby grant permission for my child(ren) to use all of the play equipment and participate in all of the activities of school.

I hereby grant permission for my child to leave the school premises under the supervision of a staff member for campus walks and on pre-announced field trips.

I understand that students may be making observations at the Center as part of class assignments.

I have no objection to my child being included in photographs, slides, or movies taken at the Grossmont College Child Development Center which might be used for purposes of interpreting the school program. I understand that any photography or observation will be done only with the consent of and under the supervision of the classroom teacher.

I understand that I must notify the Center Office of any college class-related field trips that will take me off campus while my child is at the Center.

I understand that children left after their regular contract time without permission from the Center Office will be subject to termination of child care services.

I agree to inform the Child Development Center of any and all personal changes in circumstances that would affect my status in the Center; e.g., marriage, separation, divorce, change in employment or education, change in address or telephone number.

Parent's Signature _____   Date _____

(Courtesy of the Grossmont College Child Development Center)

Department of Social Services
Community Care Licensing

IDENTIFICATION AND EMERGENCY INFORMATION
DAY CARE CENTERS

To Be Completed by Parent or Guardian

Child's Name Last	Middle	First	Sex	Telephone ( )

Address Number Street	City	State	Zip	Birthdate

Father's Name Last	Middle	First	Business Telephone ( )

Home Address Number Street	City	State	Zip	Home Telephone ( )

Mother's Name Last	Middle	First	Business Telephone ( )

Home Address Number Street	City	State	Zip	Home Telephone ( )

Person Responsible for Child Last Name Middle First	Home Telephone ( )	Business Telephone ( )

Additional Persons Who May Be Called in Emergency

Name	Address	Telephone	Relationship

Physician or Dentist To Be Called in Emergency

Physician	Address	Medical Plan and Number	Telephone ( )
Dentist	Address	Medical Plan and Number	Telephone ( )

If Physician Cannot Be Reached, What Action Should Be Taken?

☐ Call Emergency Hospital   ☐ Other   Explain _____

Names of Persons Authorized to Take Child from the Facility

(Child will not be allowed to leave with any other person without written authorization from parent or guardian)

Name	Relationship

Time Child Will Be Called For

Signature of Parent or Guardian	Date

To Be Completed by Facility Director/Administrator

Date of Admission	Date Left

LIC 700 (8/86) (Confidential)   86   41957

*This form is required for all day care centers and family day care centers.

(Courtesy of the State of California Department of Social Services)

CONSENT FOR CHILD CARE PROVIDER ACCESS TO PHYSICIAN RECORDS

I, _____, give my consent for

the following individual to have access to my child's medical records while my child is enrolled in

_____.

My child's caregiver: _____

Address: _____

Telephone Number: _____

I understand that information in my child's record will not be released to any other individuals without my specific written consent.

Signed: _____　　Date: _____
　　　　　　　(Parent/Legal Guardian)

Witnessed: _____

AUTHORIZATION FOR EMERGENCY MEDICAL CARE
(Sample)

Minor's name _____

The undersigned has entrusted the above-named minor for care with _____
child care. I hereby authorize such adult person to consent to any x-ray, examination, anesthetic, medical or surgical diagnosis or treatment, and hospital care to be rendered to said minor under the general or specific supervision and upon the advice of a physician and surgeon licensed under the provisions of the Medicine Practice Act or to consent to an x-ray examination, anesthetic, dental or surgical diagnosis or treatment, and hospital care to be rendered to said minor by a dentist licensed under the provisions of the Dental Practice Act.

A photocopy of this *Authorization for Emergency Medical Care* shall be as valid as the original.

Child's birthdate: _____

Father's work telephone number: _____

Father's Social Security number: _____

Mother's work telephone number: _____

Mother's Social Security number: _____

Father's Insurance Company and policy number: _____

_____

Mother's Insurance Company and policy number: _____

_____

Name of child's physician and telephone number: _____

_____

Date: _____   _____
                                                                Signed/Relationship

                                             _____
                                                                Signed/Relationship

_____
Child Care Provider Signature

SYMPTOM RECORD

Child's Name: _____

Date: _____   Symptom: _____

When symptoms began, how long they last, how severe, how often? _____

_____

Any change in child's behavior? _____

_____

Child's temperature _____   ☐ axillary   ☐ oral   ☐ rectal

Food and fluid intake in the past 12 hours: _____

_____

Urine, bowel movement, vomiting in the past 12 hours: _____

_____

Circle or write in other symptoms:

runny nose	sore throat	cough	vomiting	diarrhea	rash
trouble breathing	stiff neck	itching	trouble urinating	pain	

Other symptoms: _____

Exposure to medications, animals, insects, soaps, new foods: _____

_____

Exposure to other people who were sick? Who, and what sickness? _____

_____

Other problems that might affect this illness: (asthma, anemia, diabetes, allergy, emotional trauma)

_____

What has been done so far? _____

Health provider's advice for this illness: _____

Name of person completing this form: _____

SAMPLE LETTER TO PARENTS ABOUT
EXPOSURE TO COMMUNICABLE DISEASE

Name of Child Care Program: _____

Address of Child Care Program: _____

Telephone Number of Child Care Program: _____

Date: _____

Dear Parents:

A child in our program has or is suspected of having: _____

The disease is spread by: _____

The symptoms are: _____

_____ and may appear for this length of time: _____

To prevent this disease: _____

_____

_____

_____

_____

_____

_____

_____

_____

_____

_____

_____

_____

_____

_____

_____

_____

If your child has any symptoms of this disease, call your doctor to find out what to do. Be sure to tell your doctor about this notice. If you do not have a regular doctor to care for your child, contact your local health department for instructions on how to find a doctor or ask other parents for names of their children's doctors. If you have any questions, please contact:

_____ at (_____) _____
       (Caregiver's name)   (Telephone number)

(Courtesy of Pennsylvania Chapter, American Academy of Pediatrics)

INCIDENT REPORT FORM

Fill in all blanks and boxes that apply.

Name of Program: _____ Telephone No.: _____

Address of Facility: _____

Child's Name: _____ Sex: M F Birthdate:__/__/__ Incident Date: __/__/__

Time of Incident: ___:___AM/PM Witnesses: _____

Parent(s) Notified By: _____ Time Notified: ___:___AM/PM

Location where incident occurred: ☐ playground ☐ classroom ☐ bathroom ☐ hall
☐ kitchen ☐ doorway ☐ large muscle room or gym ☐ office ☐ dining room
☐ stairway ☐ unknown ☐ other (specify) _____

Equipment/product involved: ☐ climber ☐ slide ☐ swing ☐ playground surface
☐ sandbox ☐ trike/bike ☐ hand toy (specify): _____

☐ other equipment (specify): _____

Cause of injury (describe): _____

☐ fall to surface; estimated height of fall _____ feet; type of surface: _____

☐ fall from running or tripping ☐ bitten by child ☐ motor vehicle ☐ hit or pushed by child
☐ injured by object ☐ eating or choking ☐ insect sting/bite ☐ animal bite
☐ injury from exposure to cold ☐ other (specify): _____

_____

Parts of body injured: ☐ eye ☐ ear ☐ nose ☐ mouth ☐ tooth ☐ other face
☐ other part of head ☐ neck ☐ arm/wrist/hand ☐ leg/ankle/foot ☐ trunk
☐ other (specify): _____

Type of injury: ☐ cut ☐ bruise or swelling ☐ puncture ☐ scrape ☐ broken bone
or dislocation ☐ sprain ☐ crushing injury ☐ burn ☐ loss of consciousness
☐ unknown ☐ other (specify): _____

First aid given at the facility: (e.g., pressure, elevation, cold pack, washing, bandage): _____

_____

Treatment provided by: _____
☐ no doctor's or dentist's treatment required
☐ treated as an outpatient (e.g., office or emergency room)
☐ hospitalized (overnight) no. of days: _____

Number of days of limited activity from this incident: _____ Follow-up plan for care of the child: _____

Corrective action needed to prevent reoccurrence: _____

Name of official/agency notified: _____ Date: _____

Signature of staff member: _____ Date: _____

Signature of parent: _____ Date: _____

(Courtesy of Pennsylvania Chapter, American Academy of Pediatrics)

EVACUATION PROCEDURE

1. All staff must give children proper information on exiting the facility.

2. Children's activities will stop immediately at the sound of the drill, and they are to proceed to the classroom door.

3. _____ will lead children out of the facility to the designated area.
   Staff Title/Name

4. _____ will check bathrooms, closets, and hallways to assure all children have exited.
   Staff Title/Name
   (Window and doors will be closed on the way out.)

5. _____ will bring the attendance and emergency contact records to the designated area.
   Staff Title/Name

6. In case of fire, _____ will notify the fire department.
   Staff Title/Name

7. When the building cannot be reentered, children will be taken to _____.
   Name of Facility

8. Parents will be notified by telephone or radio broadcast on _____.
   Station Call Letters

9. No one should reenter the building unless given permission by the fire department.

10. _____ will complete the evacuation log at the end of each drill.
    Staff Title/Name

11. The local fire marshall will be invited to observe a drill annually, and teach staff use of fire extinguishers.

12. If there is a power failure _____ will activate the emergency lighting systems.
    Staff Title/Name
    Flashlights are available in each classroom closet.

13. If there is a severe storm or tornado, children should be taken to _____.
    Place in Facility

14. Staff should remain calm and speak to children in a reassuring manner. Take appropriate toys and books to keep children involved in an activity.

Scheduling of Fire Drills

■ Fire drills will be held monthly.

■ Drills will be held at different times during the day, after nap time, and after lunch to familiarize children with the proper evacuation procedure.

■ Select a location in the building for the site of a "pretend" fire which would change the usual evacuation route. Plan and conduct an evacuation drill using alternate exits.

(Courtesy of Pennsylvania Chapter, American Academy of Pediatrics)

(Courtesy of the Burn Institute, 3702 Ruffin Rd., Ste. 101, San Diego, CA)

APPENDIX B

PHYSICAL GROWTH
NATIONAL CENTER FOR HEALTH
STATISTICS (NCHS) PERCENTILES

- Girls: Birth to 36 Months
  (Length and Weight)

- Boys: Birth to 36 Months
  (Length and Weight)

- Girls: 2 to 18 Years (Stature and Weight)

- Boys: 2 to 18 Years (Stature and Weight)

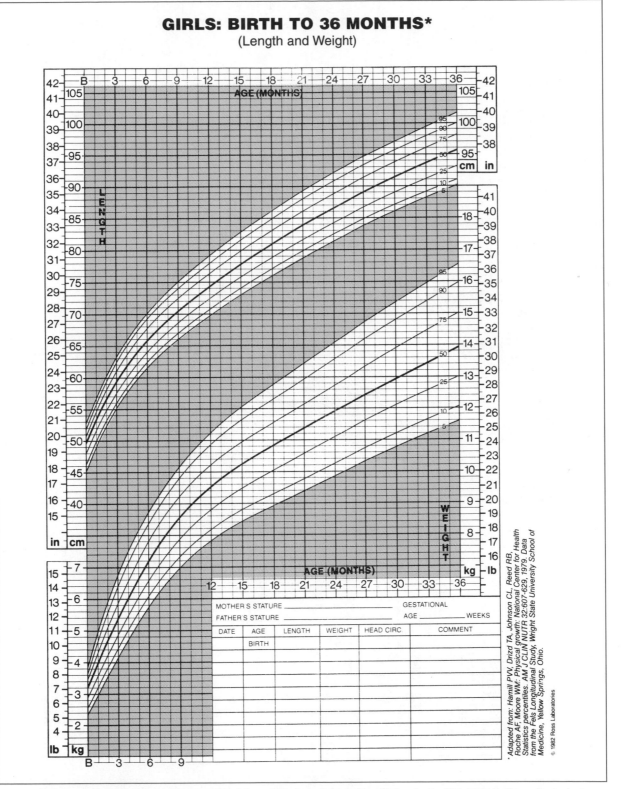

GIRLS: BIRTH TO 36 MONTHS*
(Length and Weight)

*Adapted from: Hamill PVV, Drizd TA, Johnson CL, Reed RB, Roche AF, Moore WM: Physical growth: National Center for Health Statistics percentiles. AM J CLIN NUTR 32:607-629, 1979. Data from the Fels Longitudinal Study, Wright State University School of Medicine, Yellow Springs, Ohio.

© 1982 Ross Laboratories

MOTHER'S STATURE _____ GESTATIONAL
FATHER'S STATURE _____ AGE _____ WEEKS

DATE	AGE	LENGTH	WEIGHT	HEAD CIRC	COMMENT
	BIRTH				

(Used with permission of Ross Products Division, Abbott Laboratories, Columbus, OH 43216. From Ross Laboratories. © 1982 Ross Products Division, Abbott Laboratories)

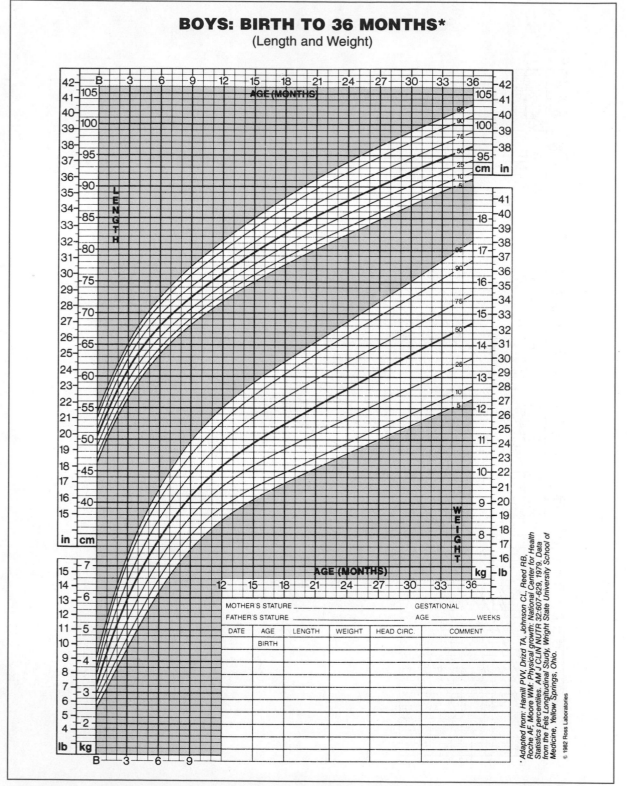

BOYS: BIRTH TO 36 MONTHS*
(Length and Weight)

(Used with permission of Ross Products Division, Abbott Laboratories, Columbus, OH 43216. From Ross Laboratories, © 1982 Ross Products Division, Abbott Laboratories)

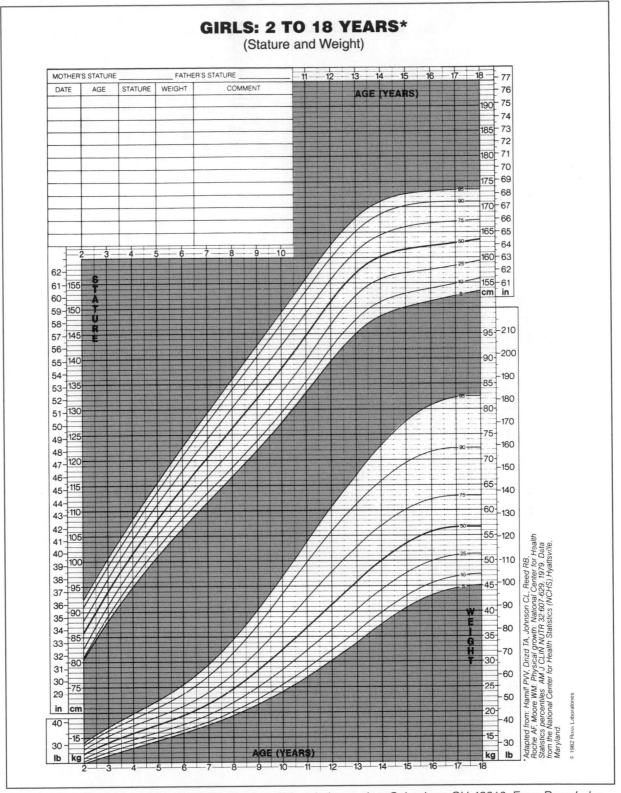

GIRLS: 2 TO 18 YEARS*
(Stature and Weight)

(Used with permission of Ross Products Division, Abbott Laboratories, Columbus, OH 43216. From Ross Laboratories, © 1982 Ross Products Division, Abbott Laboratories)

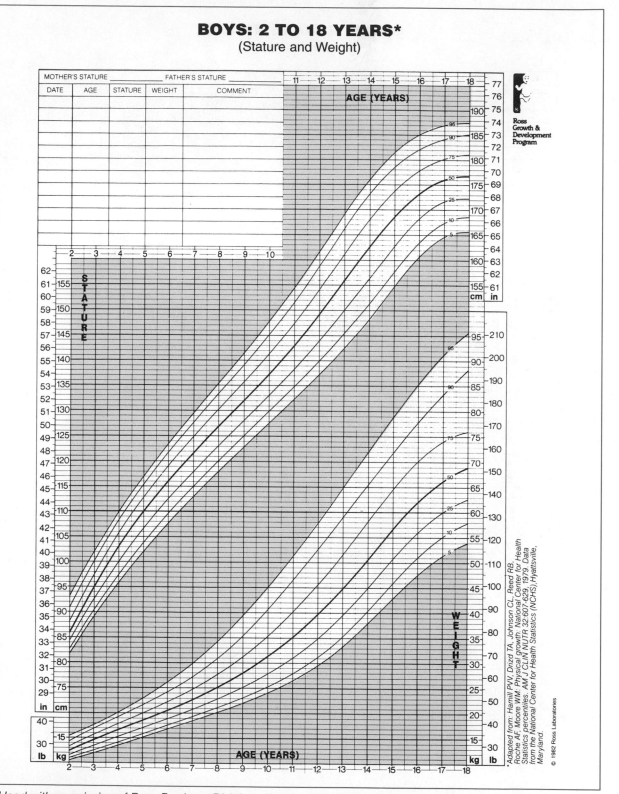

BOYS: 2 TO 18 YEARS*
(Stature and Weight)

(Used with permission of Ross Products Division, Abbott Laboratories, Columbus, OH 43216. From Ross Laboratories, © 1982 Ross Products Division, Abbott Laboratories)

APPENDIX C

CHILDREN'S DEVELOPMENT

- ■ Denver II Developmental Screening Test

- ■ Developmental Milestones—
  Birth to Five Years

- ■ Selected Screening and Assessment Tools

- ■ Suggested Readings on Children's
  Developmental Norms

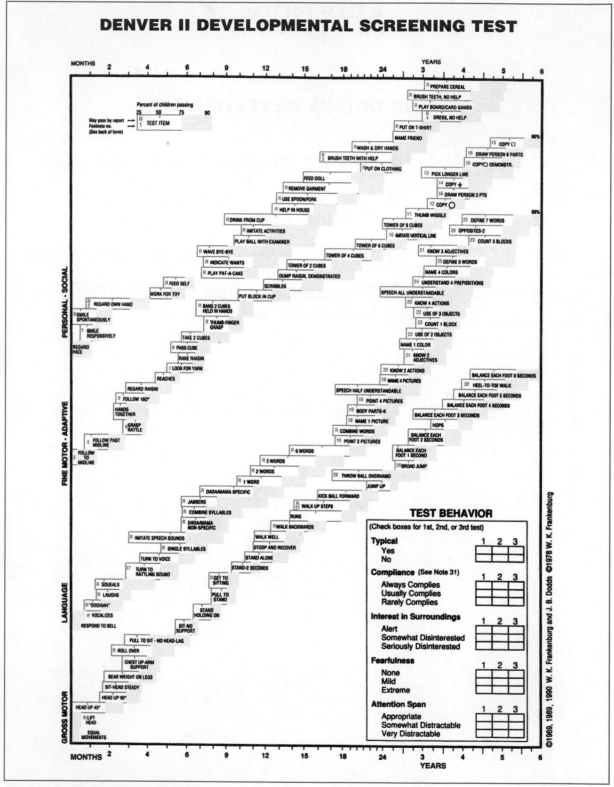

(Reprinted with permission of DDM)

Directions for Administration

1. Try to get child to smile by smiling, talking or waving. Do not touch him/her.
2. Child must stare at hand several seconds.
3. Parent may help guide toothbrush and put toothpaste on brush.
4. Child does not have to be able to tie shoes or button/zip in the back.
5. Move yarn slowly in an arc from one side to the other, about 8" above child's face.
6. Pass if child grasps rattle when it is touched to the backs or tips of fingers.
7. Pass if child tries to see where yarn went. Yarn should be dropped quickly from sight from tester's hand without arm movement.
8. Child must transfer cube from hand to hand without help of body, mouth, or table.
9. Pass if child picks up raisin with any part of thumb and finger.
10. Line can vary only 30 degrees or less from tester's line.
11. Make a fist with thumb pointing upward and wiggle only the thumb. Pass if child imitates and does not move any fingers other than the thumb.

12. Pass any enclosed form. Fail continuous round motions.
13. Which line is longer? (Not bigger.) Turn paper upside down and repeat. (pass 3 of 3 or 5 of 6)
14. Pass any lines crossing near midpoint.
15. Have child copy first. If failed, demonstrate.

When giving items 12, 14, and 15, do not name the forms. Do not demonstrate 12 and 14.

16. When scoring, each pair (2 arms, 2 legs, etc.) counts as one part.
17. Place one cube in cup and shake gently near child's ear, but out of sight. Repeat for other ear.
18. Point to picture and have child name it. (No credit is given for sounds only.)
    If less than 4 pictures are named correctly, have child point to picture as each is named by tester.

19. Using doll, tell child: Show me the nose, eyes, ears, mouth, hands, feet, tummy, hair. Pass 6 of 8.
20. Using pictures, ask child: Which one flies?... says meow?... talks?... barks?... gallops? Pass 2 of 5, 4 of 5.
21. Ask child: What do you do when you are cold?... tired?... hungry? Pass 2 of 3, 3 of 3.
22. Ask child: What do you do with a cup? What is a chair used for? What is a pencil used for? Action words must be included in answers.
23. Pass if child correctly places <u>and</u> says how many blocks are on paper. (1, 5).
24. Tell child: Put block **on** table; **under** table; **in front of** me, **behind** me. Pass 4 of 4. (Do not help child by pointing, moving head or eyes.)
25. Ask child: What is a ball?... lake?... desk?... house?... banana?... curtain?... fence?... ceiling? Pass if defined in terms of use, shape, what it is made of, or general category (such as banana is fruit, not just yellow). Pass 5 of 8, 7 of 8.
26. Ask child: If a horse is big, a mouse is __? If fire is hot, ice is __? If the sun shines during the day, the moon shines during the __? Pass 2 of 3.
27. Child may use wall or rail only, not person. May not crawl.
28. Child must throw ball overhand 3 feet to within arm's reach of tester.
29. Child must perform standing broad jump over width of test sheet (8 1/2 inches).
30. Tell child to walk forward, 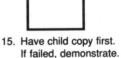 heel within 1 inch of toe. Tester may demonstrate. Child must walk 4 consecutive steps.
31. In the second year, half of normal children are non-compliant.

OBSERVATIONS:

DEVELOPMENTAL MILESTONES

Skills	Birth to Twelve Months	One Year to Two Years	
Cognitive Skills	Follows moving object with eyes. Looks directly at faces and responds to gestures. Places toy in and takes toy out of containers. Beginning of memory—object permanence. Looks for hidden objects. Listens to and follows simple directions.	Imitates adults through actions and words. Names simple objects. Listens to and follows commands and requests. Explores the environment. Acts like "little scientist." Matches simple objects.	
Language Skills	Cries, babbles, and coos. Looks at speaker when spoken to and responds using variety of sounds. Capable of vowel and consonant sounds, often using repetition. Begins to imitate sounds. Begins to use intonation for meaning.	Speaks first words. Able to speak 50 meaningful words to communicate. Identifies and names simple objects. Uses gestures to enhance communication. Indicates possession by using words *mine, me.* Uses the word *no* frequently to voice autonomy.	
Fine Motor Skills	Reaches for objects; grasps and plays with them. Puts objects in mouth. Uses pincer grasp. Shifts objects between hands. Drops objects; picks them up.	Stacks three objects, such as blocks, in a tower. Turns pages (two or three at a time). Turns door knobs. Throws small ball. Scribbles, paints with large movements, holds brush with whole hand. Drinks from a cup without help. Begins using a spoon. Places round objects into holes.	
Gross Motor Skills	Lifts head. Turns from side to side; rolls over. Sits with back straight and head steady. Able to crouch. Crawls. Pulls self up into a standing position, then walks along furniture, using both hands. Stands without support.	Takes first steps. Walks alone without help. Stands without support. Walks backwards. Walks upstairs using one hand. Jumps using both feet. Pulls and pushes toys. Throws a ball with overhand motion without falling.	
Social Skills	Smiles spontaneously. Discriminates between familiar people and strangers. Responds to own name. Understands words *no-no.* Imitates simple actions of others.	Shows emotions such as affection, joy, fear, anger, and jealousy. Recognizes self in mirror. Refers to self by name. Hugs and kisses. Throws temper tantrums. Loves to help put things away. Imitates adult activities. Initiates play.	
Self-Mastery Skills	Holds bottle. Feeds self finger foods. Holds cup with two hands; needs assistance to drink from it. Cooperates with being dressed.	Takes off shoes and other clothing; can unzip. Verbalizes needs such as food, drink, and toileting. Eats and drinks well without assistance.	

BIRTH TO FIVE YEARS

Two to Three Years	Three to Four Years	Four to Five Years
Can name and recognize one color. Matches shapes and objects by function. Stacks objects, such as blocks, five high. Responds to simple direction. Has limited attention span. Identifies objects in picture books. Can describe own activity. Begins to understand function of objects in familiar environments.	Can name and recognize six colors. Begins to understand concept of time, including past and present. Understands concept of pretending. Knows own full name and age. Attention span is somewhat longer, but easily distracted. Can match by "family" group or function.	Matches pictures of familiar objects. Draws people figures with recognizable parts. Counts to five. Knows street and town where he lives. Points to and names six colors. Matches commonly related objects. Has extended attention span. Has increased understanding of time, function, and whole and part.
Talks constantly. Refers to self by proper pronouns. Uses plurals. Uses complete sentences consisting of three to four words. Asks questions: why, where, how?	Talks in sentences. Can relate present or past experiences. Uses past tense for verbs. Has extensive vocabulary. Can repeat a song or nursery rhyme. Can understand and use size comparisons. Asks questions for information.	Has basic grammatical structure in use. Uses increasingly complex language. Has large vocabulary base. Understands more complex directions. Uses directions in play. Able to listen to long stories.
Can turn pages of book one at a time. Paints using wrist action. Holds crayon with fingers, not whole hand. Moves fingers independently of others. Strings beads. Cuts using scissors, but hasn't mastered it. Shows hand preference. Manipulates clay by rolling and pounding.	Drives pegs into holes, nails into wood. Can copy circle or cross. Manipulates clay and playdough into recognizable objects. Able to stack objects nine high. Cuts using scissors.	Cuts on a straight line. Copies simple figures. Prints a few capital letters.
Runs well. Kicks ball without losing balance. Stands on one foot. Jumps short distances with both feet. Rides a tricycle, but has not necessarily mastered both steering and peddling. Walks upstairs alternating feet. Walks on tiptoe.	Runs around obstacles. Throws ball overhand, with direction. Hops on one foot. Climbs up slide and slides down unassisted. Walks a line. Can catch ball bounced to her. Masters riding a tricycle.	Turns somersault. Walks up and down stairs unassisted, alternating feet. Jumps forward as many as ten times without falling. Walks backward in a line, heel to toe. Can swing at a stationary ball with a bat.
Better control of temper tantrums. Begins to share toys. Plays near other children (parallel play). Begins real dramatic play. Participates in group activities like circle time.	Plays with others (associative play). Able to share and take turns. Acts out whole scenes in dramatic play.	Plays with other children (cooperative play). Dramatic play resembles reality, including dressing up. Pretending is acknowledged. Acknowledges sex differences.
Understands gender identity. Feeds self. Drinks from drinking fountain. Takes off jacket or coat. Toilets with help. Opens doors.	Knows own gender identity. Buttons and unbuttons clothing. Washes hands without help. Pours well from small pitcher. Spreads with knife. Toilets without help.	Laces shoes. Follows instructions given in a group. Uses knife to cut food. Can help set table. Can help in simple food preparation. Knows name of city she lives in.

SELECTED SCREENING AND ASSESSMENT TOOLS

Bayley Scales of Infant Development
Two to Thirty Months
Developed in 1969, this tool measures mental, motor, and behavioral development. It helps to identify developmental difficulties in very young children.

Gessell Assessment Tool
Birth to Six Years
This tool was first developed in 1940 and then revised in 1980. Measures motor, adaptive, language, and personal and social behavior.

Denver Developmental Screening Test
Birth to Six Years
This tool was developed in 1967 and measures fine motor, gross motor, language, adaptive, and personal and social skills. It is best used as an indicator for further assessment needs. It is limited due to its broad spectrum.

Early Learning Accomplishment Profile
Birth to Three Years
This profile offers programming guidance for infants and young children with special needs.

Learning Accomplishment Profile Diagnostic Test
Thirty Months to Five Years
This tool measures fine motor and gross motor skills, cognition, and language development. It can also provide appropriate learning objectives and assist in measuring progress. It is intended primarily for children with special needs.

Learning Accomplishment Profile Diagnostic Screening
Birth to Five Years
This short test (15 minutes) shows cut-off points in norms that may indicate the need for early intervention. It assesses fine and gross motor skills, language, cognition, social, and self-help skills.

Uniform Performance Assessment System
Birth to Six Years
This assessment tool is based on criteria that directly refers to the areas of communication, social and self-help skills, cognition, and general motor skills.

Portage Guide to Early Education
Birth to Six Years
A checklist is the main instrument used to assess developmental skill performance. This tool also includes lesson plans and other aids to develop optimum skill building for young children.

Hawaii Early Learning Profile
Birth to Three Years
This tool, developed in 1979, measures cognition, language, social, and self-help skills as well as fine and gross motor skills.

Early Childhood Environment Rating Scale
Birth to Five Years
The primary purpose of this tool is to rate the quality of the child care or preschool setting, the materials and activities provided, children's development, and scheduling. The resulting assessment can point out areas that need improvement to enhance the child care or preschool experience.

SUGGESTED READINGS ON CHILDREN'S DEVELOPMENTAL NORMS

Ainsworth, M., Blehar, M., Waters, E., & Wall, S. (1979) *Patterns of attachment: Observation in the strange situation and at home.* Hillsdale, NJ: Erlbaum.

Bayley, N. (1969). *The Bayley scales of infant development.* New York: The Psychological Corporation.

ERIC. (1989). *Early intervention for infants and toddlers: A team effort* (#461). Urbana, IL: The University of Illinois.

Frankenburg, W.K., Dodds, J.B., & Fandal, A. (1975). *Denver developmental screening test.* Denver, CO: Ladoca Publishing.

Furuno, S., O'Reilly, D., Hosaka, C., Inatuska, T., Aleman, T., & Zeisloft, B. (1979). *Hawaii early learning profile.* Palo Alto, CA: Vort Corporation.

Harel, I., & Anastasian, N. (1985). *The at-risk infant.* Baltimore: Brookes Publishing.

Harms, T., & Clifford, R. (1980). *Early education environmental rating scale.* New York: Teacher's College Press.

Shearer, D., Billingsley, J., Froman, A., Hilliard, J., Johnson, F., & Shearer, M. (1976). *Portage guide to early education* (Rev. ed.). Portage, WI: Portage Project.

Smith P., & Pederson, D. (1988). Maternal sensitivity and patterns of infant and mother attachment. *Child Development, (59),* 1097–1101.

Terr, L., & Tyler, R. (1992, May). Prenatal drug exposure: An overview of associated problems and intervention strategies. *Phi Delta Kappan,* 705–707.

Ungerer, J., & Signman, M. (1983). Developmental lags in preterm infants from one to three years. *Child Development, (54),* 1217–1228.

Weiss, R. (1981). INREAL intervention for language handicapped and bilingual children. *Journal of the Division of Early Childhood, (4),* 24–27.

White, O., Edgar, E., Haring, N., Afflectk, J., Hayden, A., & Benderesky, M. (1981). *Uniform performance assessment system (UPAS).* Columbus, OH: Charles E. Merrill.

APPENDIX D

NUTRITIONAL ASSESSMENT TOOLS

- Hard-to-Place Foods

- Mexican American Foods and the Food Guide Pyramid

- Nutritional Breakdown of Typical Lunch Menus

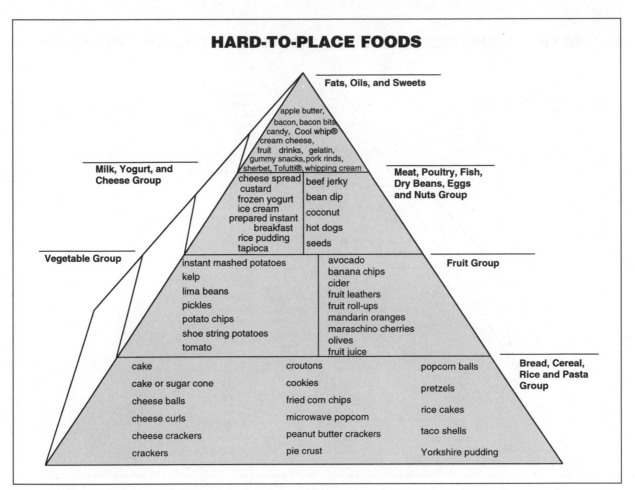

Placement of Foods on the Food Guide Pyramid (*©1993 Pyramid Packet, Penn State Nutrition Center, 417 East Calder Way, University Park, PA 16801-5633; 814-865-6323*)

MEXICAN AMERICAN FOODS AND THE FOOD GUIDE PYRAMID

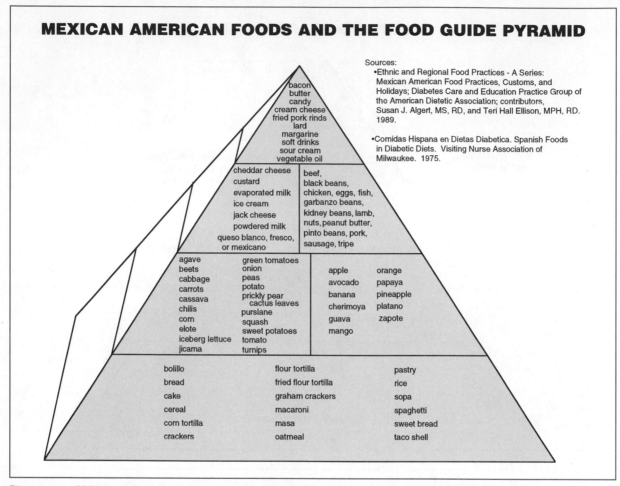

Placement of Mexican American Foods on the Food Guide Pyramid (*©1993 Pyramid Packet, Penn State Nutrition Center, 417 East Calder Way, University Park, PA 16801-5633; 814-865-6323*)

NUTRITIONAL BREAKDOWN OF TYPICAL LUNCH MENUS

HOME-PACKED LUNCH

Peanut-Butter Sandwich	Calories	Protein (grams)	Fat (grams)	% Calories from Fat	Sodium (milligrams)
(two slices white bread, 1.5 Tbsp. peanut butter, 1 Tbsp. jelly)	342	12	15	37	390
1 oz. potato chips	148	2	10	58	133
1 medium apple	125	trace	trace	5	2
2 commercial chocolate-chip cookies	90	1	4	40	70
*8 oz. 1% fat milk	97	8	2	20	118
Total	**802**	**23**	**31**	**34**	**713**

Bologna Sandwich					
(2 slices cracked-wheat bread, 2 oz. turkey bologna, .75 oz. American cheese, 1 Tbsp. mayonnaise)	420	17	28	59	1,089
1 oz. corn chips	155	2	9	53	233
8.45 oz. cranberry-apple ice drink	160	trace	trace	4	5
2 sponge snack cakes w/whipped filling	310	2	10	29	310
Total	**1,045**	**21**	**47**	**40**	**1,637**

SCHOOL LUNCH PROGRAM

Char-Patty Burger	Calories	Protein (grams)	Fat (grams)	% Calories from Fat	Sodium (milligrams)
(meat patty, whole-wheat bun, pickle, lettuce, mustard, catsup)	346	20	12	31	1,272
French fries	138	2	6	39	19
Tropical fruit mix	32	0	0	0	2
*8 oz. 1% fat milk	141	8	4	26	136
Total	**657**	**30**	**22**	**29**	**1,429**

Turkey Chili Nachos					
(turkey chili, tortilla chips)	385	16	15	35	515
Fruit cup	32	0	0	0	2
*8 oz. 1% fat milk	141	8	4	26	136
Total	**558**	**24**	**19**	**31**	**653**

FAST-FOOD LUNCH

Taco Bell	Calories	Protein (grams)	Fat (grams)	% Calories from Fat	Sodium (milligrams)
1 regular taco	180	10	11	56	276
1 order of nachos	345	7	18	46	398
16 oz. cola	150	0	0	0	15
Total	**675**	**17**	**29**	**39**	**689**

McDonald's					
1 regular hamburger	250	12	9	32	490
Medium french fries	320	4	17	50	150
*8 oz. 1% fat milk	100	8	2	20	115
Chocolate-chip cookies	330	4	15	42	280
Total	**1,000**	**28**	**43**	**39**	**1,035**

*Data for 1% fat milk vary because brands of milk differ in the amount of milk solids added.
School lunch values provided by San Diego City Unified School District food service.

Nutritional Breakdown of Typical Lunch Menus (Courtesy of Margaret Wing-Peterson, registered dietician)

APPENDIX E

SOURCES OF MATERIALS RELATED TO SAFETY, NUTRITION, AND HEALTH

Abbott Laboratories
15th and Sheridan Road
North Chicago, IL 60064
(pharmacy, nutrition, drugs)

Aetna Life and Casualty Companies
Information and Public Relations Department
151 Farmington Avenue
Hartford, CT 06156
(health and safety)

Alexander Graham Bell Association for the
    Deaf, Inc.
The Volta Bureau for the Deaf
3417 Volta Place, NW
Washington, DC 20007

Alliance to End Lead Poisoning
600 Penn Avenue, SE
Suite 100
Washington, DC 20003

American Academy of Pediatrics
141 Northwest Point Boulevard
P.O. Box 927
Elk Grove, IL 60009-0927

American Allergy Association
P.O. Box 7273
Menlo Park, CA 94026

American Alliance for Health, Physical Education,
    Recreation and Dance
1900 Association Drive
Reston, VA 22091-1502

American Automobile Association
1000 AAA Drive
Heathrow, FL 32746

American Cancer Society
1599 Clifton Road, NE
Atlanta, GA 30329

American Dairy Association
O'Hare International Center,
10255 W. Higgins Rd., Suite 900
Rosemont, IL 60018-5616

American Dairy Products Institute
130 North Franklin Street
Chicago, IL 60606

American Dental Association
Bureau of Dental Health Education
211 East Chicago Avenue
Chicago, IL 60611-2616
(dental health)

American Diabetes Association, Inc.
National Service Center
P.O. Box 25757
1660 Duke Street
Alexandria, VA 22314-3427

American Dietetic Association
216 W. Jackson Blvd.
Suite 800
Chicago, IL 60606

American Foundation for the Blind
11 Pennsylvania Plaza, Suite 300
New York, NY 10001

American Heart Association
7272 Greenville Avenue
Dallas, TX 75231-4596

American Hospital Association
1 N. Franklin, Suite 27
Chicago, IL 60606

American Institute of Baking
Consumer Service Dept.
1213 Bakers Way
Manhattan, KS 66502
(nutrition education)

American Insurance Association
1130 Connecticut Avenue, NW
Suite 1000
Washington, DC 20036

American Lung Association
1740 Broadway
New York, NY 10019-4315

American Medical Association
515 N. State Street
Chicago, IL 60610
(health, safety, and poison prevention education)

American National Red Cross
431 18th Street, NW
Washington, DC 20006

American Optometric Association
Department of Public Information
243 North Lindbergh Boulevard
St. Louis, MO 63141-7851
(eye health)

American Printing House for the Blind
1839 Frankfort Avenue
Louisville, KY 40206-3148

American Public Health Association
1015 Fifteenth Street, NW
Suite 300
Washington, DC 20005-2605

American School Health Association
7263 State, Rt. 43
Kent, OH 44240

American Social Health Association
P.O. Box 13827
Research Triangle Park, NC 27709

American Speech, Language and Hearing
Association
10801 Rockville Pike
Rockville, MD 20852-3226

The Arthritis Foundation
1314 Spring Street, NW
Atlanta, GA 30309

Association for the Care of Children's Health
7910 Woodmont Avenue, Suite 300
Bethesda, MD 20814

Association for Children and Adults with Learning
Disabilities
4156 Library Road
Pittsburgh, PA 15234

Association for Children with Retarded Mental
Development
345 Hudson Street
New York, NY 10014

Association for Retarded Citizens
500 E. Border Street, Suite 502
Arlington, TX 76010

Association of American Railroads
American Railroad Building
50 F Street, NW
Washington, DC 20001-1530

Asthma and Allergy Foundation of America
1125 15th St., NW, Suite 502
Washington, DC 20005

Better Vision Institute, Inc.
1800 N. Kent Street
Suite 1210
Rosslyn, VA 22209

Children's Defense Fund
25 E. Street, NW
Washington, DC 20001

Clearinghouse on Child Abuse and Neglect
Information
P.O. Box 1182
Washington, DC 20013

Committee for Children
172 20th Avenue
Seattle, WA 98122
(sexual abuse)

Consumer Information Center
Pueblo, CO 81009
(an index of selected federal publications)

Consumer and Professional Relations
Division of HIAA
1025 Connecticut Avenue, NW
Washington, DC 20036
(health education)

Council for Exceptional Children
1920 Association Drive
Reston, VA 22091

Cystic Fibrosis Foundation
6931 Arlington Road, Suite #200
Bethesda, MD 20814-5231

Department of Community Health
1075 Ste-Foy Road, 7th Floor
Quebec, Quebec G1S 2M1, Canada

Department of Health and Human Services
Public Health Services
Food and Drug Administration
Rockville, MD 20857

Eli Lily and Company
Public Relations Department
Box 618
Indianapolis, IN 46285

Environmental Protection Agency
401 M Street, SW
Washington, DC 20460

Epilepsy Foundation of America
4351 Garden City Drive
Landover, MD 20785

Feingold Association of the United States
P.O. Box 6550
Alexandria, VA 22306

Florida Department of Citrus Fruit
P.O. Box 148
Lakeland, FL 33802

Ford Motor Company
Research and Information Department
The American Road
Dearborn, MI 48127
(traffic safety, seat belts)

General Mills
Public Relations Department
Educational Services
P.O. Box 5588
Stacy, MN 55079
(nutrition)

Health Education Associates, Inc.
211 South Easton Road
Glenside, PA 19038-4497

Health Education Foundation
2600 Virginia Avenue, NW
Suite 502
Washington, DC 20037

Home Economics Directorate
880 Portage Avenue, 2nd Floor
Winnipeg, Manitoba R3G OP1, Canada

Huntington's Disease Society of America
140 W. 22nd Street, 6th Floor
New York, NY 10011-2420

International Life Sciences Institute
1126 16th Street, NW #300
Washington, DC 20036
(nutrition education)

Johnson and Johnson Health Care Division
New Brunswick, NJ 08903
(first aid, dental health)

Joseph P. Kennedy Jr. Foundation
1350 New York Avenue, NW
Suite 500
Washington, DC 20005
(mental retardation)

Kellogg Company
Department of Consumer Education
Battle Creek, MI 49016

Lefthanders International
P.O. Box 8249
Topeka, KS 66608
(information and supplies)

Lever Brothers Company
390 Park Avenue
New York, NY 10022
(dental health)

March of Dimes Birth Defects Foundation
1275 Mamaroneck Avenue
White Plains, NY 10605

Mental Retardation Association of America
211 E. 300 South Street
Suite 212
Salt Lake City, UT 84111

Metropolitan Life Insurance Company
Health and Safety Division
1 Madison Avenue
New York, NY 10010
(health, safety, first aid)

Muscular Dystrophy Association
3300 E. Sunrise Drive
Tucson, AZ 85718

National Academy of Sciences
National Research Council, Office of Public
   Information
2101 Constitution Avenue, NW
Washington, DC 20418
(nutrition education)

National Association for Down Syndrome
P.O. Box 4542
Oak Brook, IL 60522-4542

National Association for the Education of Young
   Children
1509 16th Street NW
Washington, DC 20036

National Association for Hearing and Speech
10801 Rockville Pike
Rockville, MD 20852

National Association for the Visually
   Handicapped
22 W. 21st.
New York, NY 10010

National Center for Nutrition and Dietetics
216 West Jackson Boulevard
Suite 800
Chicago, IL 60606-6995

National Center for the Prevention of Sudden
   Infant Death Syndrome
10500 Little Patuxent Parkway, #420
Columbia, MD 21044

National Commission on Safety Education
National Education Association
1201 16th Street, NW
Washington, DC 20036
(safety education)

National Council on Family Relations
3989 Central Avenue NE
Suite 550
Minneapolis, MN 55421

National Dairy Council
Nutrition Education Division
6300 North River Road
Rosemont Road, IL 60019-9922

National Easter Seal Society
120 W. Monroe
Chicago, IL 60606

National Easter Seal Foundation
2023 West Ogden Avenue
Chicago, IL 60612

National Fire Protection Association
1 Batterymarch Park
P.O. Box 9101
Quincy, MA 02269-9101

National Foundation for Asthma
P.O. Box 30069
Tucson, AZ 85751

National Health Council
1730 M Street, NW, Suite 500
Washington, DC 20036
(health education)

National Health Information Center
Office of Disease Prevention and Health
   Promotion
P.O. Box 1133
Washington, DC 29913-1133

National Hemophilia Foundation
110 Green Street, Room 406
New York, NY 10012

National Homecaring Council
519 C Street, NE
Washington, DC 20002

National Information Center for Handicapped
   Children and Youth
P.O. Box 1492
Washington, DC 20013

National Institute of Allergy and Infectious Diseases
Office of Communications
Building 31, Room 7A-32
9000 Rockville Pike
Bethesda, MD 20892

National Institute of Health
U.S. Public Health Service
Bethesda, MD 20014
    1. Allergy and Infectious Diseases
    2. Arthritis and Metabolic Diseases
    3. Cancer
    4. Child Health and Human Development
    5. Dental Research
    6. General Medical Services
    7. Heart
    8. Neurological Diseases and Blindness
    9. Microbiological data

National Kidney Foundation
30 E. 33rd Street
New York, NY 10016

National Livestock and Meat Board
Nutritional Department
444 N. Michigan Avenue
Chicago, IL 60611

National Lung Association
1740 Broadway
New York, NY 10019
(respiratory diseases)

National Maternal and Child Health Clearinghouse
38th and R Streets, NW
Washington, DC 20057

National Multiple Sclerosis
733 3rd Avenue
New York, NY 10017

National Pediculosis Association
P.O. Box 149
Newton, MA 02161
(head lice)

National Reye's Syndrome Foundation
426 N. Lewis, P.O. Box 829
Bryan, OH 43506

National Safety Council
1121 Spring Lake Drive
Itasca, IL 60143-3201
(safety materials, films, posters)

National SIDS Clearinghouse
8201 Greensboro Drive
Suite 600
Alexandria, VA 82102

National Society for the Prevention of Blindness
500 E. Remington Road
Schaumberg, IL 60173

National Spinal Cord Injury Association
545 Concord Avenue, No. 29
Cambridge, MA 02138-1122

National Wildlife Federation
Educational Services Section
1400 16th Street, NW
Washington, DC 20036-2266

Nutrition Information Service
234 Webb Building
Birmingham, AL 35294

Nutrition Programs
446 Jeanne Mance Building
Tunney's Pasture
Ottawa, Ontario K1A 1B4, Canada

Nutrition Services
P.O. Box 488
Halifax, Nova Scotia B3J 3R8, Canada

Nutrition Services
P.O. Box 6000
Fredericton, New Brunswick E3B 5H1,
    Canada

Office of Child Development
U.S. Department of Health and Human
    Services
P.O. Box 1182
Washington, DC 20013

Office of Civil Defense/Emergency
    Preparedness
Public Information
The Pentagon
Washington, DC 20310

Parents Anonymous
675 W. Foothill Blvd., Suite 220
Claremont, CA 91711-3416

Poison Prevention Week Council
P.O. Box 1543
Washington, DC 20013

Public Health Resource Service
15 Overlea Boulevard, 5th Floor
Toronto, Ontario M4H 1A9, Canada

Public Health Services
Public Inquiries Branch
U.S. Department of Health and Human Services
Washington, DC 20201
(health and poison prevention)

Ross Laboratories
Director of Professional Services
625 Cleveland Avenue
Columbus, OH 43216

Sex Information and Education Council of the
    United States
444 Lincoln Boulevard
Suite 107
Venice, CA 90291

State Farm Insurance Companies
Public Relations Department
One State Farm Plaza
Bloomington, IL 61701
(first aid, safety)

Sudden Infant Death Syndrome Clearinghouse
8201 Greensboro Drive, Suite 600
McLean, VA 22101

United Cerebral Palsy Association
7 Penn Plaza, Suite 804
New York, NY 10001

United States Department of Agriculture
Agriculture Research Associations
Bureau of Human Nutrition and Home
    Economics
Washington, DC 20402
(nutrition)

U.S. Government Printing Office
Superintendent of Documents
Washington, DC 20402

U.S. Office of Education
Department of Health and Human Services
P.O. Box 1182
Washington, DC 20013

Veterans of Safety
c/o Robert L. Baldwin Safety Center
Humphrey's Building
Central Missouri State University
Warrensburg, MO 64093
(accident prevention, traffic safety)

World Health Organization
Office of Public Information
525 23rd Street, NW
Washington, DC 20037
(international health)

GLOSSARY

accident—unforeseen occurrence that results in injury.

acculturated—adopting attitudes and beliefs.

activity based—activities that promote adaptive behavior.

advocate—to support or speak on behalf of another.

age appropriateness—consideration of the developmental abilities of a particular age group in the selection of toys, materials, and equipment.

agile—easy, flexible, fast movement.

amblyopia—an unequal balance of a child's eye muscles often referred to as "lazy eye." Condition is improved through the use of eye patches to enable the weaker eye to strengthen with greater use.

amino acids—organic compounds containing carbon, hydrogen, oxygen, and nitrogen; the key components of proteins.

anecdotal—a brief narrative account that describes a child's behavior that is significant to the observer.

anti-bias—an approach to curriculum that removes all inequities to race, gender, and abilities.

appraisals—regular process of evaluation of a child's health or developmental norms.

assessment—in-depth appraisal to determine if a particular health or developmental condition is occurring.

assimilate—to absorb and incorporate in order to make alike.

at risk—exposure to chance of injury, damage, or hazard.

attachment—the bond that develops between a child and another person as a result of a long-term relationship.

baby bottle tooth decay—tooth decay that results from the remains of milk left on the teeth as a result of drinking from a baby bottle.

bacteria—organisms that can survive within or outside of the body, some of which cause diseases.

basal metabolism—the amount of energy used by the body while at rest.

behaviors—actions or conduct that puts safety at risk.

blood contact—passing of germs from one person's circulatory system to another person's circulatory system via blood.

calories—the unit of measurement for the energy found in foods.

cardiovascular disease—disease resulting from impaired function of the heart and/or surrounding arteries.

caregivers—persons who care for children such as teachers, family child care providers, and nannies.

cephalocaudal—development from the top to the bottom of the body or from the head down toward the toes.

cholesterol—a steroid or fatty alcohol found in animal fats that is produced by the liver of the animal.

chronic illnesses—medical condition requiring continued treatment.

communicable diseases—a disease spread from one person to another through means of respiratory spray or infected body fluids.

complete protein—protein that contains all essential amino acids.

concrete operational stage—third stage of cognitive development in which logical ideas can be applied to concrete or specific situations.

condition—circumstance or situation under which safety is at risk.

confidential—keeping information private knowledge.

contact—touching.

coronary atherosclerosis—disease of the heart resulting in the walls of arteries degenerating due to fat build up.

coronary heart disease—disease of the arteries feeding the heart muscle.

cultural sensitivity—perceptive, responsive behavior to cultural differences.

cultural—relationship to traits and ascribed membership of a given group.

curriculum—course of study that relates to the subject being examined.

dehydrated—loss of water in the body that may impair normal bodily functions.

dental caries—tooth decay.

developmental disabilities—physical or mental incapacities that interfere with normal progress of development.

developmental norms—statistically average age that children will demonstrate certain developmental abilities and behaviors.

dilated—pupils of the eye that are enlarged due to shock or injury.

direct contact transmissions—passing of germs from one person's body or clothing to another person through direct contact.

disabled—incapacitated.

disaster preparedness—ability to be ready or prepared for any type of disaster that may occur.

disinfecting—procedures to eliminate all germs through use of chemicals or heat.

diversion—distraction of attention.

diversity—differences, variety often related to culture.

early intervention—decision to modify a child's at-risk behavior or condition in its early stage(s) in order to lessen impact of the behavior or condition on the life of the child.

ecological—dealing with the relationship of the individual to the environment.

economic—the satisfaction of the material needs of people.

emergency contact—the person or persons to notify in case of an emergency.

environment—all the conditions, circumstances, and influences surrounding and affecting the development of an individual.

environmental hazards—chance for risk resulting from environmental conditions.

ethnicity—relationship to a national, cultural, or racial group.

evacuation—removal of persons from a site where a disaster or emergency exists.

event sampling—when an observer records a specific preselected behavior as it occurs, everytime that it occurs.

failure to thrive—failure of a child to grow physically and develop mentally according to the norms. This condition may occur because of organic defects, or may be due to the lack of emotional bonding.

fat soluble—vitamins that dissolve in fat, but not in water, such as vitamins A, D, E, and K.

fecal contamination—contamination occurring through exposure to feces.

fecal-oral transmission—passing of germs from an infected person's bowel movement via the hand into another person's system via the mouth.

feedback—input.

fine motor skills—physical skills related to small body movements, particularly of the hands and fingers. These skills include using scissors, holding a crayon, or working a puzzle.

food frequency questionnaire—an estimate of the frequency of foods eaten during the period of one week.

food jag—preference for one particular food over all others, normally occurring during the preschool years.

friction—rubbing together.

functional skills—skills that allow children to adapt to their environment.

generalizable skills—common skills that can be practiced and used in different settings.

genetic—the origin of features of an individual.

germs—microscopic organisms that can cause disease.

glucose—sugar found in blood.

gross motor skills—physical skills using large body movements such as running, jumping, and climbing.

growth retardation—the hindering of progress of normal growth and development.

guidelines—statements of advice or instruction pertaining to practice.

health policies—strategies that manage health risk.

health promotion—the improvement of health conditions by promotion of healthful characteristics and customs.

health status—the condition of health of an individual.

heredity—the transmission from parent to child of certain characteristics.

holistic—consideration of the whole being in its entirety.

hygiene—protective measures and sanitary practices to limit the spread of infection and that help to promote health.

hypertension—very high blood pressure.

immigrant—one who leaves a country to settle in another.

immunization—vaccines given in order to protect individuals through the development of antibodies against specific infectious diseases.

inclusion—to include or integrate.

indicators—a sign or characteristic that signifies a problem may exist.

individualized family service plan—plan that coordinates services to meet the needs of a child with special needs and assist his or her family.

infection control—control of infectious agents by sanitary practices.

infectious diseases—diseases capable of invading the body and causing an infection to occur.

ingestion—putting into the digestive system through swallowing.

inhalation—breathing in through the nose and mouth.

injection—the force of fluid or poison into the body via a sharp object such as an animal bite or an insect bite.

injury prevention—forestalling or anticipating injury risk.

iron deficiency—lack of adequate supplies of iron needed for normal growth, development, and production of red blood cells.

isolation—situation that causes a person or persons to be set apart or separated from other people.

job burnout—inability to perform job due to excessive stress.

lactose intolerance—inability of body to process lactose found in milk and milk products.

laws—rules of conduct established and enforced by authority.

liabilities—responsible for risk.

linkages—connections that unify the caregiver, child, family, and community.

low center of gravity toy—riding toy where the center of weight is low and balanced, making it difficult to tip over.

lyme disease—disease transmitted via the bite of a tic or deer tic.

macro nutrients—major nutrients needed for the body, such as fats, carbohydrates, and protein.

malnutrion—inadequate nutrition as a result of improper diet or lack of food.

mandate—an order by law.

metabolism—chemical changes that take place as nutrients are taken into the blood, processed and absorbed by the blood, or eliminated from the body.

metabolize—change by chemical and physical processes occuring in living cells.

micro nutrients—supporting nutrients, such as vitamins, minerals, and water, needed by the body.

migrant—a transient who travels from place to place to find work.

mobile—ability to move about easily.

multi-use facilities—child care sites that are used for other functions.

nearsightedness—lack of ability to see well, other than close up.

nutrients—substances found in foods that provide for the growth, development, maintenance, and repair of the body.

obesity—condition of overweight to the extent that the body is carrying 20 percent more weight than the normal body for the size and bone structure.

objectives—goals; expected outcomes.

observation—primary means of data gathering in order to understand children's development and behavior.

orientation—meeting or discussion of a child new to care regarding health, special needs, and developmental history.

ottits media—infection of the middle ear.

overnutrition—excess intake of foods that provide more than adequate amounts of the substances needed for growth, development, maintenance, and repair of the body, often resulting in overweight.

parasites—organisms that live off of another organism.

poison control center—a resource available through a phone call in case of poisoning.

positive reinforcement—something pleasant that occurs after a behavior that increases the likelihood of the repetition of that behavior.

preoperational stage—second stage of cognitive development in which logic is limited.

primary caregiver—the person assigned to be a child's main caregiver throughout the day in order to form a positive attachment bond.

primary health assessor—caregiver who knows the children very well and can observe for health and well-being.

profusely—pouring forth freely or abundantly.

proximodistal—development of the body from the inside toward the outside or the torso through the arms and out to the fingers.

referral—sending a child for further testing or screening and making available resources that will intervene and aid risk that is posed to the child.

regional center—a center in a particular geographic area dedicated to helping families that have children with special needs. The center acts as a resource, a referral agency, and a source of support for families.

regulations—recommendations that are made a requirement by law.

rescue breathing—the process of steps to help a person who is not breathing to resume normal breathing.

resilient—the ability to recover after being exposed to risk.

respiratory diseases—diseases of the nose, ears, sinuses, throat, and lungs.

respiratory tract transmission—germs that are passed from the respiratory tract of one person through the air to another person.

risk—the chance of injury, damage, or loss.

risk management—the act of managing risk.

role modeling—behavioral example.

running records—a detailed narrative account that describes a child's behavior in sequence, as it occurs.

safety zones—areas that offer little risk.

sanitary practices—practices that remove bacteria, filth and dirt that cut down on disease transmission.

sanitized—removeal of bacteria, filth and dirt that makes transmission of disease unlikely.

secretions—saliva, mucous, urine and blood produced by the body for specific purposes.

sedentary—inactive or remaining in one location.

self-esteem—positive sense of self.

self-regulation—to control and direct actions.

sensorimotor cognitive development—first stage of cognitive development that utilizes motor abilities and senses.

shock absorbers—materials that lessen the force of a fall.

shock—an imbalance of the circulatory system as a result of injury that includes a decrease in blood pressure, a rapid pluse, and possible unconsciousness.

staff-to-child ratio—the number of staff required to provide proper care for the number of children of a certain age group.

standards—statements that define a goal of practice.

strabismus—a condition that occurs in children that causes one or both eyes appear to cross.

stress—nonspecific response of the body to any demand put on it.

survival procedures—preparation and steps to follow to stay in place in case of disaster or weather emergency.

synergy—combined effort or action.

syrup of ipecac—a liquid substance used to induce vomiting.

theme—subject being emphasized.

time sampling—occurs when an observer records a particular behavior over a specific period of time.

triggers—substances or conditions that activate a response.

travel information sheet—check-off sheet that monitors all conditions for travel safety.

twenty-four-hour dietary recall method—record of what was eaten for a twenty-four hour period that relies heavily upon memory.

undernutrition—less than adequate intake of foods that provide the substances needed for growth, development, maintenance, and repair of the body.

unintentional injury—physical injury that is the result of an unintentional event.

vaccinations—inactivated, dead, or weakened live organism or infectious diseases to which the body builds resistance.

virus—a small microorganism that is produced in living cells and that can cause disease.

vulnerability—inability to protect from risk.

water-soluble—vitamins that dissolve in water, such as vitamins B and C.

INDEX